MICHE[illegible]ULT
PHILOSOPHER

MICHEL FOUCAULT PHILOSOPHER

Essays translated from the French and German by
TIMOTHY J. ARMSTRONG

New York London Toronto Sydney Tokyo Singapore

First published 1992 by
Harvester Wheatsheaf,
66 Wood Lane End, Hemel Hempstead,
Hertfordshire, HP2 4RG
A division of
Simon & Schuster International Group

Michel Foucault philosophe was first published in French by
Éditions du Seuil, under the direction of François Ewald.
© Éditions du Seuil, 1989

This translation © 1992 Harvester Wheatsheaf

All rights reserved. No part of this publication may be
reproduced, stored in a retrieval stystem, or transmitted,
in any form, or by any means, electronic, mechanical,
photocopying, recording or otherwise, without the prior
permission, in writing, from the publisher.

Typeset in 10 on 12pt Granjon and Helvetica
by Keyboard Services, Luton.

Printed and bound in Great Britain by
BPCC Wheatons Ltd, Exeter

British Library Cataloguing in Publication Data

Michel Foucault, philosopher.
194 .
ISBN 0–7450–0884–4 hbk.
0–7450–0885–2 pbk.

1 2 3 4 5 96 95 94 93 92

Contents

4 ETHICS AND THE SUBJECT

5 RATIONALITIES AND HISTORIES

Translator's introduction

There is an irony, which would surely not have been lost on Foucault, in being the translator of texts written about texts which deal with the problems involved in writing about texts. It is hard to say whether it is in spite of or because of this irony that the exercise has proved to be both challenging and stimulating.

There are certain technical terms for which there is no immediately clear translation into English. To minimalise betrayal I have followed the practice of giving in brackets the French for the most intractable of these. For example, the terms *connaissance* and *savoir* both mean 'knowledge'. *Connaissance* means knowledge in the sense of the subject's relationship to an object and the rules which govern this relationship. *Savoir*, on the other hand, means knowledge in the sense of the underlying structure which is the precondition of any *connaissance*. Its plural form, *savoirs*, means 'forms of knowledge' or 'knowledges'.

I can only hope that, to use Foucauldian terms, the shift [*déplacement*] from one language to another has not introduced too many breaks [*ruptures*] with that which was to be signified [*signifié*] by the original writers of the papers, which in my opinion constitute a major contribution not only to research on Foucault but to philosophy and the world of ideas in general.

Tim Armstrong

Acknowledgements

This book is made up of a collection of papers read and discussed at the international meeting organised in Paris on 8, 9, 10 January 1988 by the Michel Foucault Centre. For more details about the Michel Foucault Centre, see p. 346.

The essays by Hubert L. Dreyfus, Michael Donnelly, Alessandro Pizzorno, James W. Bernauer, Mark Poster and Richard Rorty that appear in this collection were not translated by Timothy J. Armstrong. These essays were submitted for inclusion in this book by their author in the English language version herein.

Introduction

The discussions at the international conference in Paris achieved, both in range and in terms of cultural benefit, everything that could be expected from a meeting where the topic to be dealt with was a body of work such as that of Michel Foucault, dealing, as they did, with the main concerns in his work, the path which his research followed, and its impact. It was as if all those taking part had, without premeditation, already agreed to recognise that it is impossible to discuss Foucault without taking into account what he himself declares in his introduction to *L'Usage des plaisirs*: that the object of his work, what he calls 'truth games', a notion alien both to dogmatic philosophers and to his critics, can be dealt with only by 'putting them to the test, . . . this process being the living body of philosophy'. So, as they examined the way his work communicates hesitations, reservations and misgivings, and the way it has to be approached as theoretical knowledge in the process of application, all the participants felt that, like him, they were not 'living on the same planet' as those who think that the job of philosophical thought is to 'legitimise what we already know', rather than encouraging the enterprise which consists in trying to 'find out in what way and to what extent it would be possible to think differently'.

This nonconformist attitude is what sustains Foucault's passionate interest, even when dealing with traditional notions like normality, morality, transgression and regulation, in philosophically eccentric modes of enquiry and, as a result, in answers which take the form of discoveries linked with such things as incarceration and prison. Several contributions during the course of this conference showed how certain questions asked of Foucault during his lifetime and since his death – questions asked in time-honoured fashion and covering traditional territory – have become outmoded, tangential and even obsolete. It might seem astonishing, for example, to see Foucault talking of truth as a force, rather than as a norm, if one failed to realise that, from the point of view of sciences which generate technology, knowledge contains value.

With regard to the unavoidable question as to whether we should see Foucault's place as being on the inside or on the outside of philosophy proper, some have been tempted to reply that it is outside but alongside. More numerous, though, are those who consider 'outside' to be the equivalent of 'against', sensitive as they are to the fact that Foucault disparaged questions with transcendental implications, preferring those with historical implications, and censured the quest for profundity, so difficult did it seem to him to establish vantage points from which to view what lay on the surface, replacing the history of systems with the history of problematics.

The time has come to apply to Foucault's own work the methods of elucidation – namely, those of genealogy and interpretation – which he himself applied to his fields of study. Before looking to Foucault, as certain of his critics have somewhat disingenuously hastened to do, for answers to the traditional questions of philosophy – a subject which has always been considered throughout its history as a quest for truth and wisdom – it is worth meditating on the fact that he began his work with a history of madness.

Georges Canguilhem

1 MICHEL FOUCAULT IN THE HISTORY OF PHILOSOPHY

one

Archaeology and epistemology

Roberto Machado

When trying to situate Michel Foucault in the context of philosophy it is hard to avoid thinking of Nietzsche, the phenomenologists, or even Marxism.... Yet in my opinion, from a methodological point of view, the most pertinent way of situating what Foucault calls 'archaeology' is to stress his connection with the mainstream of French epistemology since Bachelard.

Epistemology, as it reflects on how scientific knowledge comes into being, judges science from a point of view which is, by nature, scientific. In order to account for the conditions in which scientific knowledge becomes possible, French epistemology takes the study of history as a privileged tool of analysis. This does not mean to say, of course, that all history of science is philosophical, but rather that conceptual philosophies like those of Bachelard, Cavaillès, Koyré and Canguilhem, because they study science in terms of its place in history, do more than simply describe inventions, traditions or authors. From an epistemological point of view, in fact, a history of science would be able to achieve its goal, which is to establish the historical nature of science, only by placing it in a philosophical perspective, and therefore by making a clear distinction between itself and historical and scientific disciplines.

It is easy to understand this situation if one bears in mind the fact that the intimate connection, if not the essential sameness, of philosophical analysis and the history of science derives from the fact that the latter poses, for philosophy, a fundamental question: the question of the nature of rationality. Science, which is a rule-governed and rule-generating mode of discourse, is, for epistemology, the home ground of truth and, as such, the means by which rationality is generated. So, if there is such a thing as a history of reason, it is only the history of science which would be able to demonstrate this and trace its development. As such, the critical dimension of the philosophical history of science does not in any way constitute a critique of science but, on the contrary, a critique of what is outside reason. It analyses the overcoming of obstacles, prejudices and myths, which make possible the progress of rationality. It is a philosophical means of clarifying the nature of knowledge using, as a norm, scientific rationality itself at its highest level of development. So epistemology is seen as a branch of philosophy which studies the question of rationality by taking scientific thought as rational thought *par excellence*. . . .

I wish here to analyse the important shift in methodological approach brought about by Michel Foucault with respect to epistemology. One will recall that Bachelard's philosophy discredits any attempt to formulate a general theory of rationalism. He thought that philosophy should follow the lead given by science, and remain on the same level as science, assimilating what it has to teach and respecting the rules it generates. From this perspective, Bachelard's epistemology can be seen as a form of 'regional' rationalism, the absence of criteria valid for all sciences necessitating the minute study of several 'regions' or areas of scientific thought.

Gaston Bachelard was concerned with sciences like physics and chemistry which can, roughly speaking, be seen as occupying the area of nature, or matter. Then Georges Canguilhem, using essentially the same methodological categories as a starting point, tackled biology, anatomy and physiology, disciplines which he refers to as 'sciences of life', thus outlining another region of scientific enquiry. Archaeological history can be understood as the investigation of a new area, all of its analyses centring on the question of man, and forming a large research project on the historical constitution of 'the human sciences' in modern times. But the specific nature of the object of study is not in itself sufficient to demonstrate the originality of archaeology. To the extent that it centres on the question of man, who is seen as a region separate from the regions of nature and of life, the archaeological process is guided by principles which are different from those of epistemological history. Archaeology, whilst keeping epistemology as a methodological reference point, assumes a different position in its analysis of rationality. Whilst epistemology postulates that science must – returning to Bachelard's expression – 'give order to philosophy', archaeology claims independence from all sciences and allows itself to criticise the very notion of rationality. In the same way, whilst epistemological history examines, on the level of scientific concepts, the production of truth in science, defined as a historical process by means of which rationality is produced and developed, archaeological history, by establishing conceptual interrelationships on the level of knowledge, does not give priority to the normative question of truth, any more than it sets out to establish a temporal order of recurrent patterns viewed from the vantage point of current scientific rationality. By neutralising the question of the essential nature of science, archaeology is able to produce a history of knowledge from which all trace of the history of the progress of reason has disappeared.

Archaeology has never either implicitly or explicitly criticised epistemology but has always aimed to suggest that epistemological history was incapable of analysing the very problems which it was able to describe. It is indeed probably one of the great riches of the archaeological method that it is a tool capable of considering human sciences as theoretical knowledge [*savoir*] by means of putting to one side the question of their scientific nature and as such avoiding the impossible challenge of having to account for recurring patterns, but without, for all that, abandoning the need for a conceptual analysis capable of establishing discontinuities.

Nevertheless, it is not purely and simply a question of a shift from the investigation of science to the investigation of theoretical knowledge [*savoir*]. The archaeological method of analysis is generally known as the 'archaeology of theoretical knowledge' but, contrary to what is often held to be the case, this denomination is not the starting point but the result of a process, itself historical, by means of which the concept of archaeology is modified, to the extent that it appears as something different in each work.

Seen in this light, *L'Archéologie du savoir* no longer comes over as the formulation of a methodology used in the various archaeological researches: *L'Histoire de la folie*, *La Naissance de la clinique* and *Les Mots et les Choses*. These are the works I wish to use to demonstrate how the archaeological method works at the very moment where (once it has been formulated) it produces concrete results. In fact it is not possible to see the methods actually put into practice in the earlier books in terms of the methodological processes put forward in *L'Archéologie du savoir*. *L'Archéologie du savoir* is not so much a conceptual explanation of what has already been achieved as a setting up of new bases for later research that archaeological history might carry out, though this in itself rapidly gives way to a new type of historical analysis of knowledge which Michel Foucault calls 'genealogy'. Conceptualism, discontinuity and normativity are the different stages of the development of archaeology that I shall be analysing, starting from points which seem to me to give the best account of its methodology and the shifts which take place in its relationship to epistemology.

Because of the extent to which it is conceptual, *Histoire de la folie* is not only different from factual histories of psychiatry; it is also critical of the methods these other histories adopt. Nevertheless, the conceptual problem is not posed in the same way as in epistemology, where the concept itself is the fundamental means by which scientific rationality is defined. *Histoire de la folie* represents an initial shift away from this sort of epistemology, radicalising the autonomy of concept as far as its relationship with science is concerned. The fact that psychiatry might not be, properly speaking, a science does not stop it from appropriating scientific concepts: it is a theoretical mode of discourse which, even if it is not scientific, can claim scientific credentials inasmuch as it comes within the parameter of medical discourse. But *Histoire de la folie* is not limited to modes of discourse which claim scientific status, since it also takes into account philosophical, literary, theological and political discourse. With the question of madness as a guiding thread, the analysis takes into consideration a whole host of different types of discourse concerned with madness. It is precisely because the analysis gives priority to the conceptual element of these forms of discourse that it is possible to make connections and establish a whole. But the concept of knowledge [*savoir*], which will become the object of archaeological investigation, has not yet been formulated in this book which, in order to separate itself off from epistemological history and define the specific nature of archaeology, is founded on the disctinction between knowing and perceiving. Epistemology affirms that science alone is capable of producing knowledge [*connaissance*]. Foucault, however, uses the term knowledge [*connaissance*] in the broader sense of a systematic theory – that is to say, the objectification by means of scientific discourse, or discourse which claims to be such, of the phenomenon of madness, as is done for example by medical, psychiatric or legal theories, which claim that they are contributing to the understanding of something which can be known about objectively, or 'positively'. This is important because *Histoire de la folie* points out precisely that the level of knowledge [*connaissance*] is insufficient to give rise to such conditions as would make psychiatry possible.[1]

How, then, can one set about analysing the way psychiatry came into being? This has to be done by some means other than taking a point of view which is either exclusively or fundamentally based on the level of theoretical discourse, since psychiatry is incapable of defining the essence of madness. As such the analysis has to be situated just as much on the level of the theoretical/practical relationship, which he refers to as the level of 'perception', established with the insane person in a situation of institutional confinement.[2] That is why archaeology researches modes of discourse linked more directly with institutional practices like the procedures adopted by the judiciary and the police or the archives of prisons, hospitals and asylums. The point is that these texts, which are unfamiliar to historians of science, are to be studied from a conceptual point of view.

It is here that the question arises as to what archaeology is. The designation appears for the first time in *Histoire de la folie*, referring not so much to a rigid, stable and precise method as to an ever-renewed requirement that scientific discourse – scientific in the broad sense of the term, including discourse which claims scientific status – should be accounted for in a particular way. The meaning of the term evolves during the course of Foucault's archaeological investigations but remains unchanged in one respect: archaeology defines a specific approach and a space appropriate to itself, but always explicitly or implicitly, referring to the epistemological history of science.

In *Histoire de la folie*, 'archaeology' has the limited and precise sense of a search for conditions which will give explanations on a deeper level than those provided by science. Hence the importance of the structural dichotomy in the organisation of the research. In this dichotomy, the area appropriate to archaeology is situated in the realm of knowledge [*connaissance*] – not only because this provides the raw material which archaeology studies but, most importantly, because it comes first in the process of revealing its true objectives. Priority is given to whatever shows a separation between the two categories, and to that which provides an explanation for this separation, or claims to do so.[3] This priority makes it possible to see here – in oppostition to histories of forms of discourse, of theories, of concepts, psychiatric or not, about madness – an archaeology of the power relationship established with the insane person, independently of the scientific reasoning by means of which the true reasoning is hidden. In *Histoire de la folie* there is no archaeology of knowledge in the sense of Foucault's later definition of the concept, though there is an archaeology of perception.

The existence of the two levels leads Foucault to criticise a 'continuist' form of history which would describe the progress of psychiatry as a linear passage from social perception to scientific knowledge of madness. Archaeology follows epistemology in criticising continuist histories, but establishes discontinuities in a different way. In *Histoire de la folie*, the breaks are general, vertical and partial.

The discontinuities might well be general, but they are still circumscribed by the question of madness and are therefore studied on the basis of the conceptual interrelationships established at a given period on the level of perception as well as on the level of knowledge [*connaissance*]. But there is also heterogeneity: between the critical awareness and tragic experience of madness in the Renaissance; between the two forms of institutional confinement in the classical age, the hospital and the Great Confinement; between legal and social awareness about madness; and between awareness of madness and awareness of impaired reasoning at the end of the eighteenth century.

The discontinuities are vertical inasmuch as the distinction between the levels of perception and knowledge [*connaissance*] brings the analysis to a point beyond that of the discourse studied. Through being deliberately situated on a level more fundamental than theories which assign to madness a specific place in a nosography, the analysis gives clear priority to the practices of confinement, so that even categories of temporary insanity and alienation appear to be constituted by the organisation, function and transformation of institutions of confinement. Yet this analysis has broader implications when, for example, the institution of the Great Confinement – the way it came into being, its decline and its transformation into the asylum system – is linked with economic, social and political factors. But the perception–knowledge [*connaissance*] dichotomy remains: nosographic theory is never related to institutional or economic considerations. Although the analysis tries to explain at once the conditions which made modern perception and knowledge [*connaissance*] about madness possible, its verticality lies in forms of discourse directly connected with perception. Psychiatry appears as a compromise between two heterogeneous elements, the abstract field of theory and the concrete space of confinement itself – or, in other terms, 'medical analysis' and 'institutional perception'.[4]

The discontinuities are partial in the sense that the historical investigation does not separate one period from another in any absolute way. Of course, what Foucault refers to as the Great Confinement constitutes a break with the situation of the insane person in the Renaissance in the same way that the asylums of Pinel and Esquirol represent a break from forms of confinement in the classical age. In the same way there are inconsistencies between psychiatric theory, classical nosography and critical understanding of insanity during the Renaissance. But the discontinuities are not total because the theories and the practices are never independent of what went before. There are always prior conditions which have implications. *Histoire de la folie* reveals a process tending towards the increased subordination of madness to the notion of reason. It criticises reason when it analyses its boundaries, the frontiers which reason establishes and moves as it tries to exclude and reduce everything which poses a threat to its sense of order. The movement of these frontiers is not of a continuous nature but tends always towards a more powerful and total domination of reason over madness. Inasmuch as it constitutes a new theory about the nature of madness and new sets of practices in the control of the insane person, psychiatry also appears as a radicalisation of a historical process of domination. It should be noted finally that the historical conditions which make psychiatry possible are institutional rather than theoretical and that it is not so much medical examination which defines, isolates and individualises the mad person as economic, political and social problems.

This leads us naturally to consider the problem of the extent to which archaeology has to be seen as normative. *Histoire de la folie* is not a normative history in the sense that it attempts to pass judgement on modes of discourse by adopting as a norm a present-day view of what science should be. The idea that science progresses, which is the essential claim of epistemology, loses all value in this form of research which, inasmuch as it neutralises the question of progress with regard to the perception of and knowledge about madness, necessarily makes the notion of historical recurrence an impossible one. None the less, the problematic caused by the notion of recurrence remains present and, in fact, provides the structure of the argument of the book, albeit in an inverted way. *Histoire de la folie* gives rise to what one might call inverted recurrence to the extent that the criterion of judgement it uses comes not from the present but from the past. It is a normative work in the sense that it detects in the history of the theories and practices related to insanity a process which reveals how a truth which arises out of and is fundamental to the nature of insanity not only remains undiscovered but is indeed covered up, because it poses a threat, a danger.

I should like to analyse this question more closely and define more exactly the sense in which *Histoire de la folie* is normative. The whole structure of the argument rests upon the existence of the fundamental experience of madness[5] – that is to say, it is seen not just as a historical pattern or something brought about by politics in practice and science in theory, or something which can be looked at in terms of the means by which it is constituted and its stages of transformation; it is seen, rather, as an originating experience more fundamental than historical patterns, which reason has covered up, masked and dominated, but without entirely destroying it: 'Completely ostracised on the one side and completely objectified on the other, madness is never shown for what it is in a language which would be appropriate to it.'[6] Foucault does not try to deal with the positive history of this original reality but is content to point out that such a thing must exist, and does so by means of reference to historical persons like Goya, Van Gogh, Nerval, Hölderlin, and Artaud. . . . He writes a critical and normative history of the negativity of insanity, using as a starting point a value taken to be positive.

Hence the importance of the hypothesis of a fundamental experience of madness: only this experience is able to tell the truth about psychiatry by placing it in the context of a historical process during the course of which insanity has been controlled more or less effectively. During the Renaissance, moral criticism designated it as being more or less illusory; in the Enlightenment, rationalism reduced it to the rank of a kind of aberration; in the modern age, finally, human sciences have pathologised it by considering it as a form of derangement. As such the production of theories about insanity appears to constitute the opposite of knowledge [*connaissance*] to the extent that it invents for it fictive essences and natures. But what is paradoxical is the fact that the aim of this sort of history is to subordinate insanity to reason and truth by developing a pseudo-science, the point of which is to ensure the domination of reason over insanity. Whichever way one looks at it, the history of insanity does not trace the progress of reason towards truth, but the progressive domination of madness so that it can be integrated into the realm of reason. This is what the history of madness comes down to: the history of the fabrication of a massive lie. In this sense, the book very much bears the marks of the epistemological project.

Naissance de la clinique is a concise text which makes no explicit mention of methodological questions except in the preface. Such questions do, however, run through the book, albeit differently from the way in which they appear in

Histoire de la folie. Next I should like to analyse the discourse of archaeological history at this new point of its trajectory, still taking as a starting point the questions of concept, discontinuity and normativity.

The archaeology of clinical treatment such as Foucault conceives it is not only very different from factual histories of medicine; it is opposed to them. Nor is it an epistemological history to the extent that archaeology does not constitute an original and specific object such as theoretical knowledge [*savoir*].[7] In order to show that the break between traditional medicine and modern medicine is archaeological, Foucault states that there has been no break on an epistemological level – that is to say, that there has been no shift from metaphorical to conceptual language, and no increase in objectivity.[8] Archaeology's aim is to produce a type of knowledge [*connaissance*] which epistemology cannot produce because the nature of *connaissance* is not scientific.

Furthermore, the thematic ambiguity between archaeology and epistemology is to be found in a terminological ambiguity. The term 'archaeology' is found in the subtitle of the book – *An archaeology of medical perception* – but it appears nowhere else in the body of the text. Yet the adjective 'epistemological' – which is associated with terms like 'medical attitude', 'medical perception', 'visible', 'invisible', or 'invisible invisibility' – is used on several occasions to designate the object of study which, from a conceptual point of view, defines the archaeological approach of the work.[9]

In *Naissance de la clinique*, archaeological history is situated on two correlated levels: perception and language. 'Medical experience', 'medical perception', 'medical look' [*regard*] ... are expressions used on several occasions as synonyms and as correlative terms to define a space within medical knowlege [*connaissance*]. In this way Foucault uses, throughout his analysis, the term 'spatialisation', meaning the constitution of a visible area or space of medical perception, a space to which modern medicine does not have privileged access. Foucault does not deny the empirical nature of modern medicine. He criticises the dichotomy of the position which supposes that the fundamental character of modern clinical practice is to give priority to the visible over the theoretical. He puts forward a hypothesis to counter this view – and this is the central idea of the book – that the change is due to a transformation in the relationship between the visible and the invisible. From this perspective, the fundamental change from eighteenth-century medicine to modern medicine takes the form of a movement from the taxonomical to the corporeal: the illness becomes spatialised within the organism. In other words, it is the contrast between a surface perception which is deliberately limited to visible symptoms and a deeper perception which, by means of the study of the sick organism, makes the invisible visible. So, it is a change in the very nature of visibility which constitutes the main characteristic of this discontinuity.

But the analysis of medical perception, and the space in which it exists, cannot be dissociated from the analysis of the language of medicine. *Naissance de la clinique* tries to show how the very concept of illness has been transformed from the classical age through to modern times – or rather, how the idea of illness as something with an independent existence has given way to the idea of the body being ill. The break caused by modern medicine is to be found in the movement from ideal to real corporeal space, and consequently the transformation of the language which is intrinsically linked to the perception of this space. As opposed to the dichotomy set up by historians when they define modern medicine as the rejection of theory and choice in favour of experience, Foucault analyses the language in its relationship to medical experience and that which underlies the experience. There is no 'spatialisation' of the pathological without 'verbalisation'. The object of archaeology is 'this region where words and things are not yet separate' – that is, 'the linking of medical language with what it describes', 'the spoken structure of the perceived', 'the fundamental spatialisation and verbalisation of pathology', 'the perception' of the doctor 'put into words'.[10]

It is in fact reflection on the intimate relationship between these two aspects which permits us to make sense of the changes which have affected and transformed the nature of medical knowledge [*connaissance*]. These changes take the form of reorganisations in the relationship between the two terms. In classical medicine, language took precedence over examination and illness was a 'rational', or 'essential' space. Perceiving an illness was the equivalent of interpreting an intelligible order of illnesses within nosographic space on the level of representation. Medical language is here, therefore, necessarily prior to perception. In clinical practice there is a balance between language and perception. Clinical experience becomes analytical because the very space in which perception takes place has a linguistic structure. In the case of anatomical medicine, what is seen is given priority over language. The identification of the space which the illness occupies as being within the sick organism destroys the ideal nature of the illness and makes it empirical. For medicine, the development of a modern language depends on our being able to see inside the substance of the body and discover what has gone wrong on an organic level.

Considered from the point of view of the reorganisation of systems of relationship between perception and language – this being the level of depth at which archaeology operates – the analysis of the changes caused by anatomically based medicine does not make appeal to any theory of historical continuity. Although the critique of retrospective history is constantly present in *Naissance de la clinique*, this critique never has recourse to the criteria of present-day science. At no point is one type of medicine considered to be explicitly superior to another. Even though Foucault on several occasions refers to his study as being epistemological, he is none the less putting forward an original type of history of medicine. However, the idea of inverted continuity which is to be found in *Histoire de la folie* disappears totally: no extramedical criteria are used to pass judgement on the rationality of medicine. The discontinuity between modern and traditional medicine – the central question of this book, which attempts to define a normativity intrinsic to medicine at different periods – is established by means of the analysis of the transformation of the concept of medical knowledge, taking as a starting point the criteria which each period considers to be true criteria, criteria which can be explained in terms of the correlation between perception and language. In *Naissance de la clinique*, these criteria are not situated in the past or in the future – and therefore exterior – but are deeply internal conditions of possibility, 'the conditions defining what can be seen as possible in terms of medical experience', or the 'concrete *a prioris*' of medical experience. This idea will reappear in a later book.

Les Mots et les Choses is Foucault's most ambitious book. It extends – not without important modifications – certain results of the preceding analyses of psychiatry and medicine to a set of principles which constitute what amounts to a general theory of human sciences. The point which concerns us is the fact that he formulates and applies the archaeological method in a way which coincides neither with preceding analyses nor with his later work.

The most important aspect of this meditation on methodology is his definition of the object of analysis as an *episteme*. This is best understood in terms of the notion of theoretical knowledge [*savoir*]. In *Les Mots et les Choses*, archaeology is a history of theoretical knowledge [*savoir*]. What gives unity to the work is the idea, which is new in archaeology, that theoretical knowledge [*savoir*] has a positive nature. Up till that point, Foucault has always used the term 'positivity' in the sense attributed to it by epistemology – that is to say, as a quality specific to scientific discourse. In *Histoire de la folie* he uses it to refer to forms of discourse claiming scientific status, as well as to scientific knowledge itself. Limiting oneself to this form of positivity, or even giving priority to it, would appear in this context to be analytically dishonest. In *Naissance de la clinique*, the adjective 'positive' is used in inverted commas and refers to modern medicine which is generally considered to be positive – that is to say, scientific – for the purpose of showing that there has been no 'psychoanalysis of medical knowledge'. Although, in these two cases, the analysis distances itself from the concept of positivity, it is only in *Les Mots et les Choses* that the concept changes its meaning with, to be precise, the introduction of the concept of theoretical knowledge [*savoir*] as the specific level of analysis and the transformation of archaeology into 'the archaeology of theoretical knowledge' [*savoir*]. Foucault now says that theoretical knowledge [*savoir*], which is the starting point of positivity, cannot be defined in terms of anything other than itself, neither by a more complete form of theoretical knowledge [*savoir*] nor by anything of a different order, like economic or social structures, which would present it only as an expression or projection of itself.

This change of direction in the project of archaeology modifies the way in which relationships are treated between forms of discourse and economic, political and institutional considerations, the importance of which diminishes during the course of subsequent research. In *Histoire de la folie*, these considerations played an essential role: in order to analyse the conditions which made psychiatry possible and the institutional practice of confinement, the modes of discourse and the way they were linked to economic changes were designated as being better able to explain the problem being studied than medical theories about madness. Priority was given to the 'perception' of the mad person rather than knowledge [*connaissance*] about madness. In turn, *Naissance de la clinique* linked different types of medicine with institutions like the hospitals and colleges or, in a larger perspective, with political changes, particularly during the French Revolution. The book showed, for example, the incompatibility between the contemporary concepts of illness and hospitals; or, again, it made connections between the state of medicine and political considerations, linked with the reorganisation of teaching, medical practice and hospitals. In *Naissance de la clinique* social practices come across as being extraneous, even though they retain some importance. It would even be possible to give an account of the general thesis of the book without making reference to them. This is because the main objective of the book – to analyse, on the level of perception [*regard*] and of language, the principles which constitute modern medical knowledge, and to define the specific nature of the break between medical knowledge and the past – required him to give priority to medical discourse. In *Les Mots et les Choses*, which studies the make-up of human sciences on the basis of a conceptual framework of theoretical forms of knowledge [*savoirs*] which constitutes the conditions which make possible the existence of these sciences, Foucault leaves totally to one side the question of the relationship between economic structures and politics. Taking theoretical knowledge [*savoir*] – and no longer perception or appearance – for the first time, in a clear and systematic way, as the specific level of archaeological analysis, Foucault tries to show the intrinsic preconditions for the birth and transformation of given forms of theoretical knowledge [*savoirs*], discrediting all forms of external history. Curiously enough, the 'genealogical approach' undertaken by Foucault just after *L'Archéologie du savoir*, which aims to explain the existence and transformation of elements of theoretical knowledge [*savoirs*] by situating them within power structures, follows a quite different direction which is, from this point of view, much closer to *Histoire de la folie*.

So it is the search for order in the way theoretical knowledge [*savoir*] is constituted that characterises the thinking in *Les Mots et les Choses*. Hence the question of the *episteme*: the *episteme* is not synonymous with theoretical knowledge [*savoir*]; it is the expression of an order, or rather a principle, through which historical order is given to theoretical knowledge [*savoir*]. This is prior to and independent of the ordering of discourse such as it is carried out by science. The *episteme* is the specific order, configuration or disposition which theoretical knowledge [*savoir*] assumes at a given period, and which confers on it a positive nature as theoretical knowledge [*savoir*].

The *episteme* has two complementary aspects which can be distinguished from one another. First of all there is the general, global aspect: 'In any culture, there is only ever one *episteme* which defines the conditions of possibility of all theoretical knowledge [*savoir*] at a given moment.'[11] For each period there is a single corresponding *episteme* which governs the totality of forms of theoretical knowledge [*savoirs*]. *Les Mots et les Choses* is not the history of a science or of a concept. Its investigations take place on a different level, on concepts belonging to different forms of theoretical knowledge [*savoirs*], attempting to establish conceptual interrelationships between them. Life, work and language, for example, are fundamental concepts of knowledge [*savoir*] between which there is no contact. But archaeology attempts to establish a relationship between them, to link them together. Archaeology attempts to find out if there are similarities between the three domains and whether or not the same type of transformation took place at the same moment in each form of theoretical knowledge [*savoir*]. The heterogeneity of the forms of discourse is replaced by a more fundamental homogeneity which reveals the elements of compatibility and coherence as well as the incompatibility and differences between different periods. The primary aim of *Les Mots et les Choses* is to reveal synchronic continuity and diachronic discontinuities between forms of theoretical knowledge [*savoirs*] and to establish the general configuration of theoretical knowledge [*savoir*] at a given period.[12]

Hence the second aspect of the notion of *episteme*: its depth. Archaeology is the historical analysis of theoretical knowledge proceeding from that which characterises it at its most fundamental level. In *Les Mots et les Choses*, surface level, at which most other historical analysis takes place, is seen in opposition to the level of depth which archaeology alone is able to give an account of. On the surface level, one comes across nothing more than opinions which can serve only to create a doxology.[13] Archaeology, on the other hand, analyses forms of theoretical knowledge [*savoirs*] proceeding from 'the historical *a priori*', which means the base element proceeding from which, in turn, the *episteme* provides the conditions of possibility of the forms of theoretical knowledge [*savoirs*] at a given historical period. Thus the notion of knowledge [*connaissance*] as having an ordering process, which characterises all approaches to natural history in the eighteenth century, is also found in attempts to analyse wealth distribution and discourse. What is more, this conception is in harmony with the theory of representation conceived as 'the general foundation of all possible orders.'[14] This is what makes it possible to talk of the *episteme* of the classical age.

In short, archaeology analyses the similarities and differences between different forms of theoretical knowledge [*savoirs*], establishing between them a 'unique network of necessary relationships',[15] the *episteme* of a period, which provides the starting point and the conditions for all that follows – that is, the historical *a priori* which reveals in depth the elementary, fundamental homogeneity.

Seen in terms of verticality and horizontality – by which is meant the global and in-depth characteristics of the theoretical knowledge [*savoir*] of a period – the *episteme* makes it possible to situate archaeology in a relationship with epistemology with regard to the way it deals with discontinuity. By analysing the nature of history on the level of concepts, epistemology denies the continuity of retrospective histories which give priority to thematic and theoretical elements. Being conceptual history, archaeology is discontinuous, like epistemology, but the form of discontinuity which it reveals is different.

We should bear in mind that epistemology takes as its object science in its historical context. It takes as its starting point the historical constitution of scientific concepts, the type of progress which characterises them, the progress made by the objectivity which they demonstrate, the way they produce truths and the criteria of rationality which they set up. Archaeology, with theoretical knowledge [*savoir*] as its object, claims independence from the aims of epistemology and affirms the priority of theoretical knowledge [*savoir*] over science. It is true that Foucault never gives priority to the question of the nature of scientific knowledge and the idea of archaeology is very much linked to the desire to escape from the epistemological process. Hence the importance of perception in *Histoire de la folie* and that of 'look' [*regard*] in *Naissance de la clinique*. Yet what now distinguishes these two types of history – and this is a fundamental new departure in *Les Mots et les Choses* – is the formulation of two specific levels of analysis: archaeology with theoretical knowledge [*savoir*] as object and epistemology with science as object.

From the point of view of the historical nature of theoretical knowledge [*savoir*], what characterises archaeology in *Les Mots et les Choses* is the fact that it analyses sets of theoretical knowledge [*savoirs*], not from the future point of view of the present day, or even of the past, but from the point of view of their own time. 'The history of theoretical knowledge [*savoir*]' can be carried out only if we proceed from that which was contemporary to it, not in terms of reciprocal influences, but in terms of that which was *a priori* present in the period in question.'[16] Archaeological history is neither evolutionary nor retrospective, nor is it interested in recurrence: it is epistemic. It does not postulate the existence of continuous or discontinuous progression, but sees discontinuity in terms of the neutralisation of the question of progress. This is possible to the extent that the present state of science no longer provides the criterion of judgement for the theoretical knowledge [*savoir*] of the past, where this knowledge [*savoir*] is not considered in relation to some goal, like the progress of truth. Yet for all that, archaeology does not seek to invalidate the legitimacy of epistemological analysis and respects the specific level on which the latter operates, and this is precisely because of the way it distinguishes between science and theoretical knowledge [*savoir*].

Finally, we come to the important problem of establishing the criteria of archaeological knowledge. Is it possible to claim that it is not normative? We probably can do so if, epistemologically speaking, we compare *Les Mots et les Choses* with history based on the notion of recurrence. In *Les Mots et les Choses* theoretical knowledge [*savoir*] of the past is never judged in terms of criteria provided by the present, and there is no trace of the notion of recurrence in its investigation of the way human sciences are constituted. No reference is made to reason, objectivity, or truth, as we would see them today. In the same way, there is nothing to suggest a progression of any kind. So the distinction between an outmoded past and a past we can still accept loses all meaning in a history attempting to define 'simultaneous systems' and 'series of mutations', by characterising a period in terms of a unique *episteme* which governs the totality of the forms of theoretical knowledge [*savoir*] and in which each new *episteme* implies a break with the past: a radical form of discontinuity.

Yet for all that, the analysis is not factual or simply descriptive. There is, in *Les Mots et les Choses*, a specific normative element present in the very concept of *episteme*. Proof of this is to be found in Foucault's insistence on the necessary character of the *episteme*. Rather than passing judgement, the normative nature of archaeology gives structure to the theoretical knowledge [*savoir*] of a period, proceeding from the theoretical knowledge [*savoir*] itself, considered in terms of its contemporary context, its generality and its depth – that is to say, in terms of the *episteme*. We should bear in mind that epistemology is not a norm which is external to science; also that present-day science provides its own norm. Archaeology abandons the criteria of truth as defined by science, particularly present-day science. Instead it brings about a double shift in the criteria it uses: from science to theoretical knowledge [*savoir*] and from the present to the contemporaneous. Without completely neutralising the question of truth, it does not take truth as a criterion by means of which science in the past should be evaluated, but tries to define it from within the theoretical knowledge [*savoir*] of the period being studied, in order to establish the conditions of possibility of the discourse which takes place. It is the period itself which, independently of science and the present day, defines its own epistemic truth criteria, the foundation of which is the historical *a priori*.

So archaeology, inasmuch as it avoids judgement in terms of recurrence, preserves the requirement for normativity which epistemology imposes, but shifts and modifies the criteria in order to establish the historical principles by means of which discourse is organised. However, this is carried out in a different way in each investigation. In *Histoire de la folie*, perception and knowledge [*connaissance*] of madness are judged from the viewpoint of an originating experience which is taken to be the norm. In *Naissance de la clinique*, an archaeological discontinuity is perceived between two historical types of medicine, starting with the idea of perception being put into language and the dimension of depth in medical knowledge; in *Les Mots et les Choses*, finally, it establishes an internal and constitutive order of forms of theoretical knowledge [*savoirs*] in their positivity, taking as a starting point the *episteme* which is conceived as the criterion for this ordering.

Therefore, to see the expression 'archaeological method' as a number of rigid procedures which can be used in the production of true knowledge would be to misunderstand the way in which Michel Foucault proceeds. Archaeological history is something which he practises at a precise and datable moment of his theoretical investigations and in his career. What is more, with the publication of *Surveiller et punir* it will be replaced by the idea of genealogy which will itself undergo important modifications. Yet one of the essential characteristics of archaeology remains the multiplicity of ways in which it can be defined, its fluidity as a mode of research which, inasmuch as it cannot be fixed into a rigid canon, means that it is able to learn from its sources. The successive shifts in archaeology are not marks of inadequacy or a lack of rigour, but illustrate the deliberate and well-considered provisional nature of the analysis. It is the idea of an immutable, systematic and universally applicable method that Michel Foucault is asking us to question.

NOTES

1. Cf. for example in *Histoire de la folie à l'âge classique*, 2nd edn, Paris: Gallimard, 1972, p. 174.
2. Cf. *Ibid.*, p. 407.
3. Cf. *Ibid.*, preface to the 1st edn, pp. i–ii.
4. Cf. *Ibid.*, p. 414.
5. This hypothesis, very much inspired by the Nietzsche of *The Birth of Tragedy*, was criticised by Foucault in *L'Archéologie du savoir* (Paris, Gallimard, 1969, p. 64). It is surely for this reason that he withdrew it from the preface in the second edition which, none the less, does not eliminate the hypothesis of an originating experience of madness which is the basis of the whole argument of the book and without which it cannot be understood in its entirety.
6. *Histoire de la folie*, p. 189.

7. This does not come across clearly without knowledge of the second edition of 1972. Foucault introduces terminological modifications. By eliminating expressions present in the first edition of *Naissance de la clinique* (Paris: PUF, 1963), like 'a structural analysis of the signified', and introducing the concept of *savoir* (theoretical knowledge) as the object of the 'analysis of forms of discourse', he was probably wishing to establish a terminological homogeneity with that of *L'Archéologie du savoir*.
8. *Naissance de la clinique*, Paris: PUF, 2nd edn, 1972, p. vi.
9. Cf. *Ibid.*, pp. 158, 169, 184, 197, 199.
10. Cf *Ibid.*, pp. vii–viii.
11. *Les Mots et les Choses*, Paris: Gallimard, 1966, p. 179.
12. This global aspect of the *episteme* was criticised in some writings on *Les Mots et les Choses*. *L'Archéologie du savoir* redefines this concept in a more limited, more specific way. By so doing, it is not criticising the concept itself so much as the fact that it had been poorly understood (cf. p. 27). It is not my opinion, however, that it is just a question of misunderstanding. For proof of this there is the fact that a defender of the work of Michel Foucault, George Canguilhem, in his most rigorous and lucid article on *Les Mots et les Choses* ('Mort de l'homme ou l'épuisement du cogito', *Critique*, no. 242, July 1967), interprets the *episteme* as a universal reference system which makes possible the variety of different forms of theoretical knowledge at a given period (p. 611), or as earth out of which only certain determined forms of discourse can develop (p. 612).
13. On the surface–depth opposition see, for example, *Les Mots et les Choses*, pp. 46, 77, 251, 278, 281–9, 328–9, 339.
14. *Ibid.*, p. 14.
15. *Ibid.*, p. 77.
16. *Ibid.*, p. 221.

SUMMARY OF DISCUSSIONS

Most of the discussion was on the relationship between Foucault and the French epistemological tradition. **Roberto Machado** admitted that his analysis was limited to two works: *Les Mots et les Choses* and *L'Archéologie du savoir*. Before *Les Mots et les Choses* the idea of an archaeology of knowledge did not exist. On the other hand, it is not possible to analyse the genealogical books (like *Surveiller et punir*) from the point of view of a comparison with epistemology – with the work of Canguilhem, for example.

Yves Roussel then put forward the hypothesis that the so-called genealogical books can also be seen in an epistemological context. Could one not compare the way they are written with, for example, the writing of Alexandre Koyré?

Roberto Machado hesitated before replying. In fact he considered that starting with *Surveiller et punir*, the work of Foucault was concerned not with theoretical knowledge [*savoir*] seen as a system of organised perceptions [*connaissances*], but with the conditions which would make theoretical knowledge possible.

By way of conclusion, **Jacques-Alain Miller** described Foucault as a philosopher who was full of surprises and inconsistent, in the positive sense of being beyond the need to be consistent: up to *L'Archéologie du savoir* he thought in terms of a unitary system, and subsequently in terms of multiplicitous systems, criticising conceptual frameworks he himself had used.

two

Notes on phenomenology in Les Mots et les Choses

Gérard Lebrun

Although Foucault does not deal directly with phenomenology in *Les Mots et les Choses*, there are a number of points at which he takes the opportunity to rebut its theses. Should these be seen merely as passing swipes taken by the archaeologist who sees himself already as being outside the mainstream of philosophical debate? This seems unlikely. If the archaeologist speaks, as it were, from the touchline, this is because he wishes to show that the mode of thought which he is situating in the 'configuration' he is dealing with is characterised by an irremediable naivety. And in the case of phenomenology, he is scarcely able to disguise the severity of his judgement. It is seen as a cul-de-sac, a mode of thinking which loses its way the moment it comes into being. For that reason, *Les Mots et les Choses* was not understood, when it first came out, as an attempt to establish a new methodology, but as an act of aggression which brought about the reaction some of us remember. This time is already long distant. The phenomenological tide is on the retreat, and *Les Mots et les Choses* has lost its polemical flavour to the extent that today's reader can easily forget – or fail to realise, depending on his or her age – that the book is combative and philosophical. Today's reader is also less sensitive to the fact that this 'archaeology of human sciences' contains at least the sketch of a history of philosophy.

Drawing attention to this fact is by no means to suggest that *Les Mots et les Choses* is primarily a book of philosophy or a history of philosophy. I know only too well that Foucault was very mistrustful, particularly of this latter discipline, and did not allow himself to practise it. But the fact still remains that in the book indications can be found of a way of rereading Descartes, Kant and Husserl. If we pay too little attention to this, there is a danger that we will reduce the book to the status of an 'archaeological montage', brilliant but somewhat arbitrary. Following this line, one would have to see Foucault as a writer uniquely preoccupied with the methodology of the human sciences, an asepticised 'Author' who was cut off from his sources and from the concerns of the moment. In the same way that it would be superficial to judge this book by a few dislocated statements taken out of context, it would also be misrepresentative to see in it only the birth of a new discipline worthy of nothing more than academic criticism. Indeed, it has not yet come to that. Recent polemics have demonstrated the extent to which Foucault remains, fortunately, an uncomfortable thinker. But it is worthwhile seeing the book in the light of the passion which enlivened it when it was written and recognising, beneath the mask of the archaeologist, a committed, keen thinker who might have been unjust, but if so, then only in the sense that 'to live is to be unjust'. That is why I have chosen to put forward three complementary polemical theses which can be extracted from the book: (1) phenomenology was not capable of understanding the nature of classical discourse; (2) phenomenology was not capable of doing justice to Kant; (3) phenomenology saw itself as the continuation of a very ancient philosophical project, whereas in fact it was very much a 'child of its time'.

I

Foucault claims that we have achieved nothing, so long as we are content simply to give the configuration of theoretical knowledge which characterised the eighteenth century some name like 'rationalistic', without going back, here as elsewhere, 'to the archaic level which makes knowledge [*connaissance*] possible, and the nature of that which can be known theoretically [*savoir*]'.[1] It is often thought that this 'rationalism' is sufficiently understood if it is seen merely as a way of 'making nature mechanical and calculable'. This is already to confuse the systematic mathematisation of empiricism (which in fact started only with Newton) and the 'universal science of measure and order', with which the *Regulae* deal. This is why there is a failure to take into account the precedence, proclaimed by Descartes, of order over measure; that is to say, the fact that mathematisation was only one of the aspects of the *mathesis* of the eighteenth century. The latter was seen at the same time as the science of equality, relative to 'simple substances' (*mathesis* proper) and the science of classification (taxonomy, or qualitative *mathesis*), which dealt with the complex nature of substances found in experience. It is not surprising, then, that this science of the general order of things should include empirical knowledge in which 'no trace of mechanism or mathematisation is to be found'.[2] In the eighteenth century there were a number of forms of knowledge which no one even thought of expressing in mathematical terms. This seems 'strange' to us because we have a distorted view of the idea of *mathesis* which was then dominant. We have lost sight of the fact that 'the analysis of representations according to their identities and their differences – that is, the ordering of things into permanent tables – situated the qualitative sciences without question in the field of a universal *mathesis*.'[3] By this means, Foucault does more than criticise a thesis of the history of ideas: he begins to reject the analysis of *mathesis* made by Husserl in *Krisis*.

When Husserl analyses in *Krisis* the 'unheard-of novelty' of the arrival of modern rationality, he identifies rationality with mathematisation such as one finds with Galileo. The world, which reason is able to dominate little by little, is a world which is in principle indefinitely open to *measure*. This is what happens when Galileo dares to extend the *a priori* which had proved its fecundity in geometry to the '*universum* of being', when he decides that the *whole* which constitutes reality must have its mathematical index. For Foucault, Husserl's interpretation distorts *mathesis*, overstressing the aspect of mathematisation. This has an effect on the way we have to view a number of points in history, as one notices if one reads the beginning of *Krisis* after *Les Mots et les Choses*. The transformation of the classical *mathesis* into a mathematising ontology does not allow one to define the full nature of the 'historical *a priori*' which *predominantly* (but not exclusively) brought about Galileo's extrapolations. What is more, his interpretation discourages us from looking for this 'historical *a priori*' – that is, from asking what it was that made irresistible the rise of the Galilean 'hypothesis' of universal inductivity, which went on to take hold of the world of intuition at a time when the performance of applied mathematics did nothing to warrant this (*Krisis*, § 9d). Why, in these conditions, should the Galilean idea have imposed itself with such a degree of force? Whence could have come this sudden conviction that there could be, properly speaking, no theoretical knowledge 'unless one were able to find a method to construct the world in a systematic way *a priori*' (*Ibid.*, § 9b)? We are told that Renaissance thinkers were 'inclined to make bold generalisations'. But is that enough to explain the fact, emphasised by Husserl, that Galileo did not even consider his astonishing gamble as a hypothesis? Galileo, again according to Husserl, proceeds with such a sense of security because he blindly takes geometry as his guiding thread, and because it does not occur to him to ask what it was that made this idealisation of geometry possible (*ibid.*, § 9h). So far so good. But again, one can ask whether this 'omission' is enough to explain his bold assumption.

From this vantage point it is possible to understand the significance of Foucault's redefinition of classical *mathesis*. If we refrain from seeing this primarily in terms of the 'hypothesis' of *a priori* mathematisation, we can find the answers to these questions – even at times in *Krisis* itself: for example, when Husserl describes the Galilean age:

> It can be seen then, in the happiness of this certitude, that this way of thinking connects that which is closest with that which is most distant, and that it extends from that which is more or less known, to the unknown. This is because it constitutes an infallible method of extending knowledge, by means of which it must be possible to know the entire Whole of being, in its totality and in the fullness of its being-in-itself – through infinite progress.[4]

This extract already sets out quite well what Foucault will mean by 'the reign of Representation'. The difference is that in *Les Mots et les Choses* this movement from the principle of being to its representation is not seen as being engendered by the ideal of mathematisation (as it was, too hastily, according to Husserl). It is now the movement itself which makes the ideal possible. It is not because he gave full confidence to 'so-called geometrical intuition' (*Krisis*, § 9h) that Galileo posited 'universal inductivity', but because he belonged to a time when 'the way of being of things and order'[5] prescribed the 'obviousness' of this region of theoretical knowledge. To sum up: (1) Foucault's analysis of the *mathesis*, following the *Regulae*, shifts the centre of gravity of classical knowledge: it is the *orderable*, not the *calculable*, which is universally guaranteed; (2) supposing that the Galilean ideal is what Husserl is describing, it is the field of Representation which accounts for the way it came into being, not Galileo's imagination, nor the notion that he had 'inherited' the geometrical *a priori* in an already consolidated form.

The polemical character of the notion of Representation appears when one looks at Foucault's analyses alongside those of *Krisis*. It could be said that both books aim to describe classical thought in its naivety. But Foucault is also concerned to respect its specific nature. He wished to understand *positively*, under the actual circumstances, why it is only 'to our way of seeing things' (as indeed Husserl recognised) that Galileo formed the boldest of hypotheses, whilst, as far as Galileo was concerned, he was doing nothing of the sort. In the same way, it is only *from our point of view* that Galileo did not even consider it worth legitimising this certainty when he posited that true being is *a priori* accessible to calculation. If this is the case, we should be wary of seeing as a philosophical error, as a lack of *thaumazein*, that which might well define the originality of an order of knowledge which is so distant from our own that it has become extremely difficult to discern the conditions by means of which it functioned.[6] Thus, when one considers the effort Foucault made to detach himself definitively from non-contemporary texts, one gets a better understanding of why it was that he formed the concept of the *episteme* and also the (paraphenomenological) concept of the 'historical *a priori*'. It was necessary to point out using new words that it is, in principle, impossible to understand the nature of a configuration of theoretical knowledge so long as one sees the way it comes into being in terms of an 'omission'; a *Verdeckung*. It is worth calling the age of Representation a 'historical *a priori*' even though this might seem disconcerting and even though the term might subsequently be abandoned; this is above all to point out to the reader that before highlighting the omissions and unthinking mistakes of classical thought, it is prudent to reconstitute the system of constraints which decreed that certain things were obvious and made certain questions impossible. If Galileo and Descartes did not baulk at what, for phenomenology, is enigmatic, this is perhaps quite simply because this *thaumazein* had no place in their structure of knowledge. Rather than enumerating the presuppositions which escaped their notice, we should begin by questioning the presuppositions which make us consider it natural that they were speaking a language which should be directly accessible to us, and that their discourse should be such as to provide, in consequence, a means of access for our criticism – without any difficulties of principle.

We can take this further by asking whether seventeenth-century thinkers were even capable of undertaking an investigation of the legitimacy of concepts or the explication of meanings. The archaeologist's answer is that they were not. The time for this sort of questioning was not yet ripe. In this case it would not be right to say that Descartes let slip the idea of transcendental thought at the very moment when he had it in his grasp, nor that Hume had already undertaken the work which would have led to its establishment, but that his empiricism stopped him from realising this. There is no need whatsoever to use their 'mistakes' to serve the purposes of *objectivism*. There is no point in regretting that Descartes missed the idea of the *transcendental ego*, when he was far from being able to foresee it. 'At that point in time' the Cogito could have appeared only as the first link in a chain of reasoning. Nor is there any reason to follow Merleau-Ponty in pointing out the abstract nature and the inadequacy of the Cartesian Cogito.

> Or rather, these objections can arise and can be justified, but from the starting point of a profoundly different form of discourse, not one whose purpose is to provide a link between representation and being. . . . So long as the classical mode of discourse lasted, it was not possible to articulate the criticism of the nature of being which the Cogito implied.[7]

Nor is there any reason to consider the God of seventeenth-century writers as a *kosmotheōros*, forged by 'overarching thought', as a result of a lack of radical criticism. If *all things* must necessarily have a place within the project of Representation, their finiteness has to be measured – in particular the finiteness of being human – against the yardstick of infinite perfection. Far from being a facile solution, theology was an integral part of the system of Representation.[8]

So it is possible to talk in terms of a failure or a block in classical thought only so long as we postulate a continuity between this form of thought and our own, a continuity which would naturally have given us the right to judge it in terms of the performance of functions which it would, however, have been quite incapable of conceiving. The moment we reject this tacit postulation, we have also to abandon the Husserlian interpretation. It is no longer possible to sustain the notion that the classical *mathesis*, perverted by 'objectivism', never managed even to begin work on the transcendental foundation of knowledge, while all the time this work was crying out to be done. It would be more rigorous, philosophically, to start from the opposite hypothesis: the reason why *mathesis* irresistibly imposed its idea of a 'true world', to the extent that it made impossible any investigation of the idea that there might be such a thing as a world 'given in advance', is that classical thought was a thousand miles away from being an effective transcendental philosophy. If this reading seems paradoxical, even provocative, this is because it disturbs the habits of thought which go back to post-Kantianism. By subjecting classical thought to forms of criticism which contained a latent yet always hidden transcendental element, all that phenomenology was capable of doing, after all, was to reinforce the way of thinking which the history of philosophy, as taught in universities, develops in us. We are so impregnated with 'Kantianism' that we are led, albeit disingenuously, to transform every classical author we study into someone who could or should have detected the problematics of transcendentalism (however much importance we might decide to attach to this). Foucault makes a clean break with this tradition. This is precisely what makes it possible for him to pay homage to Kant in a way which was no longer officially sanctioned by academia. Kantianism is seen as a revolution in thought. This idea loses its banality when Foucault reveals once more the abyss which separated Kant from the mode of thought which Kant himself called 'dogmatic' and which archaeology designates by the neutral term 'age of Representation'.

II

Again on this point, it is useful to read *Les Mots et les Choses* in relationship to Husserl. Whatever shifts and complexities there might have been in Husserl's relationship to Kant, it can be said, from an archaeological point of view, that Husserl did not fully appreciate the change which came into being as a result of Kantian criticism. This underestimation of Kant's role was probably inevitable from the moment the concept of 'objectivism' began to be used as a means of interpreting seventeenth-century thought. In fact Kant, according to Husserl, is also the victim of this same 'objectivism', which is why Kant was unable to penetrate to the core of the transcendental question, understood as the 'reflexive question about the ultimate source of the formation of knowledge' (*Krisis*, § 26). Strong evidence for this is provided by his *regressive* methodology: '*if it is necessary* that our experience should be that of objects in nature, *then* it is necessary that . . .' To commit oneself to this mode of argument is to accept more than ever the world of the 'world-given-in-advance'.

Also Husserl does not decide to recognise in Kantianism the threshold of modernity. Kant probably had the merit, he says, of distinguishing between *objective science* 'as something which is taken on loan and remains in the realm of subjectivity', and *philosophy*, which is the 'theory of how the loan comes into being' and thus unveils 'the naivety of any philosophy of nature-in-itself which claims to be rational'.[9] Does this mean that the *Critique* marks the end of the 'happy certainty' in which the classical age lived? No. Husserl refuses to go so far. He says that we should not forget that Kant saw the *Critique* as a prelude to 'a philosophy in the ancient sense of the term; that is to say one concerning the *universum* of being, and consequently also capable of reaching the *En-soi* which is rationally unknowable'[10] – that is, by any means other than those of theoretical reason. Thus, nothing had changed, 'in spite of it all', in the traditional concept of philosophising. '[Kant's] problematic occupied exactly the same territory as the rationalism running from Descartes to Wolff, via Leibniz.'[11]

It might seem that Foucault wrote *Les Mots et les Choses* in order to refute this judgement. One can, in any case, find in the book elements of a reply which Kant might make to Husserl's criticism, so closely does Kant follow the Kantian process. One would not therefore be losing sight of *Les Mots et les Choses* if one were to go on to rediscover, in Kant, the distinct pronouncement of the end of the age of Representation. Kant is aware of being the first philosopher to rectify the orientation of metaphysics by calling into question the 'assurance' of metaphysicians regarding *a priori* knowledge. Where did this 'assurance' come from? It came from the fact that these metaphysicians had been misled by the example, presented to them by mathematics, of an endless extension of *a priori* knowledge, and that they did not ask themselves what the nature of this *a priori* knowledge was, and whether or not it had any limits. It was certainly not the mathematicians' job to ask this question, 'since their concepts could not go beyond the boundaries within which the objects of thought relevant to them are given'.[12] Nor was there any reason for mathematical physics to suspect a limit to *a priori* knowledge. 'The extension of *a priori* knowledge even outside mathematics, by means of simple concepts, and the fact that this extension is a means of generating truth, are both sufficiently upheld by the concordance of judgements and principles with experience.'[13] Scientists therefore have no need to ask questions about the origins of concepts of space and time, nor about pure concepts of understanding: for them the movement from object to representation is guaranteed. And this explains their quite legitimate suspicion of any attempts at eludication. The origin and value of their concepts 'are not of any concern to them ... which they find very useful. Given all that, they do very well, provided that they do not go beyond the limits assigned to them: the limits of nature.'[14]

All in all, Galileo, for Kant, had every reason to be 'objectivist', since he was thinking within the horizons of Representation.... In metaphysics, as we know, it is a different matter. The philosopher was wrong to suppose that he was operating in the same territory as the mathematician, and that *a priori* concepts which he uses are, in principle, linked with being. That is, until the moment comes when he is finally forced to suspect that it is impossible for him, with his *a priori* concepts, to 'manage to penetrate as far as things which are not objects of experience'.[15] Then he has to be aware that the 'co-belonging of being and representation' is not guaranteed in all areas, and that it is not his business to deal with things which, by right, are knowable in themselves.

One transhistorical overview is worth another. If we accept Kant's – as Foucault does after his fashion in *Les Mots et les Choses* – we have to agree that it is not 'objectivism' in Husserl's sense of the word which is the key element, but the certainty that being can *always* be represented directly. Indeed, Kant does not make this certainty into the characteristic of an *episteme*. He attributes it to an ancient mistake which began with Plato, or rather, with the self-interpretation of Greek geometry which made Platonism possible.[16] So he recognised and at the same time misunderstood what Foucault designates as the reign of Representation. He misunderstood it inasmuch as he saw its origins in terms of a philosophical *mistake*, which could perhaps have been avoided (if Plato, for example, had not allowed himself to be won over by the enthusiasm of the Greek geometricians). Yet he recognised it to the extent that he defined it sufficiently to be able to expel from the field of play metaphysicians who should never have been there in the first place. The important thing was that he did recognise it (thereby at the same time relegating any philosophy unconcerned as to its own limitations to the category of *dogmatism*). For the first time, Foucault says, 'the space of representation' is criticised at its very foundations and questioned 'as to its rightful limitations. For the first time recognition is given to this European cultural event which took place at the end of the eighteenth century: the retreat of theoretical knowledge and thought outside the space of representation.'[17]

It is on this basis that Foucault undermines the phenomenological criticisms of Kant. To see in Kantianism a way of thinking which allowed the continued predominance of 'the evidence of objectivity' is to miss the essential point. The esential point is that, with Kant, the classical *mathesis* is swept away for ever. The postulate of integral representability is suddenly abandoned, and analyses of represented order are replaced by an analytic; that is, reflection on the conditions which make order possible, which is situated *outside* the 'table of identities and differences'. It is essential, for example, that the systematisation of nature into types and species should now be subject to a 'transcendental supposition', which is not necessarily immediately accessible to the classifier.[18] In short, representation has from that point 'lost the power, using itself as a basis, and as it itself is deployed, by a process which is self-referring, to ground the connection between its own diverse elements'.[19] So any objections addressed to Kant are, to say the least, negligible if they do not take into account the decisive nature of this 'event below'. For these critics simply fail to understand that transcendental thought arose *solely* with Kant. The most they can do is to confuse the issues. So, according to Foucault, nothing could be more unfortunate than to reproach Kant, as Husserl does, with having failed to grasp and follow the thread of the Cartesian Cogito, the very thread which Kantian critique had broken, deliberately and for ever. This is what phenomenology failed to perceive because it failed to grasp the extent of the subversiveness of Kantianism. The result was, Foucault thought, that all phenomenology could do was to gravitate around Kant, since (although it failed to realise this, which in fact reveals repeatedly its lack of 'radicalism'), archaeologically speaking, it was totally derived from Kantianism.

III

Foucault never describes a form of philosophical thought as being the victim of an *error*, in the way the 'people' and the realist philosophers were according to Berkeley; the 'dogmatists' were according to Kant, 'objectivist' thought was according to Husserl, and so on. This form of critique is always carried out by someone claiming to be redressing the 'error', and to be leading us back to the point where it could have been avoided. This *serious*[20] discourse no longer takes place in archaeology. The archaeologist does not denounce errors. The most he would do would be to speak of a distance between the task prescribed to the 'philosopher' by the *episteme* which (unbeknown to him, obviously) had brought him into being, and the absolute knowledge of which he thought himself the bearer. Since there is now no longer any question of our being able to discourse in a way which is finally liberated from all illusions and all presuppositions, we have to be content with determining just what was the function of the 'philosophy' we are dealing with, leaving to one side the claims it was making. It is obvious that these claims might not be 'true', since the very function of the philosopher is to go beyond his *episteme*.

As far as phenomenology is concerned, there are at least two ways, according to Foucault, in which it can be called 'a child of its time', and dependent on the 'underlying event' which the *Critique* instigated. First, its discourse was made possible only by the *separation of levels* between the 'field of real knowledge' and philosophical reflection – which arose for the first time in the *Critique*. In fact, the *Critique* was able to question the existence of a 'way of being common to things and to knowledge' only through its 'distancing itself in principle' in its relationship with objective sciences. And this distancing transformed our subsequent understanding of 'philosophy'. The result was the establishment of an entirely new mode of 'philosophical' discourse whose 'view of universality' was no longer the same as that of philosophies which had come before.[21] To give just one example: it was at this point that a division of labour and interests came about between the 'theoretical technician' and the philosopher. The very idea of such a division would have been quite alien to Descartes or to Leibniz. The philosopher's job, henceforth, was to be to elucidate the implicit, to detect presuppositions, and to reveal 'naivety' in all its forms. From this point of view, Husserl's critiques of Kant are of less importance than the initial *position* which he adopted and which permitted him to formulate them. Kant, we are told, had not stood back sufficiently from objectivity. But the important point is that it was only with Kant's work that, by definition, philosophical reflection became able to stand back from anything, or to stand independently at all.

Secondly, what happens in phenomenology illustrates perfectly the role of the analytic of finitude, which no transcendental philosophy can help but play. In the very concise passage where Foucault describes Husserl's place in the nineteenth-century *episteme*, he mentions two characteristics which make Husserl, archaeologically, a 'post-Kantian'. The first is the desire to *ground* ('to anchor the rightful claims and the limits of formal logic in reflection of a transcendental nature'). The second is the desire to *unveil* (to see the transcendental as being indefinitely present in the empirical).[22] It is this second characteristic which *Les Mots et les Choses* emphasises. Here, phenomenology appears above all as prefiguring the 'anthropological age'. This is an astonishing diagnostic which begins to become comprehensible only if one goes back to Kant, paying attention to the connection which is made from the beginning between the *transcendental motif* and *finitude*. The *episteme* in place at the time could not have functioned without this connection.

The coming into being of new positive elements (like the concepts of life, work, language) which to some extent are determinants of what it is to be a human being in fact posed the problem of how the human being, acclimatised as he was to this state of affairs, might discourse in a way which could be seen to be true.[23] This problem would have been insoluble if modern thought had continued to operate with the concept of *negative finitude* which classical thinkers had used (taking finitude as the sum of our imperfections, our distance from the infinitely perfect Being . . .). But this concept, as we know, only had any place or usefulness under the regime of Representation. The Kantian transcendental device makes it possible to replace this with a quite different *positive* and *grounding* form of 'finitude'. The notion of *positive finitude* is probably familiar to the reader of Merleau-Ponty. But Foucault's originality consists here in placing it at the heart of the Kantian *Critique*, exactly where the reader of Merleau-Ponty would least expect to find it: in the transcendental subject, which one should be careful not to consider as the *overview* which Merleau-Ponty tirelessly criticises. To do this would be to distort Kant and to give too much credit to 'neo-Kantian' interpretations. This, at least, is the lesson which comes out of Foucault's book. The essential point of the *Critique* is the advent of a subject who possesses *a priori* knowledge only to the extent that he is deprived of intellectual intuition; that is, to the extent that he is finite. This inexhaustibly fertile *topos* was 'necessarily' rediscovered by phenomenology, and exploited to the full. It was 'necessarily rediscovered' because of its reassertion of the transcendental, 'to the extent', Foucault explains, 'that it asserts itself against psychologism and naturalism, that is to say, from its point of departure'.[24] It is impossible for anyone who takes up the transcendental motif – and particularly for anyone who radicalises it – not to make use of the notion of a 'grounding finitude'. From the point of view of this link between the transcendental and the finite, the archaeologist does not have to go along with the criticisms which Husserl and Merleau-Ponty bring to bear against the Kantian transcendental subject and its abstraction. With regard to the constituting *ego*, and then the 'being-in-the-world', he is entitled to describe the metamorphoses of this 'non-empirical' and 'finite' subject, which Kant had situated *outside* representation, as the *fundamental element*.[25] It is true that Kant took only a few steps along the way. That much can be conceded to Merlau-Ponty. But he had established – and this is the decisive point – the apparatus by means of which phenomenology was to be able to rediscover the transcendental in the empirical, and succeed, in an indefinite way, in transforming all apparent factual truth into truth based on reason, and even, in the extreme case of Merleau-Ponty, in breaking down the barriers between these two religions.

This analysis, the severity of which appears clearly enough in the ninth chapter, at least does phenomenology the favour of allowing it to maintain its unity, and sparing it from being presented, for example, as a kind of wayward logicalism. Foucault safeguards the coherence of phenomenology. But at what cost? There are grounds enough for criticising his reading of Husserl. As has been pointed out, *Les Mots et les Choses* accurately targets the thought of Merleau-Ponty, but Foucault seems to take it for granted that Merleau-Ponty expresses the truth about Husserl's thought – though this is, as has been shown,[26] very debatable. Moreover, because Foucault sees phenomenology as being centred on the notion of a grounding finitude, he is *a priori*, and unjustly, denying the value of any reading which discovers in Husserl a treatment of the themes of metaphysics which is even deeper than the author had thought. But let us leave to one side these objections, numerous though they might be, which a historian might make regarding Foucault's reading of Husserl. Not only because an examination of this nature would go beyond our purposes, but also because it might lead us to assume that *Les Mots et les Choses* contains a *critique* of Husserl. Now, Foucault does not go on to write a critique but, as Deleuze says, a 'cartography'. To situate is not the same as to criticise, and to locate a position is not the same as to reveal presuppositions. It might still be said, though, that this process of location amounts to a brutally reductive process. But this would not be pertinent either. Indeed, it would be too weak a term to describe what amounts, quite simply, to an act of destruction. By this I mean the presentation of a philosophy in such a way as to put off possible future readers. Indeed, it might well be that in the field of the history of philosophy there have been far fewer true critiques than is supposed, and far more acts of destruction.

However this may be, we can see the point if we ask ourselves simply which way Foucault is pointing us. Once we have finished the book, what vision of phenomenology will we be left with? That of a philosophy and of two ways of seeing it. The first of these, the most clearly elucidated, is the idea of a way of thinking which has to be seen in the context of its time if we are to understand the *necessity* which brought it into being. Foucault says that the analysis of life as lived [*le vécu*] is a prerequisite of the epistemic field: it is 'quite necessary'. And so phenomenology appears, to whomsoever is able to see, as 'the instrument, very sensitive and finely tuned, of the great break' leading to anthropology.[27] The deliberately disconcerting homage which he pays to it comes down to this: that it is rooted in factitiousness (which the historical Husserl never conceded) and in the circularity between the transcendental and the empirical such as one finds in Merleau-Ponty, and that this is what made phenomenology inevitable and noteworthy. The reader might well wonder what, when it is seen in this light, has become of the traditional image of Husserl (the *épochè*, the transcendental reduction, the debate about Husserlian idealism . . .). This is the second viewpoint, about which archaeology seems to leave us in the dark. But this casualness is only apparent. If the reader goes back to Husserl's canonical texts, he will see that they too have their legitimate – though chronologically surprising – place in the archaeologist's scheme of things. One might begin by considering what guarantee there is of the 'principle of principles' in *Ideen I*; that there is 'an original donor intuition . . . which is the source through which knowledge [*connaissance*] is made known to us', and that this *parousia* is not beyond our reach. This is the *parousia* which Descartes had glimpsed, and which reduction allows us to grasp systematically and exhaustively. Yet the question is whether the exploration of this dimension is as new as Husserl claims. This is the question the reader of Foucault has to ask when he considers this second viewpoint. Because when it comes down to it, it is the resources of 'Representation', in Foucault's sense, that the phenomenologist believes himself able to use. Thus, when Merleau-Ponty assures us of the *existence*, in a sense of the term which will bear up to patient elucidation, of a place where there appears 'not only the meaning of words, but also the meaning of things',[28] he is clearly describing what Foucault calls the 'table' [*tableau*]. The question now is: what value can we attach to this postulation of absolute knowledge, after we have read *Les Mots et les Choses*? The answer is that it can only seem obsolete. If we accept the pertinence of the archaeological description, we have to admit that phenomenology, which is behind the times as far as its *episteme* is concerned, is claiming to be able to restore the Age of Representation (albeit purified, we might suppose, of 'objectivism'), and as such flies in the face of its own configuration. It is then up to the reader to judge what to make of this 'representative' daydreaming going on in the middle of the twentieth century. In any case, the reader of Foucault is left with a choice between only two views of phenomenology. Either it is an analytic of finitude, and this is the truth about the nature of the Husserlian project whose 'insidious relationship with empirical analyses of man'[29] becomes increasingly apparent; or it is a recommencement of representative discourse, which the advent of the 'anthropological age' has doomed, in advance, to failure. Otherwise it has to be seen as a 'discourse of mixed nature' which leads to an impasse or to claims which are not compatible with its time. We are locked into this dilemma by the very construction of *Les Mots et les Choses*. And this point is perhaps even more important than the centring of phenomenology on the founding notion of finitude. For the analysis of phenomenology, which is carried out in the second part, would be merely arbitrary if it had not been carefully prepared by the analysis of the seventeenth century in the first part (and this is why it is worth rereading this latter, at least once, as an anti-*Krisis*).

If we accept Foucault's description of 'Representation', and if we agree that it would be impossible for us to go back on the 'great turning point' of which Kantianism is the philosophical indicator, we can no longer raise any objections in principle against the judgement passed by the book. What we may do, though, is ask whether or not the concept of Representation was not formed in such a way as to make it possible for Foucault to discredit in advance all attempts to reconstitute absolute knowledge after Kant. The *Critique* marks the dislocation of the *mathesis* (in the broad sense which Foucault tends to give this concept). After this dislocation, it is necessarily vain to attempt to set up the Idea of an authentic *Wissenschaft* which bears the hallmarks of Platonism in the way that Husserl attempts. There is not, and there never has been, any Idea of theoretical knowledge which could, by and by, have been perceived, and which it was granted to our time, finally, to see deployed. There was only one regime of theoretical knowledge [*savoir*], of Representation, which existed, innocently, for two centuries. This was the mode of being and the order on the grounds of which knowledge [*connaissance*] spontaneously organised itself, and made it at once useless and impossible to attempt any form of transcendental grounding. Then this 'pattern' was upset, and from that point *grounding* and *unveiling* became the principal tasks for philosophers; yet at the same time these were tasks they were no longer *in a position* to accomplish. It was possible to live in the possession of absolute knowledge [*savoir*], as happened during the seventeenth and early eighteenth centuries, but once this has been lost, there is no going back. After Kant, positive finitude is the only possible grounding of the justificatory discourse, if one insists that there should be such a thing, which goes by the name of 'philosophy'. In short, if one accepts the divide between Representation and Anthropology, one also has to accept that phenomenology has to be confined to the analytic of finitude, because, from an archaeological point of view, it could never be taken seriously as the heir to Plato or Descartes.

Foucault did not, of course, design the concept of Representation, or write *Les Mots et les Choses* with the sole purpose of settling accounts with Husserl. It would not be appropriate to suggest or even set out to look for a *key* to such a rich book. It remains a fact, however, that the Representation–Anthropology divide has the effect of denying any authority to phenomenology, as if the author had *also* wanted, by means of what he wrote on this subject, to deliver himself once and for all from the influence exerted by phenomenology. What we are dealing with is a break or turning point. It is clear, however, that this notion is a delicate one, and has to be handled with care in the history of philosophy. It is not enough for a writer to 'break' openly with a tradition or with one of his predecessors in order to lose all attachment to them. In Kant's work, Leibniz remains present in texts other than those in which he is dealt with specifically, and Nietzsche's debate with Schopenhauer still continues in *The Will to Power*. Problematics and methodologies can remain impregnated with the thought of someone one has once and for all 'broken with'. This could be the case with Foucault's relationship with phenomenology. Indeed, he dissociates himself for good from the analysis of life as lived [*le vécu*], and proceeds as a 'happy positivist' to enclose Husserl in the anthropological age and push back the reign of Representation into the past. But would it be right to see here a pure and simple 'break'? Should one forget that 'historical *a priori*' is a term which originates with Husserl, not to mention the attraction which the word 'archaeology'[30] held for him? How also could one avoid being struck by the way phenomenological reduction resembles the position of detachment and neutrality adopted by the archaeologist? When the very form of thought which Foucault is showing up as naive and unaware of its position is the form of thought which saw it as its main aim to expose the traps of 'naivety', is he not, when it comes down to it, acting as the 'ultimate phenomenologist' – as someone offering a 'phenomenology to end all phenomenologies', as Dreyfus and Rabinow[31] put it? Husserl's philosophy functions in a similar way inasmuch as it is continually transgressing its own principles as a result of the radicalism of its research. 'The greatest lesson of reduction', as Merleau-Ponty said, 'is that total reduction is impossible.' Why not go one step further? The greatest lesson of phenomenology, for anyone who has managed to take the greatest possible step back from 'the obvious', would be the impossibility of phenomenology.

There is an affinity, at least a rhetorical affinity, between phenomenology and archaeology. One might think, for example, of the passage in which Foucault notes the distance he adopts in relation to immediate perception [*le vécu*]. One has to dare to ask a question, he says, which 'probably seems off the rails, so much is it out of line with what makes our thought historically possible. This question would consist in our asking whether man really exists.'[32] What is the point of this provocation supposed to be? To make the reader consider, once the initial surprise is over, how deeply 'humanist' presuppositions are rooted in his way of thinking, since to question these comes across initially as a joke. Fink uses an analogous procedure when he tries to show neo-Kantians how wrong they are to align Husserlian problematics with their own. You Kantians, he says to them, at least have the virtue of problematising 'being in general'. Yet you still think from the starting point of the world, whilst phenomenology 'questions the unity of being and the form of the world', and 'addresses itself to the question of the origin of the world'.[33] Fink does nothing to hide the hubris of this position. Yet how else can one demonstrate the way this unprecedented problematic comes into being to those who are absolutely unable, as a result of their 'attitude', even to begin to see the possibility of its existence?

It is worth considering the extent to which Foucault does reuse the framework of phenomenology and continues its task of unveiling presuppositions. One might also think of the systems of constraints, transformations and limitations which make it possible for the archaeologist to point out, in the texture of the 'configurations' he is studying, the impossibilities and connections which would remain unnoticed by anyone who was not attempting to establish, as a priority, 'conditions of possibility . . .'. These prohibitions and prescriptions, which characterise the 'historical *a priori*', abound in Foucault's analyses. It was, for example, *impossible*, in the age of Representation, to think of anything as a 'living being'; and *impossible*, in the age of Man, to preserve the application of the Cogito; and *necessary* that, in taxonomy, the knowledge of plants should have done better than the knowledge of animals; and so on. The question is whether these statements about impossibility and necessity end up controlling the nature of the final picture we get. One cannot avoid finding in these archaeological rules of exclusion at least some measure of similarity with the incompatibilities of essence, the strength of which Husserl could not have emphasised better than by invoking, rhetorically, 'God Himself' (who, if He had a body, would be able to perceive only in terms of sections).

One might object that the *Archéologie du savoir* is designed in such a way as to make it, in principle, impossible for such a *rapprochement* to be made; that the 'conditions of possibility' in question are not aspects of a *logos* but simple conditions for the appearance of forms of knowledge, and that the 'historical *a priori*' should not be considered (though this would be 'pleasant', according to Foucault) to be an 'empty form' which comes to the fore in human thought, then disappears after its reign.[34] We may agree with this entirely. Yet at this point it is necessary to distinguish between two separate things. On the one hand, the use of expressions like 'conditions of possibility' and '*a priori*' (to which Foucault has recourse in *Les Mots et les Choses* just about every time he wishes to show what is new about his way of reading history) certainly does not mean to suggest that in this book there is the equivalent of a reading of essences. Such an interpretation would result in the reintroduction, into the very heart of each *episteme*, of exactly what archaeology excludes in all its forms: the transcendental subject. Moreover, the author can in no way be held responsible for a misreading of this sort. It is not his fault if the phrase '*a priori*' is taken as 'essence' or if the 'conditions of possibility' seem to be inseparable from some 'subject' who is the bearer of them. On the other hand, the fact remains that the rules of the game which Foucault reconstitutes drastically limit the choices possible within each *episteme*. Now, what status can we give to these rules, if we are to remain faithful to the spirit of archaeology? They do not come from some *Zeitgeist*. Nor do they result from *lacunae* in information, nor from technological *backwardness*, nor from the *shortsightedness* of authors who 'have not yet foreseen that . . .' Foucault relentlessly rejects any 'explanations' based on the negative. How then are we to understand the strict ordering of possible tasks and procedures which can assure us of the originality of a configuration of theoretical knowledge?

The question becomes all the more pressing if we admit that the archaeological method cannot be reduced to the nominalistic exercise of putting things into inverted commas ('rationalism', 'biologism', 'mechanism', 'empiricism', etc.) to form macro-concepts which can subsequently be destroyed, in a way which the history of ideas and the history of philosophy often find most convenient. Indeed, it is to Foucault's credit that he forbade us to use 'philosophical' words without mentioning or researching their date of birth or the date when they came into use. Indeed, he casts suspicion on superficial panoramas with which, inevitably, theologians of meaning are satisfied. Also he enjoins us to relegate to the level of idle chitchat discourses about 'man', 'emotions', 'finiteness', and so on, which shy away from this initial philological examination. None the less, there is nothing relativistic or nihilistic in his attitude, for Foucault sweeps aside this chitchat of new metaphysicians only in order to substitute systems for the rigorous determination of theoretical knowledge [*savoir*]. These systems did not fall from the skies, and their formulation is worthy of clarification.

It is not, therefore, inconceivable that Foucault should have made use of phenomenology in the very book where he was unceremoniously sending it packing. By so doing, he did not surreptitiously become 'essentialist' but simply went back to the determinants by means of which a configuration of thought establishes that which is 'true for itself'. It is in this way that Nietzsche himself gave meaning to the notion of *a priori*:

> If we establish everything which is *necessary* according to our current way of thinking, we have proved nothing about that which is 'true in itself', only that which is 'true for us'; that is to say, that which makes our existence possible by virtue of experience – and this process is unalterable to the extent that to want to change our way of thinking about it would be impossible. This is where all *a prioris* are to be found.[35]

So, in order to bring to light these initial determinants which only chance has brought together (and certainly no source of meaning, no transcendental subject), it suits the archaeologist to have recourse to Husserlian concepts like 'horizon' or 'idealising presupposition'. It does not make one 'essentialist' to determine, with exactitude, that at a given time, human beings, in a particular area, *were bound* to develop a certain concept or, inversely, that they were *incapable* of seeing into a region of experience ('labour', 'life', 'sexuality') which nowadays is so familiar that we do not even think of seeing such things as *interpretations*. On the other hand, the notion of the *a priori* does not become unusable for having been excluded from its eternal form. It is by no means to diminish the originality of archaeology (which can too easily be said to have been a 'failure') if we study how it came into being from this point of view. This might make it into an instrument by means of which the 'history of philosophy' could be renewed, in such a way that it would pay attention, at last, to the death of what, academically, is still seen as constituting 'philosophy'.

NOTES

1. *Les Mots et les Choses*, Paris: Gallimard, 1966, p. 68.
2. *Ibid.*, p. 71.
3. *Ibid.*, p. 258.
4. Husserl, *La Crise des sciences européennes*, transl. Gérard Granel, Paris: Gallimard, 1976.
5. *Les Mots et les Choses*, p. 14.
6. *Ibid.*, p. 315.
7. *Ibid.*, p. 323.
8. *Ibid.*, pp. 327–8.
9. Husserl, *La Crise des sciences européennes*, p. 110 (§ 25).
10. *Ibid.*
11. *Ibid.*, p. 112.
12. Kant, *Progrès de la métaphysique*, transl. Guillermit, Paris: Vrin, pp. 83–4. Cf. *Critique de la Raison pure*, transl. Tremesaygue-Pacaud, Paris: PUF, p. 36.
13. *Progrès de la métaphysique*, p. 13.
14. *Critique*, p. 500.
15. *Progrès de la métaphysique*, p. 82.

16. *Critique de la faculté de juger*, transl. Alexis Philonenko, Paris: Vrin, § 62.
17. *Les Mots et les Choses*, p. 225.
18. *Première Introduction à la Critique de la faculté de juger*, § 5.
19. Cf. *Les Mots et les Choses*, p. 251. Cf. p. 255.
20. I have taken this expression from Hubert Dreyfus and Paul Rabinow.
21. *Les Mots et les Choses*, pp. 260–61.
22. *Ibid.*
23. *Ibid.*, p. 331.
24. *Ibid.*, p. 336.
25. *Ibid.*, p. 256.
26. Cf. Hubert L. Dreyfus and Paul Rabinow, *Michel Foucault: Un parcours philosophique*. Paris, Gallimard, 1984, p. 59. Jacques Derrida, Introduction to *L'Origine de la Géométrie*, Paris: PUF, 1962, pp. 108–20, 127.
27. *Les Mots et les Choses*, p. 336.
28. Maurice Merleau-Ponty, *La Phénomenologie de la perception*, Paris: Gallimard, 1945.
29. *Les Mots et les Choses*, p. 336.
30. Cf. Suzanne Bachelard, *Logique de Husserl*, Paris: PUF, 1957, p. 219.
31. Dreyfus and Rabinow, *Michel Foucault*, pp. 128, 71.
32. *Les Mots et les Choses*, p. 332.
33. Eugen Fink, *De la Phénomenologie*, transl. Didier Franck, Paris: Éditions de Minuit, 1974, pp. 119–21.
34. *L'Archéologie du savoir*, Paris: Gallimard, 1969, p. 169.
35. Nietzsche, *Le Gai Savoir. Posthuma*, transl. Klossowski, Paris: Gallimard, p. 348.

SUMMARY OF DISCUSSIONS

Various contributions led Gérard Lebrun to clarify Foucault's relationship with phenomenology. **Hubert Dreyfus** wished for clarification of Foucault's objections to Merleau-Ponty. **Gérard Lebrun** stressed Foucault's admiration of Merleau-Ponty. He wondered if Foucault had overestimated him as being the bearer of the truth about Husserl. In any case, this made it possible for Foucault to interpret the destruction of phenomenology, as a result of its tendency towards irrationalism, as the accomplishment of its destiny, to the extent that this can be seen as a transcendental philosophy with a Kantian source.

In the same way, replying to a question from André Glücksmann, **Gérard Lebrun** gave his opinion that *Les Mots et les Choses* owes nothing to Heidegger, who, in this book, undergoes just about the same treatment as Merleau-Ponty.

Jeannette Colombel noted that Foucault did not deal only with Merleau-Ponty, but also with Sartre, when confronting the problem of phenomenology. By way of reply, **Raymond Bellour** mentioned that the pages on Sartre were removed from the final version of *Les Mots et les Choses*.

three

Foucault and Marx

The question of nominalism

Étienne Balibar

It might seem strange nowadays to want to go back to the question of the relationship between Foucault and Marx (or Foucault's attitude towards 'Marxism'). It might be thought that any charm or interest this question might have possessed had been exhausted by the end of the 1970s, all the arguments having been set out at the time of the vigorous exchanges we still remember. Foucault himself commented at length on the issue in articles and interviews. At the same time, it is not difficult to imagine the irony with which he would have greeted the kind of analyses and formal interpretations which inevitably result when parallels are drawn between established works and writers in a way which takes these to be self-consistent. Although this is exactly the territory I wish to cover, I should none the less like to do so obliquely (taking, as it were, a diagonal path) in a way which will show up the main concerns in a slightly different light, in the hope of finding new questions so that the philosophical work being done on Foucault, as on Marx, can be continued.

It is tempting – perhaps indispensable if we are not to read Foucault in a merely pious way – to apply to his texts (I am thinking here particularly of his books) his own principle of analysis of the rules governing the formation or individualisation of statements [*énoncés*]: that we should look for their correlation with others, those which 'populate the margins around them', and with which they 'enter into the process of dispute and contestation', in order that we might 'rediscover how it was they came into being' (*L'Archéologie du savoir* [*AS*], pp. 128, 138, 159); also that we should, for that reason, reconnect effective statements [*énoncés*] to the discursive tactics which have come into being, and produce their effects in the context of a given strategic field; and that we should study the transformations of these tactics to see how, by the very fact that these particular affirmations have been made, the territory in which they intervene is modified. There is no question, of course, of speculating on that which is unsaid or on intentions. The affirmation of theoretical discourse, which is already of a political nature, should be taken literally within its own 'incorporeal materiality' (*AS*, p. 158). Philosophy is, as has been clear since Kant's time, a *Kampfplatz* in which there is no definitive settling of conflicts and in which, consequently, no intellectual scheme ever occupies a position which is absolutely simple and stable but develops in opposition to existing statements [*énoncés*], as a result of their incessant 'problematisation'.

If we are to see a special function in the opposition of Marx and Foucault in this perspective, something has to be made clear straight away. I shall form the hypothesis that, in ways which were constantly changing, the whole of Foucault's work can be seen in terms of a genuine struggle with Marx, and that this can be viewed as one of the driving forces of his productiveness. We can see that this struggle had already been engaged the moment he began to write *Histoire de la folie* (since, as Pierre Macherey opportunely pointed out in a recent article, it is in his repudiation of his initial adherence to Marxism, conceived of as a 'concrete critique' of alienation, that one should seek the reasons for which he henceforth 'shunned like the plague everything which arose out of dialectic materialism'). The struggle was still in progress after *La Volonté de savoir*, as is demonstrated by extracts from lectures, articles and conferences from the 1980s. None the less, this struggle is not a simple duel, for several obvious reasons. First, Foucault undertakes different programmes of work where a confrontation with Marx intervenes in a more or less decisive way and which, more interestingly, are not always addressed to the same 'Marx' or the same 'Marxism'. It is also true that the continuity of these confrontations with Marx might appear to us, in retrospect, as one of the strands which give unity to Foucault's research, from book to book and from archive to archive. Also, it is clear that the Marxist affirmations he deals with are not taken in academic isolation but are seen in conjunction, determined as they are by their usage and interpretation, so that the result is rather like an X-ray of the tissues of Marxist thought and an evaluation of the role of Marx in contemporary knowledge (the names of Sartre, Merleau-Ponty, Althusser and the Frankfurt School can serve as examples of this). But most importantly, it appears evident that for Foucault, the struggle with Marx never had an end just in itself and cannot be dissociated from other confrontations in which the role of Marx is secondary or tertiary, or even primary. We should note immediately that this situation of 'the tactical polyvalence of discourse' (*La Volonté de savoir* [*VS*], p. 132) forbids, in this respect, not only all claims to exhaustiveness but all claims that it is possible to reduce what is at stake in the combat to one sole question. As he develops his own questioning, Foucault does not cease to ask Marx questions which come from other philosophical and historical origins, just as he does not cease to ask other interlocutors, or adversaries, questions whose formulation depends on Marx.

I propose to illustrate this hypothesis by the use of one singularly striking example. It derives from the way in which, in *La Volonté de savoir*, the questions of Marxism and of psychoanalysis are interwoven. This is a polemical and at the same time programmatic work, the perspective of which was later, of course, somewhat altered. Yet its unity comes precisely from the adversaries he chooses for himself and from the way he associates them.

It is not enough to say that what Foucault is doing here is to attempt to question a particular conception of power and a certain conception of sexuality, by means of demonstrating what underlies them both (the 'hypothesis of repression') and leads them to confer on these concepts an essentialist definition. The important fact is that, throughout his work, he takes it upon himself to undermine a problematic found throughout the 'epoch', systematised in what we can call, generically, contemporary 'Freudo–Marxism' (Reich, in particular, being named on several occasions). Foucault himself points out, with precision, the major themes:

- the reciprocal implication of sexual repression and the exploitation of the workforce in capitalist society (*VS*, pp. 12–13, 150–51, 173) and the corresponding notion of sexual liberation as resulting directly from and being part of the political and social revolution (*VS*, pp. 14–15, 105, 173);
- the complicity of moral censure, the 'policing of what can be said' [*énoncés*] and the reproduction of economic relationships under the domination of the same political order (*VS*, pp. 62–4, 111–13, 132, 143);
- the homology in this respect of the global bourgeois order and the authority exercised in family and educational 'cells' by the Father-Figure who is common to both (*VS*, pp. 62–4, 111–13, 132, 143);
- the more general opposition between a natural energy tending towards the seeking of pleasure and the artificial order of institutions, the prohibition of incest and the assertion of the monogamous family and the State (*VS*, pp. 95, 107–8, 146, 151). From this comes the notion of the hypocrisy of the dominant classes (*VS*, p. 168), culminating in the fiction of a 'reality principle' against which the 'great refusal' can be opposed, the global subversion of values established by means of lies.

We might wonder why it should have been so important to Foucault to criticise these themes. The answer would probably be that Freudo–Marxism is at the same time high on the agenda of popular and academic culture; that it is a kind of geometric locus for the sort of intellectual currents which attempt to establish relationships between different disciplines, like different branches of philosophy, science and literature, militant, theoretical and aesthetic practices;

because it is, in sum, the *natural point* towards which *the alternative to human sciences* tends. The hold of Freudo–Marxism thus extends well beyond its explicit expression, encompassing current pyschological discourse every bit as much as that of the followers of Bataille. Now, Freudo–Marxism (in whatever form) is a 'reversal' of values pronounced by powerful institutional apparatuses, effectively inspiring dispute within these apparatuses, struggles whose importance Foucault recognises, but about which essentially he considers it important to find out to what extent they really do break with the forms of discourse they denounce. It would not be wrong to suppose that what Foucault – who is hardly to be suspected of conservatism – wants radically to question is the clarity and the effectiveness of a certain form of left-wing thinking or revolutionary utopianism.

Other reasons still seem to come into play. The way Foucault criticises Freudo–Marxism suggests that for him, such a 'combination' should, as a general rule, reveal precisely *how it is* that Marxism and psychoanalysis should belong to the same field of theoretical knowledge, how it is that they should, as it were, share the same pedestal. It is not certain that they can be reduced to what they have '*in common*', but it is certain that, in what they share, a form of determination must operate which is essential to both of them. Marxism and psychoanalysis cannot be interpreted in any illusory pure form, but in their use and application, and particularly in the way they are applied each in respect of the other (which gives a particular example of the way each of them works in the field of 'human sciences').

Turning the argument back on itself, it appears too that a criticism of this nature acts as a counter-proof to the autonomy of Foucault's own discourse, to the extent that it deals, at first sight at least, with the same 'objects': the institutions of power, of resistance, exclusion, social treatment of moral and sexual 'deviance' and its importance in the political economy of modern societies. Notions like that of 'normalisation' and the 'disciplinary society', put forward in *Surveiller et punir*, echo at least verbally (and this cannot have happened by chance) Freudo–Marxist themes in which a reader would not necessarily have to be naive or antagonistic to see a substitute for or generalisation of these ideas (this 'risk' will always be present in the analysis of the 'pastoral' form of power, since it is concerned with the way in which a certain regime of sexuality takes its place in the 'economy' of the modern state: see the 'Two essays on the subject of power' reproduced in Dreyfus and Rabinow's book *Michel Foucault. Un parcours philosophique*). Now the closeness of the objects and even of the words used in Freudo–Marxism and in Foucault's research (a closeness which would go even further if it appeared that Foucault was proceeding to combine anti-Freudian and anti-Marxist concepts in an *antithetical* way) is accentuated in *La Volonté du savoir* by the final emergence of the notion of 'biopower' and by the repeated designation of contemporary *racism* as the crucial phenomenon for which it should be able to account. As initially conceived, *Histoire de la sexualité* was to have ended with a volume on 'Population and races'. The place occupied by the problem of racism in the research perspectives which Foucault outlines here is considerable (*VS*, pp. 37, 56, 73, 88, 155–7, 161–8, 179 ff., 193–8). Racism can indeed be seen as the most revealing 'concrete' effect of the play of modern political technologies on the *life* of individual bodies and on the level of populations, or on the 'species' and the way it reproduces itself. Likewise it can be seen as the major indicator of how deeply anchored in the contemporary regime of knowledge–power (and even, as Foucault finally comes to specify it, 'knowledge–power–pleasure' [*savoir–pouvoir–plaisir*]) notions like 'degeneracy' and 'eugenism' have become, given that in these notions can be seen the very essence of the way the compromise is formed between the symbolism of race and the symbolism of sexuality (*VS*, p. 195). Foucault knows perfectly well that the need to account for contemporary forms of racism, their 'mass' dynamic, their hold on the individual 'personality' and their relationship with war (discussed at length in the last chapter of *La Volonté de savoir*) is at the origin of Reich's Freudo–Marxism and also that of Adorno and Marcuse (the theoretician *par excellence* of 'repressive civilisation'). He also knows that one of the most acute difficulties confronting Freudo–Marxist theorisations (in any case with Reich, to whom Foucault refers repeatedly at this point) comes from the troubling proximity of their biologism, or energism, with racist ideologies themselves. Therefore he cannot avoid asking himself: *under what conditions* does the analysis of power in contemporary societies cease to be caught up in this same ambiguity? The reason for this is that this power too would, fundamentally, be a *biopower* or power over the species, rooted in a 'biohistory' and ordering a 'biopolitics'. At this point the critique of Freudo–Marxism becomes not just a theoretical introduction but an indispensable proof in demonstrating the different nature of his own concepts and adjusting their practical effects.

It is well known how, during the course of *La Volonté de savoir*, a critique of 'the hypothesis of repression' is developed at the same time as its function is explained with regard to the economy of discourse about sex: that is, the *injunction* to talk about sex, to find out the 'truth' about it and to find in it the truth for *all people*. This injunction assures the proliferation of the discourse in question (which makes modern Western societies the most talkative in history about sex, and indeed the inventors of the notion in its generic usage) is not attentuated but, on the contrary, tactically reinforced by the way the prohibition is represented. On the basis of this characterisation, Foucault puts forward three major arguments in opposition to Freudo–Marxism:

1. First, its historical *falseness*. It is materially untrue that the society which develops from the eighteenth century, 'which can be called, as one prefers,

bourgeois, capitalist, or industrial' (*VS*, p. 92), fundamentally denied sexuality and effectively censured it. On the contrary, sexuality was something which received constant attention. And in the same way it is false that a precondition of the 'putting to work' of the working masses, the proletariat, was an emasculating supervision of the sexual body of workers (*VS*, p. 167). What is historically true is that, on the contrary, sexuality, *with* its regulatory and constraining devices (family morality, in particular the prohibition of incest, the way education was managed, medicalisation and psychiatrisation), was *imported* into the sphere of work on the basis of a bourgeois model. This happened from the moment economic relationships began to evolve towards the social integration and subtle normalisation of the workforce (and probably also towards the increasing intellectualisation of this force). Correspondingly, the 'asceticism' of bourgeois morality should be represented not as a condition of economic rationality or, inversely, as hypocrisy, but as a tactic by means of which physical pleasure can be intensified.

2. Next there is the dependence on a purely *juridical* model of power which is simultaneously limited and archaic; centred on the representation of the sovereignty of the Law (moral Law, political Law, symbolic Law). Here we are touching on the common core of psychoanalysis and Marxism which makes their combination possible, even inevitable. Each recognises its own presupposition in the other. More precisely, each recognises in the other a variation of the idea of the subjugation of individuals to a dominant power which is supposed to take the form of *obedience* (*VS*, pp. 112–13). In opposition to this, Foucault – from the time of *Surveiller et punir* at least – never ceases to put forward the idea of 'discipline' (though in fact for him this idea goes back a long way: see, for example, *Histoire de la folie* on the 'positive' meaning of the power of confinement; or *L'Ordre du discours* on the 'affirmative power' which genealogy attempts to describe).

We should note that from the moment the idea of subjugation–obedience comes in, together with that of *alienation*, there is a profound relationship between them (since obedience, in the last analysis, has to be founded on the interiorisation of the Law which arises out of external authority; since in this way it determines a split in the subject which can take on the privileged form of the body–soul duality, but which is also found in the public–private duality or in the dualism of State–society). In the belief that it is able to *discover* an explanatory principle in the homology of State and moral censure, Freudo-Marxism – and in general all the variations of the repressive hypothesis – do nothing more than *repeat* the imaginary schema already present in an identical form in each of their two composing parts.

3. Taking a step further, then, we can see, throughout the length of the text of *La Volonté de savoir*, a systematic criticism of what I should be happy to call – referring to a philosophical tradition which very early on attracted the

attacks of materialists (Lucretius) – *the principle of social homoeomery*: by which I mean the idea that, in the social (or political, or cultural) 'whole', the 'parts' or the 'cells' are necessarily *similar* to the whole itself. As it happens, the focus of Foucault's criticism (in this sense a materialist criticism) concentrates on the question of the *family* (though it also touches on other institutions and apparatuses, like those of the school and medicine). Foucault stresses the strategic role of the family (its moralisation and its medicalisation) in the apparatus of the regulation of populations which forms one of the essential powers of the 'bourgeois' State; also it is important for him to show that the family is simultaneously the locus of institutional perversion (*VS*, pp. 50 ff.), the hysterisation of the woman's body (*VS*, pp. 131, 138, 146), the space which is the opposite to psychiatric space (*VS*, pp. 147–8), the central concern in the competition between holders of professional knowledge about man (*VS*, pp. 131, 138, 146), the means of socialising reproductive activity and, in particular, the locus of the juridical 'recoding' of bodily techniques in general into forms of alliance or kinship (*VS*, pp. 138, 142–50, 165). It is for all these reasons that the family *cannot* be considered as the reduced *image* of the global society. 'The family does not reproduce society, and the latter, by corollary, does not imitate it' (*VS*, p. 132). The family is a 'local centre' of power–knowledge (*VS*, p. 130), but not a monad *pars totalis* of 'the society', and its strategic importance lies not in its resemblance but in its specific nature or in its difference. Therefore it is no more the case that the family is a little State than that the State is a large patriarchy.

Now this analysis can be generalised immediately with regard to *all* institutions whose practices contribute to the production of this complex object referred to as 'sexuality', and it forms an essential part of the criticism of the representation of power as 'a general system of domination exercised by one group or element on another, the effects of which, seen in terms of successive amplifications, are supposed to run through the whole social body' (*VS*, p. 121) – or, in other words, of the social organism (an organism in which, rather than the model of the body, one should see a perpetuation of the idea of the soul or the spirit). This illustrates concretely the need for what Foucault calls *nominalism* (*VS*, p. 123), even though this reduces the critical effect of some of *his own* formulations. In *Surveiller et punir* he had written, during the course of his description of panoptism: 'What is surprising about the fact that prisons resemble factories, schools, barracks, hospitals, all of which in turn resemble prisons?' (*Surveiller et punir* [*SP*], p. 229). And even though he clearly warned the reader to be wary of the temptation to see in the 'panoptic view' anything other than a *programme*, immediately subject to the variables of what might happen when it is put into practice in a given field of resistance, he none the less presents prison as a 'carceral archipelago' (*SP*, p. 304) made of several concentric circles of institutions, or disciplinary practices constituting 'a means towards the perpetual surveillance of the population: an apparatus which makes it possible to control, by means of offenders themselves, the whole social field' (*SP*, p. 287). As such it comes across as the starting and finishing point of all the varieties of normative power, the totality of which constitutes a 'disciplinary society'. After this, Foucault seems to break with the idea that the definition of large-scale 'diagrams of power', proper to a given society, could be founded on the formal homology of institutions (in which there is always the idea that each of them is a piece in the greater mechanism *of* power, or that it participates in the generic essence of power). It seems that he adopts instead the thesis of the '*equivocal nature of power*' and goes on to study the historical articulation of its different practices, which in turn implies – in a way which designates a break with the philosophical tradition running from Kant to Marx (or at least the 'young Marx') – that there is no longer such a thing as *the* practice of power, but *practices*, each specified by its own 'technology'.

Yet this critique goes back to, and helps to define more precisely, a fundamental theme which could be said to have run through the whole of Foucault's work, in counterpoint with his critique of humanism and of the 'anthropological circle': the critical investigation of 'political psychologism' in the broadest sense of the term. By this is meant both the idea that historical and social processes have their roots and conditions of possibility in the way individuals are determined, whether this be freely or by means of constraint (an idea to which 'sexual psychology' or a psychology of sexual personality brings an extra dimension of apparent objectivity), and the symmetrical idea according to which the psychology, behaviour or awareness of individuals reflects the functional positions they occupy in the field of institutions or political contradictions (Marxist 'class consciousness' was often no more than a variant of this idea). Foucault never ceased to explore the origins and institutional forms of this mirror-relationship; that is, he never ceased to ask why it is that in contemporary society – especially since the more society 'modernises itself' the more it 'politicises itself' – politics (be this the practices of a government or the forms of resistance these cause) is projected into psychology and constrains individuals to identify with a 'self' (or a 'group self') in order to act as social beings. What are the models of subjectivity which individuals have to imitate in order to be able to take part in these practices? In this respect, the utopian politics of Freudo–Marxism seem to be a simple reversal of values, yet they none the less remain totally caught up in the psychopolitical framework and thus reveal the psychologism inherent in its two parents, Marxism and psychoanalysis.

Here, in any case, the symmetry ends. In the context of *La Volonté de savoir*, Marx and Freud become the objects of totally different treatments. It is not my aim here to try to see if one is more correct than the other, but to describe the way in which this asymmetry demonstrates Foucault's discursive strategy.

It seems that this strategy (as a result of the initial objective of the 'history of sexuality') is *directed first against psychoanalysis*. This is because psychoanalysis postulates that sexuality has no history (or that sex is the one thing in the whole of history which transcends history, according to the schema of the enunciation of the limits of human finitude which is described in the final pages of *Les Mots et les Choses*). But it also seems that since the critique of psycholanalysis is carried out *by means of the use*, *to some extent*, of Marxism (or, if one prefers, by turning certain affirmations which are associated with it in the Freudo–Marxist mix) against psychoanalysis itself, it is necessary also to challenge the whole transcendental aspect of Marxism, present in the very language of historical immanence (the idea of a historical *law*), which would reduce its critical power to nothing. Thus, depending on the vantage point one adopts (I will not dare go so far as to say one's preference for 'Marx' or 'Freud' as theoretical reference points), one could begin to feel either that the main point is the break with Freud, to which the critique of Marx is only a means, or that the critique of Marx is so thoroughgoing that it *necessitates* a definitive settling of scores with psychologism which includes psychoanalysis. And here, naturally, it is the whole apparatus of 'the political history of truth' (*VS*, p. 81) which is at stake; the idea of reversing the traditional idea of a truth which is supposed to be 'fundamentally related to freedom', to show that 'truth is not free by nature, nor is error servile, but its production is completely enmeshed in power relations'. Psychoanalysis, as Foucault sees it, poses a fundamental obstacle to this critical thesis, because it is completely caught up in the practice of *confession*, and also in the denial of this practice, because it makes of sex itself the truth which 'demands' to be liberated; whilst Marxism *can* make a decisive contribution, provided that it is possible to dissociate it from that part of itself which identifies the *telos* of liberation with the final manifestation of truth: the part which is rooted, in the last analysis, in the hypothesis of repression.

Would this mean that the critique of psychoanalysis is situated in the category of *ideology*? Foucault has always challenged the term (and does so again here: *VS*, pp. 91, 129, 135, 168), though there is a brief but notable exception, in *L'Archéologie du savoir*. But this is not always for the same fundamental reason. A retrospective overview would show, it seems to me, that the Marxist notion of ideology (such as Marx puts forward in *The German Ideology* – that is to say, not so much as a reflection, but rather as the social being's 'consciousness of self', or as the abstraction of the 'language of real life') was always bound to figure, even if only implicitly, in the same field of discourse and knowledge [*savoir*] which makes it possible for archaeology to criticise scientific claims. The movement is made, in any case, from a problematic of sign and representation to a problematic of practice. Rereading

Naissance de la clinique – a book which does not address itself directly to Marx, and with good reason, but where the historical categories of cultural experience are inflected in the direction of an analysis of institutional practices – there is no escape from the conclusion that Marx's 'language of real life' would appear to Foucault as a scarcely transformed variant of Condillac's 'language of action' (and consequently the whole theory of ideology as that which is left behind by [. . .] Ideologists), in which History is substituted for Nature in the role of originating experience, and the reciprocal mutual relationship between sign and thing would close into oneness. On the contrary, rereading the analyses of the 'production of discourse' which follow on from *L'Ordre du discours*, it appears that what causes the problem in the notion of ideology is its anthropological presupposition, its implicit reference to a subject's alienation, including that which comes in the form of 'misunderstanding', or 'illusion', as implied by relationships of domination. Between these two critiques, *L'Archéologie du savoir* represents a fleeting moment of unstable equilibrium (which is also the only moment at which Foucault refers to Marx, Freud and Nietzsche as being on an equal footing as initiators of the 'decentring of the subject'). The Marx to whom Foucault has recourse at this point, in order to describe the 'incision' between ideologies and sciences in the history of discursive formation, is none other than the Marx transformed by Althusser into a theoretician of the articulation of practices, amongst which therefore 'discourse practices' would also figure. But the moment is unstable, because the designation of the formation of discourse as the formation of ideologies always tends to collapse the articulation of power and theoretical knowledge [*savoir*] into an articulation of misunderstanding and understanding (in the sense of *connaissance*). From that point, the unity of 'power–knowledge' [*pouvoir–savoir*] shifts the question of ideology to a point where all practices are equivalent with regard to their truth, rather than substituting for it another name to serve as a critique of the forms of knowledge [*connaissance*]. Every practice, as an exercise in power, implies norms of truth, procedures of dividing between truth and falsehood; and (scientific) knowledge represents in this respect only one form of power exercised amongst others.

Although psychoanalysis is not to be criticised as an 'ideology', Foucault none the less clearly does put forward – in ways which very much call to mind the critique of speculation as it is found, for example, in *The German Ideology* – a genesis of sex as 'ideal point', 'the most speculative, ideal, the most interior element', 'the imaginary point' or 'imaginary element' about which the historical apparatus of sexuality orders individual experience (*VS*, p. 172). And he tells us that this genesis is valid at the same time as 'an archaeology of psychoanalysis'. Psychoanalysis can escape the hold of this *idea* of sex neither theoretically (since, for psychoanalysis, sex is the epitome of truth itself) nor practically (since the psychoanalytic technique depends entirely on sex being banned and on the injunction to return it to its rightful place). The result of this is that the hypothesis of pyschoanalytic nominalism is quite simply absurd, whilst a Marxist nominalism can at least be considered.

The rejection of Freudo–Marxism can, then, be read as a simple introduction of a Marxist criticism of psychoanalysis:

> There are those who think it is possible to denounce at the same time two symmetrical hypocrisies. . . . This is to misunderstand the process by means of which, on the contrary, the middle classes, through an arrogant political affirmation, endowed themselves with a sexuality about which they liked to do a lot of talking. The proletariat refused to accept this sexuality from the moment it was imposed on them for the purpose of subjugating them. If it is true that 'sexuality' is the sum of the effects produced in bodies, ways of behaviour, and social relationships, by a certain apparatus which arises out of complex political technologies, it must be remembered that this apparatus does not act symmetrically on either side and that it does not produce the same effects. It is therefore necessary to return to formulations which have for a long time been disparaged [*sic*]; it must be said that there is a middle-class form of sexuality and that there are different forms of sexuality in different social classes. Or rather, that sexuality is originally and historically bourgeois, and it brings about, during the course of its successive shifts and transpositions, effects specific to its class. (*VS*, p. 168)

This is precisely one of the shifts to which Foucault refers in order to explain, if not how exactly psychoanalysis came into being (since psychoanalysis is present as an object of knowledge [*savoir*] throughout the history of the objectification of sex, the whole history of the articulation of sex, word and prohibition), then at least the time and place of its formation.

In the same way that sexuality exists as a substance, or rather a 'class body' (*VS*, pp. 164 ff.), so too the very substance of psychoanalytic discourse and practice cannot be dissociated from a class position, in the sense of a place which it occupies in the strategic relationships between the classes (*VS*, pp. 170 ff.). Previously, Foucault had argued at length against the idea of a parallel between the political repression of poor classes and the control of sex (*VS*, pp. 158 ff.). As soon as it became necessary to conceive of the family as a place where the apparatus of sexuality is *intensified*, sexuality came to be seen as constituting primarily a bourgeois *privilege*, both from the point of view of pleasure and from the medical point of view, and as such it became a fundamental element of bourgeois culture. Yet it also becomes the basis of State racism, rooted in the middle classes and linked with heredity and eugenics:

> And this process was linked to the movement by means of which it affirmed its difference and its hegemony. It should probably be conceded that one of the primordial forms of class consciousness is the affirmation of the body; at least

> this was the case for the middle classes in the course of the eighteenth century; it changed the blue blood of the nobles into a healthy organism and a healthy form of sexuality; it is understandable why the bourgeoisie took so much time and put up so much silent opposition before it recognised the bodies and sexuality of other classes – exactly those classes which it was exploiting. (*VS*, pp. 166–7)

The industrialisation, urbanisation and social conflicts of the nineteenth century called this privilege into question and brought about the extension of the 'sexual body' to the whole social body (*VS*, p. 169) – that is to say, the extension of the family, medical and demographic techniques of sexualisation. The *class division* then shifts: no longer bearing on whether or not a sexual body experiences pleasure, but on the way in which the interdiction is imposed and treated: 'Those who had lost the exclusive privilege of nurturing their sexuality have, henceforth, the privilege of being more able than others to test out the nature of the interdiction, and of being in possession of the method by means of which the repression can be countered' (*VS*, p. 172). At the same time, amongst the middle classes, psychoanalysis takes pride of place as a critical method in the apparatus of psychiatry, and the lower classes are stigmatised as hotbeds of 'racial' degeneracy and subjected to administrative and judiciary controls designed to drive out incest and the like.

This situation of psychoanalysis in terms of social class is only one of the two sides of the criticism. On the other side, which deals formally with the *underlying ideas* of psychoanalysis, a thematic approach not dissimilar to that of Marxism is also at work. Or rather it is here that the reference to Marx inevitably has to be seen to enter into the analysis of ideas. In the psychoanalytic representation of sex founded on the interplay of that which is hidden and that which is manifest, of desire and law, of death and family being fundamentally linked, it is necessary, according to Foucault, to see, rather than the simple following through of the development of the disciplines by means of which the body is normalised, a return to the juridical model, or rather to the 'juridical discursive model' (*VS*, p. 109) of power over the practices which give rise to this. One might be tempted to see this as a contradiction internal to the rules and norms, such as was analysed in more detail in *Surveiller et punir* (in which he showed first that 'the power of the Norm' was in opposition to 'the power of the Law', (*SP*, pp. 185–6), and then that in disciplinary power – that is, normative power – there is the 'surplus power' or the 'supplement' which alone confers on juridical fictions their hold on reality by *creating a juridical reality* (*SP*, pp. 224, 251, etc.). Moreover, it is by referring to this critical turnround, which is carried out in the name of law or of its juridical idea, during the course of which it attacks the very disciplines out of which it none the less proceeds, that Foucault highlights what he calls the 'political honour of psychoanalysis' (*VS*, p. 197) and its practical and theoretical opposition to fascism, which goes back to the very source of his initial break with the organicism of the 'grand system' of perversion, heredity and degeneration (*VS*, pp. 157–8).

Therefore, at the heart of this (psychoanalytic) idealism, there figures the undisputed power of the *juridical idealisation*; the historically constituted imaginary notion of sovereignty. Foucault describes this power as an illusion, but only to the extent that it perpetuates an anachronism:

> A normalising society is the historical effect of a technology of power centred on life. Compared with societies such as we knew them until the eighteenth century, we have entered into a phase of juridical regression; the written Constitutions throughout the world since the French Revolution, the Codes which are drawn up and revised, the whole relentless and noisy legislative activity which takes place should not create any illusions: these are all forms of activity which make an essentially normalising power acceptable. (*VS*, p. 190)

But for a few words ('life' instead of 'work', 'normalisation' instead of 'economic', though in both texts there is talk of production, or rather, productivity) we are, it seems, curiously close to Marxism, the sort of Marxism which, like Marx in *Poverty of Philosophy*, puts forward the idea that 'the windmill will give you a society with sovereignty and the steam mill will give you a society with industrial capitalism' and denounces Proudhon's 'fiction of the personal society'; the same Marxism which, along with Marx in the *Eighteenth Brumaire* and Lenin in 1905, describes the 'constitutional illusions' of revolutionaries, repeating the forms of the struggle against feudalism; and indeed the same Marxism which, along with the Marx of *Capital*, describes in factory legislation an effect of permanent 'excess' in power relations over and above the juridical forms of contract.

None the less, we have now gone as far as we can go. And this is not only because Foucault describes Marxism, indirectly, as caught in its own trap with regards to the *State*, where the monarchical sovereignty is represented in a way which results in the State being condemned to oscillate between the idea of all-powerfulness and the idea of its being radically without power, or as having a purely parasitic function, according to an all-or-nothing dialectic (already in *Surveiller et punir*, discussing the ideas of Rusche and Kircheimer, Foucault had systematically opposed the law of 'all-or-nothing' with regard to control or destruction such as one might imagine regarding State apparatuses, and the diffuse network of effective 'micro-powers', which act even on the level of bodily contact (*SP*, pp. 29 ff.). For one could go so far as to interpret this dependence of Marxism on the juridical illusion (or the 'decisionist' illusion, founded on the antithesis of law and violence) which he himself criticises, as an internal inconsistency, or the point where his analysis of exploitation and his analysis of the State get out of synchronisation. So a part of Marxist discourse could be interpreted as *an internal debate about the juridical representation of power*, which is symmetrical in the sense of the internal debate which psychoanalysis extends into disciplinary practices and forms an integral part of nineteenth-century humanist socialism:

> Another type of criticism of political institutions appeared in the nineteenth century: a criticism which was far more radical since its aim was to show not only that real power was beyond the rule of law, but that the system of law itself was nothing more than a means of exercising violence, of annexing it to the profit of some rather than others, and calling into being, in the guise of a general law, the asymmetries and injustices of domination. But this critique of law is still founded on the assumption that power must, by essence, be exercised according to some fundamental law. (*VS*, p. 117)

Foucault himself suggests ways of getting out of this mirror-relationship between law and the critique of law. He does so in *Surveiller et punir*, taking up Marx's analyses in *Capital* regarding the division of labour in production, in order to show how disciplinary procedures increase the utility of the body of workers by neutralising their resistance, and more generally how this permits the unification of the two processes of the accumulation of labour and the accumulation of capital (*SP*, pp. 221 ff.). 'Discipline' and 'micro-power' therefore represent *at the same time* the other side of economic exploitation and the other side of juridico-political class domination, which they make it possible to see as a unity; that is to say, they come into play exactly at the point of the 'short circuit' which Marx sets up between economics and politics, society and State, in his analysis of the process of production (thus permitting us to see it in terms of a 'practice'). Foucault does this again, but in a different way, in *La Volonté de savoir* when, to his own ends, he uses the notion of *hegemony* in a way which puts one very much in mind of Gramsci. Here in fact the point is to cease representing classes as subjects or as castes (*VS*, p. 125), and above all to incorporate in their very definition the complexity of power relations and the multiplicity of the forms of conflict and resistance (*VS*, p. 126) in a way which makes it possible to get away from the 'great binary division' (*VS*, p. 127) in which the necessity for a final crisis and collision is always ideally contained. The 'social hegemonies' (*VS*, p. 122), or the 'hegemonic effects' which make up the 'great dominations' (*VS*, p. 124) and constitute the 'focal points of resistance' on the basis of which a network of institutions and disciplinary practices spreads throughout the whole of society (*VS*, p. 169) have to be conceived of not as given in advance but as results or as resultants; 'terminal forms', which are at the same time differential or relational forms. In the same way, revolutions have to be conceived of as 'strategic codings of points of resistance' (*VS*, p. 127) – in other words, as the effects of contingent integration, not predetermined (we should note here that Lenin, about whose 'theory' of the 'weakest link' Foucault had occasion to be ironical ('Pouvoirs et stratégies', an interview with J. Rancière, *Les Révoltes logiques*, no. 4, Winter 1977) had, for his part, written:

> to imagine that one army will take up position in a given place and will say, 'We are for socialism', and that another army will take up position in another place and will say, 'We are for imperialism', and that then there will be a social revolution . . . is to be a revolutionary in words only and to understand nothing of what a real revolution is. [*Oeuvres*, vol. XXII, p. 383]

In short, these corrections no doubt go against the grain of the imaginary historical eschatology which Marxism puts forward, but they are by no means incompatible with the strategic analyses which Marx uses, any more than they contradict the idea of 'overdetermination' which Althusser had used for purposes analogous to the critique of 'Marxist' teleology.

What, on the other hand, marks an irreducible divergence is the very idea of *the structure of social conflict* which Foucault puts forward. This divergence does not consist of the alternatives of 'local' and 'global' (between the micro-physics and macro-physics of power, so to speak), but rather bears on the opposition between the logical structure of *power relations*, in which 'contradiction' is at best only one particular configuration, and the logic of *contradiction*, in which the 'power relation' is only a strategic moment. For Marx, as for Foucault, in the last analysis, it would be right to suggest that 'power relations do not exist in a position exterior to other types of relations . . . but that they are immanently present amongst them' (*VS*, pp. 123–4), or again that 'power comes from below' (*VS*, p. 124). That is to say that all its effectiveness and reality comes from the material conditions in which it is exercised; *a fortiori* it would be correct to say that 'where there is power there is resistance' (*VS*, p. 125). But these arguments are *not understood in the same way*. One could say that Foucault understands them simply *as having an external nature*, which means at the same time that 'the opposing aims' in a strategic conflict destroy, neutralise, mutally reinforce or modify one another, but do not form a superior unity or individuality. On the contrary, for Marx, the condition for the development of a conflict is the *interiorisation of the relationship* itself, in such a way that the antagonistic terms become the functions or the bearers of the relationship. This is why it is not essential to the Marxist representation of the class struggle to describe society empirically as characterised entirely by 'a binary and global opposition between the dominators and the dominated' (*VS*, p. 124), but it is absolutely essential for it to conceive of class relations as being internally irreconcilable, as relations from which the dominated can escape only by destroying the subjugating relationship itself, and thereby transforming themselves into different individuals from those who 'constituted' that relationship.

Paradoxically, perhaps, this divergence – with the result that, with Foucault, one always has the impression that it would be possible in some way to shift the terms of a conflict to create a different outcome – echoes a divergence which runs in the opposite direction with regard to *practices*. For Marx, the practice is *par excellence* an *external* production, which produces effects outside itself and consequently also produces effects of subjectification (the conflict which develops in the area of the 'means of production'), whilst for Foucault, power is a productive practice which acts in the first place *on bodies* themselves, aiming initially at individualisation or subjectification (one might go so far as to say a 'practice for the self' or 'of the self'), in consequence producing effects of an objective nature, or knowledge [*savoir*]. What this comes down to is that Foucault's logic of power relations is underpinned by the idea of a plasticity of life, whilst the Marxist logic of contradiction (which interiorises power relations) cannot be dissociated from its immanence within the structure.

This long discussion, based on a rereading of *one* of Foucault's texts, will perhaps make it possible for us to glimpse a little more concretely the complex form in which his relationship with Marx can be seen, at a point which is, admittedly, privileged. But I believe that the lesson can be generalised. A similar strategic complexity, albeit differently organised, characterises each of the phases of his work, such as they can be traced from one book to the next. I would be happy to put forward the idea that this strategic complexity follows a general format, which is repeated several times, in which a movement is made from a *break* to a tactical *alliance*, the first involving a global *critique* of Marxism as a 'theory'; the second a partial *usage* of Marxist tenets or affirmations compatible with Marxism. One might even suggest that the latter become at the same time more and more limited and more and more specifically Marxist. Thus, in contradictory fashion, the opposition to Marxist 'theory' grows deeper and deeper whilst the convergence of the analyses and concepts taken from Marx becomes more and more significant. It should be added that it is not when Foucault most often quotes Marx that he most uses him, nor is it when he has been reading Marx most closely that Foucault puts forward the most radical critiques of him (it would be worth making a detailed study just of all the quotes from and references to Marx).

Like Marx, and yet in a different way from Marx (which is why it becomes necessary to see them in opposition to one another), Foucault, with a century's distance from Marx, created what he himself calls 'philosophical fragments in historical building sites' (*L'Impossible Prison*, p. 41). The same questions come into play. These are, first, that of philosophy in the form of the philosophy of history (and here there is probably only one problem, or rather this form of philosophy has only one problem: the particular nature of 'bourgeois' society and its successive political forms); and, second, history as investigation and as historical writing (there are obviously several forms of both). For a century the question has constantly been raised as to whether Marx's work should be considered as the culmination of the philosophy of history or as the start of a different, non-philosophical relationship with history. Foucault himself participates in this investigation. But the difference between him and so many others (I am tempted to say nearly all the others) is that having formulated a purely theoretical reply (which can be found in the famous pages in *Les Mots et les Choses* on the 'storms in a children's pool') he pursues it in a practical form, by remaking, on the basis of different objects of study in a different setting, the 'jump' from philosophy to non-philosophy, which suddenly reveals different aspects of philosophical questions (like questions of truth, power and practice and questions of time and the subject). Given this, if our aim is to determine in what way our philosophical horizon is irreversibly post-Marxist (in both senses of the expression), reading Foucault will give us a privileged vantage point.

Yet one could go further. Inasmuch as it is true that Foucault's discursive tactics can, to an extent which is essential to them, be analysed as 'anti-Marxist', certain common ground between them has to exist. Inasmuch as it is true that the *shift* in philosophy as practised by Marx and by Foucault involves, in a nutshell, the need which has existed for a century to move from a philosophy *of* history to a philosophy *in* history, it is necessary, in the rigorous form of a series of dilemmas (*either* Marx, *or* Foucault), that the main lines of tension of a theoretical field should become apparent and, eventually, definable. This field must, in some form, *already exist*, and it must already have been traversed and particularised. None the less it must remain to a large extent *to be discovered* and defined cartographically. Perhaps it could be referred to as the field of 'historical materialism'. Marx, of course, did not himself use this expression to characterise the philosophical position implied by his critical analysis of capitalist society, but came very close to it and never actually challenged its usage. In any case, it does indicate less poorly than any other term the point of interest and the philosophical anchorage in its object which the theory creates for itself: the *material nature* of the class struggle, and therefore the contradiction, the *necessity* of historical transformation (by means of contradiction and in the field of the 'social relations' constituted by the class struggle). Hence the open philosophical question, which remains aporetic, as to whether it is possible to conceive of a dialectic which does not include the imagined anticipation of the end of its contradictions, but consists simply of the analysis of movement at a given moment, according to its internal determination. Central to this difficulty is the concept of 'social relations', or contradiction as a structure internal to power relations. This is what sustains the Marxian notion of historical materialism. This then is what, more and more explicitly, Foucault questions. At the (provisional) point of his evolution on this question (in *Surveiller et punir*, *La Volonté de savoir*, and similar texts) he developed ideas which it would not be wrong to refer to by the name of 'historical materialism', but in a way which is opposed, in each of the ways in which it is meant, to Marx: *materiality* is seen not as the materiality of 'social relations' but as the materiality of the apparatus and practice of power, inasmuch as it affects *bodies*; *historicity* is seen not as the historicity of contradiction (whether this be viewed as an instance of the totalisation of different forms of struggle or as an instance of the interiorisation of their necessity) but in terms of the historicity of the *event*; the improbable outcome of various strategies of repression and of multiple and partially uncontrollable forms of subjugation. Hence the overt philosophical aporia which becomes possible for Foucault, which, as I see it, is not situated so much in the difficulty of seeing the 'transformation' on the basis of the 'microphysics of power' (thus, in aleatory terms) as in terms of the following difficulty: how can one consider the categories of forms of history, taking as a point of departure the material nature of the body, *without* at the same time including historical events within the bounds of the metamorphoses of *life*, which is another, different form of teleology?

Inasmuch as Marx's historical materialism remains haunted by the spiritualism of philosophies of history (the contradiction, necessity, immanence of a structure seen as the logic or the discursive nature of historical time), the question has to be asked as to what it is in Foucault's 'materialism' and 'historicism' that leads to its immediate proximity to vitalism, or indeed biologism. The objection could be made here that Foucault avoids this problem by means of his positivism (a term which was used to attack him and which he took on board and made use of) or, better still, by his *nominalism*. There are two good reasons for using this term. Not only does the practice of 'historical nominalism' make idealised notions like 'sex', 'reason', 'power' or 'contradiction' impossible, but it also *forbids* one to pass directly from the material nature of bodies to the ideal nature of life, whilst others are unable to desist from moving from the material nature of social relations to the ideal nature of dialectics. All the same, an interdiction, even one formulated for one's own purposes, is never more than an ambivalent injunction. It does not make the question go away, but merely holds it in check. Moreover, the situation *can be reversed*. We might suppose that Marx could answer the criticism as follows: 'You claim that, in place of a substantialisation of the concept of power as a "thing" which can be appropriated, and in place of the (juridical) idealism which identifies all power as the emanation of sovereignty, you are establishing an analytic of power which makes explicit its *purely relational* nature. Now, when I analysed capitalist exploitation as a process of the consumption and reproduction of the workforce and as a permanent excess in the forms of contract and exchange, not only was I doing nothing other than just what you say, but I virtually drew the consequences by means of which the ambiguities of your "materialism" can be criticised in advance. I agree with you entirely that historical *individuals* are *bodies* subjected to disciplines, but I put forward the idea that these "bodies" themselves, in the particular situation of their class (and why not sex, knowledge, or culture), must themselves be thought of *in relational terms*. Therefore it is I who am the most thoroughgoing nominalist, the least metaphysical, of the two of us.'

In my opinion, the point is not to divide up concepts like 'body' and 'relationships' and to assign them to one side or the other – at least not without further examination of what they imply – but simply to make clear the question which I have just formulated in an abstract way. In the critique of philosophies of history, from Marx to Foucault, there is always the question of *the nature of the material*, and therefore of 'materialism'. As to the consideration of the historical in its material context, or as 'material', one is clearly faced with an ambiguous undertaking, which is prone to various forms of reversal. One might agree to call upon *nominalism* as a supplement to materialism necessary to stop a particular form of materiality – economic, political, or discursive – from turning back into metaphysics. Yet the Marx/Foucault confrontation shows that there are at least two ways of being a nominalist. Therefore there are two ways of practising philosophy *in* history, as opposed to philosophies *of* history. It is in the gap, in the active opposition between these two (at least) ways that, today, it is the lot of philosophy, as far as its relationship to historical knowledge is concerned, to find itself situated. It is therefore an immense advantage to be able to make use of the work of Michel Foucault as a point of leverage. Instead of just chewing over the work of Marx, and finding oneself caught in an equivocal search for a point of leverage *in Marx* in order to form a critique *of Marx*, we now have at our disposal two sets of theories, which are simultaneously disjointed and necessarily in confrontation with one another, and therefore of a 'heretical viewpoint' about which the questions of a field of theoretical knowledge can be formed.

SUMMARY OF DISCUSSIONS

The debate bore directly on the central theme of Étienne Balibar's contribution – that is, the existence of Foucault's thought of a materialism appertaining to bodies, and the possibility of a limiting positivity. . . . **François Wahl** said that he was not sure he understood the term 'materialism of bodies': given that the notion of body maintains an infranoumenal status in Foucault's writing, it is still not put forward as a material affirmation.

Étienne Balibar recognised this. In Foucault's work, the problematic of the nature of material appeared before the problematic of the nature of the body. Étienne Balibar was simply trying to reflect on the discriminating value that the notion of body seemed to possess in the practice of writing history in relation to a Marxist or Marx-orientated vision of the immanence of structure in historical contradictions.

Raymond Bellour referred to the passage in *La Volonté de savoir* which defines the history of mentalities as the history of bodies at their most material. In these few lines one senses in Foucault the desire to approach as closely as possible to the real; to the nature of the material.

Fati Triki then read aloud a long quotation from Foucault in order to clarify his relationship with Marxism, which was one of standing to one side rather than one of combat.

four

Michel Foucault and psychoanalysis

Jacques-Alain Miller

'Foucault', says Maurice Blanchot,[1] 'was never all that passionately interested in psychoanalysis.' He was right. None the less, the archaeology of human sciences in *Les Mots et les Choses* (1966), and therefore the perspective in which human sciences have to be seen for the purposes of archaeology, is entirely and explicitly ordered by psychoanalysis, by psychoanalysis and ethnology, though the way they are linked together is such as to favour psychoanalysis rather than ethnology. Foucault was never all that passionately interested in psychoanalysis. Maurice Blanchot says so, and there is no doubt about it. None the less, psychoanalysis is at the heart of the project which seems to have occupied Foucault throughout his later years: namely, the history of sexuality.

The position occupied by psychoanalysis in *La Volonté de savoir* is symmetrical and inverse to the position it occupies in *Les Mots et les Choses*. It is no longer the guiding principle of the enquiry but the object of the enquiry. It does not guide the archaeologist, but is subject to his counterattack. It is not praised. On the contrary, it is crushed with sarcasm. It is no longer in a position to foresee the next break in the basic make-up of theoretical knowledge [*savoir*], when it could well be the fate of man to be wiped away 'like a face drawn in sand at the edge of the sea'. It is seen as belonging to a structure whose historical emergence is contemporary with the human sciences; it arises out of a retrospective view of history, which archaeology is to deal with in such a way that we might free ourselves from it.

Tomorrow, or the day after tomorrow, when the fundamental layout of knowledge [*savoir*] has changed, perhaps this shift in the work of Foucault, between 1966 and 1976, will appear to the future archaeologist as the privileged indicator of the moment when the practice of psychoanalysis fell definitively into disuse, deprived of meaning and of hope, becoming as anachronistic for us today as initiation. Maybe. And in the same way that Foucault, at the beginning of *Naissance de la clinique*,[2] gives us texts to read by Pomme from 1769 and by Bayle from 1825, to show us the full extent of the division between them, it might well be that a future archaeologist will place one Foucault text from 1966 and another from 1976 at the beginning of a book called *The Death of Psychoanalysis*. Maybe. The possibility exists. Psychoanalysis does, after all, contain within it the knowledge of its own mortality. Freud knew this and said it. Maybe it was with the idea of perpetuating his discovery and invention that Freud endeavoured to protect it in the form of an institution, denounced by Lacan as having the same structure as the Church.

What interests me here is not any desire to contradict Foucault. If that were the case, I should say so. I did in fact once do just that, when Foucault was spending an evening with us – his friends from the Department of Psychoanalysis[3] – in order to discuss his *La Volonté de savoir*, which had just come out. I do not want to contradict him now but to follow through what he says, his method, and the problems he faces when he takes it upon himself to overturn the perspective in *Les Mots et les Choses*, and to write, in turn, an archaeology of psychoanalysis, as though psychoanalysis were something dead or about to die. I am interested here in his procedures. I shall begin by clarifying the contrast with the procedures he used in 1966. In *Les Mots et les Choses*, Foucault proceeds by way of extraction. He defines the notion of man, which all human sciences take for granted, in the context of the ensemble of human sciences. What he calls 'man', the 'man' of the human sciences, would have been unthinkable during the classical age, and is absent from it; that is, from the *episteme* of Representation. The concept emerges at the end of the eighteenth century, and in the first years of the nineteenth. Already there are some human sciences, which have become counter-sciences, which are bringing about its dissolution. This amounts to the dissolution of their object of study.

On the one hand, in *La Volonté de savoir*, Foucault does not proceed by means of extraction; he proceeds by means of inclusion. On the basis of psychoanalysis, he invents a vaster ensemble in which psychoanalysis is, in turn, situated. He calls this the 'apparatus of sexuality'. Next we should consider how it is that, starting with psychoanalysis, Foucault obtains this apparatus of sexuality, in which he situates psychoanalysis as one composite part amongst others. In fact he does so by drawing on one key aspect, relevant for the purpose of inclusion in archaeology, which is summed up in the syntagma: 'talking about sex'. As soon as this key element has been isolated, all kinds of different forms of theoretical knowledge [*savoirs*], practices, institutions, forms of behaviour, become apparent. These might be considered to be contrary to psychoanalysis and yet, by virtue of this common trait, this attribute, they can be grouped alongside it to form an ensemble which, heterogeneous though it might be, can be given a name – it should not be forgotten that Foucault is a nominalist. That name is: 'the apparatus of sexuality'. Now that it has been situated in this new object, which has been created before our very eyes, psychoanalysis immediately loses the very uniqueness which psychoanalysts flatter themselves that it possesses. It can be seen as sharing common ground with the forms of discourse and practices which it called into question from the moment of its birth, yet which can now be seen as calling it into question, since the place of psychoanalysis in history is established and might well be in a state of decline.

'Sexuality', in *La Volonté de savoir*, warrants the same inverted commas as the term 'man' in *Les Mots et les Choses*. It is not something which nature simply presents us with, but it is a name which, Foucault says, can be given to a historical apparatus [*dispositif*], which came into being at about the same time as the apparatus of 'man'. It is just as recent and perhaps just about as close to being swept away. In the same way that Foucault was able to say that 'man' is an invention, the recent date of which the archaeologist can quite easily show, he says that sexuality is originally, historically, bourgeois, and that it dates from the middle of the eighteenth century. And even if he does not foretell its end with the same assurance, he hopes this end will not be long in coming, and sees the first signs of its approach. It is therefore by the expedient of this invented object, which he calls the 'apparatus of sexuality', that Foucault undertakes what he himself calls the archaeology of psychoanalysis. To quote him: 'The history of the apparatus of sexuality can be seen in terms of an archaeology of psychoanalysis.'[4]

The Foucault effect – by which I mean the effect of the truth of the enquiry or the experiment with which he is proceeding – is always at its most telling when archaeology shows us, from both sides of a break, a movement being eclipsed; the interplay of absence and presence. 'Man', for example, is a presence on one side of the modern (anthropological) break and an absence on the other side. Or again, and simultaneously, clinical medicine is absent on one side and present on the other side of the same break. And, to begin with, it might seem as though the same were true of sexuality, such as it is found, redefined, in *La Volonté de savoir*. The most precious lesson of the project of *Histoire de la sexualité* is, in my opinion, the following. Foucault's object, created on the basis of psychoanalysis, slowly but surely destroys the framework, the limitations and the categories of his own archaeology, and this is precisely because Foucault, its inventor, subjects himself to it and assumes its own logic. As such it takes one aback to realise that his superb archaeological machine, which had triumphed successively in the case of madness, clinical medicine, the human sciences and prison, here comes to grief and decomposes because of the effect of the very object it set for itself, when it took psychoanalysis as its starting point.

The apparatus of sexuality comes to the fore at the end of the eighteenth century. Yet it is already present from the middle of that century, and in fact, from the moment one takes the notion of 'talking about sex' as the key element, the whole of Christian discourse on the flesh becomes swallowed up in the archaeological structure, and then the originating network of ideas has to be sought even further back. It is here that a kind of slide is set in motion, which uproots the archaeological process and also the processes of epistemic scansion that directed the enquiries into medicine and the sciences and kept archaeology secure, making possible the flawlessly binary linking together of successions of presences and absences, absences and presences. These scanning processes are corroded, as if by acid. Once corroded, they teeter and collapse.

'Sexuality' emerges in the middle of the eighteenth century. But it had been expanding increasingly, Foucault says, since the seventeenth. Then it is necessary to go back to the Council of Trent, to the practice of penitence, the examination of conscience and spiritual direction. And from there, because spiritual direction itself has a history, the archaeologist finds himself dislodged from the form of archaeology he is used to, and projected with irresistible force back to the Greeks and the Romans. This will remain one of Foucault's greatest lessons: that he did not recoil from the consequences at this point, and take the easy way out by wrapping the job up on the cheap; that he did not hang on to the branches when the very ground of his archaeology was disappearing beneath his feet; and that he did not tie himself down, by means of a grandiose gesture of denial, to the infernal logic he himself had stirred up. And indeed, Maurice Blanchot might well ask him, posthumously, why not ancient Judaism, where sexuality plays an important role, and whence the law originates? There is a programme here for five thousand years' worth of archaeology which would probably lead right back to Ancient Egypt, which exercised such a powerful fascination over Freud.

The process seems to imply that Foucault's archaeology had met in this object a transhistorical thoroughfare which continually led beyond and outside itself. One might well wonder if the epistemic structures of archaeology were designed to deal with something like a religion, for it is by this religious archaeology of psychoanalysis that what I have just referred to as Foucault's slide is set in motion. It was this consideration which led directly to a kind of archaeology of religion which drew it irresistibly out of its original territory – that is, the modern age beginning with the classical age of the eighteenth century and going right up to our own contemporary age. Yet Foucault did not give in. The artful archaeologist did not hand in his resignation straight away because of the truth-effect he had produced, which turned on him, like the sorcerer's apprentice, in such a surprising way. This, together with the fact that Foucault persevered in order to give us *L'Usage des plaisirs* and *Le Souci de soi*, is an achievement which must be admired by all those for whom thought is an ethical concern.

Foucault himself notes the change in his research, such as it appears in the last two volumes of *Histoire de la sexualité*. It takes on, he says, a completely different form. A completely different form indeed! It seems as though the central notion of 'talking about sex' had turned out to be too slender to support the archaeological project, so that Foucault had found it necessary to add another which, little by little, superimposed itself more and more over the first; this new notion being 'talking about the self'. The term 'power', on the basis of which the object of sexuality was problematised in the first volume, yields priority of place in the succeeding volumes to the question of the subject.

Of course, the term 'subject' is not absent from *La Volonté de savoir*, but it occurs in an incidental manner; and the idea of power is present in *L'Usage des plaisirs* and *Le Souci de soi*, but in an interiorised form, at the very heart of the workings of the self on the self. The introduction to *L'Usage des plaisirs* is unequivocally about the broadening of the terms of the investigation beyond the sexuality of the subject, to the constitution of the self as subject.

On rereading this introduction it becomes clear that the markers are there which show the extent to which what occupied Foucault during his last years was an explication which runs parallel to the work of Lacan. Foucault never quotes him, neither in *Les Mots et les Choses* nor in *Histoire de la sexualité*, and professed not to understand him. I still recall his saying to me in 1972, after we had spent a day at the *Salpêtrière*, where I had accompanied him as he went through the Charcot archives, 'One of these days you'll have to explain Lacan to me.' This makes no difference, however, to the fact that one has not fully grasped *L'Histoire de la sexualité* unless one recognises in Foucault, not an explication of Lacan at all, but an explication which runs alongside Lacan. This is not because Foucault's subject had become the same as Lacan's. Foucault's subject recognises him/herself as a subject, and this – from 1958 at least – was no longer the sort of subject Lacan was dealing with. On the contrary, the reason is that Foucault found it necessary to revise the nature of the self in a history which had taken as its starting point the notion of an apparatus designed in such a way that the self would not have to be taken into account. This was because it was intended to concentrate on practices of an external nature.

Maurice Blanchot comments on the difference in style in the last books. He says they are at rest, without the passion which runs through Foucault's other texts. This is true. But how can we explain this sudden calming down in the very work which, in the heat of its sarcasm, affirmed its ambition to set us free? Foucault referred to *L'Histoire de la sexualité* as a counterattack against the apparatus of sexuality. He wrote in the final pages of *La Volonté de savour* that 'the point of leverage for the counterattack against the apparatus of sexuality had to be not sex as desire but bodies and pleasure'. Bodies and pleasure.

Indeed, Foucault's archaeology had from the beginning always been a form of counterattack. It always needed a point of leverage. In *Les Mots et les Choses*, the counterattack against the human sciences used concrete disciplines as its point of leverage: the triad of linguistics, ethnology and psychoanalysis. I would go so far as to say that his Archimedes' point was Lacan. Would it not be true to say that his counterattack against the apparatus of sexuality, with psychoanalysis at its heart, has as its point of leverage no discipline, no practice, other than the utopia of a body outside sex, whose various pleasures depend on nothing but the unifying rule of castration? This point of leverage is, of course, very slender. It is nothing more than a subdivision of perversion which, in *La Volonté de savoir*, Foucault saw only as a utopian viewpoint necessary in order to think in terms other than those of psychoanalysis. And it was precisely the need for this initial point of leverage which precipitated archaeology rapidly backwards in a movement which was unstoppable and limitless. Yet if this movement is seen as stopping in Ancient Greece, perhaps this is because Foucault discovered there, within and not beyond the contemporary epoch, the point of leverage he needed. For my part, I see this final calming down of his quest not in terms of a happy sexuality but in terms of a body capable of multiple pleasures; that is, in terms of the realisation of this utopia, where the things of love do not form an ensemble unified by the function of the castrated phallus. This takes place at a point beyond the break with the modern world for which Foucault was always hoping for himself and for his archaeology; at a point beyond, from which he would be able to turn back and look at our epoch in order to describe its end. Yet this point turns out not to be beyond, but to be figured in Greece.

NOTES

1. Maurice Blanchot, *Michel Foucault as I imagine him*, Montpellier: Fata Morgana, 1986.
2. Michel Foucault, *Naissance de la clinique*, Paris: PUF, 1963, pp. v–vi.
3. 'Le jeu de Michel Foucault', *Ornicar? Bulletin périodique du champ freudien*, no. 10, July 1977.
4. Michel Foucault, *La Volonté de savoir*, Paris: Gallimard, 1976, p. 172.

SUMMARY OF DISCUSSIONS

Two themes emerged from the discussions: the historical nature of sexuality and the relationship with religion.

Rainer Rochlitz was astonished at the claims made by Jacques-Alain Miller, who was actually suggesting that Foucault was making a negative statement about the nature of history in that he wanted to situate castration in history and yet was unable to do so. Yet surely it would be worthwhile to situate the birth of psychoanalysis at a certain moment within history, relating it to certain social structures?

Jacques-Alain Miller replied, not without irony, that the notion that sexuality is historical is by no means shocking to a psychoanalyst. It is quite clear that psychoanalysis was born on the terrain of the natural sciences. One might wish that there were in the hall a pupil of Foucault prepared to carry out an archaeology of psychoanalysis, who would look for the conditions which made it possible somewhere between religion and science. Replying to **Jeannette Colombel**, Jacques-Alain Miller specified further that he did not think psychoanalysis tended to normalise sexuality.

Anne Kerien wanted to reaffirm this. After all, sexuality became historically problematic at the time of the women's movement, the FHAR (Homosexual Front for Revolutionary Action) and other contempoary movements.

It was the word 'religion' which caused **François Wahl** to intervene. This word 'religion' is used by Jacques-Alain Miller in order to speak of the way archaeology drifts off course when it considers sexuality. Yet Foucault is dealing not with religious practices but with prescriptive discourse, and this by no means constitutes a break with archaeology. Having said that, though, **Miller** replied, it was none the less the way the flesh was institutionally controlled which interested Foucault, and it was the Catholic religion which drew his interest towards Antiquity. **Paul Veyne**, for his part, was of the opinion that 'religion' was not a concept for Foucault. This was not the problem he was dealing with, even if the Christian religion was later to monopolise ethical prescriptiveness.

André Glücksmann concluded as follows: when Foucault distinguished between two forms of the erotic, Socrates' ascetic form of the erotic and Plutarch's harmonious form, perhaps this also explained the opposition between Freud and Jung. If so, then Foucault would not just be offering an explanation in parallel to Lacan's, but would actually be explaining him.

five

Inside or outside philosophy?

L'Archéologie du savoir, L'Usage des plaisirs, Le Souci de soi

François Wahl

The question as to what conclusions can be drawn from Michel Foucault's practice of 'history writing' is not an immediately obvious one. The difficulty is of course, one of circularity. In order to find out whether the archaeologist's *method* – which is in other ways perfectly clear – is rooted in a choice which is in the last analysis philosophical, it is necessary to have an adequate definition of philosophy itself. Yet it is not certain that a definition of this kind could be obtained except by means of an investigation from a viewpoint which was close to philosophy, yet at the same time distinct from it. This viewpoint would in fact be very much like that of archaeology. In their treatment of subjects from the mastery of pleasure to the problem of self, Foucault's last two books proceed and take support from *material* which for Antiquity was of a philosophical nature from the point of Antiquity, and which from our point of view traces the genealogy of concepts like desire and the subject, which are central also to what we call philosophy. It does not follow, though, that the treatment to which Michel Foucault subjects them is in itself necessarily philosophical. And even if this treatment can be said to be philosophical, the question still remains as to whether this means what was considered to be philosophical in the fourth century BC, or in the second century AD, or whether it means philosophical in terms of the major philosophical problems as we understand them today, or again in terms of a successor to what we call philosophy, which is yet to appear. Then again, there has existed – especially in the last few centuries – such a thing as a *history* of philosophy. The field of this history of philosophy – large-scale systems and their short-term and long-term succession

Note. References are designated as follows. *AS*: *L'Archéologie du savoir*; *UP*: *L'Usage des plaisirs*; *SS*: *Le Souci de soi*; *CP*: *Ceci n'est pas une pipe*; and *DF*: Gilles Deleuze, *Foucault*.

– as well as its rules – from philology to architectonics – are well established. Yet the history of theoretical knowledge [*savoir*], the power and practices conducted by Michel Foucault, cannot be confused with this history of philosophy. His form of history is concerned less with systems and more with the exercise of power, and we cannot be sure whether this history is being juxtaposed with the history of ideas or whether at times its aim is to replace it.

Viewed from the *inside of* Michel Foucault's practice, it might well be that none of these questions is either really pertinent or important: or maybe they have just been put off until later. But from an *exterior* viewpoint, for those of us whose job it is to take measure of what he achieved in his work and the changes it has brought in its wake, each of these questions is essential to the location of Michel Foucault's work in relation to other orders of discourse.

To start again in a less academic and more topical way: if I say 'this is not a philosophy', should this be understood as meaning 'this is *and* this is not (philosophical)', like language from the viewpoint of the represented object which gives itself to language, distant but not separated from it: like a similarity which is affirmed but then suppressed by negation, such that the object common to both escapes notice? Perhaps what we find between philosophy and archaeology is a correspondence crossed by a 'narrow divide of absence', a joint cut out by the 'incision' of discourse into the form of things. In short, between archaeology and philosophy, perhaps what we see is an interplay of equivalences and criss-crossings, an interplay of *ordered* shifts, but one which is at the same time thrown into confusion by new forms of *instability*.

I

1. In the structure – the recapitulatory structure – of *L'Archéologie du savoir*, the effects of the difference in *method* between archaeology and philosophy are made clear in an obvious way. Foucault does this with such clarity that one hesitates to restate them.

(a) Philosophy is, next to literature, history and religion, one of the 'major types of discourse' (*AS*, p. 33) which tradition has accustomed us to seeing in opposition to one another. Archaeology casts doubt over this notion of their 'individuality': the 'ensemble of affirmations' with which it deals are, throughout history, continually regrouping and then re-separating. Philosophy is, after all, a 'discursive fact' which is not substantially different from all the others; neither is it more intrinsically determined.

Philosophy is, from that point, nothing more than a 'surface' (*AS*, p. 38) phenomenon; the effective unities of discourse have to be traced *beyond* and ways of seeing links between them have to be sought *elsewhere*. At each point what has to be dealt with is the dispersion of affirmations [*énoncés*], 'the population of events in the space of discourse in general: at each point one is looking for the conditions which make it possible for the rules to appear'.

What is more: the classical way of reading philosophies is a form of translation; it seeks meaning and then refers this meaning to the subject who is subsequently included as part of it. One senses that in the eyes of Michel Foucault the process is always hermeneutic. The archaeologist, on the other hand, proceeds *on the level* of the affirmations [*énoncés*], such as they were made, in order to analyse the particularities and the exclusions: the contingent necessity. In place of the synthetic character of the project, he substitutes the 'forms of regularity' (*AS*, pp. 41, 49) which order the *game* of a form of discourse.

(b) It is not with regard to philosophy but with regard to madness, clinical medicine and language that, in order to describe the sum total of affirmations [*énoncés*] linked to each of them, Michel Foucault challenges the pertinence of a *unity of object*, of a *homogeneity of style*, of a *conceptual system* or of a *thematic identity*. But it is clear that this quadruple refutation would also be valid for what one might call 'the' philosophical. Instead of, and in the place of, what he four times over rejects, the archaeologist encounters – in the criss-crossing of forms of knowledge [*savoirs*] – a 'space where various objects become visible and continually transform themselves and one another' (*AS*, p. 46), where the viewpoint itself is ordered by unstable hypotheses; where what determines whether or not the objects will group is not their fixed (or otherwise) coherence, but their 'simultaneous successive emergence' (*AS*, p. 49). Here the same theme could be modelled on different discursive formations, and the same formation could be ordered on the basis of opposing choices. The key word, then, is no longer architecture but 'dispersion' and 'distribution' (*AS*, p. 52).

(c) Hence, finally, the four hypotheses with which the archaeologist himself works: (i) the archaeologist should position himself not within the discourse but 'on its boundaries', in the shifting interplay of relationships which preside over his *practice*; (ii) the archaeologist should refrain from referring, even implicitly, to a formation as being constituted by a subject (probably of a transcendental nature) but should trace in the formation a diversity of positions, thus bringing about a *'discontinuity' in the subject* (*AS*, p. 74); (iii) the archaeologist should see common ideas circulating (even at the very heart of a formation) not in terms of the non-contradiction of the concepts, but of a process of 'rewriting' (*AS*, p. 80), bearing witness to a (lacunary) organisation at a level which one might call *preconceptual* (*AS*, p. 81); (iv) the archaeologist should account for the diffraction of theories which are underpinned by the same formation, not in terms of a diversity of opinions but in terms of the 'functions of the *possibilities* [*AS*, p. 93] of this discourse', at the heart of the discourse itself.

2. Archaeology, then, is neither philosophy – held in place by the chain of meaning, of the transcendental and of the subject – nor science, setting out on the surface the way its concepts are linked together presupposing a theoretical homogeneity; archaeology is a *positive* task – the forms of discourse are given – and its positive nature is not articulated in the way it surveys a state of affairs, but in the conditions which make it possible for a *practice* to operate. The discourse is seen at each stage in terms of the operation of the rules which brought it into being.

In other words, from the archaeologist's viewpoint *everything which is said is a specific action*. This explains the discreet (and rarely noted) presence of Austin in the final pages of *L'Archéologie du savoir*. It might well be that archaeology arises out of a theoretical option, and that this is the option of the *performative*.

(a) Of course, archaeology is not a science. It does not cover the same territory as disciplines established by science; it often outlines heterogeneous discursive practices in the various processes or hypotheses of a science at a given period. Yet it would not be possible either to claim that the way it is constituted is totally alien to science, since the foundations of science are, after all, what archaeology is bringing to the fore.

This is what leads Michel Foucault to put forward, as the proper field of the investigations of archaeology, the notion of theoretical knowledge [*savoir*]. A form of theoretical knowledge [*savoir*] 'is that which one can speak of in the context of a discursive practice such that this practice becomes, as a result, specified' (*AS*, p. 238); and 'it is also the space in which the subject can position him/herself in order to speak of the objects with which s/he is dealing in his/her discourse'; and 'finally, a form of theoretical knowledge [*savoir*] is defined in terms of its potentiality for use and appropriation' by means of its connectedness with other practices and other forms of discourse. (This enumeration, of course, satisfies the archaeologist's four critical principles.) In short, we are now no longer in the classical field of knowledge [*connaissance*] (and its subject), but in the territory which proceeds from the discursive nature of science (a territory where production occurs by means of *the discourse itself* and where the subject can never 'play the leading role' [*AS*, p. 239]. Theoretical knowledge [*savoir*] is opposed to science in the same way that the complexity and density of the interplay of *discursive practices* is opposed to 'transcendental narcissism' (*AS*, p. 265).

(b) It is none the less the case that archaeology is based on an 'enveloping theory' (*AS*, p. 270). The point is to demonstrate the conditions in which a discursive practice *is exercised* or, in other words: 'to show that *to speak, is to do* something' (*AS*, p. 272). To investigate theoretical knowledge [*savoir*] is therefore to have made a choice; and this option is, in the last analysis, the performative option.

It is an option which, of course, theoretical knowledge [*savoir*] transforms, since it no longer refers it back to any subject, and as such decentralises the option. This is indeed exactly how Michel Foucault is able to say that the field of investigation is no longer a philosophical one. What we are left with – and this is the essential point, so it is meant neither in the trivial nor in the formal sense of the term – is a *wager* – to be justified by results – on the field of investigations where all emergence of meaning is rooted. This is neither transcendence nor transcendental; but since it is situated beyond the factuality of regularly occurring features, and beyond the description of an ensemble of affirmations, a 'conversion in one's way of seeing' (*AS*, p. 145) becomes necessary, in order to locate, on the 'periphery' (*AS*, p. 147) of the discourse in question that which orders its very existence: such that to say becomes to do, and the function of discourse is to be reversed into a *practice*.

The result of this is that, if it were absolutely necessary to locate *L'Archéologie du savoir* in the topography of 'philosophical options', it would not be, as is sometimes claimed, on the side of nominalism, but on the side of *pragmatism*. Not in the sense of an acting 'I', but in a sense in which each affirmation [*énoncé*] has to be understood in terms of the affirmations which created it and those which it, in turn, creates. *Doing* is inherent in the *discursive*.

II

It might, as I said, seem legitimate to ask whether, in *L'Usage des plaisirs* and *Le Souci de soi*, concepts which arise directly out of philosophy do not come to the surface: essentially as a result of the problematisation of the *self* or 'subjectification'.

The fact that the question has arisen can be seen from the efforts which several people have made to resolve it – or to deflect it. In the finest, and indeed the most philosophical, of the books on Foucault, Deleuze makes the observation that the point is the existence of a third axis, which goes beyond the axes of knowledge [*savoir*] and power. He goes on to suggest that the 'inside' (*DF*, p. 104) can be read as a movement from the exterior to the interior, where the outside remains unchanged, and becomes 'the inside of the outside' (*DF*, p. 105), an interiorisation of the outside. This certainly does not mean that the Self is seen as having a unitary nature, but that 'that which is Other is re-doubled'. The great merit of this proposition is that it constitutes a *systematic* encompassing the whole of Michel Foucault's work.

It is, I believe, necessary to see how far these two claims can be taken – first the claim that Michel Foucault has taken terms from philosophy; secondly the claim that underlying his discourse there is a systematic order which is, properly speaking, philosophical.

1. I shall take as a starting point a possible misreading of Deleuze's propositions – a mistake which, once resolved, will make it possible to understand its implications more clearly. To some, Deleuze's formulation might sound singularly like an affirmation [*énoncé*] of psychonalysis, whereby the subject is alienated only from the Other and has no message to formulate except the inversion of the Other. Of course, this is not what Deleuze is saying, but the difference clarifies the issue: redoubling is not a form of alienation; at the very most it is a means of constitution and, given that the Other is active within the Self, it cannot be true that it is present in the form of an absence. In other words, if one can speak of a continuity from the first to the last in Michel Foucalt's work, this again is to be found in his *positivity* which (this being the absolutely crucial choice he makes) links sexuality to *pleasure*, and not to the negative transcendence of desire; it is found also in his *pragmatism*, in that the history of sexuality is not the history of how sexuality was represented at each period (i.e., of that which was understood about it at the time) but the history of the *rules of conduct* on which sexuality was based. In other words, it is not so much a question of what was (or is), but rather of what was done, as it was being done.

Having established this, it seems to me that to seek further unity in Michel Foucault's work would be to fail to take account of what made it so empirical, open, discontinuous and, as Michel Foucault said, so surprising for himself. The subject he was working on confronted him with a new dimension of the Self. He took this into account without (so far?) trying to integrate it into anything like a system. As always, he took his lead from the facts of the discourse he was studying – which in this case was prescriptive discourse – trying to find inconsistencies in it, whatever they might be. The Self is a concept which belongs to the practice in which sexuality is inscribed. This was also a new piece of data, whose compatibility with the others was not (so far?) in question.

This, of course, is not to deny the massive action of the impersonal Other within the Self. This is because Michel Foucault is exploring collective practices, the regulations they imply, and the way forms of stand-in ethics can arise out of them. The point is that the Self is nothing more than a form called into being by the totality of these practices, the concept which they need in order to be able to link themselves together. Here again, that which appears as an object or a theme of knowledge is nothing more than the reverse side of a network of relationships and exclusions, convergences and lacunae, formed by the 'pre-concepts' of the pragmatic.

2. At the same time we find here the question of the way in which *L'Usage des plaisirs* and *Le Souci de soi* are related to philosophical texts solved in advance.

Indeed, Xenophon, Plato, Plutarch, Seneca and Epictetus are taken as examples. But Michel Foucault makes it quite clear from the beginning that the concepts which he takes from them are significant only to the extent that they make it possible to construct 'a history of sexuality as *experience*, if one understands by experience the correlation, in a culture, between domains of knowledge [*savoir*], types of normativity and forms of subjectivity' (*UP*, p. 10). If the aim of the history of sexuality is to 'define the *conditions* in which the human being 'problematises' what he is . . .' (*UP*, p. 16), this problematisation is revealed as 'linked to an ensemble of *practices* which have indeed been very important in our societies: they are what one might call the *arts of existence*'.

This is why the point of departure is not taken in the Eros but in the *aphrodisia*, the 'work' and 'acts' of Aphrodite. This also explains why the problematic of sex in Antiquity is seen as being haunted by the fear of the excess to which the body can lead and by the medical control of this through proper regulation of relationships with women and young boys, and the requirement that sexual relationships should take place with the right partner at the right time. This problematic is gradually subsumed into the requirement for self-mastery and for care to be taken of the Self. Such are the fascinating revelations about the practice of sex in Antiquity and its prescriptive core. But these are made in a field which is quite clearly chosen and which again can be seen as the field of the *pragmatic*.

Now, the axis about which philosophy has been constructed since Antiquity was not that of experience taken in itself, but that of its relationship with knowledge [*connaissance*], and through knowledge with *truth*. Michel Foucault states this directly: he wants to write a history 'which is not a history of that which is supposed to be true in knowledge: but an analysis of *truth games*' (*UP*, p. 12). This is a remarkable formulation which sets out the whole difference: he is not concerned with truth such as it is posited *before* (and beyond) experience, but such as it *comes into play* in practices and through the interpretation of these practices.

3. There remains the view of the erotic in the *Symposium*. Michel Foucault is far from denying that this requires separate treatment, because this time it is the body as such which has to be *bypassed*, and sexuality which has to be led back within the reach of *truth*.

It was on the basis of this that a whole philosophical tradition, from Diotimo-Platonism onwards, took it upon itself to believe in the reality of the idealisation–sublimation of love: the soul as more than the body, *philia* as better than *eros*, austerity and abstention as realisations of love 'in its essence' (*UP*, p. 256): in short, what one might describe as a (if not the) transhistoric position of philosophers with regard to the things of sex. And *in one sense*, this is a correct view: precisely because what was being dealt with here was the discourse of *philosophy* and not the implication of practices.

But, as Michel Foucault shows so well, once placed in the context of prescriptive writing, even the philosophical project turns out to be conditioned by the practices of the period. Here it is the question of the *style* and not the application of a code (*UP*, p. 269); going beyond the body is a *luxury* (*UP*, p. 274); if it is important that the lover should determine 'in himself . . . the being and the form of his love' (*UP*, p. 261); if, between the lover and the loved one, love is supposed to be 'convergent' (*UP*, p. 261), the sexual ethic remains problematised 'like the relationship for a free man between the exercise of his liberty, the forms of his power and his access to truth' (*UP*, p. 277). Michel Foucault was struck and probably surprised that, from ancient right up to quite recent historical times, a certain relationship between negative prescriptions, a certain parallelism of moral hierarchies, has always existed; but he also shows that distances of this nature established in the context of sexuality do not in the last analysis even have any meaning, ordered as they are by a different problematisation of *experience*.

There is, of course, more to come: elaboration does not in itself amount to interiorisation (*UP*, p. 277); the Platonic problematisation of sexual behaviour does not amount to its re-elaboration 'proceeding from the soul of desire' (*UP*, p. 268). I am not even sure myself whether, to be precise, Michel Foucault does not himself go a little too far when he speaks of 'man's investigation of himself as *desiring subject*' (*UP*, p. 269). There certainly does exist nowadays a reading of the *Symposium* as a treatise on desire in which the *agalmata* represent the lost object (for Lacan: [*a*]) and Socrates' work represents the embodiment of the truth that love has nothing to give except precisely that which it lacks. This is an interpretation which I would be far from considering to be without interest or to be without a great deal to offer. But that aside, as Michel Foucault's work has amply demonstrated: it functions only on the basis of a retrospective reinterpretation. For Plato, intemperance is not alienation but weakness: if Poverty is the mother of Eros, this is because it seeks an object or a complement which is exterior to it, and not because it lacks something within; finally, it distorts the meaning of *ēpithumia* to translate it, in the traditional way, as 'desire': most accurately, it would have to be seen as the racing of the horse of the heart. A philosophy which is developed on the basis of making an effort to take oneself in hand could not be linked to a philosophy of the self's loss of self.

The same has to be said of the Stoic systematisation 'in which the *relationship of the self to the self* was intensified and given value' (*SS*, p. 57). If, for Epictetus, man is 'the being who has been given over to the concern for self' (*SS*, p. 61), the one who can 'freely make use of himself' (*SS*, p. 62), thanks to his reason which is 'capable of taking itself as well as all besides as an object of study' (*SS*, p. 59), it must be understood that this definition of 'man' (*SS*, p. 60) amounts to an *injunction* to 'live, constantly taking care of oneself' (*SS*, p. 62), 'transforming oneself' and 'returning to oneself'. This injunction, in turn, is not abstract but already present in a whole series of *exercises* (*SS*, p. 63): ways of ordering occupations, filling time (including on the social level) with 'useful tasks' (*SS*, p. 66), caring for oneself to prevent illness (the school is a 'dispensary for the soul' (*SS*, p. 71); knowing oneself is an 'art . . . with precise procedures' (*SS*, p. 74): learning, in spite of all misfortunes, to do without the superfluous, 'examining' (*SS*, p. 78) one's day, questioning the legitimacy of the way things are presented (*SS*, p. 80). Philosophy can assign to reason the *truth* about man (*SS*, p. 82); *practice*, for its part, organises a 'trajectory' in the face of which sexuality remains 'a form of violence, of excess' (*SS*, p. 85), and anything which opposes it is a possession, in the juridical sense of the word, of the self, the victory being a 'concrete relationship which makes it possible to *enjoy the self*' (*SS*, p. 82). This much is clear: this enjoyment is an addition *of the practice* to the philosophy of the period; and it is still further from ours since for us enjoyment is, on the contrary, a loss of self.

4. Again, this does not mean that in the view adopted by Michel Foucault there is no *choice* which can be called philosophical.

This happens from the moment the word *pleasure* is adopted. After all, one hardly comes across the term *hēdonē* at all in the texts studied in *L'Usage des plaisirs*, and for good reason: for the free man, allowing oneself to be submerged by the movements and transports of the body and heart presents an image of disorder and agitation which he can only contemplate with fear. The reason Michel Foucault chooses the term 'pleasure' is obviously to separate off Antiquity from 'our' conceptualisation of *desire*. He has definitively shown, in my opinion, the irreducibility of the divide. Yet it seems to me that, in speaking of pleasure, he himself opted for a reading which is to some extent retrospective, the paradigm of which might well be said to date from eighteenth-century empiricism. Take the subject of the texts Foucault studies. They have a great deal to say about ways of training oneself to contain pleasure: their understanding of sexuality – although it is not tragic, as is later the case – is still far from sharing the euphoria which at a later time will accompany the word 'pleasure'. In fact, the choice of this latter is made on principle, and the principle is an *ethical* one. To put the matter clearly: Michel Foucault wanted, in this way, to establish his position *with regard to the present*.

This much has to be said of the 'question of self' (*SS*, p. 273). Since it is essential to the practices of mistrust regarding the body and to the search for a privileged relationship with and conformity to nature, it expresses itself in the form of a need to 'keep control of oneself'. It is the reverse side of the 'style of sexual behaviour' where disquiet and vigilance are to be seen. As such, this question is posed in terms which remain *positive*. On the one hand, Michel

Foucault insists: if these forms of behaviour result in exercises like the examination of conscience, the struggle against all *pathein*, the necessity to know oneself and even to filter the way one sees things; and if the point of all this is to 'keep control of oneself' (*SAS*, p. 273), 'not to accept in one's relationship with oneself anything other than that which is dependent on free and reasonable choice' (*SS*, p. 81), then what we are dealing with is, in the last analysis 'the elements which constitute moral *subjectivity*'. This shift is summed up perfectly in the notion of *concern* for self. Only, when authors of the imperial period talk of the *ēpimēlēia hēautou*, of the *cura sui*, of caring *for one's soul* (*SS*, p. 59), for that which is, for each person, 'the most important *object*, perhaps, with which he could be concerned' (*SS*, p. 63), one feels that they are directing the efforts of a *concrete* subject in such a way that he should come to grips with the task of appropriation *of the self by the self*. (Here it would be worth stopping to consider the use of the genitive in nearly all these examples.) This is not, however, exactly what is meant by the *Self* in the universal sense of the concept. Here again, Michel Foucault definitively marks the difference between this kind of asceticism and the guilt, the obsession with intention and understanding, and the seeking for a universal code which characterise Christianity. Although Antiquity deals with the question of the Subject, who becomes the 'desiring subject', it does so only to the extent of elucidating the 'genealogy' of this subject. It seems to me that in fact, *for today's purposes*, on the question of an ethic for our time, Michel Foucault is as reticent on the question of the definition of the Subject by means of self-constitution as he is on the question of the value to be attached to desire. In other words, by introducing the self, he wanted to displace a problematic which had become at the same time epistemological and ontological and refer it back to a much more strictly *practical* conception of ethics. *Technē tou biou*.

III

How, then, can *the history of philosophy* be situated in relation to the project of *archaeology*?

To begin with, it should be borne in mind that the history of philosophy can exist on two levels. It can be the history of a progression, branching off and proceeding in fits and starts towards the *True*. Or it can be seen as a chain of *systems*, which can be studied on the one hand each from within, purely from the point of view of internal coherence, and on the other from a point of view which sees them as belonging to a common textual pool, in which a degree of intertextuality is to be found.

1. From the first point of view, inasmuch as the history of philosophy is taken as the history of successive definitions and constitutions of Truth, it has always

operated on several fields. These are those of knowledge [*connaissance*], conditions, limits, and also the values governing action (Ethics) (*AS*, p. 26), and indeed the totality of the factors determining a given state of a culture. From this point of view, archaeology does not bring about a radical break. I have already mentioned that in the last analysis it goes back to the way practices function at the heart of theoretical knowledge [*savoir*] . Deleuze, for his part, stressed that it is of a double nature, in that on the level of enunciation the discursive object is in juxtaposition with the visible object. So there is an archaeology of the visible which is inseparable from the archaeology of theoretical knowledge [*savoir*]. It should be added that Foucault's archaeology deals not only with this doubling up of theoretical knowledge [*savoir*], but also with power and, as we have seen, with the prescriptive.

The fact remains that history is organised around progress and presupposes a certain degree of *continuity*. On this point, as far as the acquired knowledge of archaeology is concerned, a comparison with Freud can clarify matters: the difference is not insignificant, even if this is seen in terms of the metaphors which are used to interpret the word 'archaeology'. For Freud, the archaeologist is someone who *digs* in search of that which lies *below* in order to find one town hidden beneath another. (I am not saying that the Freudian process can be reduced to this alone, but there is no doubt that this is the underlying image.) For Michel Foucault, the archaeologist is someone who *moves aside* and reveals another organisation which follows different *alignments*. Remaining within the metaphor of the town, the process which Michel Foucault uses puts one in mind more of the kaleidoscoping of a map like that of Paris, the centre of which is constantly changing, from one side of the Seine to the other and back again. From this point of view it would be absurd to suggest that a former state of knowledge [*savoir*] (or power, or the subject) constituted the 'deep–seated' root of another: of course they succeed one another, but they are *different*.

Now, if, rather than the setting in of 'stubborn processes of becoming' (*AS*, p. 10), one comes across 'disconnections' (*AS*, p. 9) in patterns; and if, rather than the continuing history of an object, one bears witness, as a result of 'interruptions' (*AS*, p. 17), to its disappearance and replacement: if, instead of the evolution of a concept, one comes across, as one reaches 'the inflections of the curve' (*AS*, p. 17) and the 'inversion of a regulatory movement', a shift in this concept so that it takes on a different form (the same characteristics no longer being the pertinent ones), within the context of a different field (such that it is no longer the same structures which are problematical), and when the constitution of 'series' and the way they are linked changes into 'series of series' or 'tables' (*AS*, p. 13) – it is clear that archaeology is dealing essentially with '*breaks*' (*AS*, p. 9) and 'redistributions' (*AS*, p. 11): 'the problem is no longer that of the tradition and the tracing of it, but the way it is formed and delimited' (*AS*, p. 12), where what is at stake are the 'shifts in level and synchronisation

[. . .], particular forms of retentivity, and the types of relationship which are possible' (*AS*, p. 18). That is to say, the nerve structure of the knowledge [*connaissance*] in question, in the succession of *epistemes*.

Instead of progress, then, one finds rupture; instead of an extended, coherent structure, one finds the interplay of disconnected series. What, then, can be said to remain of a history of philosophy? How can one talk of a reinterpretation or rearticulation of the same concept, from one philosophy to the next, if, in fact, one is not dealing with the *same* concept, taken as it is from a different state of rules of behaviour and theoretical knowledge [*savoir*], and treated in a different style? Moreover, what if the concepts themselves are not linked to one another in their surface use but spring from shifting layers of substrata, thus making any total overview impossible? And again: if 'philosophy' (*AS*, p. 16) is constructed each time on a different order of theoretical knowledge [*savoir*] (or power, or of the prescriptive), an order which could not be called total, but global, such that it roots itself in this knowledge, or sets itself up against it, then how can philosophy be talked about in the *singular* and be inferred from the notion of continuity? All this is well known, but it has to be called to mind in order to conclude that archaeology is a *deconstruction* of the history of philosophy.

It is in this way that Michel Foucault found a point of departure in the Heideggerian deconstruction of metaphysics; and when, nowadays Rorty challenges the notion of the mind as 'a mirror of nature', he is re-echoing Foucault's temporalisation of discursive systems. It is self-evident that when the scaffolding has been thrown down in this way, the whole edifice of philosophy has to be reconstructed.

2. There is also the view – and this is the other way in which its history can be seen – that philosophy is a *particular* order of discourse (which is not, of course, eternal; and which, for us, came into being in what was perhaps a contingent way in Greece). From this point of view, philosophical discourse can be seen as having a *subject*, in the sense that all forms of discourse have one; the subject who is the bearer of affirmations [*énoncés*] and is an essential part of its structure (including its verbal structure), who is indeed represented by its structure. This form of discourse can be seen as attempting to speak of the *Real*: by describing it, deducing it, or by means of reduction. Seen in this way, it is on the basis of its continuity of status that it is able to constitute an *event* at each of its historical phases, which cannot be foreseen in terms of the global movement which will make it run obliquely to a state of theoretical knowledge [*savoir*] (or power, or practices), and tear itself away on the basis of the new situation of the *archē*. In this way, finally, the systems form amongst themselves what amounts more or less to a further *system*, to the extent that they return to certain positions and that several of them repeat – from one period to another

– the same type of construction, the same sort of movement, such that essential relationships are present transhistorically.

One might object to this that Michel Foucault did not tackle the status of philosophical discourse head on, and that we cannot know whether or not he would have done so. But is true that he dealt with it *obliquely*. It is certainly to philosophy that he was referring in his critique of history, history such as is founded on 'the long series constituted by the *progress of awareness*, or the *teleology of reason*, or the *evolution of human thought*' (*AS*, p. 16). It was certainly philosophy that Michel Foucault had in mind when he wrote: 'if the history of thought . . . were able to weave, around what men think and say, obscure syntheses which anticipate what will become of him, prepare him and lead him indefinitely towards his future, it would provide a privileged shelter for the *sovereignty of consciousness*.' Where, except in philosophy, does one find this 'founding function of the *subject*' (*AS*, p. 21) which claims that one day it will be able to 'appropriate to itself once again [those things being kept at a distance by the difference], restore its mastery and find in it what could be referred to as its true dwelling place' (*AS*, p. 21)? In the last analysis, it is philosophy which, 'in the reassuring form of sameness', makes our relationship with the past 'a memory' (*AS*, p. 14) and conserves truth on the basis of anthropological constancy.

Even on the level of its specific discursive nature, the history of philosophy, like the philosophy of history, acts on presuppositions which are exactly those which the archaeologist questions.

But at this point we have to consider whether we are dealing with philosophy in a general sense or with *a* philosophy? After all, what Michel Foucault designates as the 'other' is *par excellence* the Hegelian model. And one might put forward the idea that in Michel Foucault's ordering notion of 'thinking of the Other' (*AS*, p. 22), it is *yet another philosophy* which is being affirmed. This philosophy would have been initiated by Marx (his shift of emphasis to the relations surrounding production), Nietzsche (genealogy as opposed to origination) and Freud (consciousness's inability to take account of sexuality), not forgetting Guéroult and his 'architectonic' (*AS*, p. 12) of systems, for which all that is relevant is the 'internal coherency, axioms, deductive chains and compatibility', which are constituted on each occasion into an irreducible unity. Hence one might say that the establishing of breaks which constitute archaeology operates with a certain degree of homogeneity within its given field, with a relative persistence in the nature of the questions it asks. This can be seen at the point where Michel Foucault writes that his work is situated 'in the field where the questions of the human being, awareness, origin and subject become manifest, entangled, and specified' (*AS*, p. 26). It seems at this point that the undertaking of archaeology separates itself from the principle of thinking in terms of *Sameness* – in order to denounce the ideology of so doing, but also to make new use of the terms involved in this form of thought, and to show that they can be reused in a different way.

3. On this basis, a final question can be asked: if one thinks in terms of the Otherness of Sameness, is one *thinking* differently? Apparently not. The impression the archaeologist gives of having shifted his position is in the last analysis a way of reproaching historians (including historians of philosophy) for *bad* thinking, and for having been prisoners of an ideology: for holding on to what they saw as knowledge [*connaissances*] without seeing, below the surface, the operation of discursive practices; for investigating intentions rather than the rules of behaviour; for presenting us with a memory to be interpreted, instead of the mutual resistance of fields which need to be linked together. Continuing this process of demystifying criticism, Michel Foucault is – to take an extremely lofty view – a Cartesian thinker; what he tries to track down is confusion between levels and timescales; what he seeks is the clarity which positivity can bring to the pragmatic.

This is not to say that he did not set in motion a number of philosophical shifts which have radical implications for philosophy. To think in terms of the Other is to finish with the idea of the *One*: in the interlinking movement of affirmations is affirmed a multiplicity where there is no oneness, which is only ever organised in a temporary and partial way. If one moves towards rules of behaviour which are tied to the mastery and approbation of the self, there is no further need for the narrow processes of blame or indeed for that which is, *par excellence*, the *Within*. To undertake a history of problems and the redistribution of practices which order them is to render the notion of a changeless *Truth* meaningless.

But these three breaks – which cut diagonally across the paths of critical retreat which are more or less similar in other contemporary authors – can be understood in Michel Foucault's case only in terms of the pragmatic: from the practices of discourse to the practices of action, and always in terms of the changing rules which cause them to act upon one another. And the way in which he reaches this point is not, as has been maintained, nihilistic, but by means of an original process of argumentation. This is the double rejection of *similitude* and the notion that similitude could be established *affirmatively*. In the place of the former we find a slender thread of absence; and instead of the latter, eating away at it, a tremulous uncertainty. 'Nothing less was needed to break down the fortress where resemblance was the prisoner of affirmation' (*CP*, p. 101). In his article about the statement *this is not a pipe*, he argues (*CP*, p. 103) that because the sign is not 'separated' from the thing, and because it is, in turn, a sign, and because between the two signs the 'Same' is without the idea of 'As if' (*CP*, p. 99), the negation is inscribed in the very heart of the relationship. All there is is discourse, a 'clouded' (*CP*, p. 100) space without foundation, where correspondences cover over slippages in an indefinite way. The inconsistency, the break, the undermined affirmation, the disontologisation of rules – all these are germinal movements in a form of thought which explores discourse without claiming to found it. As a result of this, in the progress and perhaps in the shift in position of the enquiry, the performative, prescriptions which are inscribed in practices and in an actively uncentred history reveal themselves to be the operatives in the workings of the discourse.

In this sense, then, Michel Foucault can be seen as making a contribution to the field of philosophy. For him, the Same is always being worked away at by the Other; the Other is delivered from the process of dialectic reconciliation; discursive space is isolated by non-unitary multiplicity, which is a multiplicity not of states but of deeds. The thought of Michel Foucault is that of the pragmatic of diversity.

six

On the ordering of things

Being and power in Heidegger and Foucault

Hubert L. Dreyfus

The most central and obscure notion in Heidegger's writings is Being, and the same could be said of the notion of Power in the works of Foucault. For both thinkers these are not traditional stable entities. Heidegger offers a history of Being [*Seinsgeschichte*] in order to help us understand and overcome our current technological understanding of Being; and Foucault analyses several regimes of power in the course of his genealogy of the biopower which, he claims, dominates modern life.

These rough parallels suggest that it might be illuminating to see how far the comparison of Heidegger's 'Being' with Foucault's 'Power' can be pushed. Do these terms designate equivalent functions? To what extent do Heidegger's epochs of the history of Being match Foucault's regimes in the history of Power? To what extent do these two histories lead us to see our current cultural condition in similar ways? How does each envisage resistance?

Lest the striking difference in Heidegger's and Foucault's politics and life-styles make this project seem hopeless from the start, we must remember Foucault's comment on Heidegger in his last interview:

> For me Heidegger has always been the essential philosopher.... My entire philosophical development was determined by my reading of Heidegger.[1]

The other major influence was, of course, Nietzsche. Foucault tells us in the same interview: 'I am simply Nietzschean, and I try to see, on a number of points, and to the extent that it is possible, with the aid of Nietzsche's texts ... what can be done in this or that domain.'[2] But it was through Heidegger that Foucault came to appreciate Nietzsche. 'It is possible that if I had not read

Heidegger, I would not have read Nietzsche. I had tried to read Nietzsche in the fifties but Nietzsche alone did not appeal to me – whereas Nietzsche and Heidegger, that was a philosophical shock!'[3]

I THE FUNCTIONING OF BEING AND POWER

It is important to realise from the start that for Heidegger Being is not a substance or a process. Being, in the sense relevant here, is short for the understanding of Being, the truth of Being or the meaning of Being.[4] For Heidegger all these terms call attention to the context in which people and things show up and can encounter each other. In *Being and Time* he shows that all human activity presupposes such a context in which objects and actions make sense – a context that both opens up and limits the kinds of objects that can be dealt with and the possible ways of dealing with them.

Heidegger is interested only in the most general characteristics of our understanding of Being. He notes, however, that this understanding is embodied in the tools, language and institutions of a society and in each person growing up in that society. These shared practices into which we are socialised provide a background understanding of what counts as objects, what counts as human beings and ultimately what counts as real, on the basis of which we can direct our actions towards particular things and people. Thus the understanding of Being creates what Heidegger calls a clearing [*Lichtung*]. Heidegger calls the unnoticed way that the clearing both limits and opens up what can show up and what can be done, its 'unobtrusive governance' [*Waltens*] (*Letter on Humanism*, p. 212).

Many of Foucault's difficult remarks concerning power make sense if we take him to be getting at a similar social clearing with an emphasis on the way embodied, everyday practices produce, perpetuate and delimit what people can think and do. And since Foucault is not interested in how *things* show up but exclusively in *people's actions*, 'Power', which is normally used to describe the way governments govern people's actions, seems an appropriate, if perhaps misleading, name for this selective aspect of the clearing. Foucault attempts to ward off any misunderstanding:

> By power, I do not mean 'Power' as a group of institutions and mechanisms that ensure the subservience of the citizens of a given state. By power, I do not mean, either, a mode of subjugation which, in contrast to violence, has the form of the rule. Finally, I do not have in mind a general system of domination exerted by one group over another. . . . The analysis, made in terms of power, must not assume that the sovereignty of the State, the form of the law, or the overall unity of a domination are given at the outset; rather, these are only the terminal forms power takes.[5]

Each age has its distinctive form of power:

> [T]o live in society is to live in such a way that it is possible to act on each other's actions. A society without power relations can only be an abstraction.[6]

For Foucault, as for Heidegger on Being, power is neither a fixed entity nor an institution:

> One needs to be nominalistic, no doubt; power is not an institution, and not a structure; neither is it a certain strength we are endowed with; it is the name that one attributes to a complex strategical situation in a particular society.[7]

It is sometimes difficult to separate Foucault's discussion of those characteristics which belong to power *as such* from those which belong to the stage of power in which we now live. The best general description of power is found in Foucault's essay 'Le sujet et le pouvoir'. There, he clearly thinks of power not as a substance or process or force but as a clearing which, by opening up a finite field of possibilities, governs actions while none the less leaving them free.

> [S]omething called Power, with or without a capital letter, which is assumed to exist universally in a concentrated or diffused form, does not exist. Power exists only when it is put into action. . . . It is a total structure of actions brought to bear upon possible actions . . .
>
> Power is exercised only over free subjects, and only in so far as they are free. By this we mean individual or collective subjects who are faced with a field of possibilities in which several ways of behaving, several reactions and diverse comportments may be realized. [T]o 'conduct' is at the same time to 'lead' others . . . and a way of behaving within a more or less open field of possibilities. The exercise of power consists in guiding the possibility of conduct and putting in order the possible outcome. Basically power is less a confrontation between two adversaries or the linking of one to the other than a question of government. . . . To govern, in this sense, is to structure the possible field of action of others.[8]

We should not be surprised that in Volume II of *Histoire de la sexualité*, Foucault speaks in Heideggerian terms of his later work analysing power. He first reminds us that 'the proper task of a history of thought, as against a history of behaviors or representations, [is] to define the conditions in which human beings "problematize" what they are, what they do, and the world in which they live.'[9] He then puts this in later Heideggerian terms as a receptivity to being:

> [It was a matter of] analyzing, not behaviors or ideas, nor societies and their 'ideologies', but the *problematizations* through which *being offers itself as having to be thought* – and the *practices* on the basis of which these problematizations are formed.[10]

II *SEINSGESCHICHTE* AND GENEALOGY

The space that governs human activity by determining what counts as a thing, what counts as true/false and what it makes sense to do, is not static, nor does it have abrupt discontinuities, but it does fall into a distinguishable, if overlapping, series of epochs.

Both Heidegger and Foucault, no doubt influenced by Nietzsche, begin with a prehistory in pre-Socratic Greece. Heidegger devotes many pages to showing that although pre-Socratic thought did not encompass the clearing [*Lichtung*], it did not deny it either. Their sense that what showed up as present depended upon what was not itself present is preserved in their understanding of the truth of Being as *alethia* or unconcealment. But this understanding was lost when Socrates and Plato took Being to be the ground of the phenomena, and truth to be the correspondence of propositions to an independent reality.

> [T]here has historically been a withdrawal of Being itself; there has been an abandonment by Being of beings as such. . . . Consequently, and from that time on, Being itself has remained unthought.[11]

Foucault's references to this first stage of our culture are much sketchier than Heidegger's, but he too points to the emergence of theoretical knowing among the Greeks as the great turning point in our history. The pragmatic and poetic discourse of early Greek civilisation was destroyed by the rise of theory: 'The Sophists were routed . . . [from] the time of the great Platonic division onwards, the [Platonic] will to truth has had its own history. . . .'[12] This change presumably altered all aspects of Greek life. For example, Foucault tells us that 'When Hippocrates had reduced medicine to a system, observation was abandoned and philosophy introduced into medicine'[13] or '. . . the West has managed . . . to annex sex to a field of rationality . . . we are accustomed to such "conquests" since the Greeks. . . .'[14]

Heidegger, in keeping with his concerns as a philosopher, has an elaborate account of the epochs of Being associated with the words *physis*, *idea* and *energeia*, and of the radical break between pre-Socratic *physis* and all later names for Being. He stresses the difference between the pre-Socratic understanding of Being and our own. For the pre-Socratics:

> [t]hat which is, is that which arises and opens itself, which, as what presences, comes upon man as the one who presences, i.e., comes upon the one who himself opens himself to what presences in that he apprehends it. . . . To be beheld by what is, to be included and maintained within its openness and in that way to be borne along by it, to be driven about by its oppositions and marked by its discord – that is the essence of man in the great age of the [pre-Socratic] Greeks.[15]

In his published works Heidegger has much less to say about the Platonic and Aristotelian epochs and relatively little to add about the Romans, except that the translation of Greek terms into a philosophy expressing Roman practices lost the original sense of words such as *theoria*, which once focused the Platonic Greek understanding of Being.

By medieval times the clearing [*Lichtung*] had been completely forgotten and Being was equated with substances grounded in a supreme Being:

> For the Middle Ages . . . to be in being means to belong within a specific rank of the order of what has been created – a rank appointed from the beginning – and as thus caused, to correspond to the cause of creation. . . .[16]

Foucault, too, has little to say about Greek philosophy. He does, it is true, briefly describe hierarchical, monarchical power at the beginning of *Surveiller et punir*. What interests us is, in any case, how Heidegger's and Foucault's concerns converge upon the transformation which issues in the modern world and our current understanding of human beings.

Heidegger begins by telling us that 'Metaphysics grounds an age, in that, through a specific interpretation of what is, and through a specific comprehension of truth, it gives to that age the basis upon which it is essentially formed' ('The age of the world picture', p. 115). Foucault says, more narrowly: 'In any given culture and at any given moment, there is only one *episteme* that defines the conditions of possibility of all knowledge whether expressed in a theory or silently invested in a practice' (*Les Mots et les Choses*, p. 179 [ET: *The Order of Things*, p. 168]).

Both view the account of representation in the classical age as the crucial but unstable beginning of modernity – a starting point that is not yet clear about its radically new understanding of Being – a new understanding that finally becomes explicit in Kant's interpretation of *man*.

At this point the parallel between the two thinkers comes into sharp focus, as can be seen when we compare Heidegger's account of the origin of man in 'The age of the world picture' and Foucault's account in *Les Mots et les Choses*. Heidegger tells us of a radical transformation in our understanding of being which took place in the seventeenth century: 'What it is to be is for the first time defined as the objectiveness of representing, and truth is first defined as the certainty of representation in the metaphysics of Descartes . . .' (p. 127). The age of representation differs in fundamental ways from all other ages:

> What is, in its entirety, is now taken in such a way that it only is in being to the extent that it is set up by man, who represents and sets forth. The being of whatever is, is sought and found in the representedness of the latter – the fact that the world becomes picture is what distinguishes the essence of the modern age. (pp. 127–30)

Foucault, always more concrete, brilliantly analyses a representative picture, *Las Meninas*, where representation in its various forms is literally pictured. In *Las Meninas* the aspects of representation – the subject matter of the painting – have been dispersed into three separate figures. Their representations are spread out in the picture itself. These aspects are the producing of the representation (the painter), the object represented (the models and their gaze), and the viewing of the representation (the spectator). Each of these separate functions can be and has been represented by Velázquez. This dispersion of representation is necessary so that all these functions can be laid out in an organised table. The price paid for this success is that the activity of representation, the unified temporal unfolding of the functions of representation, cannot be represented on the table. And it is this tension which produces the instability in the painting and in the *episteme*. The central paradox of the painting turns on the impossibility of representing the act of representing.

The answer to this paradox is that man does not only copy the order; he produces it. Heidegger explains:

> To represent means to bring what is present at hand before oneself as something standing over against, to relate it to oneself, to the one representing it, and to force it back into this relationship to oneself as the normative realm. . . . What is decisive is that man himself expressly takes up this position as one constituted by himself and that he makes it secure as the footing for a possible development of humanity. . . . ('The age of the world picture', p. 132)

As Foucault puts it:

> Man appears in his ambiguous position as an object of knowledge and as subject that knows: enslaved sovereign, observed spectator, he appears in the place belonging to the King, which was assigned to him in advance by *Las Meninas*. . . .[17]

With Kant, man becomes both the source of the meaning of objects and an object in the world, and philosophy becomes anthropology. In Heidegger's terms:

> [O]bservation of and teaching about the world change into a doctrine of man, into anthropology. . . . The name 'anthropology' as used here does not mean just some investigation of man by a natural science. . . . It designates that philosophical interpretation of man which explains and evaluates whatever is, in its entirety, from the standpoint of man and in relation to man.[18]

> Anthropology is that interpretation of man that already knows fundamentally what man is and hence can never ask who he may be. . . .[19]

Philosophy, according to Kant, awakens from its dogmatic slumber, only to fall, according to Foucault, into an anthropological sleep. Heidegger and Foucault thus both reach rhetorical heights as they look forward to the end of humanism. Heidegger:

> Man cannot, of himself, abandon this destining of his modern essence or abolish it by fiat. But man can, as he thinks ahead, ponder this: Being subject as humanity has not always been the sole possibility belonging to the essence of historical man, ... nor will it always be. A fleeting cloud shadow over a concealed land, such is the darkening which that truth as the certainty of subjectivity ... lays over a disclosing event that it remains denied to subjectivity itself to experience.[20]

Or Foucault:

> As the archaeology of our thought easily shows, man is an invention of recent date. And one perhaps nearing its end.
>
> If those arrangements were to disappear as they appeared, if some event ... were to cause them to crumble, as the ground of Classical thought did, at the end of the eighteenth century, then one can certainly wager that man would be erased, like a face drawn in sand at the edge of the sea.[21]

In the last stage of their thinking, both Heidegger and Foucault realise that man is, indeed, being wiped out, but this only reveals a long-term process which is by no means encouraging. Heidegger and Foucault see us as caught in especially dangerous practices which, both suggest, produced man only finally to eliminate him, as they more and more nakedly reveal a tendency towards the total ordering of all beings – a tendency that became possible as soon as the Greeks forgot the truth of being and substituted the will to truth. Heidegger calls this current understanding of Being technological, and he is concerned to show how it distorts our understanding of *things*; Foucault calls it disciplinary biopower and focuses primarily on how it distorts the social order and our relation to other *human beings*. Both hold that it distorts our understanding of ourselves and leads to a pervasive sense of distress.

Heidegger, for a time, like many current critics of the modern age, was under the illusion that the danger was that man was dominating everything and exploiting all beings for his own satisfaction[22] – as if man were a subject in control, and the objectification of everything were the problem. As Foucault points out in *Les Mots et les Choses*, with the help of Heideggerian hindsight, in *Being and Time* and even after his 'turning', Heidegger himself was still caught up in the Kantian doubles. Indeed, as late as 1940 Heidegger still held that from the beginning of modernity up to the present, man has been in control:

> Western history has now begun to enter into the completion of that period we call the *modern*, and which is defined by the fact that man becomes the measure and the center of beings. Man is what lies at the bottom of all beings: that is, in modern terms, at the bottom of all objectification and representability.[23]

But by 1946 Heidegger clearly distances himself from this view. He interprets Rilke, for example, as criticising the objectification of all beings:

> It is by the positioning that belongs to representation that Nature is brought before man. Man places before himself the world as the whole of everything objective, and he places himself before the world.
>
> Where Nature is not satisfactory to man's representation, he reframes or redisposes it.
>
> The whole objective inventory in terms of which the world appears is given over to, commended to, and thus subjected to the command of self-assertive production.
>
> Modern science and the total state, as necessary consequences of the nature of technology, are also its attendants. The same holds true of the means and forms that are set up for the organization of public opinion and of men's everyday ideas. . . . At the bottom, the essence of life is supposed to yield itself to technical production.[24]

But Heidegger himself is clear that all this exploitation and control is not man's doing, and man never was anything but an effect of other forces.

> Even this, that man becomes the subject and the world the object, is a consequence of technology's nature establishing itself, and not the other way around.[25]

Thus, in his final analysis of technology, Heidegger is critical of those who, still caught in the subject/object picture, think that technology is dangerous because it embodies instrumental reason.

> The current conception of technology, according to which it is a means and a human activity, can . . . be called the instrumental and anthropological definition of technology.[26]

Modern technology is 'something completely different and therefore new'.[27] The essence of modern technology is ordering for its own sake:

> Everywhere everything is ordered to stand by, to be immediately at hand, indeed to stand there just so that it may be on call for a further ordering. Whatever is ordered about in this way has its own standing. We call it the standing-reserve [*Bestand*]. . . . Whatever stands by in the sense of standing-reserve no longer stands over against us as object.[28]

The goal of technology, Heidegger tells us, is more and more flexibility and efficiency simply for its own sake: '[E]xpediting is always itself directed from the beginning toward furthering something else, i.e., toward driving on to the maximum yield at the minimum expense.'[29] Heidegger sees this modern understanding as gradually absorbing both subjects and objects.

> The subject–object relation thus reaches, for the first time, its pure 'relational', i.e., ordering, character in which both the subject and the object are sucked up as standing-reserves. That does not mean that the subject–object relation vanishes, but rather the opposite: it now attains to its most extreme dominance. . . . It becomes a standing-reserve to be commanded and set in order.[30]

> If man is challenged, ordered, to [optimize everything], then does not man himself belong even more originally than nature within the standing-reserve? The current talk about human resources, about the supply of patients for a clinic, gives evidence of this.[31]

In spite of Heidegger's self-critique, and his correction of his early view that domination by man was the problem, Foucault too, in the social realm, went through a stage where he thought the problem was that some men or classes dominated and excluded others, and only later saw that exclusion, calling for the liberation of the repressed, was not the problem. Power is not an instrument for exclusion which has fallen into the wrong hands, but a pressure towards ever-greater optimisation. Sex, for example, becomes 'a thing to be not simply condemned or tolerated but managed, inserted into systems of utility, regulated for the greater good of all, made to function according to an optimum'.[32] Thus Foucault's auto-critique:

> We must cease once and for all to describe the effects of power in negative terms: it 'excludes,' it 'represses,' it 'censors,' it 'abstracts,' it 'masks,' it 'conceals.' In fact, power produces; it produces reality; it produces domains of objects and rituals of truth. The individual and the knowledge that may be gained of him belong to this production.[33]

> At bottom, despite the differences in epochs and objectives, the representation of power has remained under the spell of monarchy. In political thought and analysis, we still have not cut off the head of the king. Hence the importance that the theory of power gives to the problem of right and violence, law and illegality, freedom and will, and especially the state and sovereignty. . . . To conceive of power on the basis of these problems is to conceive of it in terms of a historical form that is characteristic of our societies: the juridical monarchy. Characteristic yet transitory.[34]

> The theory of sovereignty . . . does not allow for a calculation of power in terms of the minimum expenditure for the maximum return.[35]

III OUR CONTEMPORARY UNDERSTANDING OF BEING/POWER

In their final analysis of our current situation, both Heidegger and Foucault contend that, in spite of the appearance that we have passed through several epochs, since the classical age our modern Western practices exhibit an underlying, continuous directionality, a 'destining' (Heidegger), a 'strategy without a strategist' (Foucault). Heidegger and Foucault agree that this directionality of our practices has reached a final phase in this century. In the way it now regulates our most important practices, its underlying direction has become clear. Our culture is facing the greatest danger in its history, for, while previous clearings [*Lichtung*] were static and partial, leaving a certain leeway for the way things and human beings could show up and be encountered, our current understanding is progressively taking over *every* aspect of the natural and social world.

Unlike the hierarchical, top–down order of the medieval understanding of Being and of monarchical power, which was centralised but not extended to all details of the world, the modern understanding of Being/Power is bottom–up, levelling and totalising. Heidegger emphasises the totalisation in his phrase 'total mobilisation', while Foucault includes both totalising and levelling in referring to 'normalisation'.

Normalisation is more than socialisation into norms. Such socialisation is the way the understanding of Being or Power governs the actions of the members of any society. Normalisation, however, is uniquely modern. 'A normalizing society is the historical outcome of a technology of power centered on life.'[36] In this understanding, which has emerged more and more clearly since the classical age, norms are progressively brought to bear on *all* aspects of life.

To understand how normalisation works we have to bring Foucault's insight into the way the human sciences serve to extend social norms, together with Heidegger's account of the technological understanding of Being underlying modern science. To begin with, for Heidegger science is a form of technology. According to Heidegger this can be seen in the modern understanding of theory: '[T]he "theory" that modern science shows itself to be is something essentially different from the Greek *theoria*.'[37] What is original in modern theory is the totalising. Since Galileo, scientific research has been based on the idea that there must be *one system* into which all of physical reality must be made to fit:

> [E]very procedure ... requires an open sphere in which it moves. And it is precisely the opening up of such a sphere that is the fundamental event in research. This is accomplished through the projection within some realm of what is – in nature, for example – of a fixed ground plan of natural events. The projection sketches out in advance the manner in which the knowing procedure must bind itself and adhere to the sphere opened up. This binding adherence is the rigor of research.[38]

This is what Heidegger means when, in speaking of Descartes, he describes representing as 'forcing things into our normative realm'.

Heidegger's understanding of modern science is exactly like Thomas Kuhn's in *The Nature of Scientific Revolutions*. What Heidegger calls research, Kuhn calls normal science. Normal science operates by setting up a *total* interpretation of some region of reality and then attempts to show that the anomalies that emerge can be fitted into the general account. Normal science assumes beforehand that the general plan is correct, and thus that the anomalies have no truth to tell – that in the end, all anomalies must be brought under the law. Normal science progresses precisely by causing and overcoming anomalies. Foucault sees that modern norms supposedly grounded in science likewise produce anomalies and then take every anomaly, every attempt to evade them, as occasions for further intervention to bring the anomalies under the scientific norms. This is normalisation.

Normalisation, according to Foucault, serves not to objectify, exclude, coerce or punish, but rather to enhance life. Power creates docile bodies and self-absorbed, analytical deep subjects so as to further the range of the human sciences, with no other goal than ever-greater welfare for all. It has become self-evident to us that everyone should get the most out of his or her possibilities, and that the human sciences show us the way to do this. The resulting practices Foucault calls biopower. It is a power

> working to incite, reinforce, control, monitor, optimize, and organize the forces under it: a power bent on generating forces, making them grow, and ordering them, rather than one dedicated to impending them, making them submit, or destroying them.[39]

Their common critique of technology/biopower does not lead either Heidegger or Foucault to oppose the use of technological devices and specific welfare practices. Heidegger is clear that it is the *technological understanding of Being*, not *technology*, that causes our distress. (That the technological understanding of Being can be dissociated from technological devices is clear if one looks at contemporary Japan, where a traditional, non-technological understanding of Being – or, perhaps better, no understanding of Being at all, since it seems that the Japanese have no single unified understanding of reality – exists alongside the most advanced high-tech production and consumption.

> [T]he essence of technology is by no means anything technological. Thus we shall never experience our relationship to the essence of technology so long as we merely conceive and push forward the technological, put up with it, or evade it. Everywhere we remain unfree and chained to technology, whether we passionately affirm or deny it.[40]

Heidegger uses and depends upon modern technological devices like anyone else, and he does not advocate a return to the pre-technological world of

Ancient Greece. Foucault, like Heidegger, is, of course, not opposed to modern medical technology, and specific welfare practices like mass vaccination. He is, however, opposed to taking it for granted that welfare practices, based on the human sciences, should, in the name of efficiency and optimisation, be extended without critical questioning to all aspects of our lives.

IV WHAT RESISTS AND WHY

Whereas Foucault is concerned solely with what is happening to *people*, Heidegger is concerned almost exclusively with what is happening to *things*.[41] And each sees what is endangered as at the same time a source of resistance.

Heidegger is not against modern science, but he is critical of the way its methods, legitimate and successful for dealing with physical reality, are carried over into other aspects of human practices so that all things become mere resources for more and more flexible and total organisation. Yet he holds that things can never be completely understood by science, nor totally controlled. Their resistance is not the passive resistance of prime matter, but an active withdrawal. Heidegger calls this function 'earth':

> Earth ... shatters every attempt to penetrate into it. It causes every merely calculating importunity upon it to turn into a destruction. This destruction may herald itself under the appearance of mastery and of progress in the form of the technical-scientific objectivation of nature, but this mastery nevertheless remains an impotence of will. The earth appears openly cleared as itself only when it is perceived and preserved as that which is by nature undisclosable, that which shrinks from every disclosure and constantly keeps itself closed up.[42]

This refusal of things to fit into some preordained total plan reveals things not just as anomalies but as the source of other ways of seeing things. Just as for Kuhn anomalies sometimes contain a resistance that forces a revolution in science in which the anomaly is no longer an anomaly but a paradigm case of a new truth, so for Heidegger the resistance intrinsic to things holds open the possibility of a saving breakdown of the total ground plan of modern culture, provided we are open to things in their resistance.

> When and in what way do things appear as things? They do not appear *by means of* human making. But neither do they appear without the vigilance of mortals. The first step toward such vigilance is the step back from the thinking that merely represents ...[43]

Instead we must preserve the endangered marginal and local element: 'Here and now . . . in simple things . . . we may foster the saving power in its increase.'[44]

People, however, unlike things, organise themselves, and Foucault not only shows us in detail how human beings come to impose norms on themselves; he finds in them a resistance to biopower parallel to that Heidegger finds in things:

> [T]here is indeed always something in the social body, in classes, groups and individuals themselves which in some sense escapes relations of power, something which is by no means a more or less docile or reactive primal matter, but rather a centrifugal movement, an inverse energy, a discharge. There is certainly no such thing as 'the' plebs; rather there is, as it were, a certain plebeian quality or aspect. There is plebs in bodies, in souls, in individuals, in the proletariat, in the bourgeoisie, but everywhere in a diversity of forms and extensions, of energies and irreducibilities. This measure of plebs is not so much what stands outside relations of power as their limit, their underside, their counter-stroke, that which responds to every advance of power by a movement of disengagement.[45]

For both Heidegger and Foucault these strange notions are presumably meant to encourage us to pay attention to what remains of the different, the local, and the recalcitrant in our current practices. But Heidegger and Foucault are faced with a dilemma concerning the status of those marginal practices which have escaped or successfully resisted the spread of technology/biopower. While they remain dispersed, these practices escape totalisation but offer little resistance to its further spread. However, if Heidegger or Foucault were to focus on them in an ordered way, even in the name of counter-tradition or resistance, they would risk being taken over and normalised.

When it comes to the difficult question of just why and how, then, we should resist, Heidegger and Foucault finally take quite different paths, each of which has its advantages and drawbacks. Heidegger, unlike Foucault, has an account of why the technological understanding of Being causes human beings distress. For Heidegger human beings, whether they realise it or not, are the recipients of all understandings of Being. Human practices have been receptive to at least two radically different understandings of Being in our culture, and could receive many others. Human beings who explicitly see and reflect on this happening Heidegger calls 'thinkers', but all human beings are essentially receptive. Although the current understanding of Being as the total ordering of everything for its own sake conceals the fact that that it is received, not controlled, human beings none the less remain recipients. Heidegger holds that realising this would weaken the hold of our technological understanding of reality, but because technology actively blocks the possibility of this realisation and its expression in our practices, we experience distress.

In the last analysis Foucault is more radical than Heidegger in that, consistent with his opposition to *all* totalising, he avoids any account of what human beings essentially are and are called to do, whether that be Nietzsche's call to constant self-overcoming or Heidegger's claim that Being demands total receptivity. Although Foucault does attempt to be receptive to the problematisations in our current practices 'through which being offers itself as having to be thought', he does not claim that in so doing he is fulfilling his human essence. This, of course, denies him any account of why biopower should be felt as distressing and so be resisted, but it enables him to avoid adding one more universal norm, while still engaging in active resistance to current levelling or totalising practices.

NOTES

1. Michel Foucault, 'Final interview', *Raritan*, Summer 1985, p. 8. Interview conducted by Gilles Barbedette and published in *Les Nouvelles*, 28 June 1984.
2. *Ibid.*, p. 9.
3. *Ibid.*
4. Later Heidegger distinguishes the understanding of Being from Being which 'sends' various understandings. In his middle period he speaks of Being in a way which covers both meanings. 'Being . . . is not God and not a cosmic ground. It is furthest from all beings and yet nearer to man than any being' (*Letter on Humanism*, p. 210).
5. Michel Foucault, *L'Histoire de la sexualité I: La Volonté de savoir*, Paris: Gallimard, 1976, p. 121 (English translation [ET]: *The History of Sexuality I: An introduction*, New York: Vintage, 1980, p. 92).
6. Michel Foucault, 'The subject and power', afterword in Hubert L. Dreyfus and Paul Rabinow, *Michel Foucault: Beyond structuralism and hermeneutics*, Chicago: University of Chicago Press, 2nd edn, 1983, pp. 221–2.
7. *Ibid.*, p. 93.
8. *Ibid.*, pp. 219–21.
9. Michel Foucault, *L'Usage des plaisirs*, Paris: Gallimard, 1984, p. 16 (ET: *The History of Sexuality II: The use of pleasure*, New York: Vintage, 1986, p. 10).
10. *Ibid.*, p. 17 (ET: p. 11 [emphasis added]).
11. Martin Heidegger, *Nietzsche, Volume Four: Nihilism*, New York: Harper & Row, 1982, p. 215.
12. Michel Foucault, *L'Ordre du discours*, Paris: Gallimard, 1971, pp. 18–19.
13. Michel Foucault, *Naissance de la clinique*, Paris: PUF, 1963, p. 55 (ET: *The Birth of the Clinic*, New York: Vintage, 1975, p. 56).
14. Michel Foucault, *La Volonté de savoir*, pp. 102–3 (ET: p. 78).
15. Martin Heidegger, 'The age of the world picture', in *The Question Concerning Technology and Other Essays*, New York: Harper Colophon, 1977, p. 131.
16. *Ibid.*, p. 130.
17. Michel Foucault, *Les Mots et les Choses*, Paris: Gallimard, 1966, p. 323 (ET: *The Order of Things*, New York: Vintage, 1973, p. 312).
18. Heidegger, 'The age of the world picture', p. 132.
19. *Ibid.*, p. 153.
20. *Ibid.*
21. Foucault, *Les Mots et les Choses*, p. 398 (ET: p. 387).

22. Heidegger himself was caught up in the subjectivist understanding of the human condition in *Being and Time*.
23. Heidegger, *Nietzsche*, p. 28.
24. Martin Heidegger, *Poetry, Language and Thought*, New York: Harper & Row, 1971, pp. 110–12.
25. *Ibid.*
26. Martin Heidegger, *The Question Concerning Technology*, New York: Harper Colophon, p. 5.
27. *Ibid.*
28. *Ibid.*, p. 17.
29. *Ibid.*, p. 15.
30. Martin Heidegger, 'Science and reflection', in *The Question Concerning Technology*, p. 173.
31. Heidegger, *The Question Concerning Technology*, p. 18.
32. Foucault, *La Volonté de savoir*, pp. 34–5 (ET: p. 24).
33. Michel Foucault, *Surveiller et punir*, Paris: Gallimard, 1975, p. 196 (ET: *Discipline and Punish*, New York: Pantheon, 1977, p. 194.
34. Foucault, *La Volonté de savoir*, p. 117 (ET: pp. 88–9).
35. Michel Foucault, 'Two lectures', in *Power/Knowledge*, New York: Pantheon, 1980, p. 105.
36. Foucault, *La Volonté de savoir*, p. 190 (ET: p. 144).
37. Heidegger, 'Science and reflection', p. 166.
38. Heidegger, 'The age of the world picture', p. 118.
39. Foucault, *La Volonté de savoir*, p. 179 (ET: p. 136).
40. Heidegger, *The Question Concerning Technology*, p. 4.
41. Occasionally in passing Heidegger notes the social consequences of the technological understanding of Being. He once speaks of practices dedicated to 'the organized establishment of a uniform state of happiness for all men' (*What is Called Thinking?*, New York: Harper & Row, 1968, p. 30) and adds that in this pursuit man is turned into yet another resource:

    Man, who no longer conceals his character of being the most important raw material, is also drawn into this process.

    Since man is the most important raw material, one must reckon with the fact that some day factories will be built for the artificial breeding of human material . . . ('Overcoming metaphysics', in *The End of Philosophy*, New York: Harper & Row, 1973, pp. 104, 106).

42. Heidegger, 'The origin of the work of art', in *Poetry, Language, Thought*, p. 47.
43. Heidegger, 'The thing', in *Poetry, Language, Thought*, p. 181.
44. Heidegger, *The Question Concerning Technology*, p. 33.
45. Michel Foucault, 'Power and strategies', in *Power/Knowledge*, p. 138.

SUMMARY OF DISCUSSIONS

Dreyfus's contribution provoked quite vehement reactions, all of which questioned the grounds on which he drew the parallel between Foucault and Heidegger. Thus **Dominique Janicaud** questioned him on the Heideggerian idea of thought, of '*Denken*' taken as '*Danken*'. Dreyfus agreed that there was no equivalent in Heidegger. None the less, in Foucault as in Heidegger there was an ontological distinction: in the case of Foucault it is the difference between the field which governs the acts of all persons and the specific way in which each person acts.

Michel Karkeits suggested that we should go beyond Heidegger and look to Nietzsche in order to understand Foucault's notion of power. If one does so one realises that it is impossible to reconcile the two opposites of Heidegger's notion of 'Being' and Foucault's notion of 'Power'.

Yves Roussel questioned Dreyfus briefly as to whether there was in Heidegger's work any single element which could be compared to or seen as providing a parallel with Foucault's practice as a historian.

In one sense, **Hubert Dreyfus** replied, Heidegger turns history into the history of Being. But Foucault considers details in particular, particular practices; so Foucault is certainly a historian in a sense that Heidegger is not.

2 STYLE AND DISCOURSE

one

On Foucault's concept of discourse

Manfred Frank

According to Lichtenberg's aphorism, the hollow sound which is made when a book hits a head is not always caused by the book. Yet one should not be too quick to conclude the opposite. If a community of researchers feels perplexed when faced with a somewhat vague key concept in an author's work, this is not always the fault of that community of researchers. It seems to me that for those who are opposed to hermeneutics, this is the situation with the term *Diskurs*. The extremely frequent and still growing use of this term, in literary criticism in particular, makes it clear that an epistemological problem (or, more prudently, a need) does exist, which it is supposed to remedy. Nevertheless, this is not enough to disarm the objection that the term's semantic field is so imprecise that any use of it is bound to be unclear. For this objection immediately undermines the critical or polemical bite (against the concept in terms of the comprehension of its meaning) imputed to it by the few who make use of it. For if we do not know what the criticism is directed against, the vague debate about it cannot be advanced any further, let alone settled.

I am not, of course, speaking of the use of the French noun '*discours*', whose meaning is limited to various conventional, political and literary contexts, but rather of the special use by means of which it became the substance of the theoretical programme which Michel Foucault for a time termed 'archaeology'. The meaning of this concept is scarcely any clearer than that of *Diskurs* (which is, in German, if anything somewhat more awkward). It is still worth asking which elements are supposed to be present in the received semantic of '*discours*', in a way which led Foucault to choose it as the appropriate candidate for the semantic reformulation which he proposes.

'Discourse' is taken from the Latin *discursus*, which in turn comes from the verb *discurrere*, meaning 'to run hither and thither'. A discourse is an utterance, or a talk of some length (not determined), whose unfolding or spontaneous development is not held back by any over-rigid intentions. Holding a 'discourse' is not the same as holding a conference. In the French context, 'discourse' comes quite close to terms like 'chat', 'chinwag', 'free conversation', 'improvisation', 'exposé', 'narration', 'peroration', '*langage*', or '*parole*'. Its everyday use is a long way from the definition which Habermas gives it, according to which discourse would have to be seen as the form of language in which claims to validity are founded. This definition is closer to the way Foucault uses it, first in the sense that discourse is resistant to rigid regulation, but also because it is situated more or less halfway between a norm-following linguistic system and a purely individual use of language. In present-day French, a discourse is neither a simple and singular combination of words (in the Saussurean sense of '*parole*') nor, on the other hand, is its meaning confined only within rules which have a controlling force in a linguistic system. They are not simple and singular combinations of words because intersubjective relationships are involved. At the same time their meaning is not exhausted purely in terms of linguistic rules, since this meaning arises out of a freedom which, though not without rules, could not be summed up exclusively through the concept of grammatical rules.

I shall attempt in what follows to isolate three levels of usage of the word 'discourse' in the theoretical texts of French structuralism and neo-structuralism. Only the two latter will be concerned with Foucault's own work, which does not in the slightest way disown the work of those who preceded and made his work possible. The first level is taken from my reading of the first volume of *Anthropologie structurale* by Claude Lévi-Strauss.[1] In my opinion the role played by Lévi-Strauss as precursor in the terminological transformation of the term 'discourse' into a term which contains within it a complete theoretical programme has been underestimated.

I

One of the magical formulae which structuralism took from the published versions of Saussure's *Cours* is that language is to be seen not as a substance but as a form. It is well known that, taking Saussure and the phonology of Trubetskoy as a starting point, Lévi-Strauss tried to discover algebraic structures and transformation groups in different types of relationship. Group relationships are indeed seen as obeying rules which are regulated in a way which is analogous to language, but not – in our sense of the term – discursively. This is why I shall be directing my attention here to the application of this programme to linguistic forms like myths.

Saussure had already situated general linguistics under the heading of a 'semiology' which he defined as 'a science which studies the life of signs at the heart of social life; it should form a part of social psychology, and in consequence, of general psychology. . . . It should tell us what signs consist of and what laws control them.'[2] Lévi-Strauss then suggested that the law according to which the meaning of a social sign was the effect of differential relations to other signs could be extended *by analogy* to other social systems, and in the last instance to the totality of the productions of the 'unconscious mind',[3] whose activity consisted in 'imposing forms on a content'.[4] If we add that this content was something not previously articulated, we find that we have returned immediately to the beginning of Chapter IV of Saussure's *Cours*, where the principle of the articulation of signs is set out: mind is in itself as amorphous as sound, and this is why something has to intervene between the two: the schematism of articulation. This makes it possible to refer a perceptible sound back to a signification which is not perceived by the senses. Lévi-Strauss applied to his own procedure the idealist term of 'schematism', notably in a famous passage in *La Pensée sauvage*, from which I shall quote here only two sentences:

> Without calling into question the incontestable primacy of infrastructures, we believe that between praxis and practices a mediator always come into play, which is the conceptual scheme by the operation of which a material object and a formal object, neither of which has any independent existence, complete one another as structures, that is to say as elements which are at once empirical and intelligible. It is to this theory of superstructures, which Marx barely sketched, that I wish to contribute.[5]

The fertile potential of the transference of the Saussurean theorem of articulation into the context of social structures is not, however, what I wish to deal with here. It seems to me that it was Lévi-Strauss's transference of the structuralist process to the analysis of myths that stimulated Foucault, in a decisive way, to develop his analytic of discourse. Myths are, after all, narrative texts which, unlike linguistic relationships or social structure, are rooted in the domain of language.[6]

Now there is an essential difference between the internal form of a language and a myth. Though myths are effectively linguistic forms (and are as such likely to be encompassed by the concept of language) they are still events on the level of *parole*: they arise out of discourse [*il[s] relève[nt] du discours*].[7]

This is how we come to encounter this concept, which is to occupy a central place in the language game of neo-structuralism. Lévi-Strauss introduces it as follows: a myth, he says, is a self-enclosed series, not of isolated signs, but of sentences. Inasmuch as it is a narrative it is a linguistic event, but not an event whose successive elements could be removed from their situation in time without doing harm to the whole. The linear nature of the signs – especially that of the succession of sentences – means that each of these elements has a temporal index; it is therefore not reversible. On the other hand, the elements of a structure, the values and the differential relationships, are defined in a recursive manner; they can be inverted without problems: the matrix which produces them as events is itself strictly non-temporal. This difference was set out by Saussure himself using the (clumsy) terms 'synchronic' and 'diachronic'. Lévi-Strauss remembered at this point that the concept of structure, which lay close to hand yet had not been used in a deliberate way, still bore within it the idea of multiple divisions: it is a form which can be seen to be constituted by different levels.

I shall explain this briefly. It was Émile Benveniste who, in his principal work,[8] introduced the concept of levels of constitution and explained it as follows: Saussure's idea, according to which linguistic signification comes by means of the phonic differentiation of signs, should be taken further. There must be, finally, several levels on which this abstract concept could be applied: first on the phonetic level on which the sounds of a language can be distinguished; then the phonological level on which the 'distinctive features' of national languages can be specified, and in terms of which their incompatibilities and potential for combination can be established; then the morphemic level where the smallest signifying parts and unities can be ordered (verb endings, for example); then the syntactic level where words are distinguished and combined in syntagms and sentences; and finally the contextual level on which the semantic nuances of expressions are taken into account in the context of other syntagms, and so on. So it is possible to distinguish between relationships established between elements at a certain level (like phonemes) and relationships established between elements from two different levels (like those between words and sentences). Benveniste calls the first type of relationship 'distributional' and the second 'integrative'. A linguistic structure would therefore be the sum total of the relationships which exist not only between the elements on one level but also between those on different levels of constitution.

In any case, as a linguist, Benveniste limits himself to the level of the constitution of the sentence; the totality of linguistic rules cannot go beyond this level. Myths, on the other hand – as *discourse* structures – are of such a nature that they do not have phonemes, morphemes or syntagms as their smallest constitutive unit, but sentences. Now Lévi-Strauss goes further: why not move on to a third level of constitution: 'a stage beyond *langue* and *parole*, that of "discourse"' ('the myth as this mode of discourse . . .'[9])? Here, then, we would have an initial definition – still crude – of one of the key concepts of neostructuralism: discourse is a linguistic structure whose smallest constitutive parts are sentences or, as Lévi-Strauss puts it, a structure which is made up not of small but of large units.

Having established this, we now need to bear in mind the other characteristic of (mythical) discourse: the way its one-dimensional nature seems to distinguish it from the system of language. Looked at more closely, this dimension is not of such great import as the following formulation shows:

myths do order their units, like the word [*parole*], in a chronology of succession; but this chronology is of a particular type. Mythical time is always already in the past or, more precisely, a timeless past time. There would be no sense, then, in disputing the succession of the order of events in the narration, nor would there be any sense in affirming that the succession of narrative elements took place at a time which was in fact historical. Now this is precisely a condition of the succession of sentences in *parole*. Although a mythical event is in the past, it can be reproduced at any time: it is in the past and at the same time, so long as it is rooted in the collective belief of a population, present in a way which is outside time – like, for example, the announcement of the Birth of the Divine Child which is repeated each Christmas. That, again, is what myth has in common with *langue*.

> This double structure, which is at the same time historical and ahistorical, explains the way in which myth can arise simultaneously out of the domain of *parole* (and can be analysed as such) and out of the domain of *langue* (in which it is formulated) whilst at the same time demonstrating on a third level the very characteristic of an absolute object. This third level also has a linguistic nature, but it is none the less distinct from the other two.[10]

What we are dealing with here, then, on this third level of language [*niveau de langage*], is the *level of discourse*, and we should bear this in mind.

I should like to make the clearest possible distinction between these different points. Myths share with linguistic systems a property which means that their elements possess a value (or a meaning) which is not based on themselves but comes about by virtue of the relationships which are set up between them: that is to say, both are structures. At the same time myths, as discourses, are structures made up of large units, or transphrastic units, which is what distinguishes them from languages [*langues*]. If, however, they are still to be analysed structurally, recourse has to be made to an analogy which Lévi-Strauss sets out in two stages:

> (1) like all linguistic phenomena, the myth is formed by constitutive units; (2) these units imply the presence of those which normally come into the structure of the language, that is phonemes, morphemes and semantemes. But the relationship of these units to semantemes is the same as the relationship of semantemes to morphemes, which is likewise the same as the relationship between morphemes and phonemes. Each form differs from the one which precedes it through its possession of a higher degree of complexity. For this reason, we can call the elements which are found in myths (and which are the most complex of all): large constitutive units (or mythemes).[11]

It is in this passage that the idea comes into being of what will later be called 'the linguistics of discourse'.[12] It was Barthes who formulated this hypothesis most clearly (although all he had done was to repeat what Lévi-Strauss had already said). Here is an extract:

> It is well known that linguistics stops at the level of the sentence: this is the last unit which it considers itself to have the right to deal with; ... And yet it is obvious that discourse itself (consisting of sentences grouped together) is organised and that by means of this organisation it appears as a message from another language, which is superior to the language of linguisticians: discourse has its units, its rules, its 'grammar'; going beyond the sentence and yet composed uniquely of sentences, discourse has by nature to become the object of a second form of linguistics. ... If one were to put forward a working hypothesis for an analysis of this, an immense task with infinite material, the most reasonable way forward would be to postulate a homological relationship between the sentence and discourse on the grounds that the same formal relationship seems to regulate all semiotic systems, whatever their substance and dimension: discourse would be seen as a large 'sentence' (the units of which would not necessarily be sentences), just as the sentence, with certain specifications, is a small discourse.[13]

Lévi-Strauss calls the smallest units of myths 'mythemes'. They share with the constitutive units of discourse the property of being sentences ('it would therefore be necessary to look on the level of the sentences'), but they can be fundamentally distinguished from specifically literary texts in that they do not demonstrate any style:[14]

> Myth could be defined as the mode of discourse where the value of the formula *traduttore, traditore* tends practically towards zero. ... The substance of the myth is found neither in the style nor in the syntax, but in the story which is told through them.[15]

It is this property which makes them even more similar to the constitutive units of a purely formal system of rules such as we find in language [*langue*] – for in language [*langue*] too, the *way* an individual speaker comes to master language is completely disregarded.

II

It is on the basis of these considerations that the 'Preface' of *Les Mots et les Choses: Une archéologie des sciences humaines*[16] was written. In this essay, of course, Foucault to a very great extent refrains from using the expression 'discourse', preferring the term 'episteme of the classical age', and as he does so he is taking a new step. No one has yet managed to clarify exactly what this step consists of. This is how it seems to me.

Starting from a biographical note (the idea of writing *Les Mots et les Choses* apparently came to Foucault on reading a text by Borges, who quotes a certain Chinese encyclopaedia which presents a taxonomy of the animal kingdom structured according to heterogeneity,[17] Foucault reasons from non-necessity – that is to say, from the historical relativity of our own schemes of thought: we react with amused astonishment to whatever fails to correspond to our schemes of classification, and consider it 'unthinkable'. This predicate reveals a state of affairs which is simple but fundamental: our thought moves in relation to the ordering of a group of symbols by virtue of which the world is disclosed in a way which is on each occasion linguistically and culturally specific. We can call discourse – in an approximate way which is still rather vague – a symbolic order of this nature which makes it possible for all subjects who have been socialised under its authority to speak and act together; in which case we can suppose that each discourse *always* has an order, but not necessarily that there is a *single* order for all discourses. If there were such an order for all discourses – in the sense of a *caracteristica universalis* – then we would be able to codify an absolute *a priori*. The historical relativity of discourse leads us, on the contrary, to talk of a 'historical *a prioris*', the plurality of which underlies its relativity.[18]

But of what does this order consist? Foucault's evocative way of putting it is not very satisfactory:

> This order is at once that which gives things, as it were, their internal law, the secret network according to which they somehow look at each other, and also that which exists only through the grid of looking, of attention, of language; and it is only in the white squares of this grid that it shows itself to be present in depth, waiting in silence for the moment when it will be enunciated.[19]

Further on we are told that discourses are second-degree orders and are situated somewhere 'in the middle' between the reversible order of language [*langue*] and the irreversible order of the word [*parole*], as Lévi-Strauss suggested in the case of mythical narrations. Thus, if I am not mistaken, this second-degree order, this 'middle region', means something like this: no culture offers us a simple and one-sided picture of what we know of as 'fundamental codes, those which order language, its perceptive schemes, its exchanges, its techniques, its values, the hierarchy of its practices'.[20] Nor is culture identical to scientific or cultural theories which either justify this order on the basis of a principle or examine it in terms of a systematic conceptualisation – that is, which establish, by means of reflection and systematisation, a position in relation to the (already existing) order of that which is to be found in the world. The 'empirical' and the 'philosophical-theoretical' visions of order are seen rather as extremes between which a third view – the one we are seeking – is to be found; one which Foucault says 'is no less fundamental', although its architecture is less rigid and as a result more difficult to analyse.

> It is here that a culture, as it moves out of synchronisation with the empirical orders prescribed to it by its primary codes, establishes an initial distance between itself and them, causes them to lose their initial transparency and ceases to allow a merely passive relationship between itself and them, liberating itself sufficiently to be able to affirm that these orders are perhaps not the only possible ones or the best, in such a way that it finds itself faced with the raw fact that there are, underlying its spontaneous orders, things which are in themselves orderable, and which belong to a certain mute order, or more briefly *that there is* order. It is as if, as it frees itself on the one hand from the linguistic, perceptive and practical grids, culture superimposes over these a second, neutralising grid which, by replicating the first, causes them to appear [*sic!*] and at the same time excludes them [*sic!*], finding itself at the same time face to face with the raw material of the order. It is in the name of this order that codes of language [*langage*], perception and practice are criticised and rendered partially invalid. It is on the grounds of this order, which is seen as fertile soil, that general theories of the order of things and the interpretations which these call for are developed. Thus, between the already codified perception [*regard*] and reflexive knowledge [*connaissance*], there is a middle region which generates order through the very nature of its being.[21]

I suppose that what Foucault is referring to, when he talks of this middle order, are those culture and epoch-specific interpretations of the world which are on the one hand 'more confused and obscure' than what he calls the level of knowledge [*'connaissances'*] – that is, scientifically guaranteed knowledge; yet are on the other hand more concrete and more rich than the 'primary codes' which uniformly determine our language, our modes of intercourse, our perceptions and our social nature. They could be seen as being in part related to Husserl's *Lebenswelt* ('world of life'), and in part also in terms of the orders traditionally called *Weltanschauungen* ('world-views') or 'ideologies'. Foucault says that they can 'present themselves as the most fundamental [area of order]': they are more trustworthy, more commonly used, more deeply rooted, even more reliable than the words, the perceptions and even the gestures by means of which they find expression; they are more solid, more original, more archaic and, so to speak, 'more true' than the theories which attempt to supplant them by means of exhaustive and explicit explanations; they are, so it seems to me, quite comparable to the Heideggerian *Welt* ('world') – understood as the articulation of *Bewandtniszusammenhang* 'connections of relationship', and they are also 'pre-ontologically' prior to the knowledge of signs and forms of life as well as scientific reflection and formalisation. However this may be – and it is of course annoying not to be quite certain what the exact object of scientific analysis is – it is with the divisions between these orders that Foucault's book deals. They are termed 'historical *a prioris*' which – in advance of any scientific analysis – provide the empirical and positive conditions of possibility according to which a particular civilisation organises its speech, sets up its processes of exchange, lives its social life, sees its world, etc. Here too Ricoeur's formula is appropriate: 'a Kantianism without a transcendental subject'. Foucault sets himself apart from the epistemological and socio-epistemological projects of Bachelard, or indeed the *Annales* group, to the extent that he does not deal with established science and 'objective' knowledge but explores the underlying discursive conditions which determine how these, amongst other things, as well as all pre-scientific orders, came into being (they are only partially reflected and fulfilled in *epistemes*, which are the actual knowledge forms). As such, he is more interested in the conditions which make it possible for the structures to arise than in the structures themselves; only one should not see the term 'constitution' in the sense of a historical or transcendental-historical 'derivation'; because for Foucault the foundation of the constitution of an order is never a subject, but yet another order: in the last instance this would be the order of the discourse with its *regard déjà codé* (already coded look). For the same reason it is also impossible to describe the succession of 'positivities' – in the Hegelian sense – as a goal-orientated process:

> There is therefore no question of describing forms of knowledge [*connaissances*] in terms of their progress towards an objectivity in which our science today could finally be recognised; what I should like to shed light on is the epistemological field, the *episteme* in which forms of knowledge, seen outside the context of any criteria referring to their rational value or to their objective forms, break free from their positive aspect and can be seen in terms, not of their growing perfection, but rather of their conditions of possibility; in this story, what should appear, in the space of knowledge [*savoir*], are the configurations which have given rise to the various forms of empirical knowledge [*connaissances*].[22]

III

It would be pleasing to learn more details about the theoretical procedure relevant to the concept of archaeology. Foucault allows his readers to do this only in a later book which is, so to speak, his '*Discours de la méthode*', the *Archéologie du savoir*.[23] I wish to refer to this text in the third section of my semantic reconstruction.

Whilst in *Les Mots et les Choses* discourse was described very much as a homogeneous order – though of course not one which could be reduced to the structure of *langue* – when we come to the *Archéologie du savoir* it is the concept of discontinuity which comes to the fore. This means not only discontinuities *between* different discourses which appear in historical succession (this requirement was already present in *Les Mots et les Choses*) but also discontinuities between discourses which exist contemporaneously with one another. The discourses are also multiplicitous synchronically; symbolic orders existing at the same point in time are not subject to one and the same rule of formation.[24] This differentiation makes it possible to dismiss the idealistic notion of a completely homogeneous *Zeitgeist* and of a universal history which can be related narratively in terms of a 'global history'.[25] At the same time doubt is cast upon the subsumption model of cognition. According to this model, historical or linguistic events are cases which come under general concepts and, in the last analysis, general rules, and can therefore be deduced if one has mastered these latter. The *Archéologie du savoir* – and even more so the inauguration speech at the Collège de France[26] – emphasise the 'specific events',[27] the *événements singuliers*,[28] which cannot be integrated and cannot be decoded simply as the application of a uniform and universal regularity. The analytic of discourse, Foucault says,

> has led to the *individualisation* of different series, which are juxtaposed with one another, which succeed, overlap and criss-cross without it being possible to reduce them to a linear schema. Thus, instead of this continuous chronology of reason, which is invariably traced back to an inaccessible origin, to some founding moment of its beginning, there appear scales of time which are sometimes brief, distinct from one another, *not conforming to a single law*, often bearing within them a type of history which is individual to itself, and irreducible to the general model of a consciousness which acquires, progresses and remembers itself.[29]

Alongside the principle of the individuality of events, we find that of exteriority.[30] We are so used to seeing individuality as a special case of subjectivity (and/or internality) that we are initially confused by the association of individuality and exteriority. Yet what Foucault actually means by this is only one aspect, already implied in the notion of the singularity of the individual: the individual's irreducibility to a unified discursive principle, or to an 'internal' core of meaning to be found in the discourse. What the rule of the exteriority of discourse means, then, is: 'not moving from the discourse towards its internal, hidden core, towards the heart of the thought or the meaning, which is manifest in it'.[31] So the procedure of the analytic of discourse is external because it wishes to leave the series [*série*] of single events, mutually irreducible (in terms of a deductive or teleological principle), just as they are, 'external' to any totalising general concept.

Then of course there is the question of methodology: scientific explanations assume general concepts, and that whatever cannot be derived from them is not explained. Referring to Foucault's archaeology of knowledge Jean Piaget talked of a 'structuralism without structures'; and Foucault himself claims that it was by no means his intention to establish uniformity or to master individual historical events by inferring them from transcendental or universal categories, or from rules of formation.[32] But how can we talk of several discourses existing next to one another? Each discourse can as such be inferred only in the light of a meaning-unity which is valid for its criterion of recognisability. And this consequence cannot be escaped by multiplying discourses. In other words, a multiplication of codes from which the events can indeed be deduced is not yet a fundamental departure from the code-model of classical structuralism; the only difference is that instead of *one* global code, *a lot of* small codes are at work – as is analogously the case in Roland Barthes's analysis of Balzac's *Sarrasine*.[33] These rules of generation – however much they are multiplied – are in fact indispensable if there is to be any sense in Foucault's subsequent theory that each discourse operates in the service of a will to power, and consequently in terms of strict and brutal rules of exclusion. So it can be seen that the radicalism of the departure from universals is inconsistent.

This is not the case only for the rules of formation of subdiscourses which are discontinuous with one another, but even more so for the collective singular 'discourse' itself. It is true that Foucault's concept of epochs in *L'Archéologie du savoir* is not as monolithically closed as in *Les Mots et les Choses*: yet it does operate – in a way which is certainly hard to see through – with global concepts of unity. In the Introduction Foucault explains that he does not want to split up the unity of history and its great epochs simply by making anarchistic gestures, but that he is looking for regularities by means of which discontinuous series map on to one another ('the vertical system they are capable of forming'). It is this talk of a *vertical system* holding together various series of histories occurring at the same time[34] which demonstrates most clearly that the total discourse – as an ensemble of disconnected subdiscourses – is thought of as an order. According to the logic of the metaphor, it runs perpendicular to the individual histories and goes through them like a skewer. If there were no such thing as this skewer, then there could be no (albeit uniquely characteristic) science which could be distinguished from the purely random.

The extent to which this is the case is demonstrated by the concretely continuous methodological procedure of *L'Archéologie du savoir* which, in fine structuralist tradition, breaks down the concept of discourse into its smallest constitutive parts, which are not phonemes or morphemes, but sentences. Foucault calls these *énoncés*, 'statements'.

What Foucault has to say about these is not only very unclear but also – albeit in a way which is sometimes confused – very stimulating. Elsewhere[35] I have attempted a patient and sympathetic reconstruction of Foucauldian methodology. Here I shall have to work with simplifications.

Concentrating on his wish to save individual phenomena from being reduced to cases of a code, Foucault seeks to locate a founding concept – *le discours* – somewhere between structure and event. Discourse is not subject to the 'structure–becoming opposition' [*opposition structure–devenir*].[36]

Why not? Because 'archaeology' deals with 'discourses', the elements of which are not 'types' but individuals. Though discourses are to be seen as generalities in comparison with their elements, they are still individualised generalities: systems of a nature which is different from that of logic.

What, then, are discourses? Foucault concedes that he has used this central notion in at least three clearly distinct ways:

> Finally, instead of making the rather hazy meaning of the word 'discourse' more distinct, I think that I have multiplied its meanings: sometimes using it to mean the general domain of all statements [*énoncés*], sometimes as an individualisable group of statements [*énoncés*], and sometimes as an ordered practice which takes account of a certain number of statements [*énoncés*].[37]

In all three cases, discourses are seen as something like frames; and what they enclose are statements [*énoncés*]. We would know more about these if we knew more about what an *énoncé* is. This is because a higher-order system can be understood only in terms of the mass of elements enclosed within it.

Foucault gives a series of negative answers to this question. *Énoncés*, he says, are not propositions, sentences [*phrases*] or speech acts.[38] Elements of these three categories are conventionalised and can be generated on the basis of underlying rules like, as it were, 'atoms of discourse' [*'atomes du discours'*].[39] Not even this is appropriate for *énoncés*, because they – quite unlike strict taxonomical systems – are 'individualised'.[40] Thus they cannot be deduced simply from universals like 'grammar' or 'logic'.[41]

'Individualised', then, means: not predictable from the point of view of their structure, and contingent with respect to the way they happen to be [*ihres So-Seins*]. Foucault says this expressly when he differentiates an *énoncé* (as an element of discourse) from events in language [*parole*] (that is, as elements of language [*langue*]). Thus the term *énoncé* is to account for the never-decreasing distance between that which could be said according to the rules of language [*langue*], convention (*the pragmatic*) and correct thinking (*logic*) and that which actually *is* said. The *énoncé* keeps this distance bound to certain forms of order, each of which could be described, in the strict structuralist sense of the word, as a system.

This leads to another characteristic of the *énoncé*. Again it can be seen in contrast to events in the language system. It is essential that all system-events should be repeatable without noticeable depreciation in meaning; elements of systems are in fact not individualities but types (or schemata) which can be reproduced in the appropriate context as being exactly what they are (even contexts, when rule-governed, are types). This is what is said, in contrast, about the *énoncé*:

> An *énoncé* exists in a way which makes any notion of its reappearance impossible; and the relationship it has with what it enunciates is not identical to a set of rules of usage. What we find is a one-off relationship: and if under these

> conditions an identical formulation reappears – even if the same words are used, even if we find substantially the same nouns, even if in total it is the same sentence – it is not necessarily the same *énoncé*.[42]

At the same time the *énoncé* cannot be individualised as radically as the act of enunciation which, because of the irreversibility of the extension in time, lies outside any form of systematic control: 'The *énoncé* is obviously an event which cannot be repeated; it has a situational singularity which cannot be reduced'.[43] Yet it is still maintained that *énoncés* are the elements of discourses:

> Now the *énoncé* itself cannot be reduced to this pure event of enunciation, for in spite of its materiality [that is to say, its spatio–temporal index], it can be repeated. . . . And yet it cannot be reduced to a grammatical and logical form because, to a greater degree than a grammatical or logical form and in a different way, it is sensitive to differences in matter, substance, time and place.[44]

So the statement [*énoncé*] is somewhere between the exclusive singularity of the enunciation and the repeatability in form, if not in meaning, of a linguistic or logical or in some other way systematisable schema. The same *énoncé* can be produced in several different enunciations, whilst at the same time, in each of several repeated and correctly formed sentences [*phrases*], each having the same meaning, a different *énoncé* might be being expressed.

Discourses may well, then, be intermediate orders of a special nature in which all possible exceptions and specific cases are valid: if they were completely without generative rules they would be as imaginary as Dali's malleable clocks.

In order to guarantee this (minimal) repeatability, we need to have recourse to an *order* which encodes also the element of discourse, the *énoncé*, as a *schema* which is certainly infinitely sensitive, susceptible and changeable, but still remains a *schema*. In fact Foucault draws this conclusion in two steps. In the first he refers back to the metaphor of the *vertical* grouping of *énoncés* – by which he seems to mean that *énoncés* are not produced by a singular mode of generation but come into being according to various associated domains ['*domaine[s] associé[s]*'],[45] various context-rules and various modes. Again, Foucault believes that he can explain the systematic uncontrollability of the individual by means of a multiplication of the codes of the reference system. But even with so many 'vertically' grouped systems, the spell is still not broken of a code-model of intersubjectively binding rules of input and output encompassing all these systems (without which the underlying power of discourses would be incomprehensible).

However, discourses are ordered in yet another respect. Foucault speaks (1) of an 'order of institution' [*ordre d'institution*] to which discourses are subject as elements identical to one another,[46] and (2) of a 'field of usage [*champ d'utilisation*], in which the *énoncé* is invested'.[47] Institutions and fields of usage are certainly more subtle orders than formalised grammar; yet they are still orders. When Foucault ascribes to them a 'status which is never definitive, but modifiable, relative and always capable of being called into question',[48] he could mean this only in the context of a hermeneutic of divination, which discloses innovations in meaning which are unpredictable in any systematic way; in the epistemological context of an analytic of discourse, such innovations would necessarily rigidify in the inflexible structure of an institutional doctrine which, in the framework of an 'apparatus of torture' [*dispositif de torture*], would not permit individuals and innovation.

In this way we can understand the sense in which Foucault – in spite of his rhetorical pleading for discontinuity and multiplicity of meaning – can still talk of the *unity* of an 'archive', where 'archive' is defined as the totality of all discursive regularities which characterise an epoch in a way which is not unlike that of the classical *Zeitgeist*. It is only in this sense that the concepts of 'discursive formation' and 'rules of formation' become comprehensible, especially if one bears in mind the following definition:

> The rules of formation are the conditions of existence (but also of coexistence, maintenance, modification and disappearance) in a given discursive distribution.[49]

Again the metaphor of a 'vertical system of interdependence'[50] between subsystems of discourse is used as a means of reconciling the idea of the radical discontinuity of these subsystems with the idea of the unity of the archive. I shall not go into further details here, but attempt to make a critical résumé.

Foucault's concept of discourse is in opposition to the Hegelian and (in Dithey's sense of the word) hermeneutic levelling and uniformalising of the complexity of history. I shall leave to one side here metaphysical implications like the way structure is seen in relation to meaning or the way the non-original nature of the subject is seen in relation to symbolic orderings on the grounds that these are ephemeral and grounded in a predetermined historical configuration. (The analysis of the thesis that meaning is grounded in signs would bring to light the notion that one cannot describe a written sign or sound configuration without using predicates taken from the sphere of consciousness – which is precisely what the polemic which criticises the role of the subject opposes; I shall deliberately disregard this dimension of the analytic of discourse on the grounds that it is a purely rhetorical epiphenomenon.) Instead of this I wish to point out what is in my opinion the critical point of the theory of discourse. The definition (unclear though it is) of discourse as a singular, systematically ungovernable and multiple connection of talk stands in extreme contrast to the method of discourse analysis as a (non-hermeneutic but strict) science. In this way discourses can be described and analysed, as Foucault himself does, only if they are constructed according to principles of formation, which contradicts our definition of them.

It is well known that Foucault reflected on this contradiction in his inauguration speech to the Collège de France. Here he attempted to ground the methodologically indispensable thesis of the order of discourse in a theory of power, claiming that discourses are not ordered *per se*, but through the intervention of a will to power. He sees them as functioning as brutal restrictions and systems of exclusion, which owe their unity to the ties of their 'disseminality' which *L'Archéologie du savoir* was committed to ascribing to them. If this thesis were grounded, the untenable consequence would follow that the scientific credentials of the analytic of discourse could be guaranteed only through the repression of this will to power, which so overwhelmingly subjects and ties the disseminality of our talk to the restrictiveness of systems of exclusion. As such the analytic of discourse would be forced into an appropriation of the subject (whose existence it incidentally denies) as a transcendental condition before it could proceed.

One might take it, then, that Foucault was using the term 'discourse' with a view to criticising it in a way which would lead to subsequent clarification: as a term from which we need to escape. Yet this is by no means the case. In *L'Archéologie du savoir* he explains that discourses are inescapable.[51] What keeps them alive and brings about their unity – their conditions of possibility, so to speak – 'also belongs to the realm of the discursive'. There would be no point, then, from which Foucault could pronounce a criticism of discourse – if there were such a thing.

Foucault never freed himself from this contradiction. In order to do so he would have had to establish his theory of discourse on a quite different epistemological basis to that of a code-model (even one involving the multiplication of discourses). Derrida, for example, showed that Foucault's metaphor of a policing of discourse[52] becomes objectless when the scientific-theoretical preconditions are changed – preconditions according to which the meaning-identity of an *énoncé* cannot be ascertained even under conditions of total determination:

> If the police are always standing in the wings, this is because convention is essentially transgressable and precarious *in itself*. The moment reiteration establishes the possibility of parasitism, of a certain kind of fabrication which, because it is part of the system of rules (regarded as being vertical) and conventions (regarded as being horizontal), actually ends up altering these rules and conventions; the moment that this parasitism and this functionalism becomes capable of adding an extra parasitic or fictional structure, what I call elsewhere an 'extra-code' [*supplément de code*], *anything can happen against the policing of language*. . . . Anything is possible except an exhaustive typology which claims to

limit such powers of grafting or fabrication to a logical analytic of distinction, opposition and classification.[53]

The 'order of discourse', then, is no phantom, but its being-status is purely virtual, whilst its reality involves the permanent change and re-creation of discursively constituted meaning (yet not in a way which can be tied down or bound to any will to power).

NOTES

1. Claude Lévi-Strauss, *Anthropologie structurale*, Paris, 1974.
2. Ferdinand de Saussure, *Cours de linguistique générale*, Paris, 1980, p. 33.
3. Lévi-Strauss, *Anthropologie structurale*, pp. 28, 37, 40–41.
4. *Ibid.*, p. 28.
5. Claude Lévi-Strauss, *La Pensée sauvage*, pp. 28, 37, 40–41.
6. Here I am leaving to one side the criticism made by Lévi-Strauss (analogous with the fundamental ideas of Saussure) of the conception according to which myths reflect contents of some nature (social, for example) and are as such analysable on the basis of their content or the history of their motifs. The form of myths and language [*langue*] in fact depends upon the actual schematism of articulation, according to which the meaning and the expression (signified and signifier) are not 'positive' and 'simple magnitudes' but arise out of the differential relationships between 'values': in short, they detach themselves as the effects of linguistic form. It is through the work of the 'unconscious mind' that similarities originate between the mythological narratives of different peoples, the contents of which may be extremely different.
7. Claude Lévi-Strauss, *Anthropologie sociale*, p. 320.
8. Émile Benveniste, *Problèmes de linguistique générale*, Paris, 1966, pp. 122 ff.
9. Lévi-Strauss, *Anthropologie sociale*, p. 232.
10. *Ibid.*, p. 231.
11. *Ibid.*, pp. 232 f.
12. Roland Barthes, *Introduction à l'analyse structurale des récits*, *Communications*, no. 8, (1966), pp. 1–27, esp. p. 3.
13. Barthes, *op cit.*, p. 3.
14. Lévi-Strauss, *Anthropologie sociale*, pp. 232 f.
15. *Ibid.*, p. 232.
16. Michel Foucault, *Les Mots et les Choses: Une archéologie des sciences humaines*, Paris: Gallimard, 1966.
17. *Ibid.*, p. 7.
18. *Ibid.*, p. 15.
19. *Ibid.*, p. 11.
20. *Ibid.*, p. 12.
21. *Idem.*
22. *Idem.*

23. Michel Foucault, *L'Archéologie du savoir*, Paris: Gallimard, 1969.
24. *Ibid.*, p. 18.
25. *Ibid.*, p. 17.
26. Michel Foucault, *L'Ordre du discours*, Paris: Gallimard, 1971.
27. *Ibid.*, p. 55.
28. *Ibid.*, p. 56.
29. Foucault, *L'Archéologie du savoir*, p. 16.
30. Foucault, *L'Ordre du discours*, pp. 55 f.
31. *Ibid.*, p. 55.
32. Foucault, *L'Archéologie du savoir*, pp. 264 f.
33. Roland Barthes, *S/Z*, Paris 1970.
34. Foucault, *L'Archéologie du savoir*, p. 96.
35. Manfred Frank, *Was is Neostrukturalismus?*, Frankfurt-am-Main 1983, pp. 226 ff.
36. Foucault, *L'Archéologie du savoir*, p. 20.
37. *Ibid.*, p. 16.
38. *Ibid.*, pp. 107 ff.
39. *Ibid.*, p. 107.
40. *Ibid.*, p. 111.
41. *Ibid.*, p. 111.
42. *Ibid.*, p. 138.
43. *Ibid.*, pp. 133 f.
44. *Ibid.*, p. 134.
45. *Ibid.*, p. 115.
46. *Ibid.*, p. 136.
47. *Ibid.*, p. 137.
48. *Ibid.*, p. 135.
49. *Ibid.*, p. 53.
50. *Ibid.*, p. 96.
51. *Ibid.*, p. 100.
52. Foucault, *L'Ordre du discours*, p. 37.
53. Jacques Derrida, *Limited Inc.*, Supplement to *Glyph*, no. 2, Baltimore, MD: Johns Hopkins, 1977, p. 72.

SUMMARY OF DISCUSSIONS

[NOTE: these discussions were on an earlier form of the paper presented at the conference. This consisted essentially of only the first two sections.]

Manfred Frank's paper drew the participants' attention to the use of the word 'discourse', and it was this which gave rise to most of the contributions. To begin with, **Michel Karkeits** wished to be clear as to why Foucault abandoned the term 'discourse', using instead the term *savoir* after he had written *L'Ordre du discours*.

Manfred Frank took the opportunity to remind us that his paper was more relevant to the use of the term in Germany than to the attitude of Foucault himself. As to Foucault, one might suppose that by introducing this concept of the 'will to power' he made it unnecessary to use the term 'discourse' as having a coercive nature.

André Glücksmann gave a few indications as to the meaning of the word '*discours*' in French, and its philosophical implications. He felt that the reference to Lévi-Strauss was not enough. Returning instead to the translation of the word *logos*, he showed that '*discours*' has to be understood as a 'dialectic' in the post-Platonic sense of the term, and thus contains within it the suggestion of 'trying out', which is fundamental in philosophy. **Manfred Frank** agreed, but pointed out a difficulty. Because of their Latin linguistic origin, the French will associate this idea of 'dissemination' with the word '*discours*'. Discourse in the German, Habermassian sense, on the other hand, has a more 'police-orientated' meaning linked with the need to account for the reasons why a certain proposition might or might not be true.

Rainer Rochlitz returned to Michel Karkeits's question. In Foucault's texts written in the 1970s the idea of discourse loses its autonomy and is seen rather as dependent, finally, on the practices and mechanisms of power. Towards the end of his career, the idea of the autonomy of discourse returns, though this is still seen as an emanation of practices.

Manfred Frank agreed. The texts of the 1970s reintroduced certain categories which transcend discourse: power, compulsion, instinct, and so on. But he felt it would be too early to give an interpretation of the final stage of Foucault's evolution. . . .

Paul Veyne, for his part, saw no more than expediency in the use of the word 'discourse'. Why should it be that Foucault used this word rather than words like 'practices', 'archives' or 'presuppositions' to designate this thing in which we are to recognise positive finitude or rarefaction? Maybe he was just sensitive to the linguistic fashion in France at the time, and there is nothing more to it than that.

two

On Michel Foucault's philosophical style: Towards a critique of the normal

Miguel Morey

> If no one sought pleasure (or joy);
> if repose (satisfaction) and balance
> were all that counted, the present
> that I bring would be vain. This
> present is ecstasy, the lightning at
> play within it . . .
> Georges Bataille, *Le Coupable*

> If I pronounce only the words 'I am speaking', I am threatened by none of these perils; and the two propositions which are hidden in this single pronouncement ('I am speaking' and 'I say that I am speaking') are not compromised in any way. I am protected by an immovable fortress in which the affirmation affirms itself, exactly adjusting itself to itself, crossing no boundaries, and banishing all danger of error since I am saying nothing beyond the fact that I am speaking. The presupposition-cum-object and that which pronounces it are communicated without obstacle and without reticence, not only from the point of view of the statement [*parole*] in question, but from the point of view of the subject articulating the statement. It is therefore true, invincibly true, that I am speaking when I say that I am speaking.[1]

I should like to study Michel Foucault's style from the point of view of the generality of this notion 'I am speaking', and in so doing to go back to 'his initial options'. It seems to me that in his critique of the normal a concern can be found which runs throughout his discourse, together with the position from which the notion 'I am speaking' originates and the schema which governs the form and the content of his discourse.

I

On the subject of Kant's text *Was ist Aufklärung?* Foucault wrote:

> There exists in modern and contemporary philosophy another type of question, another mode of critical interrogation: the one which came into being precisely with the question of the *Aufklärung* or in the text on the Revolution; this new critical tradition asks the question: what is our present? What is the present field of possible experiences? This has nothing to do with an analytic of truth, but is rather a question of what one might refer to as an ontology of the present, an ontology of ourselves, and it seems to me that at the moment this is the philosophical choice which confronts us: one could opt for a critical philosophy which would appear as an analytical philosophy of truth in general, or one could opt for a critical way of thinking which would take the form of an ontology of ourselves, of an ontology of the present; it is this form of philosophy, from Hegel to the Frankfurt School, via Nietzsche and Max Weber, which founded the form of reflection in which I tried to work.[2]

The text should also be quoted where Foucault characterises – unfortunately, for the last time – his procedure with that of another text parallel to his own, which enriched its meaning:

> But what is philosophy today, I mean philosophical activity, if it is not work which is critical of thought itself? And what is it if, instead of legitimising that which we already know, it does not consist in finding out how and how far it might be possible to think differently? There is always something laughable about philosophical discourse when it attempts, from the outside, to lay down the law for others, to tell them where their truth really lies, and how to find it, or when it takes it upon itself to make clear what it is in their procedures which can be seen as naive positivity. Yet it is the right of philosophical discourse to explore that which, in its own thought, can be changed by the use of a form of knowledge [*savoir*] which is alien to it.[3]

'Telling of the present' and 'thinking differently' are interdependent. They define the task which, nowadays, can be characterised as 'philosophy'. They make possible an initial approach to Foucault's work. To begin with, what we are dealing with is a *telling*, the truth-telling of the *parrhesia*, a telling whose requirement for existence is this 'otherwise', breaking with the normality of the telling of the *doxa*, a telling about and against what is said and what must be said, a telling which seeks out its possibility in the 'otherwise' of the *doxa*. It could be that this 'otherwise' might be possible only in the movement which runs through the sombre volume of received tellings, like lightning in a dark sky.

There is probably no single and certain way for this telling to achieve its truth. There are, however, criteria for moving in the direction of this 'otherwise'. We can find here the old Nietzschean probity: it is simple, Nietzsche seems to be saying; all we need to do is to *stop lying*. All we have to do is to guard against the sort of inertia which leads us to say what we are expected to say and repeat a normalised 'telling' which takes the place of thought. Hence the negative character of the references in most of Foucault's research. What we are confronted with is a procedure which aims to suspend the way of telling that dominates an area of study, a way of telling which, since it is there, demands repetition.[4]

But truth-telling has to bear on the present. It should not be confused with the past, with the weight of the past on the present, the inertia of the normal in the social and the insistence of a memory always ready to recognise itself in what is happening. Thought, even when it takes on the form of historical discourse, has to function according to a regime of anti-memory.[5] This is because, in the same way that ethnologists denounce ethnocentricity, Foucault, considering history as a kind of ethnology interior to our culture,[6] denounces the convenience of a form of historical memory which disguises horrors as errors in order to legitimise a present which is subject to the presumption of the normal and the powers of the norm. Nietzsche should again be quoted, bearing in mind the 'content' of Foucault's discourse (*the present*) and his critique of all retrospective rationality:

> All things which last for a long time become progressively so well imbued with reason that it becomes incredible that they might have originated in a way which was other than reasonable. Is not the precise history of how something came into being almost always resented as being paradoxical and sacrilegious? Does not the good historian basically spend his time *contradicting*?[7]

So the injunction to 'tell of the present' and to 'think differently' opens on to a place of combat against the normal, against the norms of telling and the so-called normality of our present, in order to set in motion this 'thinking differently' which is in fact the passion for thinking clearly and decisively.

II

'Thinking differently' and 'telling of the present' imply breaking with the habit of taking the normal as the criterion of the real and untangling the confusion of the normal with the *present* as something which is at the same time *a priori* and given. If Foucault was able to say that power produces the real, this is because he characterises power as the power to normalise, as normalising power.[8] It is well known that a norm: (1) conforms to habits; (2) conforms to a rational principle; (3) conforms to history or to tradition. As such, a normalising power acts on the formation of habits, on rationalising principles and historical legitimisations. Foucault finds in these things his objects of study: in the archaeology of knowing [*savoir*], the genealogy of power, the critique of anatomical politics; and especially in the places where they intersect: when a historical legitimisation functions in the formation of habits, or when it suggests itself as a rationalising principle, and so on.

Nineteenth-century grammarians used these three criteria (habit, rational principle and history or tradition) in order to justify the idea of the linguistic norm. The way in which this notion has been debated since Saussure illustrates Foucault's criticism. Thus, whilst linguisticians state that the correction of the *parole* of a given period does no more than consecrate errors and mistakes of the preceding period, Foucault denies the rational origin of these norms: when linguisticians state that these incorrect forms use the same linguistic procedures as the correct forms,[9] Foucault refuses to eulogise the 'other', that which opposes the norm in the form of an inversion of it.

III

The norm is sometimes identified with the 'statistical mean', and it is claimed that it can be used as a descriptive concept. We say that a thing is normal if it can be assimilated to the mean of other objects belonging to the same class. But numerical superiority leads to the 'normal' becoming the normative: the law which leads us to do the same as everyone else.... Foucault finds in the circularity of this mixed, bastardised use of the descriptive and the normative a privileged opportunity to analyse knowledge–power relations. Thus knowledge [*savoir*] tells us what 'everyone'[10] thinks, whilst power invites us to put this into practice. The notions of political management of populations and of biopolitics give a good example of this type of critique of the normal.

IV

The normal is simultaneously a modality of the object and a regime for perception. It is that which, in a given domain, is invisible because it has not been hidden. This is why criticising the normal in the present consists of (1) separating out the notion of the normal from the present; (2) seeing the normal as the effect of the complex practices of normalisation (whether or not these are discursive); (3) examining conditions of possibility, in the sense of the Kantian critique. But because of the equivocal nature of the normal (descriptive and normative, rational and historical at the same time) the 'critique' brings about a Nietzschean effect: the overturning of idols.

V

The critique which Foucault carries out against the prestige of the norm and of the normal takes the form of a discourse outside norms, as a working process by means of which one places oneself outside the normal. In short, it takes the form of a strategy. This means that Foucault has to place himself in a relationship of exteriority regarding both the norms of analysis proper to the areas which he is studying and the general norms controlling forms of 'academic discourse'.[11] Instead of a picture of thought guided by the idea of *con-sensus*, Foucault tries to provoke *dis-sensus*: to exercise his right to take up a position elsewhere. His writing procedures (the discourse of *dissensus*) and his objects of study (madness, prisons, sexuality . . .) unfold in a maliciously self-referential way: as if his language were suddenly becoming transparent in order to show what has become invisible as a result of being seen; as if he were speaking about nothing more than his own writing procedures, of the conquest of the conditions he sets for making any utterance.[12]

Foucault also sets himself aside from the norm by the status of his discourse. He does this by deploying, as opposed to the form of normative discourse, descriptive discourses which have less to do with *telling* than with trying out *ways of telling*.[13] *L'Archéologie du savoir*, itself an essay in methodology-fiction, a strict poetical rendition of his previous procedure, does not found a theory but explores possibilities.[14]

The non-normative character of Foucault's discourse is distinguished, finally, by a sort of 'suspension of judgement' when faced with the question of alternatives, by his desire not to propose 'global solutions' to problems which he is announcing or denouncing: to imagine another system that still belongs to the present system.[15] Was what he dreamt of a form of perception which would in itself possess the power to destroy?[16]

VI

With Foucault, the desire to break free from the normal is not marked only by his abnormal academic discourse, a discourse which is purely descriptive, not normative, and hostile to the position of any 'alternatives'. The critique of the norm is also characterised by the way in which he controls the hidden presence of the normal, as presuppositions, in the discourse; and in his choice of his subjects.

As a subjective presupposition, the normal takes on the form of phrases like '*everyone knows*' and '*no one can deny*'.[17] The argument 'through force of numbers' is here, in fact, nothing more than the argument through which those who arrogate to themselves the right to speak in the name of the greatest number exercise their authority. Foucault never ceases to show them his disdain.[18] In opposition to this Foucault lays claim to the idea of theory as a 'tool-box'[19] and to the notion of the 'specific intellectual'.[20]

The objective presupposition of the norm consists in justifying it rationally and giving an absolute value to rationality. However, this value is deprived of its prestige the moment the scale of analysis is increased, as it was by Nietzsche[21] or Bataille.[22]

Foucault uses the same procedure: he 'begins' his books by stating that their object of study is a 'recent invention' and ends by announcing the *possibility* that 'it might soon be at the end': 'Perhaps by remembering that the men we once were believed that there is a truth on the other side at least as precious as that which they had already sought on earth, in the stars and in the pure forms of their thought. . .'. This procedure, which employs the notion of untimeliness, has two effects on the present: it presents itself as an anonymous and innovatory voice; and it makes our habitual perception of objects (madness, sickness, man), the discourse which upholds them (psychiatrically based science, medicine, human sciences) and the institutions which embody them (the asylum, hospital) all seem strange.

In a word: we have to think that everything we think today will be thought of in a different way tomorrow, in terms of a way of thinking which has not yet come into being.[23] How, then, could there be any philosophical task other than to tell of the present?

The subjects with which Foucault chose to work always aim at one of the modes of presence of the normal in the present; hence his 'topicality'. These are interventions against the normal, carried out with a desire to go to the secret of their origin in order to show that there is no secret.

From his very first book, the problem is posed: 'How is it that our society came to give sickness a sense of deviation and to the sick person a status which excludes him? And how in spite of that does our society come to express itself in morbid forms in which it refuses to recognise itself?'[24] The last words in *Histoire de la folie* pick up on the same problem:

> This is the trick and new triumph of madness: this world which believes itself able to measure madness and to justify madness through psychology in fact needs to justify itself in the face of madness since in its strivings and in its debates it measures itself in terms of the excesses of such works as those of Nietzsche, Van Gogh, and Artaud. And nothing in it, especially not what it knows of madness, can assure it that it is justified by its works of madness.[25]

Although in his early books it is the pairing of the normal and the pathological which is the object of problematisation – and this without the least connivance of reference groups (discourse and institutions) which decide on the normal and the way in which it is to be applied – in the latter books the object is man himself to the extent that he is the effect of the normalising processes which the human sciences and disciplines exercise over him. *Historie de la sexualité* studies the processes of normalisation linked with the 'sexualisation' of bodies and of populations. Foucault always targets and problematises the production of a certain normality, the division between the normal and the abnormal and the weight of the normal on the present. We should bear in mind the fact that when he was asked about this choice of subjects, Foucault replied simply: 'I am interested in sexuality because it has made a lot of people suffer.'[26]

The criticism Foucault directs on the present bears witness to the obvious irritation he feels at confusion between the normal and the moral, the movement from a morality of virtue to a morality of normality put forward as progress. He derides present-day man, who asks himself in the grandest of solitudes, and as if for the last time: Am I normal?

Hence the importance which Foucault attaches to the criticism of our desire to have norms, to be normalised, and to see our differences recognised as normal. His criticism is addressed also to those who dream of seeing the usual authorised as the norm and as a means to the fulfilment of liberty, as a means to emancipation. Talking of the apparatus of sexuality, Foucault concludes: 'The irony inherent in this apparatus is that it leads us to believe that in it our "liberation" is at stake.' It is hardly surprising, then, that the question he tackles in his final books is the question of ethics.

VII

It might be said that norms are necessary for all human conduct, for the regulation of social life, and that Foucault himself needs them in order to be able to carry out his enterprise. To answer questions about the legitimisation of *Les Mots et les Choses*, Foucault wrote *L'Archéologie du savoir*: here, though, where one might expect to find norms, one finds procedures; and where one expects the closed structure of theory, one encounters space crowded with possibilities.

Those who seek out norms in Foucault's procedures are like those who expect him to formulate alternatives: the question is always that of the position from which a pronouncement is being made. It makes rather more sense to ask which of the rules Foucault suspends amongst those which produce normality in the reference groups to which he is supposed to belong (as a philosopher, a historian, an intellectual, a left-winger, and so on). His discourse appears as a discourse which eschews all complicity; it is a non-complicitous discourse.[28]

Inasmuch as philosophical discourse cannot be expressed without the affirmation of some norm or another, it inevitably becomes complicitous. Those who accuse Foucault of irresponsibility deserve to have the question thrown back at them: 'responsible', but to whom? The State? Philosophy? Everyone? Who is a thinker supposed to be responsible to?

There will always be enough norms – too many. Behind the question of Foucault's responsibility one finds, again, the question of alternatives: '. . . because, after all, you've got to do something with the inane, with offenders . . .'. But something is already being done with them, and whatever this might be is found to be normal, because something has to be done. But is it normal to find this normal?

Foucault's challenging of the normal is always localised, even though its effects are general. The local character of the things with which he deals, and his understanding of his own procedure as being one amongst others, provide an answer to those who deny the possibility of talking and acting outside all norms. Foucault's discourse impugns the form of the general. To the sort of approach which asks: '. . . and what if everyone did the same thing?', the reply can be given, with a Nietzschean laugh: 'When all the customs and the morals on which the power of gods, priests, and redeemers depend are finally reduced to nothing, when, therefore, morality in the ancient sense of the word is dead: what will come? . . . Well, what exactly will come?'[29] Well, what will happen? Maybe the present will be released from the weight of the past?

If there must be norms, they have to be invented: new syntheses of habits and modalities of relations with others; new possibilities of ethical and political life. These norms have to arise out of practices and experiences. In a reply to a question on the future of socialism and of the Revolution, Foucault replied by contrasting 'experience' with 'utopia'. Maybe the future society is being mapped out by new forms of awareness and new types of individualisation through drugs, sex or communal life. If socialism were to come into being, it would not be as a utopia but on the basis of experience.[30] Foucault's political practice, designated 'individualistic', meets this requirement. If human action has to be carried out on the basis of norms, the practice of liberty is the unconditional norm . . .

Foucault hides; he does not explain the position from which he is speaking. Although he denounces modern power as the practice of a certain seeing-without-being-seen, he himself does not allow himself to be seen. His discourse is a-confessional, his voice is without inflection; he is a historian to philosophers and a philosopher to historians; an intellectual, but an intellectual of a specific nature who does not say what he thinks but wonders if it might not be possible to think it.[31]

When we ask about the position from which a pronouncement is made, we are asking: 'In whose name are you speaking?' Foucault is not speaking in the name of anything or anyone. And yet we recognize ourselves in his discourse, his struggles, his way of asking questions. . . . In spite of his determination to make history into a form of antidote to memory, there is in his writings, in his essays, a core of meaning which we can recognise. Although Foucault can give the lie to the meaning which history and memory lay claim to and which form the normality of our present,[32] he is not able to do so without giving a certain meaning to our history, without creating a fable which he offers up for us to recognise. This fable, too, is linked with the denunciation of norms.[33]

Concepts like power always have a double layer of meaning: 'power' is the name of a game which can be determined as to its truth; it is also something which is recognised as being *intolerable*. Power can be recognised in the truth of the way it functions, and at the same time it is resented as that which is considered to be *the* (our, current) problem: 'They are intolerable: courts, the police, hospitals, asylums, schools, military service, the press, the television, the State, and first and foremost, prisons.'[34] If we recognise ourselves in Foucault's discourse, this is because what today, for us, is intolerable is no longer so much *that which does not allow us to be* what we are, as *that which causes us to be* what we are.

This curious equivocation in the way he proceeds explains why it is that one seeks in vain, in Foucault, the methodological discourse of post-structuralism or the political 'alternative' of post-May '68. Foucault's discourse can be used only locally in the field of epistemology and politics. Those who have attempted to apply his procedures mechanically or to deal with his discourse in an academic way have not met with any greater success. His theoretical procedures are as 'individualistic' as his political practice.

Would it be right to call Foucault's writings *récits*? Maybe. In any case, his work, seen as a simple exercise of the notion 'I am speaking', is situated elsewhere. He never ceased to produce that which was 'otherwise'. This is why there is, in certain areas in which he worked, talk of *before* and *after* Foucault. He never ceased to break with norms, and what he said about Pierre Boulez should be applied to him too:

> What he expected of thought was exactly that it should allow him continually to do something other than what he was doing. In the game which he was playing, which was so regulated and so considered, he asked of it that it should open up new space. Some accused him of technical gratuitousness; others accused him of excessive theorising. But for him it was essential to think of the exercise in which he was engaged in a way which was as close as possible to its internal necessities, yet without yielding to any of them as if they were sovereign requirements. What role can thought play in what one does if it is to be neither know-how nor pure theory? Boulez showed the answer: to give us strength to break the rules in the very act which brings them into play.[35]

NOTES

1. 'La pensée du dehors', *Critique*, no. 299, 1966.
2. 'Un cours inédit', *Magazine littéraire*, 1984, p. 207.
3. *L'Usage des plaisirs*, Paris: Gallimard, 1984.
4. Cf. the themes and notions parenthesised in *L'Archéologie du savoir*, the postulates about power which *Surveiller et punir* suspends. Cf. also Gilles Deleuze, *Foucault*, Paris: Éditions de Minuit, 1986.
5. 'Nietzsche, genealogy, history', *Hommage à Jean Hyppolite*, Paris: PUF, 1971.

6. *Les Mots et les Choses*, Paris: Gallimard, 1966.
7. *Aurore*, vol. I, no. 1.
8. *Surveiller et punir*, Paris: Gallimard, 1966.
9. Cf. for example W. Warburg, *Problèmes et Méthodes de la linguistique*, Paris, 1946, and H. Frei, *La Grammaire de fautes*, Belgrade, 1922.
10. That is to say, the reference group(s) which propose that we should recognise ourselves as subjects.
11. The function of the author, the quoting and referencing policy, the secondary bibliography, the supposed dignity of the object of study, legitimisation by a recognised method, complex strategies of alliances with a 'school', etc. Cf. *L'Ordre du discours*, Paris: Gallimard, 1971.
12. In *Oublier Foucault*, Jean Baudrillard sometimes touched on this problem. But his desire to undermine Foucault stops him from grasping its full complexity.
13. This is what characterises, for Robbe-Grillet, the 'true' writer; see *Pour un nouveau roman*, Paris: Éditions de Minuit, 1963.
14. Deleuze, *Foucault.*
15. Conversation with M.–A. Burnier and P. Graine, *Actuel*, no. 14, 1971.
16. *Naissance de la clinique*, Paris: PUF, 1963.
17. Gilles Deleuze, *Différence*, Paris: PUF, 1968.
18. 'An example: if prison doctors were not as cowardly as they are (and I am not going to withdraw that phrase), they could, simply by telling the truth, shake up the system to a considerable extent. Their cowardice has, I think, been immense . . .' (conversation with A. Krywin and F. Ringelheim, *Pro-Justitia*, no. 3/4, 1973).
19. 'The point is not to construct a system, but an instrument: a *logic* appropriate to the power relations and the struggles which are going on around them; this sort of research can take place only one step at a time, on the basis of reflections (which of necessity have to be historical in some respects) on given situations' ('Power and strategies', a discussion with Michel Foucault, *Les Révoltes logiques*, no. 4, 1977).
20. 'A new mode of "liaison between theory and practice" is established. Intellectuals have acquired the habit of working not in the realm of the "universal", the "exemplary", the "right-and-true-for-all", but in determined sectors, in precise points where they have been positioned either by the conditions of their work or by the conditions of their lives (where they live, hospital, asylum, laboratory, university, family or sexual relationships). They certainly gained a more concrete and immediate awareness of struggles going on. And in this way they have encountered problems which were "non-universal", often different from those of the proletariat or the masses. And yet they really did get close to these, I believe, for two reasons: because they were dealing with real, material, everyday struggles, and because they often came across, albeit in a different form, the peasant classes or the masses (the multinationals, the judiciary and police system, property speculation, etc.); this is what I call the "specific" intellectual as opposed to the "universal" intellectual' (Conversation with M. Fontana, *L'Arc*, no. 70, 1977).
21. 'In a distant corner of the universe amidst the brilliant light of innumerable solar systems, there was once a star on which intelligent animals invented consciousness. This was the most arrogant and deceitful moment in the history of the universe: but it was only a moment. There was barely enough time for a few sighs from nature

before the star grew cold and the intelligent animals had to die' (*Über Wahrheit und Lüge*).

22. Cf. his parody of economics generalised to a Universal scale, confronted with the so-called rationality of the system of restraint.
23. This might be a terrible formulation, but it tells us, like a promise, that there will be a future. If it is not the superman, it is man (such as we are), overtaken, outmoded.
24. *Maladie mentale et Psychologie* Paris: PUF, 1954.
25. *Histoire de la folie à l'âge classique*, Paris: PUF, 1954.
26. Conversation with A. Berton. Video of the University of Louvain. Transcription in *Quaderns de l'obra social*, no. 26, 1984.
27. *La Volonté de savoir*, Paris: Gallimard, 1976.
28. Regarding *Surveiller et punir*, Deleuze wrote: 'There is in Foucault's position a theoretical revolution which takes place not only against bourgeois theories of the State but against the Marxist conception of power and relationships with the State. It is as if, when it comes down to it, something new has surfaced since Marx. It is as if the complicity surrounding the State had been broken' (*Foucault*).
29. *Morgenröte*, I, 96.
30. Conversation with M.-A. Burnier and P. Graine.
31. *Les Révoltes logiques*, no. 4, 1977.
32. He challenges, for example, the so-called sense of origin or original sense in order to affirm the truth of coming into being, of emergence; by opposing the discourse of *for all time* with the question *since when?*; saying that history has to make us know and not recognise (ourselves), etc.
33. This could be formulated as follows: 'It is wrong to say "with a certain famous post-Hegelian" that the concrete existence of man is labour. For the life and times of man are not by nature labour, they are: pleasure, discontinuity, celebration, rest, needs, appetite, violence, deprecation, etc. Capital is supposed to transform all this explosive energy into a continuous labour force continually available on the market. Capital is supposed to synthesise life into a labour force, in a way which implies coercion: that of a system of appropriation.' And he adds: 'If it is true that the economic structure characterised by the accumulation of capital has the property of being able to transform the labour force into a productive force, then the power structures which have the form of appropriation have the ultimate aim of transforming living time into a labour force. Appropriation is the correlative in terms of the power force. Appropriation is the correlative in terms of the power of that which, in economic terms, is the accumulation of capital.' Cf. *Le Pouvoir de la Norme* (undated). In relation to this problem, cf. M. Morey: 'Erase una vez ... M. Foucault y el problema del sentido de la historia', in *Discurso, Poder, Sujeto: Lecturas de M. Foucault*, University of Saint Jacques de Compostella, 1977.
34. *Intolerables: les prisons*, Paris, 1971.
35. *Nouvel Observateur*, no. 934, 2–8 October 1982.

SUMMARY OF DISCUSSIONS

The debate was dominated by a question posed by **Manfred Frank**. He sees in Foucault the undeniable presence of an ethic. Frank wondered what the basis of this ethic was, what it was that formed the foundation of Foucault's commitment. This had necessarily to be a norm. But what kind of norm?

Various contributions were made in an attempt to reply to this question, defending the possibility of commitment without founding norms.

Thus **Miguel Morey** suggested the choice of a form of commitment which would take on the form of non-complicity, the localised contesting of norms. **François Ewald** recalled that for Foucault the norm is not a universal, general, ahistorical form. His commitment followed the desire to make the production of truth into an event.

Étienne Balibar took this further. The important point was not the foundation of commitment but the way in which it comes into operation and its material conditions of possibility. The nature of this contribution, as Foucault clearly stated, was the contribution of the intellectual; as for the material conditions of possibility, again it is 'intelligence', 'hearing the roar of battle'.

Jeannette Colombel saw in this the criteria which separated off previous philosophies (from Hegel to Sartre) from Foucault's philosophy. There is no need for a positive value in order to continue the struggle. Maybe from now on that which is evidently 'intolerable' will take the place of what for Descartes was the undoubtable.

Paul Veyne concluded laconically that this was the intractable problem of what, for Foucault, constituted truth-telling.

three

The Word of God: 'I am dead'

Denis Hollier

Valéry was mistaken. The only thing a page of literature can say is: I am not a page of literature. The writing is imperceptible. True literature, if such a thing exists, begins with resistance to literature. This is probably how Foucault came to wear the mask of the historian.

On the back cover of his last two books, *Le Souci de soi* and *L'Usage des plaisirs*, the same aphorism of Char is reproduced: 'The history of man is a long succession of synonyms of a single word. To contradict this is a duty.' By 1984, a lot of time had passed since Foucault had last quoted Char. It was also a long time since he had spoken of duty. The fact that, in order to be understood, this imperative had to be expressed by means of the borrowed voice of a poet suggests, at least indirectly, an affinity between literature and the existential stylistics on which, according to *Le Souci de soi*, the possibility of escaping from the great synonymic confinement, the possibility of suspending, interrupting, the synonymic reign of expressibility, would depend. This synonymic concatenation – concatenation of synonyms, concatenation by synonym – evokes the moral imprisonment which is the conclusion of *Histoire de la folie*. Can a homonymic imperative be opposed to this imperialism of synonymy? This resistance to synonymy can be seen in Foucault's interest in the secret rhymes of Roussel and that other homonymic outburst, Brisset's giddying grammar of God.

Those who were students at the time will remember Foucault's first texts on literature, his articles on Bataille, Blanchot, Klossokowski, and on *Tel Quel*. The romanticism of *Histoire de la folie* allowed texts, in the face of which we had been paralysed, reduced to silence, at last to begin to speak. None of these articles has lost the imprudent nature they demonstrated at the time – this spark of enthusiasm, as Lacan would have said; Lacan probably had a lot of trouble with the way Foucault later did everything he could to avoid them, to avoid recognising them, and having to recognise himself in them. The assurance of their lyricism, their unbridled, authoritarian pathos, the exasperated quality of their abstraction – which was frenetic even when they were at their most erudite – and the brusqueness of their hyperbole burst through alongside the carefulness which already promised to be the regime of his future audacity.

Who is speaking in these texts? How many Michel Foucaults would it be necessary to construct in order that they should figure in at least one of his complete works? What would be their exact place in the complete works of all the Michel Foucaults? I do not know if he officially disowned them, but he set around them signs of the greatest distance. On the basis of this distance, Foucault's own question can be turned back on him: What is an author? What nowadays is perhaps most striking about his work is in fact the insurmountable distance he adopts from himself, as if his grammar were that of dissent. Hence the impression one gets that the distance anyone might want to adopt from him would remain small in comparison with the distance Foucault has already established from himself. More distant from himself than we will ever be, he forestalls us, circumvents us, condemning us to an interior distance, holding himself back in a distance without interiority.

A passage from Caillois's essay on the praying mantis is devoted to mimesis.[1] Caillois interprets this – as in his contemporary essay on legendary neurasthenia – in terms of sexuality and the death instinct. In this case he sets up the most baffling labyrinth, an infinite series of mirrors where life and death play with one another, one against the other, and one into the other, at last ending up lost in one another. Caillois's essay is the foundation of modern reflection on simulation.

It all begins, very reasonably, with a situation of danger in which death is used as a defence mechanism: in order to save its life, the mantis plays dead. The second stage is already more out of the ordinary. It is also more difficult to interpret in utilitarian terms of external ends and the struggle for life: a first step towards gratuity and simulation brings about a communication between mimesis and the notion of expenditure. The mantis is now really dead. But an automatic reflex makes it possible for it to carry out various activities: walking, getting its balance when necessary, carrying out various forms of behaviour aimed at self-preservation (including self-mutilation), mating, nest-building, and so on. Life was imitating death. Now it is death which is imitating life. The insect, like the Marathon runner, has not noticed that it is no longer alive. It is dead but too busy; it has not had the time to realise that it is no longer alive. It has not read its death announcement. And it continues to exploit the posthumous fringe of its living present. But things do not stop there.

The final degree is reached when, amongst the signs of life that the dead insect continues to give, there appears what Caillois calls 'sham corpse-like immobility'. This is the return to the starting point. The insect is playing dead again. But now it *is* dead. It has lost the life which it is continuing to protect. In death, Caillois says, the mantis is simulating death. It is dead and says so. Now it is death which is imitating itself in the very centre of life, a life which is reduced to act as a mirror to death. In death, it feigns life only because in life it feigned death. It is a double death, simultaneously real and feigned: the corpse pretends to be what it is. Blanchot, later, associated this collapse of space in cadaverous simulation with the access to literary space.[2] Death by resemblance.

Caillois would probably have given Blanchot the manuscript of *Histoire de la folie*[3] to read.

One of Foucault's first publications, the preface to his translation of Binswanger's *Rêve et l'Existence*, which appeared in 1954, also set up a labyrinthine series of mirror games in which the vital distinction is displaced. Foucault takes it upon himself to dissociate dream from sleep, to undermine any relationship between them. Though carried along by opposing existential vectors, sleeping and dreaming arise out of heterogeneous orders (as madness and unreason are seen to do some years later). Although they coexist, their simultaneity will never be sufficient to form a whole. It implies no complementarity and no synonymy. For if the sleeper, in his way, acts dead, this death, precisely because it is false, places sleep in the service of life. Dreaming, on the other hand, by animating the inertia of sleep, reduces life to a state of reflection and for this reason belongs to the side of death. In these pages Foucault refers explicitly, as did Caillois's 'praying mantis', to *Beyond the Pleasure Principle*: all Foucault retains of the manifestations of dream life is the 'repetitions of dreams of death', which is precisely where psychoanalysis very nearly came to grief. What would a dream be which did not belong to anybody? Is it necessary to be in order to dream? Dreams, he says, never come to satisfy the desires of a living person. They insert in life an enclave which says: 'I am dead'. He writes:

> At the deepest point of his dreaming, what man meets is his death. . . . If in sleep consciousness falls asleep, in dreams existence wakes up. Sleep moves in the direction of the life which it prepares for, which it looks to and which it prefers; though it has the appearance of death, this is through a trick of life which does not want to die; it 'plays dead' but does so 'out of fear of death'; it remains in the order of life.
>
> Dreaming has nothing in common with sleep; dreaming moves up the slope which sleep descends towards life, it moves towards existence and there, in broad daylight, it sees death as the destiny of liberty: for dreaming in itself, and through all the meanings of existence which it bears within itself, kills sleep and the life which falls asleep. This is not to say that sleep makes dreaming possible, for dreaming is that which makes sleep impossible, by awakening it to the light of death. (*Rêve et l'Existence*, pp. 70–71)

In these lines, the heterogeneousness of existence and life can be seen as paralleling that of dreaming and life: it is precisely because it is situated on the side of 'existence' that dreaming is fundamentally the dream of death and that – similar in this way to the Hegelian–Kojèvian desire for recognition, and similar also to the mimetic excesses of Caillois's insects – it designates what Foucault calls 'an absolute boundary to the biological principle of satisfying desire'. It matters little here whether satisfaction is defined in physiological or psychological terms, or whether it is situated under the pleasure principle or the reality principle. In both cases, desire is linked to life. This is why the dream world escapes its influence.

This description is not unlike one put forward by Lévinas a little earlier[4] of the experience of existence without an existent, the impersonal spontaneity of a consciousness experiencing the horror of *there is* in the insomniac dream of a desubjectivised consciousness. Blanchot, in turn, one year after the publication of *Rêve et l'Existence* (which he had probably not read), took up these ideas again in the appendix of *L'Espace littéraire*, where he opposes sleep and dreaming: 'I sleep,' he says, 'but it is the night that dreams.

Caillois quotes Valéry: 'The verb *to dream* has almost no "present tense". *I dream*, *you dream*, these are rhetorical devices, for the person speaking is a person who is asleep or at least someone who should be.'[5] Are they, though, just rhetorical devices? Terror also has its devices (the most current of which says: 'I am not a page of literature').

Anyone who says: 'I am dreaming' is practically not saying it, is saying almost nothing, is not really saying it. He says it but does not think it. He says it without thinking it. It is an empty phrase. You are not there. I sleep, but it is the night that dreams. The message refuses to support the subject who pronounces it. The subject is emptied of his words, not because he is dreaming but because he says so. His words cannot support him. Dreaming escapes the regime by means of which experiences can be expressed in a way which the first person can demonstrate to be authentic. Like death. The verbalisation of these things implies what Foucault calls in his essay on Bataille a 'scission', an abuse of language, 'where', he says, 'the subject who speaks is bound to disappear'.[6]

In Foucault's historical references, the turn of the eighteenth century (the revolutionary period, the turning point between the eighteenth and nineteenth centuries) has a pivotal function. The most important motifs of his work meet there to sketch, at the intersection of the *Aufklärung* and the Terror, of Kant and Sade, a period with contradictory characteristics.[7] It is the age of the invention of man and his death, of the humanisation of punishment and the cruelty of knowledge, of anthropological slumber and the great Romantic fear. This period is the point of conclusion for the *Histoire de la folie*, and the point of departure for *Naissance de la clinique* and *Surveiller et punir*. It is also to this period that '*Le langage à l'infini*' traces the birth of literature,[8] which is said to appear as a result of the relationship between death and language which articulates terror (as a feeling) and the Terror (as a revolutionary period). Its birth is illustrated by the proliferation of 'terror novels' – not only those of de Sade, but those of Reveroni de Saint-Cyr, Bellin de Labordière and other Gothic writers. In *Les Fleurs de Tarbes*, Paulhan contrasted terrorists and rhetoricians. According to Foucault, literature transforms this contrast into a dilemma: the library, the movement of language to infinity, the movement to the literary infinity, has as its specific regime the simultaneousness of rhetoric and terror and the simulation of terror by rhetoric. It is this double *simul*, simultaneousness and simulation, which also defines the relationship between literature and politics.

In 'La littérature et le droit à la mort', Blanchot had already seen it as the task of Terror (both the feeling and the revolutionary period designated by its name) to ensure the communication between politics and literature. The central figure of this text was a Lazarus who, in many respects, seems himself to belong to the literature of horror, to the world of the black novel, to the Goyaesque shades which seem to haunt the works of the great fear – an anti-Paschal Lazarus, a Lazarus of the Antichrist: resurrection has no hold on this refractory, bloodless and faceless corpse, this mouthpiece of the formless: 'the Lazarus of the tomb,' writes Blanchot, 'and not the Lazarus brought back to daylight – who already has the stench of death about him, who is Evil, the Lost Lazarus and not the Lazarus who has been saved and brought back to life'. He is the bearer of a revelation which is made 'on the basis of the non-existence of the one who makes it', and in his word that which gives life to the word dies. 'Literature now moves out of the hands of the writer.' 'It is *my* consciousness *without me*.'[9] Through his non-living voice and his non-living speech, lifeless and without presence, Lazarus repeats: 'I am dead'.

It is precisely on the basis of this terrorising and Lazarean desubjectivation and depersonalisation that Blanchot sees the literary as communicating with the political. It is in fact necessary to think in terms of the terrorist, to see Saint-Just as Lazarus. For the terrorist is not the one who causes terror to reign: he does not affirm himself on the basis of terror and he does not exercise terror for his own profit. Nor does he claim to be capable of changing a life or transforming a world with which he has broken: he claims only one thing, the right to death. And he claims it in the first instance for himself. Terror demands the non-existence of the one who brings about its reign. Literature begins with the fascination of the terrorist's renunciation of existence, of a biography, which is another name for the death of the author. 'When the blade fell on Saint-Just and on Robespierre,' Blanchot wrote, 'in some ways it struck nobody. The instigators of Terror, in their lives, act not as living men in the midst of living men, but as beings deprived of being . . .'

Foucault's definition of literature as an inverted performative, as the lingusitic regime of precipitous and acephalous phrases, owes much to these pages of Blanchot. For him it is always defined in terms of a pragmatic, as a negative linguistic performance, as an act of language in the performance of which the first person disappears. The effect appropriately achieved by modern literary affirmation is in this sense exactly the opposite to that of Scheherazadean storytelling or of narrative by means of which the accused attempts to secure a royal pardon.[10] The examples here are those of Flaubert, Proust and Kafka, who are condemned to death by their work, and write to secure the right to death. 'Where a work had the duty of creating immortality, it now attains the right to kill, to become the murderer of its author' (*Language, Counter-Memory, Practice*, p. 117).

The notion of the death of the author does not, in this sense, open up literary space to the positivity of historical enquiry. It does not imply a transfer of authority in which the disciplinary contextualisation of the works replaces the author with non-subjective contingencies, which cannot be formulated exclusively in terms of Taine's trinity of race, moment and milieu. On the contrary. Literature resists (Char would say: contradicts) anthropological sleep so radically that, in the preface to Binswanger, dreaming goes beyond physiological sleep. *Naissance de la clinique* deprives the scalpel of its value as a cutting edge; it is no longer seen as cutting, since all it can do is follow the lines of wounds which are already there, guided by the course which the illness takes. In the same way, when criticism triumphantly announces the death of the other, all it is really doing is repeating without knowing it, the idea which itself gave birth to literature.

Nor does the death of the author open the way to formalism. As soon as he is called upon to define literature, Foucault reminds us of the intransitive experience of the existence of language. No triumphalism of form results from its relationship with itself or from these intransitive recesses. He never links this intransitiveness to the modernist affirmation of formal independence. The self-referentiality which is a major symptom of the exhaustion of the realm of that which can be expressed says less about the disappearance of the object than it does about the disappearance of the subject. The mirror is an apparatus in which the author disappears. There are no forms, only the formless, which triumphs in the mirror of the death of the author.[11] It brings to the same level what Foucault calls the mirroring of the formless; the being of the murmur. As the locus of inexpressive excess, literature is seen as the ensemble of propositions which are incompatible with a subject. 'I am dreaming', 'I am dead': no one ever says that. 'The subject who speaks ends up vanishing.'

This formulation, which we find in '*Préface à la transgression*', has to be seen in its context. It appears in a special number of *Critique*, published in homage to Bataille: a speaking subject who in fact had just disappeared. And, in his contribution, Foucault justifies what he says in terms of the circumstances in which he says it. He says he had set himself the task of rereading Bataille 'from the point of view of the place where his recent death had situated his language'. In '*Le langage à l'infini*', which dates from the same period, he says, along the same lines: 'Death is probably the most essential of the accidents of language.' '*Préface à la transgression*' is the analysis of one of these accidents: the effects of Bataille's death on his language; what happened to language as a result of the death of the author.

On his mother's death, Roussel had a windowpane placed in her coffin. What was the function of this glass? Who was it meant for? For her? For him? Was it so that he would be able to continue to see his dead mother, or was it rather so that he would still be able to be seen by her, to be exposed to the absence of her look?

Foucault is only indirectly interested in Roussel's language games. His reading does not begin with the procedures themselves but with the way the procedures are revealed simultaneously with Roussel's suicide – that is, the simultaneousness of the author's death and the readability of the work. Foucault says that it is Roussel's death which is, in the last analysis, the ultimate key to the procedure; it is the ultimate driving force of the various mechanisms, linguistic and otherwise, which are at work in his novels. Suicide is the true response to the title of the book which he brought into being: *Comment j'ai écrit certains de mes livres*. The Surrealists applauded Roussel's work: they did not wait for his death in order to admire it. Foucault's interest begins in the notion of '*How I wrote some of my books*'. But his interest in *Comment j'ai écrit certains de mes livres* arises every bit as much out of the revelations in the text; from the fact that they are made, in the first person, by a dead person: 'the *récit* in the first person of the posthumous revelation' (p. 195).

Blanchot (following Leiris) draws a parallel between Roussel and Proust. None the less, Martial Canterel, the inventor of *Locus Solus*, is not a priest of refound time. And this is why, as Foucault's reading suggests, the mechanisms of *Locus Solus* and those of *Comment j'ai écrit certains de mes livres* shed light upon one another. In Canterel's thanatonic park, this morgue for agitated corpses, none of the dead people he exhibits comes back to life; none of his curiosities is redeemed, saved or resurrected. There is no redemptive virtue in the way he tinkers with them. He is not interested in overcoming death, merely in conserving it. The injections of *vitalium* and *résurrectine* open the doors not to 'life refound' but to plasticised, vitrified and conserved death. The posthumous and silent contortions of Danton's mouth have nothing of life in them, and even less of the afterlife. One should rather talk of the hyper-dead, in this *Luna Park* of hyper-dying. Canterel is not Doctor Pascal. 'The grand, leisurely pace of *Locus Solus*,' Foucault writes, 'its "emptiness", is that of an

Easter Sunday which remains empty. Canterel tells us to look amongst the dead for the one who is there; that is where he is, he has not been resurrected' (p. 110). What survives death is the movement of life into death, which he continually re-enacts. But there will never be a movement in the other direction, from death to life. Instead of life refound, one finds its homonym: life indefinitely lost, death indefinitely repeated. Good Friday is desanctified because no Easter Sunday connects it to the dialectic synonymy. *Locus Solus*, the Sunday of death.

Returning to Caillois. Though dead, the praying mantis continued, just as when it was alive, to pretend to be dead. Canterel's panes of glass reflect the interplay of matching mirrors. In them the dead repeat the movements they made before they died, but amongst these movements the only ones they repeat are those by means of which, during their lifetime, they belonged to death. All that death retains of life is that which was already posthumous about it. Foucault writes:

> That which in life which is repeated in death, is death itself. The scene death plays as it imitates life imitates death in a way which is as lifelike as it had been when lived in life. The boundary which *résurrectine* could not abolish repeats life in death and in life that which was already dead. (p. 111)

Blanchot's Lazarus would not be out of place in Canterel's garden.

The extent to which *Raymond Roussel* and *Naissance de la clinique* are twin books has never been pointed out. They are both organised around the same central argument: death as the key to reading. It was the suicidal publication of *Comment j'ai écrit certains de mes livres* which made Roussel's work readable. The posthumous text reveals the immense lesion which formed the secret nerve structure of the work. With the change in medical perception brought about by Bichat's anatomical pathology, *Naissance de la clinique* revolves about another type of medical perception: the lesions discovered on the corpse by the autopsy produce, retrospectively, the number of the symptoms of the illness.

Foucault contrasts Cabanis and Bichat. For the first, 'the knowledge of life was rooted directly in the essence of the living person'. Life and knowledge of life, welded together through their synonymous connection, thus have a common origin. After Bichat, the inverse becomes true: 'The knowledge of life has its origins in the destruction of life.' Foucault develops this contrast:

> From the foundations of the Renaissance right up to the end of the eighteenth century, the knowledge [*savoir*] of life (the equivocal genitive of the expression suggests the synonymity of knowledge about life and knowledge of life) was seen in terms of the circle of life turning in on itself and reflecting itself; from the time of Bichat, its relationship with life has shifted and it is separated from it by the uncrossable boundary of death, in whose mirror it looks. (p. 147)

Between life and the knowledge of life, the uncrossable mirror of death interposes its reversible surface. *Raymond Roussel* was saying exactly the same thing: 'as if perception, in order to see what there is to see, needed the duplicative presence of death' (p. 77). Duplicative presence: a presence reduplicated by the simultaneity of its semblance.

In *Naissance de la clinique*, the Lazarean 'I am dead' does none the less undergo a shift, moving from the register of the readable to that of the visible. The critique of phenomenological expressivism no longer attacks the living word but the living eye. Foucault uses a number of different formulations to account for an experience of perception which could be said to escape from phenomenologising fundamentalism, and speaks of a perception which could be said to be made 'from the point of view of the dead person', 'on the basis of death', 'on the basis of the corpse'; a perception which again, he says, would have 'invested death in its way of seeing', a 'perception of which death would be the bearer'. All these formulations make the disappearance of any seeing subject the correlation of the advent of absolute visibility. The visible, which is deployed for the sake of no one, affirms 'death as the absolute point of view on life' (p. 156). Medical perception, Foucault continues, 'is no longer that of a living eye but the perception of an eye which has seen death' (p. 146).

This is a fine contrast. Yet under the cover of the antithesis, something is hidden. There is a surreptitious change of subject. *Noli me legere*. A dead angle, a blind spot, brings about the transition of the living eye into any eye which has seen death. There are two eyes. The first shows its subject to be alive; but the second has no subject. The organ of vision is present (one eye) but there is no one there to use it. The anatomical–pathological conversion in the same way brings about a movement from perception defined by its subject (who is alive) to another which is alive from the point of view of its object (this perception has seen death). '*Préface à la transgression*' takes up once more this anti-phenomenology of perception. In Bataille's novels, Foucault traces the patterns in an extraordinary ballet where the eye makes a show of its blindness to an absence of perception. One of these patterns (which is a variation on the lens which Roussel places in his mother's coffin) consists in an unsocketed eye being confronted with the empty eye-socket, 'the globe of darkness whose sphere is closed by the unsocketed eye which stands before it, depriving it of the ability to see and yet offering to this absence the spectacle of the unshatterable core which now imprisons the dead vision'. Rousseau dreamed of theatre without actors. Rousseauism, in the emptiness of this theatre without spectators, gives rise to the experience of theatricality with the death of God; the theatrical exacerbation of exhibitionism without anyone to witness it. A spectacle is offered to an absence, something is being shown to no one, nothing.

After 1966, Foucault's language becomes more sober. His break with literature takes place between *Naissance de la clinique* and *Surveiller et punir*. It can be glimpsed in the difference between the confessional scenes which are analysed in the two books: they are on opposite sides of a stream which is not deep. From one book to the next, Foucault turns his back on terror, on the association of literature and the thematic of death. The macabre and the morbid were essential categories in *Naissance de la clinique*. *La Volonté de savoir* denounces the 'morbid indecencies' in *Surveiller et punir*, separates itself from retrospective views which invoke de Sade or Bataille, and proclaims the 'disqualification of death' in modern political space. This theoretical promotion of life is not obviously accompanied by any 'biophilia' (on the contrary, the counterpart of the analysis of biopowers is a political critique of the discipline of biology), but it does make it possible to break away from the problematic of self-referential mirrors, be they those of death or those of writing.

The doctor in the *Clinique* does not try to make the sick person speak. He does not consult him, he does not say a word to him; the living person's awareness of himself does not enter into the examination to which Laënnec subjects him. As for Bichat, he tries to make his corpse speak, to discover in it the lesions which will retrospectively give a language structure to his illness. The context of the confessional scenes in *Surveiller et punir* is totally different. Here the word is linked to the life of the body. The point is to make it speak before death gets hold of it. The threshold of enunciation then takes a decisive step backwards: it is situated below, on this side of the boundary which separates life and death. Unlike the sick person, the criminal 'comes to play the role of living truth'. The system of justice needs a 'speaking body', and only a living body can speak. Thus the speech acts of *Surveiller et punir* no longer have anything 'literary' about them: the condition for their performance is the life of the speaker, the speaking subject and his presence in what he says. The technology of confession is not content just to make living bodies speak; it forces the bodies which it makes speak to live. 'The only way truth can exercise its full power is for the criminal to take back on himself responsibility for his own crime, and put his own name to the learned and obscure constructs of information' (p. 42).

Running parallel to this internal disaffection in *Surveiller et punir* with the literary structures of posthumous (or morbid) enunciation, there is also the fact that the book is not accompanied by a literary double. *Moi, Pierre Rivière* does not bear the same relationship to it that *Roussel* bore to *Naissance de la clinique*. There is a way in which Pierre Rivière's text is of a literary nature, but for this precise reason it remains contemporary in its format with *Naissance de la clinique*, not with *Surveiller et punir*. The way in which Foucault, in his commentary, describes the complex ensemble constituted by the murder and the narrative of Rivière brings out the analogy of its mechanism to the one formed by the ensemble of Roussel's suicide and his *Comment j'ai écrit certains de mes livres*. Foucault described the memoirs as a text which arose out of Leiris's 'tauromachic' writing,[12] in the performance of which the death of the author is an integral part. He does everything he can to give the author a suicidal dimension which will cause him to enter into the category of 'the posthumous revelation of the first person': Rivière presumably continued to live after the publication of his memoirs, 'but', Foucault tells us, 'a newspaper report tells us that in his prison he considered himself already dead' (p. 175).

A brief return to the notion of 'I am dead' had made an appearance in the conclusion of the analysis of 'Corporal Punishment'. This section of *Surveiller et punir* sets up a confessional apparatus which no longer has anything to do with the literary (or the posthumous). This brief return to the posthumous Cogito occurs in a context which turns it into an explicit farewell to literature. He is dealing with fly-sheets, cheap magazines, and ballads which glorify crime. There is no longer any question of confessing under torture. The dead murderer himself sings his glory and proclaims, in the first person, his crimes and their expiation. Foucault quotes one: 'On the day of the execution, / it will hardly be believed, / I was seen without emotion, / making honourable amends, / At last I sat on the cross / showing no fear' (p. 70).

This is how Foucault came to assume the historian's mask.

What is an author? *Moi, Pierre Rivière* answers this question in two ways. By publishing the memoirs, Foucault demonstrates by example. He dismantles the means by which an author invents, produces and constructs himself. So it is a kind of applied exercise in authorisation. '*What were Sade's papers before he was consecrated as an author?*' The archive is authorised when it finds a reader. Foucault authorises Rivière, he authorises the document by publishing it, by causing it to accede to the mode of being 'for someone'. On this level the publication of the memoirs is a sort of ironical and positivistic demystification of a form of literature which is bound to the authorial function. The posthumous invention of Pierre Rivière (like that of Sade) demonstrates the death of the author. A subject is not needed; no one is needed for an author to be created. The authorial function is the effect of a mechanism of reception, of ideological control. The whole process unfurls in the positive sociohistorical reality of ideological analysis. It is the external abstraction of the enunciator.

But it was preceded by his internal abstraction.

Pierre Rivière considered himself already dead.

And Sade did not wait to disappear and to be carried off by the mechanism of authorisation in order to present *La Philosophie dans le boudoir* as 'a posthumous work by the author of *Justine*'.

NOTES

1. *Le Mythe de l'Homme*, Paris: Gallimard, 1938.
2. 'La ressemblance cadavérique', in the appendix to *L'Espace littéraire* entitled 'Les deux versions de l'imaginaire'.
3. Cf. Blanchot's slim volume published by Fata Morgana.
4. *De l'existence à l'existant*, Fontaine, 1947.
5. Caillois, *L'Incertitude qui vient des rêves*, Paris: Gallimard, 3rd edn, 1956, p. 89.
6. 'Préface à la transgression', *Critique*, no. 195–6, August–September 1963, p. 759.
7. 'Préface à la transgression' associates the names 'Kant and Sade' in order to give a date to the experience of finitude and being which is 'essential to our culture'.
8. 'Perhaps the threshold of the existence of what can strictly be termed "literature" is to be found here, at the end of the eighteenth century . . .' ('Le langage à l'infini', *Tel Quel*, no. 15, 1963, p. 52).
9. 'La littérature et le droit à la mort', in *La Part du feu*, Paris: Gallimard, 3rd edn, 1949, p. 317. For Blanchot the motif of terror goes back to the critique of the transcendental *ego*, the presence of the phenomenological consciousness to itself, as tackled by Sartre in 'La transcendance de l'*ego*' and in the final pages of *La Nausée*. Cf. Hollier, 'I've done my act. An exercice [*sic* [*Tr.*]] in gravity', *Representations*, no. 4, Autumn 1984.
10. Literature is contemporary to what might be called, making a variation on Brisset's title, 'the grammar of God'. The proposition 'I am dead' has to be understood, alongside *Madame Edwarda's* 'I am God', as one of the variants of 'God is dead'. These different pronouncements are transformed according to a logic which is the logic of the phantasm. *Eritis sicut dii*: it would be divine to say 'I am dead'. Hence the laughter of the gods at the idea that they might exist, the diabolical laugh of God as He pronounces a sentence which is acephalous. In this sense again, literature can be seen as a long attempt to resist synomymy, the personalisation of the unnameable, and the anthropologisation of death.
11. It is in this sense that terror and self-referentiality stand shoulder to shoulder, since terror is nothing but the exoteric version of self-referentiality and the library is the place of the pure forms of terror. Transgression, initiated by sexuality, culminates in a language which talks about itself. The sexual terror of the writings of de Sade is only an introduction to the hell of libraries whose heart is Mallarmé-like. 'Sade and Mallarmé with their books, with the Book, are by definition the hell of Libraries' ('Distance, aspect, origine', *Critique*, no. 198, 1963, p. 938). Cf. Hollier, 'The death of the Author', *Raritan*, vol. V, no. 1, 1985.
12. At the end of the 'Préface à la transgression', Foucault refers back to Leiris's 'tauromachic' writing (see *Language, Counter-Memory, Practice*, p. 51). This model is also essential to Foucault's reading of Roussel, to which it explicitly refers on several occasions. The same intricate, labyrinthine relationship between death and writing is to be found at the centre of the introductions to the volume of *Moi, Pierre Rivière* in which Foucault shifts the emphasis by talking about the impossibility of separating murders from the narration of them.

SUMMARY OF DISCUSSIONS

Denis Hollier had located a noteworthy break in Foucault's work with regard to his attitude towards literature, and it was this break which brought about the first questions. **Walter Seitter** wondered if, as Hollier stated, literature really ceases to play a certain doubling-up role in Foucault's books after *Naissance de la clinique*. Why shouldn't a text like Pierre Rivière's be seen as playing this doubling-up role? Or again, Herculine Babin's? Could not his non-scientific affirmations, the shout of the 'people', continue to be seen as having something in the nature of a doubling effect in his work?

Denis Hollier observed that the text of Pierre Rivière interested Foucault to the extent that it was posthumous; the literary production of the text of Pierre Rivière implies its origination in death. It is true, though, that there is no sudden break: *Surveiller et punir* is the locus of the change in which Foucault ceases to think about the relationship between language and death and begins to think of the question of life in terms of political systems.

A contributor in the auditorium mentioned Kant, Nietzsche and Bataille. It was by means of reference to these authors that Foucault put forward the problem of that which it is 'impossible to say' in Western culture and in modern times; that which has to be expressed in figures which are not within the competence of rhetoric, although they are classed as literary.

Denis Hollier pointed out that one finds explicitly in *La Volonté de savoir* an ironic reference to those authors who continue to seek authorisation from de Sade and Bataille. There is undeniably a break which can be associated with these proper names and the theme of transgression; Hollier simply took the risk of associating this break with the distancing of literary discourse.

Gérard Lebrun then asked Hollier about a point of history. Could Foucault be situated in the same critical movement regarding the transcendental ego in which Sartre operates? Sartre was the first to try to express a fact of consciousness avoiding the first person. In this there was an important movement which began in about 1930. Similar considerations led **Paul Veyne** to remind us of the fascination which Foucault felt for Blanchot around 1955. Would he have been sensitive to the theme which was at that time in fashion: poets had the idea that communication was a chain of murders, the poet dying in the poem which itself kills the reader. . . ?

four

Oneirocriticisms

Walter Seitter

A dream is something conscious.
Jacques Lacan,
15 December 1954

From 1954 up to the last volumes of *L'Histoire de la sexualité*, Michel Foucault placed his books under the banner of René Char.

In 1954, he published two books: *Maladie mentale et Personnalité* and a long introduction to Ludwig Binswanger's *Rêve et Existence*. As a heading to this introduction Michel Foucault used a quotation in which René Char speaks about dreams; at its very centre is the word 'VIVRE' in capitals.[1] Thus the poet is seen as the pathfinder to this recently discovered key to dreams.

On 5 February 1960, in North Germany, Michel Foucault completed the introduction to *Histoire de la folie* with a quotation from René Char expressing 'the most urgent and the most circumspect definition of truth'.[2] Now it so happens that Michel Foucault opens the chapter on '*the Great Confinement*' with an analysis of the *Méditation* where Descartes convinces himself that there is a principle of truth. This analysis was criticised by Jacques Derrida.[3] In his reply,[4] Michel Foucault insists on the Cartesian distinction between the illusion of madness and the vision of dreams, and writes a sentence which might sum up his oneirology if there were such a thing: 'The oneiric imagination is pinned in a precise way to one's perception of the present.'[5]

Le Souci de soi (1984) opens with an analysis of the most famous oneirocriticism in Antiquity, that of Artemidorus. The work has a quotation from René Char on its back cover.[6] It is situated outside the text, like the headlights of a car disappearing into the darkness of the night.

The poet provided the philosopher with flashes of illumination. They are to be found throughout the length of his work for thirty years, every time Michel Foucault deals with dreams or dream thoughts.

The first stage was the publication in French of a German book, a book which was part of a series of translations of German texts by Viktor von Weizäcker, Emmanuel Kant and Leo Spitzer. Though Michel Foucault did not translate Binswanger's text, he seems to have been the driving force behind the publication.

It is remarkable that in 1954 Michel Foucault should have taken up this text by Ludwig Binswanger, which was written in 1930, during Freud's lifetime. Two years earlier Ludwig Binswanger had written a study entitled *Wandlungen in der Auffassung und Deutung des Traumes von den Griechen bis zur Gegenwart*.[7] In it he traced the changes in the way dreams had been conceived of in the Western world since Homer. He distanced himself from Freud who, he considered, had not paid sufficient attention to the long history of the interpretation of dreams, the only period which the latter had really studied being that which came immediately before his own time. It was following on from this study that Ludwig Binswanger was to write the article *Traum und Existenz*, where he formulated specific statements about dreams. Meanwhile he had read Husserl, Heidegger and Löwith. According to Foucault, this text is the first that Binswanger had written in his own style: that of *Daseinsanalyse*.[8]

This text of Foucault's probably demonstrates his preference at the time for the philosophy of Heidegger, which he saw as superior to psychoanalysis. But Binswanger's text is not the application of a philosophy. It takes as its starting point a study of metaphor dealing with expressions like 'falling', 'flying' and 'hovering' which come from the sphere of spatio-sensitivity and concern the qualities and events of the soul. In daily language and in poetic language, these expressions have a metaphorical usage which is affirmed in dreams, where these situations are experienced as modes of existence. Foucault takes up this theme and explains that Binswanger is demonstrating 'a plasticity of dreams and of expression'.[9]

In this text, Michel Foucault gives an initial sketch of the genealogical method which he will use right up to the end. It is not yet seen as being in opposition to supra-historical discourse. He uses it in a fairly traditional way: in fact, as a means of researching a tradition. Foucault states that with his 'plasticity of dreams and of expression', Binswanger is picking up the threads of a tradition left to one side by nineteenth-century psychology, a psychology which Freud did not always manage to go beyond, which saw the dream as a rhapsody of images. If dreaming were nothing more than that, a psychological analysis of the dream could hope to be exhaustive, whether this analysis took the form of a psychophysiology or a study of meanings. But the dream is something other than a rhapsody of images, it is an absolutely specific form of experience. Psychology can approach dreams only in a secondary and derivative way. In *Traum und Existenz* Binswanger takes up this tradition. The wealth of the content of dream experience is demonstrated by its irreducibility to the psychological determinations despite attempts made at such a reduction. There is an old idea, constantly present in the literary and mystical traditions of the Graeco-Latin period, that only 'morning dreams' have a valid meaning.[10]

The genealogical sketch which Foucault makes does not obey any chronology; it moves back and forth between Romanticism and Antiquity, concentrating on 'Cartesian and post-Cartesian texts', from Spinoza to the age of French classicism.[11] Although he takes up the history which Binswanger had traced in his previous work, he refuses to write a history in the proper sense of the term.

Foucault discusses Freudian theory on the basis of the very same problem as that which faces genealogy: the problem of time. He notes that Freud would have had to be aware:

> in dreams of signs of the dreamer himself putting himself on the inside of the oneiric drama, as if it were not sufficient for the dream merely to symbolise and tell in pictures the story of former experiences, as if the dream were doing a tour of the whole of the subject's existence, in order to reconstitute its dramatic essence in a theatrical form. This is what happens in Dora's second dream. Freud must have recognised in retrospect that he had not grasped the whole meaning of this dream. . . . Like her loss of voice and her coughing fits, Dora's dream did not refer only to the history of her life, but to a whole mode of existence of which this story is strictly only a chronicle: an existence where the alien sexuality of the man appears only in the guise of hostility, constraint and incursion, culminating in rape; an existence which could not even be realised in the close and parallel sexuality of the woman, but which invested the most profound meaning in breaking off relationships, one of the most decisive of which was to put an end to the psychoanalysis. One might say that Dora was cured, not in spite of the interruption of the psychoanalysis, but because, when she took the decision to break it off, she committed herself in a final way to the solitude which her nature, up to that point, had been leading to in an irresolute way.[12]

With regard to a case related by Binswanger, Foucault explains:

> The essential point of a dream is not so much what it brings back from the past but what it announces of the future. It foresees and announces the moment when the sick person finally delivers up to the psychoanalyst the secret which the sick person does not yet know and yet which is the heaviest burden of his or her present; this secret is designated by the dream in the very nature of its content by the exactness of a detailed image; the dream anticipates the moment of liberation. It foresees the story, rather than being just the repetition of a traumatic past.[13]

In the fourth part, Foucault develops an analytic of existence according to the three dimensions of light and darkness, closeness and distance and rising and falling. He sees a 'chronology of spatial progression' as corresponding to the second category: in it, time develops only as a point of departure and of arrival; it becomes exhausted as the progression is made; and, when it starts again, this is in the form of repetition, return, and of a new beginning. In this essential direction, time is in its essence nostalgic, seeking to close in on itself, to recover itself by going back to its roots in its own origins.[14]

The term 'nostalgia' suggests a parallel between the temporality of the dream and that of psychoanalysis; the term links in with the temporality which we find in Foucault's own genealogical work, which goes back to things past, often forgotten. How could a historical reconstruction be anything other than nostaligic? Added to this is the fact that, since ancient texts which deal with the past are always beautiful in themselves, enthusiasm for the past is almost inevitable. Binswanger gets out of this by declaring that, after all, the Ancients were not scientific. Foucault forestalls nostalgia by darting about from one point to another, and especially by means of his principal theme: that dreaming has an ethical content.[15] The dream, which is 'without complicity with sleep', is man's confrontation with his destiny.[16] At its origin is that which Foucault calls imagination. It is not the invasion of images, but it addresses itself to someone and has to be seen from the point of view of an exchange.[17] The dream is an expression of the imagination which has itself to be expressed as a style, through language, as a work of art, or as an ethic. The dream is labour[18] and happiness.[19] But though it is happiness, it is a present happiness, not a past one.

I mentioned Foucault's dispute with Derrida regarding dreams. Foucault's third period of dream literature is marked by his study of Artemidorus' oneirocriticism. Most probably he was studying it not with regard to its dream content but with regard to its ethical content, on the basis of the sexual viewpoint favoured by Freud.[20] In any case, Foucault has something to say on the principle of there being keys to dreams and rightly insists on the profound distinction between Artemidorus' view of dreams and Freud's unitary theory. In his translation – here again we meet Foucault as translator – of Artemidorus' concepts, Foucault can be seen as moving alongside – and even going further than[21] – Lacan, who had – in 1954, as it so happened – taken seriously the difference between the desire dream and the punishment dream, saying that this latter 'does not so much represent a chastisement as the revelation of the being . . . , the being moving on to a new phase'.[22] In Artemidorus there are two dream categories. One corresponds more or less to that which holds the monopoly in Freudian thought and which Lacan calls the 'desire dream' [*rêve de désir*]. Foucault calls it the 'dream of desire' [*rêve du désir*].[23] The other sort he calls 'the dream of being' [*songe de l'être*].

So the way Foucault deals with dreams can throw some light on his undertaking, which was that of a '*Wächter über die Nacht der Menschen*'.[24]

NOTES

1. 'In the age of man, I saw rising and growing on the dividing wall between life and death, a ladder which grew more and more stark, which bore a unique power to tear out: this was the dream. . . . Now the darkness parted, and TO LIVE became, in the form of a rugged allegorical asceticism, the conquest of extraordinary powers which we feel running through us in a confused way but to which, because of our lack of loyalty, pitiless discernment and perseverance, we can only give incomplete expression' (René Char, *Partage formel*, XII, *Œuvres complètes*, Paris: Gallimard, coll. 'Bibliothèque de la Pléiade', 1983, p. 160).
2. 'I took away from things the illusion which they create in order to keep themselves from us and I left them the part of themselves which they yield to us' (René Char, *Suzerain*, in *Poèmes et Prose*, p. 261).
3. 'Cogito et *L'Histoire de la folie*', *Revue de métaphysique et de morale*, no. 3–4, 1964.
4. 'Mon corps, ce papier, ce feu', in Michel Foucault, *Histoire de la folie à l'âge classique*, Paris: Gallimard, 1972, pp. 583 ff.
5. *Ibid.*, p. 588.
6. 'The history of man is the long succession of synonyms of a single word. To contradict this is a duty' (René Char, *Recherche de la base et du sommet*, p. 766).
7. Berlin: Springes, 1928.
8. Ludwig Binswanger, *Le Rêve et l'Existence*, Paris: Desclée de Brouwer, 1954, p. 14.
9. *Ibid.*, p. 42.
10. '*Die Träume der Gesunden sind Morgenträume*', said Schelling, and Jamblique: 'A dream cannot be considered to be divine if it takes place amongst the vapours of digestion' (*Ibid.*, p. 44).
11. Binswanger, p. 46.
12. *Ibid.*, pp. 76–7.
13. *Ibid.*, pp. 82–3.
14. *Ibid.*, pp. 99–100.
15. *Ibid.*, p. 65.
16. *Ibid.*, pp. 69, 71.
17. *Ibid.*, p. 125.
18. *Ibid.*
19. *Ibid.*, p. 128.
20. Which he was none the less unable to appreciate, the chapters on sexual dreams being omitted from the German translation.
21. From 1954 Foucault continued Lacan's work in a progressive way, because he was neither a disciple nor a follower of Lacan.
22. Jacques Lacan, *Le Séminaire*, I, *Les Écrits techniques de Freud*, Paris: Éditions du Seuil, 1975, p. 297.
23. Michel Foucault, *Histoire de la sexualité* III, *Le Souci de soi*, Paris: Gallimard, 1984, p. 23.
24. This is the title of an article by Foucault which appeared only in German, in *Unterwegs mit Rolf Italiaander*, Hamburg, 1963, p. 48. In the text, Foucault says of Rolf

Italiaander that he is 'a spirit of daylight who knows how to keep watch over the night of men'. The formula echoes Max Weber's observation in which he talks of this task: '*Wächter zu sein in einer sonst allzu finsteren Nacht*'. For Foucault, perhaps dreams were lights in the darkness.

SUMMARY OF DISCUSSIONS

Following Walter Seitter's remarks, **Paul Veyne** and **François Ewald** intervened to point out that Foucault had opposed the republication of this preface to the work of Binswanger, but that one could find in it a positive and non-interpretative view of dreaming which is in harmony with the rest of Foucault's work. **Walter Seitter** confirmed that he perceived echoes of this youthful text in Foucault's most recent texts.

five

Towards fiction

Raymond Bellour

I should like to talk about the word *fiction* and try to discuss the ways in which it is attractive, how much weight we should attach to it, and the way it is related to reality.

Twelve years ago, when *Surveiller et punir* had just come out, Jacques Revel, in answer to a question, wondered: 'What if Foucault is telling us stories? Or, to put it more nobly: what if he is constructing fictions?'[1]

I do not want to ask whether or not, in their relationship with the histories of historians, Foucault's stories, his archaeologies, should count as fictions, even if the answer to this question were to end up being 'yes'. I should simply like to try to locate the importance of the word fiction for Foucault's work. Revel, moreover, added: 'No ill intent should be seen in this question; since Freud, at least, we have known that fiction, like history, is a system of intelligibility – and that is not such a bad precedent.'

The first point is to recall the extent to which Foucault, as he developed this system, or these systems, of intelligibility, found himself more or less drawing support from, or at least often spending time over, authors, works (mostly literary but sometimes visual) and names which presuppose what amounts to a universe of fiction (both in the banal sense of the term and also in the sense in which he understands it). This is a precondition of the way he deals with them. It is not a question of asides, complements, ornaments or parallelistic ramblings. It will be easier to appreciate this when these dense texts have been brought together in what would amount to two weighty tomes, constituting (with *Raymond Roussel*) more than a quarter of his work. Foucault is addressing a question to philosophy which, from another point of view, he has already addressed to history. The point here is to give consistency to this question, though it will not be possible to develop it as it will or should be developed. For schematic purposes this process can be broken down into three stages which simultaneously show a real evolution and an obstinate truth to himself.

I

Fiction. Foucault used the word itself most of all (it seems to me) in the years (1960–67) when he was putting together the essential elements of what Jean Roudaut so appropriately termed his 'imaginary library' (in one of the rare texts which tried to assess what I am trying to shed light on).[2]

Let us first of all hear what Foucault had to say in 1963 (on the subject of Robbe-Grillet and the novelists of *Tel Quel*. I think this is his longest sustained passage on the word fiction as such):

> What if the fictive were neither the beyond nor the intimate secret of the everyday but the arrowshot which strikes us in the eye and offers up to us everything which appears? In this case the fictive would be that which names things, that which makes them speak and that which gives them in language [*langage*] their being already apportioned by the sovereign power of words. . . . This is not to say, then, that fiction is language [*langage*]: this trick would be too easy, though a very familiar one nowadays. It does mean, though, more prudently, that there is between them a complex sense of belonging, a mutual support and an element of contention; also that, in a way which lasts as long as it can keep the words going, the simple experience of picking up a pen and writing creates . . . a distance which belongs neither to the world, nor to the unconscious, nor to perception, nor to inwardness, a distance which, in its barest form, offers a criss-crossing of lines of ink as well as an entanglement of thoroughfares. . . . And if at last anyone were to ask me to define the fictive, I should say, albeit rather tactlessly, that it was the verbal nerve structure of that which does not exist, such as it is.
>
> I should want to do some paring away, in order to allow this experience to be what it is (to treat it, then, as fiction, since it does not exist, which we already know): I should like to pare away all the contradictory words which might cause it to be seen too easily in terms of a dialectic: subjective and objective, interior and exterior, reality and imagination, all these should be dealt with or abolished. This whole lexicon of mixture would have to be replaced with the vocabulary of distance and thus show that the fictive is a distancing which is appropriate to language – a distancing which has its place in it but which also puts language on display, disperses it, redivides it and opens it up. Fiction is not there because language is distant from things; but language [*langage*] is their distance, the light in which they are to be found and their inaccessibility, the simulacrum in which only their presence is given; and all such language [*langage*], which instead of putting this distance to one side maintains itself in the distance and the distance in itself, and which talks of this distance whilst advancing within it, is a language [*langage*] of fiction. As such it can be found equally throughout all prose and all poetry, all novels and all reflective writing.[3]

This is what he had to say three years later on the subject of Jules Verne: 'In all works which have the form of a narrative, *story* [*fable*] should be distinguished from *fiction*. The story is that which is recounted. . . . Fiction is the regime of the narrative, or rather the various regimes according to which it is recounted.'[4] Fiction is an 'aspect' of the story: what lies behind the story [*l'arrière-fable*] is the exchange of voices which forms the texture of the fiction.

Thus, from both points of view, fiction does not depend on events (real or imaginary) linked together in a narrative; but on the distance which language sets up in relation to itself when it discovers in itself unknown properties and produces unsuspected new deals. It is clear that by saying this, as he speaks of the fiction of others, Foucault is also speaking to himself. He seeks to define a regime which would be his own (and that of certain of his contemporaries). This is a regime which it is impossible for him to characterise without making reference to writers. Yet he also knows that it cannot be exactly the same as the regime of the writer whose starting point in writing fiction is the story (even though, in the greater number of writers in which he is interested, the story can be reduced more or less to nothing more than the abstract locus of a fictional game).

Such is the movement (which is both other and the same, described on several occasions) which makes it possible for him to see in history (historical history, which is his true story) successions which he brings together, connects, groups, develops (according to a process which is like the way the voices in an opera work together, or like serial music, or again, to give a more directly realistic example, Eisenstein's montage of attractions, provided that one removes from this his obsession with dialectic).

Is this not the way fiction functions, seen in a way which attaches itself internally to the archive (or to certain archives) which have inherited the name of an author? (Foucault says in *L'Ordre du discours*: 'The author is that which gives to the troubling language of fiction its unities, that which knots it together coherently, and inserts it into the real'.) And does not this function also designate at the same time the function of discourse which takes possession of the archive, every archive, in order to trace in it lines of readability and visibility? A function of fiction, which is to be found whenever discourse reflects on itself, provided that one enters into the spirit of the game being played (which means at the same time: the pleasure which one takes in it and the empty space which one recognises to be in it)? Fiction, the Borgesian word *par excellence*, is summed up entirely in the famous sentence in the preface to *Les Mots et les Choses*: 'The birthplace of this book is a text of Borges'.

In this first stage, then, Foucault wrote a lot about literature (and painting) but also used it as a means. On the one hand, he published a large number of articles on works and on authors in which he was still trying to bring to the fore the role of fiction, in the context of their excessive quest for the 'being of language'. These articles (on Hölderlin, Rousseau, Bataille, Klossowski, Crébillon and J. Reveroni de Saint-Cyr, Robbe-Grillet, Roger Laporte, the novelists of *Tel Quel*, Mallarmé, Jules Verne, Blanchot, Flaubert . . .) can be seen alongside his own books. The excess which Foucault emphasises is set out, schematically, in two major forms: transgression and going back over the same material (Bataille and Blanchot); repetition and reduplication – spaces and successions (Flaubert, Roussel).

These texts, then, run parallel to the books. But we should not forget, as we all know, that one book which is on the subject of an author, Roussel, is treated in an individual way, and runs parallel to itself, if one can say that. This book is situated at a strategic moment, between *Histoire de la folie* and *Naissance de la clinique* on one side and *Les Mots et les Choses* on the other. Foucault used the book on Roussel to show, in what was perhaps his last interview, that he was maintaining a profound and quite singular relationship, at once intimate and gleeful, with the boundaries of the secret. It was as if he had found in it a kind of moving image of his own way of conceiving and thinking. This book, which was written very quickly, with reference to nothing other than its own object of study to which Foucault applied himself with concentrated enthusiasm, was also his first book on methodology, a sort of first version of his *Archéologie du savoir*.

On the other hand, in his books proper, his archaeologies, his main works, writers of fiction occupy a position which is pivotal, mirror-like and ambiguous: they are treated at the same time as elements of his own story and of his fiction, yet in a way which never deprives them of their own fiction. Though they constitute archives amongst archives, they are at the same time difficult to reduce to archives: as such they function just as well as archive-mirrors (producing the effects of projection and refocusing: *Le Neveu de Rameau* in *Histoire de la folie*, *Les Ménines* in *Les Mots et les Choses*) or as vantage-point archives (that is to say, as a distancing which is different from that of his own language – Nietzsche is the prime example; he will remain for a long while a figure who is 'non-archaeologisible').

II

In the second phase, this relationship of mutual envelopment and distorted mirroring becomes blurred. The reasons for this on a political level are well known, as are the theoretical reasons. But they can be expressed also in terms of the logic of fiction, as a deepening of the idea of thought as fiction proper – that is to say, having recourse only to the elements of the story being dealt with – and as violence being done by fiction to the story.

There are in fact no literary or artistic archives in Foucault's work from *'L'Archéologie du savoir* onwards. And, for the rest, the archives which could be called the 'famous' archives thereafter fall into line with those 'less famous' archives which form the basis of the order of discourse and its genealogy (like de Sade and Bataille, who were previously the subversive heroes of archaeology, and are seen in *La Volonté de savoir* in terms of a 'historical revision'). And parallel to this the problem, in itself, of the need for an archaeology of the authorial function is posed; that is to say, an evaluation of the relationship between the story and fiction in archaeology's own terms, this relationship having until then served it as a mirror function. Yet this archaeology does not really need to be developed (any more than Barthes's famous project on scientific writing). This is because the most vivid material for such an archaeology, the turning of the story into fiction, happens more than anywhere in Foucault's own books. As such they become more and more sensitive and more and more abstract, more and more fictive, even though their fiction is as true – that is to say, as present and as effective – as fiction can be. This is shown *par excellence* in *Surveiller et punir*.

Fiction understood in this sense possesses a virtue in comparison with the history which it is, without being so. It does not bring to the fore that which is in the past in order that the effect of it should return to the present. What it brings to the fore is that which is in the process of happening. Thus it is most true for the time in which it is practised because it incorporates the shift between times in the very way in which it is constructed, and converts this into space (which is both visible and readable).

Barthes expressed this when he said of *Histoire de la folie*: 'the newest thing there is about this project is the sense of vertigo'.[5] Paul Veyne, fifteen years later, compared Foucault to Cézanne in order to describe the effect of the 'strange pictures' produced by the 'pictorial method' of archaeological description. 'These are pictures of a world which we know: Foucault is no more a painter of abstracts than Cézanne; the countryside of Aix can be recognised, only it is invested with a violent sense of feeling; it seems to have risen up out of an earthquake.'[6]

This sense of feeling, this quaking, is fiction operating as reality, affirming itself as the only reality possible. Fiction becomes the break between self and self, as between other moments, high points, phases, the sentences of discourse which invent themselves by means of discourse. It is at the same time a law of composition and of grouping; an ethic of self-invention.

But in this same movement, as if to give it more clarity, by an effect of pure reflection (from a distance, to be precise), Foucault writes the two texts on literature and on art which most perfectly express (since his book on Roussel) his conception of fiction, the conception of his fiction.

Right in the middle of his 'political period', at the same time as he is polishing up his increasingly positive instruments of archaeological analysis, Foucault ecstatically groups together in Jean-Pierre Brisset's extraordinary books, *La Grammaire logique* and *La Science de Dieu*, elements of a phonetic-semantic mechanism which discovers, in the most extreme separation that language can establish from itself, the principle of regulated-deregulated fiction. The very terms that Foucault uses can be seen as being in parallel with his formulation of a theory of grouping in *L'Archéologie du savoir*, which is developed and refined in *Surveiller et punir*. For example: 'Between one word and another there are swarms of episodes – battles, victories, confinements and persecutions'; 'the word exists only in order to be at one with a shout, a murmur, a command or a narrative'.[7] And this is a distancing of the same sort ('the point of incursion of poetry and time which is no more, yet repeated') as that which converts each operation of the story into fiction. Foucault also takes measure of the vertiginous mirroring effect of this distancing by allowing himself to slip into the labyrinths through which Magritte, as a painter, traps the representation of things and words ('*This is not a pipe*').

None the less, even then there is a way to pass from the 'neutral' archive to the 'magnetically charged' archive. (The problem of how to link them preoccupied Foucault a great deal, very concerned, as he was from a certain point, to avoid any impression of idealism, or of recourse to the metaphysical, or any collusion with thought about the text or writing.) A sort of point of resolution, which is simultaneously ideal and ambiguous, is to be found in the memoir of Pierre Rivière. This text is in the first instance an archive, in the full sense that Foucault attaches to this: as it becomes part of the trial, it produces the event which is the object of his discourse – that is, the crime. Then it becomes literature, but still as an archive: the murder narrative of Rivière belongs to a genre, and fits into the discursive regularity of those 'narrations which thus form a popular memory of crimes'. But it is still literature from whatever point of view one looks at it, due to the proper value of language and verbal machinery, bearing the voice of a subject who is moving towards his dissolution, his death, before coming back from this death, changed, abolished in words. 'Let me be honest,' Foucault writes as he situates the objective reasons of the archaeological work carried out on the basis of the Rivière affair. 'Maybe that was not what detained me for a year as I studied these documents. But simply the beauty of Rivière's memoir.' Let us pause on this word beauty. In a context like this it does not mean a banal force, but that something essential is at play which leads in the direction of the aesthetic.

The essential point is that this movement, through the aesthetic, duplicates the passage through the political and towards the ethical in such a strict and pointed way. The aesthetic does not come in order to play a balancing or compensatory role, nor is it to be seen as a supplement to politics and ethics, nor as constituting the outward appearance of these: it informs them. It is at the same time their concern and their style. It is what makes them possible, visible and readable in the proper sense of this word in the context of Foucault's books. It is therefore what makes them effective.

III

The distance (which could be called the principle of fiction) now becomes the departure of the project of the history of sexuality in the direction of Greece, Rome and the Middle Ages. The texts, philosophical or literary (Plato, Artemidorus) are able to return freely to these ages, without any tension, mirror effects or overhanging. They are able to do this the more easily since they come from a period when writing was not affected by the separating functions which gradually formed throughout history, culminating in the nineteenth century. They do this also because they bear within themselves (with no utopia other than that which consists in being able to write this movement into a book) the idea of a world where a more direct implementation of writing by thought could be possible.

To continue with Paul Veyne's metaphor, one could say that despite the wealth of their material these books put one in mind of Cézanne's water-colours, which came after his oil paintings, where a landscape is evoked where spacious areas of blue blend into the white of the paper. A space is created where empty areas are as important as those which are full.

Is not something similar designated by the aphorism of Char which is written on the back of these volumes? 'The history of man is the long succession of synonyms of a single word. To contradict this is a duty.' This boils down to saying that it is necessary to maintain, rediscover and order spaces between words and even within them, so that thought can proceed and be made visible. These words could be in stories, fiction, history or philosophy.

As for literature and art proper, Foucault published nothing in these years as far as I know (at least not in French), other than a text to introduce the photos of Duane Michals.[8] But it is all there. 'The indiscreet desire to make a narrative of things.' The value of experience. The taste for disappearance. The effects of dissociation. The prescription of the invisible ('not to fix the image, not to tie it down, but rather to expose it to invisible breaths'). The eluded event. And then there are words (which provide the title of the text): the 'thought emotion' which, Foucault writes, is stronger than time, aging and death, since only its experience (which is the same as that of art) has the capacity to speak of these things (as he used to say at the time of *Tel Quel*: 'speaking thought, thinking speech'). And in order to give more force to his approach, and to catch up with art on all sides, at the beginning of the article Foucault inserts Duane Michaels's work in a succession which was perhaps suggested to him by Michals but which at the same time becomes, in its own right, a suggestion for an artistic trail to follow and also Foucault's personal sequence of art as experience, both in its initial experience and in its continuation. 'Magritte, Bob Wilson, *Under the Volcano*, *La Mort de Maria Malibran* and, of course H.G. [Hervé Guibert]'. That is a painter, a theatre producer, a great modern novel, a film, and a contemporary novelist.

What could be said of the authorial function of a writer who, as he put together histories in philosophy, was actually constructing fictions? It seems to me that Foucault does show us the way in one of the procedures which are familiar in his work, when one ends up twisting one's neck in order to try to see oneself (as when he says, for example, that perhaps we will not know what madness, sexuality and so on were), though sometimes he does practise this method without saying so. In his description of levels of authorial functions he suggests that our age (that is to say, still, the age which began in the nineteenth century) had witnessed the appearance of what he wishes to call 'founders of discursivity'.[9] 'These authors', he writes, 'are not only the authors of their works, their books. They have produced something more: this is the possibility of regulating the formation of other texts. . . . they established an indefinite possibility of discourse.' It is in this way that he situates Marx and Freud ('the first and the most important') and emphasises that, contrary to the novelist who makes it possible for analogies with his work to come after him, the founder of discursivity makes a certain number of differences possible; whilst yet contrary to the foundation of a science, 'the discourse which is established is of a heterogeneous nature to its subsequent transformations'. It remains withdrawn, or overhangs it. That is why, he adds, it is possible to 'go back to' these heroes of a new genre: the 'bolted door of forgetting' is incorporated in their work, making any return to their work impossible and yet bringing about this return at the same time. And this return becomes 'something like a sort of enigmatic knitting together of the author and the work'.

It could well be that the work, which is at the same time philosophical and literary, of transforming history into fiction, with the profound singularity that this implies, is what contributes most vividly to making Michel Foucault one of these founders of discursivity (and that this should be, precisely, the aspect which bears within it the fatality of forgetting and returning). Like Marx, Freud, and some others. After all, that is what Jacques Revel foresaw.

NOTES

1. 'Foucault and the historians', conversation with Jacques Revel by Raymond Bellour, *Magazine littéraire, spécial Foucault*, no. 101, June 1975.
2. Jean Roudaut, 'Bibliothèque imaginaire', *Magazine littéraire, spécial Foucault*, no. 207, May 1984.
3. 'Distance, aspect, origine', *Critique*, November 1963, pp. 20–22.
4. 'L'arrière-fable', *L'Arc, Jules Verne*, no. 29, 1966.

5. Roland Barthes, 'De part et d'autre', in *Essais critiques*, Paris: Éditions du Seuil, 1964, p. 172.
6. Paul Veyne, 'Foucault révolutionne l'histoire', in *Comment on écrit l'histoire*, Paris: Éditions du Seuil, 1978, p. 241.
7. '7 propos sur le 7e ange', in Jean-Pierre Brisset, *La Grammaire logique* followed by *La Science de Dieu*, Paris: Tchou, 1970, pp. xi, xii.
8. 'La pensée, l'émotion', *Duane Michals*, Musée d'art moderne, 1982.
9. 'Qu'est-ce qu'un auteur?', *Bulletin de la société française de philosophie*, meeting of 22 February 1969.

SUMMARY OF DISCUSSIONS

Raymond Bellour's paper brought the first day of the conference to an end; only **Walter Seitter** addressed a question to him, asking him why Foucault used the noun 'discursivity' in order to describe certain types of discourse, and if there was not a degree of irony in this description of discourse and repetitions.

Raymond Bellour saw no irony of that nature. As for the term 'discursivity', maybe something fundamental was at work here: the idea that words are there to be tried out.

3 POWER AND GOVERNMENT

one

What is a dispositif*?

Gilles Deleuze

Foucault's philosophy is often presented as an analysis of concrete social apparatuses [*dispositifs*]. But what is a *dispositif*? In the first instance it is a tangle, a multilinear ensemble. It is composed of lines, each having a different nature. And the lines in the apparatus do not outline or surround systems which are each homogeneous in their own right, object, subject, language, and so on, but follow directions, trace balances which are always off balance, now drawing together and then distancing themselves from one another. Each line is broken and subject to *changes in direction*, bifurcating and forked, and subject to *drifting*. Visible objects, affirmations which can be formulated, forces exercised and subjects in position are like vectors and tensors. Thus the three major aspects which Foucault successively distinguishes, Knowledge, Power and Subjectivity are by no means contours given once and for all, but series of variables which supplant one another. It is always in a crisis that Foucault discovers new dimensions, new lines. Great thinkers are somewhat seismic; they do not evolve but proceed by means of crisis, in fits and starts. Thinking in terms of moving lines was the process put forward by Herman Melville, and this involved fishing lines and lines of descent which could be dangerous, even fatal. Foucault talked of lines of sedimentation but also of lines of 'breakage' and of 'fracture'. Untangling these lines within a social apparatus is, in each case, like drawing up a map, doing cartography, surveying unknown landscapes, and this is what he calls 'working on the ground'. One has to position oneself on these lines themselves, these lines which do not just make up the social apparatus but run through it and pull at it, from North to South, from East to West, or diagonally.

The first two dimensions of a social apparatus [*dispositif*] – or those to which

* *Translator's note*: There is, in English, no straightforward way of translating *dispositif*, the implications of which are developed in this chapter. I have used the terms 'social apparatus' or 'apparatus' as the closest available equivalent.

Foucault draws our attention in the first instance – are curves of visibility and curves of enunciation. The apparatuses are like Raymond Roussel's machines, such as Foucault analyses them; they are machines which make one see and speak. Visibility cannot be traced back to a general source of light which could be said to fall upon pre-existing objects: it is made of lines of light which form variable shapes inseparable from the apparatus in question. Each apparatus has its way of structuring light, the way in which it falls, blurs and disperses, distributing the visible and the invisible, giving birth to objects which are dependent on it for their existence, and causing them to disappear. This is the case not only for painting but also for architecture: like the 'prison apparatus' as an optical machine, used for seeing without being seen. If apparatuses have a historical nature, this is to be found in regimes of light, but also in regimes of enunciation. Affirmations [*énoncés*] in turn can be traced back to lines of enunciation over which the differential positions of their elements are distributed; and, if the curves are themselves affirmations [*énoncés*], this is because *énoncés* are curves which distribute variables and because a science, at a given moment, or a literary genre, or a state of law, or a social movement, can be defined precisely by the regimes of enunciations to which they give rise. They are neither subjects nor objects, but regimes which must be defined from the point of view of the visible and from the point of view of that which can be enunciated, with the drifting, transformations and mutations which this will imply. And in every apparatus [*dispositif*] the lines break through thresholds, according to which they might have been seen as aesthetic, scientific, political, and so on.

Thirdly, a social apparatus [*dispositif*] consists of lines of force. It could be said that they proceed from one unique point to another in the preceding lines; in a way they 'rectify' the preceding curves, they draw tangents, fill in the space between one line and another, acting as go-betweens between seeing and saying and vice versa, acting as arrows which continually cross between words and things, constantly waging battle between them. The line of force comes about 'in any relationship between one point and another', and passes through every area in the apparatus. Though invisible and unsayable, it is closely knitted in with the others, yet separable. It is these lines that Foucault is interested in tracing, and he finds their trajectory in Roussel, Brisset, and in the painters Magritte and Rebeyrolle. This is the 'dimension of power', and power is the third dimension of space, internal to the apparatus, variable to the apparatus. It is formed, like power, out of knowledge [*savoir*].

Finally, Foucault discovered lines of subjectification. This new dimension has already given rise to misunderstandings, the reasons for which are hard to see in precise terms. More than anything else, the discovery of this new dimension arose out of a crisis in Foucault's thought, as if it had become necessary for him to redraw the map of social apparatuses [*dispositifs*], to find for them a new orientation in order to stop them from becoming locked into unbreakable lines of force which would impose definitive contours. Leibniz gave exemplary expression to this state of crisis which sets thought on the move again when one thinks a resolution has been found: we thought we were in port, but we were cast back out into the open sea. Foucault, for his part, was concerned that the social apparatuses [*dispositifs*] which he was analysing should not be circumscribed by an enveloping line, unless other vectors could be seen as passing above or below it. Maybe he is using the term 'breaking the line' in the sense of 'bypassing it'. This bypassing of the line of forces is what happens when it turns on itself, meanders, grows obscure and goes underground – or rather when the force, instead of entering into a linear relationship with another force, turns back on itself, works on itself or affects itself. This dimension of the Self is by no means a pre-existing determination which one finds ready-made. Here again, a line of subjectification is a process, a production of subjectivity in a social apparatus [*dispositif*]: it has to be made, inasmuch as the apparatus allows it to come into being or makes it possible. It is a line of escape. It escapes preceding lines and escapes *from* itself. The Self is neither knowledge nor power. It is a process of individuation which bears on groups and on people, and is subtracted from the power relations which are established as constituting forms of knowledge [*savoirs*]: a sort of surplus-value. It is not certain that all social apparatuses [*dispositifs*] comprise these.

Foucault designates the Athenian city as the first place in which subjectification was invented: this is because it is, according to the original definition which he gives to it, the city which invented the line of forces which runs through the *rivalry of free men*. Now, from this line which makes it possible for one free man to command others, a very different one branches off which has it that a man who commands free men has to be seen as a master of himself. It is these optional rules of self-mastery which constitute subjectification, and this is autonomous, even if it is subsequently called upon to inspire new powers. One might wonder if these lines of subjectification do not form the extreme boundary of a social apparatus [*dispositif*], and if perhaps they sketch the movement of one apparatus to another, in this sense preparing for 'lines of fracture'. And lines of subjectification have no general formula, any more than the other lines. Though cruelly interrupted, Foucault's research would have shown that processes of subjectification could take on quite different forms from the Greek mode: for example in Christian social apparatuses [*dispositifs*] in modern societies, and so on. Can one not think of apparatuses where subjectification does not come about through aristocratic life or the aestheticised existence of the free man, but through the marginalised existence of the 'outsider'? Thus the Sinologist Tokeï explains how the liberated slave somehow lost his social status and found himself thrown back on an isolated, lamenting, *elegiac* existence, out of which he was to shape new forms of power and knowledge. The study of the variations in the process of subjectification seems to be one of the fundamental tasks which Foucault left to those who would follow him. I believe that there is great fecundity in this form of research, and that current projects concerning a history of private life only partially cover it. The creators of subjectivity can sometimes be the nobles, those who, according to Nietzsche, say 'we the good . . .', but in different conditions they are the excluded, the bad, the sinners, the hermits, or monastic communities, or heretics: a whole typology of subjective formations in a moving apparatus. And everywhere there are mix-ups to sort out: the productions of subjectivity escape from the powers and the forms of knowledge [*savoirs*] of one social apparatus [*dispositif*] in order to be reinserted in another, in forms which are yet to come into being.

These apparatuses, then, are composed of the following elements: lines of visibility and enunciation, lines of force, lines of subjectification, lines of splitting, breakage, fracture, all of which criss-cross and mingle together, some lines reproducing or giving rise to others, by means of variations or even changes in the way they are grouped. Two important consequences arise for a philosophy of social apparatuses [*dispositifs*]. The first of these is the repudiation of universals. The universal, in fact, explains nothing; it is the universal which needs to be explained. All the lines are lines of variation, which do not even have constant co-ordinates. The One, the All, the True, the object, the subject are not universals, but singular processes – of unification, totalisation, verification, objectivation, subjectification – present in the given apparatus. Also each apparatus is a multiplicity in which operate processes of this nature still in formation, distinct from those operating in another. It is in this sense that Foucault's philosophy can be referred to as pragmatism, functionalism, positivism, pluralism. Perhaps it is Reason which poses the greatest problem because the processes of rationalisation can operate on segments or on regions of all lines under consideration. Foucault pays homage to Nietzsche regarding the historical nature of reason; and he suggests the importance of epistemological research on the different forms of rationality in knowledge [*savoir*] (Koyré, Bachelard, Canguilhem) and of sociopolitical research into modes of rationality in power (Max Weber). Perhaps he was reserving the third line for himself: the study of types of 'reasonableness' in subjects he was dealing with. But what he essentially refuses is the identification of this process with Reason *par excellence*. He challenges any attempt to restore universals in reflection, communication or consensus. One might say in this respect that his relations with the Frankfurt School and the successors of this school were a series of misunderstandings for which he was not responsible. And, just as he does not admit of a universality in a founding subject or in Reason *par excellence* which would make it possible to judge social apparatuses [*dispositifs*], he also does not admit of universals of catastrophe in which reason becomes alienated and collapses once and for all. As Foucault said to Gérard Raulet, there is not a bifurcation in reason, yet reason is forever bifurcating; there are as many bifurcations and branchings as there are foundations, as many collapses as there are constructions following the breaks brought about by the apparatus, and 'there is no sense in the propositions according to which reason is a long narrative which has now come to an end'. From this point of view, the question raised in objection to Foucault – the question as to how the relative value of a social apparatus [*dispositif*] can be assessed if one cannot evoke transcendental values by way of universal co-ordinates – is a question which leads us backwards and which, in itself, also risks meaninglessness. Does this mean that all social apparatuses [*dispositifs*] are equally valid (nihilism)? It has been a long while since thinkers like Spinoza and Nietzsche first began to show that modes of existence have to be assessed according to immanent criteria, according to their content of 'possibilities', liberty or creativity, without any appeal to transcendental values. Foucault even makes allusion to 'aesthetic' criteria, which are understood as criteria for life and replace on each occasion the claims of transcendental judgement with an immanent evaluation. When we read Foucault's last books, we have to do our best to understand the programme which he is placing in front of his readers. Could this be the intrinsic aesthetic of modes of existence as the ultimate dimension of social apparatuses [*dispositifs*]?

The second consequence of a philosophy of social apparatuses [*dispositifs*] is a change in orientation which turns one's interest away from the Eternal and towards the new. The new is not supposed to mean the same as the fashionable but, on the contrary, the variable creativity which arises out of social apparatuses [*dispositifs*]. This fits in with the question which began to be asked in the twentieth century as to how the production of something new in the world might be possible. It is true that, throughout his theory of enunciation, Foucault explicitly impugns the 'originality' of an *énoncé* as being something which is of little relevance and interest. All he wishes to consider is the 'regularity' of *énoncés*. But what he understands by regularity is the sweep of the curve which passes through singular points or the differential values of the ensemble of enunciations (in the same way that he defines power relations by means of the distribution of singular elements in a social field). When he challenges the originality of an *énoncé*, he means that a contradiction which might arise between two *énoncés* is not enough to distinguish between them, or to mark the newness of one with regard to the other. What counts is the newness of the regime itself in which the enunciation is made, given that such a regime is capable of containing contradictory *énoncés*. One might, for example, ask what regime of *énoncés* appeared with the social apparatus [*dispositif*] of the French Revolution, or the Bolshevik Revolution: it is the newness of the regime that counts, not the newness of the *énoncé*. Each apparatus is thus defined in terms of its newness content and its creativity content, this marking at the same time its ability to transform itself, or indeed to break down in favour of a future apparatus, unless it concentrates its strength along its harder, more rigid, or more solid lines. Inasmuch as they escape the dimensions of power and knowledge, the lines of subjectification seem particularly capable of tracing paths of creation, which are continually aborting, but then restarting, in a modified way, until the former apparatus is broken. Foucault's as yet unpublished studies on various Christian processes probably open a number of different avenues in this respect. Yet it would not be right to think that the production of subjectivity is the territory only of religion: anti-religious struggles are also creative, just as regimes of light, enunciation and domination pass through different domains. Modern forms of subjectivation no longer resemble those of Greece any more than they do those of Christianity, and the same goes for their light, their enunciations and their forms of power.

We belong to social apparatuses [*dispositifs*] and act within them. The newness of an apparatus in relation to those which have gone before is what we call its actuality, our actuality. The new is the current. The current is not what we are but rather what we are in the process of becoming – that is the Other, our becoming-other. In each apparatus [*dispositif*] it is necessary to distinguish what we are (what we are already no longer), and what we are in the process of becoming: *the historical part and the current part*. History is the archive, the drawing of what we are and what we are ceasing to be, whilst the current is the sketch of what we are becoming. In the same way, history or the archive is what still separates us from ourselves, whilst the current is the Other with which we are already coinciding. It is sometimes thought that Foucault paints a picture of modern societies in terms of disciplinary social apparatuses [*dispositifs*], in opposition to older social apparatuses [*dispositifs*] in which sovereignty is the key concept. Yet this is by no means the case: the disciplines which Foucault describes are the history of what we gradually cease to be, and our present-day reality takes on the form of dispositions of overt and continuous *control* in a way which is very different from recent closed disciplines. Foucault agrees with Burroughs, who claims that our future will be controlled rather than disciplined. The question is not whether this is worse. For to ask this would be to make appeal to ways of producing subjectivity which would be capable of resisting this new form of domination, ways which would be very different from those which were formerly exercised against disciplines. Would this mean a new light, new enunciations, new power, new forms of subjectification? In each apparatus we have to untangle the lines of the recent past and those of the near future: that which belongs to the archive and that which belongs to the present; that which belongs to history and that which belongs to the process of becoming; *that which belongs to the analytic and that which belongs to the diagnostic*. If Foucault is a great philosopher, this is because he used history for the sake of something beyond it: as Nietzsche said: acting against time, and thus on time, for the sake of a time one hopes will come. For what appears to be the present-day or the new according to Foucault is what Nietzsche called the unseasonable, the uncontemporary, the becoming which bifurcates with history, the diagnostic which relays analysis with other roads. This is not to predict but to be attentive to the unknown which knocks at the door. Nothing shows this better than a fundamental passage in *L'Archéologie du savoir*, which is valid for the rest of Foucault's work:

> As such the analysis of the archive comprises a privileged region which is at the same time close to us, but different from our present; it is the border of the time which surrounds our present, jutting over it and describing it by means of its otherness; it is that which is outside us and delimits us. To describe the archive is to set out its possibilities (and the mastery of its possibilities) on the basis of forms of discourse which have just recently ceased to be our own; the threshold of its existence is established by the break which separates us from what we can no longer say, and from that which falls outside our discursive practices; it begins with what is outside our own language [*langage*], its locus being its distance from our own discursive practices. In this sense it becomes valid as a diagnostic for us. This is not because it makes it possible for us to paint a picture of our distinctive traits and to sketch in advance what we will look like in the future. But it deprives us of our continuities; it dissolves this temporal identity in which we like to look at ourselves in order to conjure with breaks in history; it breaks the thread of transcendental teleologies; and at the point where anthropological thought questions the being of man or his subjectivity, it vividly draws attention to the other, to the outside. Understood in this way, the diagnostic does not establish the facts of our identity by means of the interplay of distinctions. It establishes that we are difference, that our reason is the difference of forms of discourse, our history is the difference of times, that our selves are the difference of masks.

The different lines of an apparatus [*dispositif*] divide into two groups: lines of stratification or sedimentation, and lines leading to the present day or creativity. The last consequence of this method concerns the whole of Foucault's work. In most of his books he specifies a precise archive, with extremely new historical methods, regarding the General Hospital of the seventeenth century, the clinic of the eighteenth century, the prison of the nineteenth century, the subjectivity of Ancient Greece, and then Christianity. But that is one half of his task. For, through a concern for rigorousness, through a desire not to mix things up and through confidence in his reader, he does not formulate the other half. He formulates this explicitly only in the interviews which take place contemporary with the writing of each of his major books: what can be said nowadays about insanity, prison, sexuality? What new modes of subjectification can be seen to appear today which, indeed, are neither Greek nor Christian? This last question, notably, haunts Foucault till the end (we who are no longer either Greeks or Christians . . .). Right till the end of his life Foucault attached a lot of importance to interviews, in France and even more so abroad, and this was not because he had a taste for them but because in them he was able to trace these lines leading to the present which required a different form of expression from the lines which were drawn together in his major books. These interviews are diagnostics. It is rather like the situation with Nietzsche, whose works are hard to read unless one sees them in the context of the *Nachlass* contemporary with each of them. The complete work of Foucault, such as Defert and Ewald conceive it to be, cannot separate off the books which have made such an impression on all of us from the interviews which lead us towards a future, towards a becoming: the underlying strata and the present day.

SUMMARY OF DISCUSSIONS

Michel Karkeits noted that Gilles Deleuze did not use the word 'truth'. Where should one situate the notion of truth-telling which Foucault talks of in his last interviews? Is this an apparatus [*dispositif*] in itself? Or is it a dimension of all apparatuses?

Gilles Deleuze replied that for Foucault the true has no universal nature. The truth designates the ensemble of the productions which come about inside an apparatus [*dispositif*]. An apparatus comprises truths of enunciation, truths of light and visibility, truths of power, truths of subjectivation. Truth is the actualisation of the lines which constitute an apparatus. To extract from the ensemble of apparatuses [*dispositifs*] a desire for truth which could move from one to the other as something constant would be without meaning in Foucault's work.

Manfred Frank observed that Foucault's philosophy belongs to a post-Hegelian and post-Marxist tradition which wished to break with the universal in Enlightenment thought. None the less, one finds in Foucault all kinds of universals: apparatuses [*dispositifs*], discourses, archives, and so on, which prove that the break with the universal is not a radical one. Instead of one universal, there are several, on different levels.

Gilles Deleuze stressed that the true frontier is between constants and variables. The critique of universals can be translated into a question: how is it possible that anything new might come into the world? Other philosophers, like Whitehead and Bergson, made this the fundamental question in modern philosophy. It matters little if general terms are used in order to reflect on apparatuses [*dispositifs*]: they are names given to variables. All constants are done away with. The lines which make up the apparatuses demonstrate continuous variations. There are no more universals – that is to say, there is nothing except lines of variation. The general terms are the co-ordinates which have no meaning other than to make possible the estimation of a continuous variation.

Raymond Bellour wondered where it would be appropriate to situate

Foucault's texts on the subject of art: on the side of the book, and therefore of the archive, or on the side of the interviews, and therefore of the current.

Gilles Deleuze recalled Foucault's plan to write a book on Manet. In this book, Foucault would probably have analysed more than the lines and the colours, the way Manet structured light. This book would have belonged to the side of the archive. The interviews would have redeemed from the archive the lines characterising our present.

Foucault might well have said: Manet is the painter who ceases to be. This does not detract from Manet's greatness. For the greatness of Manet consists in what it was to become Manet at the moment he painted. These interviews would have consisted in showing the lines of breakage and of fracture which have led to artists nowadays entering into regimes of light which can be said to be different – that is to say, light has a different form of becoming.

For the arts, too, there is a complementarity in the two aspects of the analytic (that which we are, and by dint of this what we are ceasing to be) and the diagnostic (the becoming other to which we are heading). The analytic of Manet implies a diagnostic of what becomes of light, starting with Manet and following on from him.

Walter Seitter was surprised at the 'physicalism' which ran through Gilles Deleuze's presentation.

Gilles Deleuze did not accept the expression to the extent that it implied that in regimes of light there might be such a thing as a raw light which could be stated in physical terms. The physical is the threshold of that which is visible and that which can be stated. There is nothing given in an apparatus which can be taken to be in some kind of raw state. But light does have a physical regime – lines of light, waves and vibrations: why not?

Fati Triki wondered how and where the demolition of modern techniques of servitude could be introduced into the concept of social apparatuses [*dispositifs*]. Where could the practices of Michel Foucault be situated?

Gilles Deleuze indicated that there was no general reply. If a diagnostic was to be found in Foucault, it was in the need to locate, for each apparatus, lines of breakage and fracture. Sometimes these were situated on the level of powers; at other times on the level of knowledges [*savoirs*]. More generally, it should be said that the lines of subjectivation indicate fissures and fractures. But one is dealing with a form of casuistry. Evaluations must be made according to the case, according to the content of the apparatus. To give a general reply would be to undermine a discipline which is as important as that of archaeology, the discipline of the diagnostic.

Fati Triki wondered if Foucault's philosophy could succeed in breaking down the barriers of the Western world. Could it be seen as a philosophy *extra muros*?

Gilles Deleuze replied that for a long time Foucault limited his method to short sequences in French history. But in his latter books he envisaged longer sequences, starting with the Greeks. Could the same extension be made geographically? Could methods analogous to those of Foucault be used to study oriental social apparatuses [*dispositifs*] or those of the Middle East? Certainly so, since Foucault's language [*langage*], which sees things in terms of parcels of lines, as entanglements, as multilinear ensembles, does have an oriental feel to it.

two

A power without an exterior

François Ewald

In *Surveiller et punir* Michel Foucault described an initial stage in the grouping of norms in the modern sense of the term as *disciplines*. He demonstrated how they extended progressively in the course of the seventeenth and eighteenth centuries, and how they spread across the whole ensemble of the social body, 'the formation of what one might in general terms call the disciplinary society'.[1]

This diffusion came about by means of three principal modalities. The first, and probably the most important, is to be found in what Foucault calls the functional inversion of disciplines:

> Originally they were required to neutralise dangers, to keep useless or agitated populations in their place and to avoid the problems caused by assemblies of too great a number; from then on, though, since they became capable of so doing, they were required to play a positive role, increasing the potential utility of individuals.[2]

We see, then, a movement from discipline as a blockade given completely to negative functions like stopping evil, breaking communications, suspending time, to discipline as mechanism.

The second modality:

> The emigration of disciplinary mechanisms. Whilst disciplinary establishments multiply, their mechanisms have a certain tendency to become de-institutionalised, to step outside closed fortresses and to circulate in a 'free' state; massive and compact disciplines decompose into supple processes of control, which can be transferred and adapted.[3]

Disciplines are no longer the prerogative of certain institutions which are 'closed, established within boundaries', and every institution becomes capable of using the disciplinary schema. Disciplines become ubiquitous and liberated, no longer addressing only someone who is to be punished or a particular evil which one wishes to contain; they are placed at the service of the good, the good of all, of all socially useful production. Disciplines are addressed to all people, without distinction. 'Finally, the mechanisms of discipline are established as means of state control'[4] by means of the organisation of a centralised police force whose task is to exercise a 'permanent, exhaustive and omnipresent surveillance capable of making everything visible'.[5] Hence the conclusion which constitutes one of the major themes in *Surveiller et punir*: not only did the generalisation of the schema and the technologies of discipline make prison possible, but in itself it presented to modern society its true picture of itself: 'Why should we be surprised if prisons resemble factories, schools, barracks, and hospitals, all of which resemble prisons?'[6]

Foucault did not mean by this that 'disciplinary society' was a society of generalised confinement. Probably he meant the opposite. In fact the diffusion of disciplines demonstrates that their techniques are alien to the principle of confinement or, more exactly, that with disciplines confinement is no longer of a segregational nature. What makes society, as it were, disciplinary is precisely the fact that disciplines do not create partitions. On the contrary, their diffusion, far from dividing or compartmentalising, homogenises social space. The important element in the disciplinary society is the idea of society: the disciplines create the society; they create a sort of common language between all sorts of institutions, making it possible for one to be translated into another.

Prison does not escape from this: the disciplinary element is what makes prison the exclusive instrument of the administration of punishment, and it does so without alienating the social element. This is how prison can claim to re-educate the criminal and see as its end product the socialisation of the offender. Because the juridical apportionment in the deprivation of liberty no longer designates a share in the real. It is a 'false' apportionment, an artificial apportionment which no longer involves anything either on the side of the mechanisms of power, or on the side of the objectivation of the criminal. What characterises prison is the fact that the juridical aspect is of a purely surface nature and has no function in the substance of what goes on. It should not be allowed to mask the fact which, for Foucault, characterises the modern age: the fact of the redundancy of the disciplinary, of the great disciplinary continuum. Disciplinary society is a society of absolute communication: the diffusion of disciplines makes it possible for everything to communicate with everything else according to an interplay of redundant elements and infinite homologies.

The norm, or the normative, is at the same time that which makes possible the transformation from discipline as blockade into discipline as mechanism, the matrix which transforms the negative into the positive, and is to make possible the generalisation of the disciplinary as that which is instituted as a result of this transformation. The norm is precisely that by means of which and through which society, when it becomes a disciplinary society, communicates with itself. The norm links disciplinary institutions of production, of knowledge [*savoir*], wealth and finance and makes them *interdisciplinary*, homogenising social space even if it does not unify it.

Foucault describes three major disciplinary instruments: hierarchic surveillance, normalising sanctions, and examination.[7] It is perhaps less a question of three instruments than of three uses of the same technology which lies at the basis of the norm. In a certain way one is not dealing with instruments aiming to resolve the traditional problems of power: ordering multiple elements, linking the whole with its parts, placing them in relationship one with another. The normative puts forward a particular solution to this old problem: we have already seen that this composition operates according to a principle of production (and not of repression) – producing, raising value, intensifying rather than constraining, forbidding, stopping; but also this ordering occurs according to the logic of *individualisation*. Foucault continally returns to this point: discipline 'manufactures' individuals; it is the specific technique of a power which takes individuals at one and the same time as objects and as the instruments by means of which it is exercised.[8] But this axis of individualisation is not and cannot be the only one: the norm is at the same time the link, the principle of unity – of communication – between these individualities. The norm is the reference which is instituted when the group finds itself objectivised in the form of the individual. The norm is at the centre of a form of communication without origin and without subject.

The normative schema rests on the whole economy of *visibility*.

> The exercise of discipline supposes an apparatus which constrains by means of the interplay of perception [*regard*]; an apparatus where the techniques which make it possible to see produce the effects of power, and where in return the means of coercion make clearly visible those to whom they are applied.[9]

Normative disciplines principally mobilise space and architecture. We need to try to find out why it should be that the norm implies such a use of *architecture*, stones and walls. The importance of architecture comes from the fact that it takes the place of the king. In normative space architecture is no longer – or is no longer exclusively – the expression of power. It takes its place. It moves to the centre. It *is* the power itself. Architecture is the instrument, the technique, the apparatus by means of which, in the absence of a sovereign, and correlative to the individualisation of the subjects, there exists the possibility of an *objectivity* in the self's judgement of the self; by means of which this objectivity – the principle of communication, the value of values, meaning of meaning – could be constituted by means of a mechanism of self-reference. Architecture makes it possible for the objectivity of a judgement of the self on the self to be without external reference, just a judgement of self by self.

In fact, 'examination – disciplines – inverts economy and visibility into the exercise of power'.[10] This inversion designates practically a double process. First the institution of a one-dimensional space of visibility, where the axis of verticality – up and down – disappears, leaving purely horizontal vision; next, and as a result of this, comes the institution of lateral and relative visibility. That is to say, in disciplinary or normative space there is nothing to take the place of the sovereign. Perception [*regard*] itself becomes invisible: 'Disciplinary power is exercised by making things invisible; on the other hand, it imposes on those whom it subjugates a principle of obligatory visibility.'[11] Visibility is no longer the visible origin which can be situated; for it has no source other than those whom it makes visible, thus visible to themselves.

In the pre-disciplinary (pre-normative) order, the sovereign organises – for example, in the ceremony of torture and capital punishment – the sumptuous spectacle of his own presence. 'Until then the role of political ceremony had been to provide for the presentation, at the same time excessive and ordered, of power; it was a sumptuary expression of power, an expenditure which was at the same time exaggerated and codified and from which power drew its vigour,' Foucault[12] says; and by way of synthesis:

> Traditionally power is that which is seen, that which shows itself, that which makes its presence felt, and, paradoxically, that which reveals the principle of its strength in the movement by means of which it deploys that strength. Those on whom it is exercised can remain in the shade; they receive light only from that part of power which is conceded to them, or from the reflection of it which, for a moment, they might bear.[13]

We should be clear about the function of this presentation: it reminds people of their place, and gives everyone their identity. The individuality of power is maximal, to the extent that it is on the basis of its unity, its identity, that each individual is able to perceive his own identity.

With disciplines, according to the logic of the norm – 'the reversal of the political axis of individualisation'[14] – the shade becomes the light. 'In discipline, it is the subjects who are there to be seen. This light ensures the control of the power exercised over them.'[15] Each individual is to be objectivised according to an infinite principle of individualisation. Each individual becomes *a case*. Therefore each is always different, different from the other (and from himself). How can this individualisation operate, this individualisation of the normative?

The answer is that it occurs according to a purely lateral and relative logic. Normative individualisation comes about without any reference to any nature or essence in subjects. It does not have the form of a specification: it does not aim to reveal qualities that the individual might himself possess and which could thus be seen as characteristics of his type or of his nature. Disciplinary individualisation occurs without the supposition of any knowledge [*savoir*]. It is an individualisation which is positive and without metaphysics, an individualisation which is substanceless, rather like the way, in the system of language, in which the opposition between signifiers can never be traced back only to differences, unless one can fall back on the notion of the signified having a substance. It is a pure relationship. It is a relationship without support. Normative individualisation is itself also diacritical, lateral and relative.[16] It is purely comparative. Meaning is created only by spaces within it (rather than *exploits*).[17] Disciplines individualise and never cease from so doing; yet this individualisation does not occur by means of categories, only on the interior of categories. Always present and always starting afresh, it makes appeal to no knowledge exterior to that which it makes visible. Hidden worlds, the internal and secrets are finished with. The age is one of purely positive forms of knowledge [*savoirs*]. Normative knowledge [*savoir*] appeals to nothing exterior to that which it works on, that which it makes visible. What precisely is the norm? It is the measure which simultaneously individualises, makes ceaseless individualisation possible and creates comparability. The norm makes it possible to locate spaces, indefinitely, which become more and more discrete, minute, and at the same time makes sure that these spaces never enclose anyone in such a way as to create a nature for them, since these individualising spaces are never anything more than the expression of a relationship, of a relationship which has to been seen indefinitely in the context of others. What is a norm? A principle of comparison, of comparability, a common measure, which is instituted in the pure reference of one group to itself, when the group has no relationship other than to itself, without external reference and without verticality.

From the analysis which Foucault carries out in *Surveiller et punir*, two other characteristics of the norm, or the normative, can be deduced. First of all, normative individualisation is not exterior. The abnormal does not have a nature which is different from that of the normal. The norm, or normative space, knows no outside. The norm integrates anything which might attempt to go beyond it – nothing, nobody, whatever difference it might display, can ever claim to be exterior, or claim to possess an otherness which would actually make it other. Georges Canguilhem demonstrated this in the context of his analysis of monsters; when one thinks in terms of norms, the anomaly is not abnormal. It does not bear witness to a difference which would be seen as so strong that partitions would have to be seen in nature; the difference manifests a possibility. Isidore Geoffroy Saint-Hilaire said: 'There is no exception to the laws of nature, there are exceptions to the laws of naturalists.' It is not the exception that proves the rule. Rather, the exception is within the rule.

Therefore the line from the abnormal to the normal is not a definite one. It cannot be traced back to anything in nature. The abnormal is the norm: both the giant and the dwarf, the idiot and the genius. But this does not mean to say that, in normative space, there is no possible division, that there is no place for a process of valuing. The practices of the norm are not relativistic. The normal is opposed to the abnormal. But this division is of a special kind: it is formulated in terms of thresholds and boundaries. It is precisely a problem of knowing how to effect the division between the normal and the abnormal. It must be understood, though, that it can never express a law in nature; it can only formulate a pure relationship between the self and the group.

Hence the implication concerning the treatment of the *abnormal*. As Foucault writes: 'To punish is to exercise'.[18] Disciplines do not act by means of segregation but through intensification. In a disciplinary society – and this is its principle– the treatment of those who have been declared to be criminals is no different from that which applied to the good citizen. 'Disciplinary punishment is, for a large part at least, an isomorph of obligation itself; it is less the vengeance of the contravened law than its repetition, its redoubled insistence.'[19] Also, if prison constitutes a disciplinary space, this is not because it is founded on the *juridical* deprivation of liberty but because within its confines the means by which normal individuals are manufactured are repeated and insisted upon. When the disciplines become normative, the disciplinary institutions become isomorphs of one another. When the whole society becomes normative, each institution – armed forces, school, workshop, prison – becomes redundant in its relationship to the others.

'Norm' should not be confused with 'discipline'. Disciplines target bodies, with a function of training them; the norm is a measure, a means by which the common measure is produced. It is at the same time that which makes things comparable and that which individualises them: a principle of visibility, resulting from the pure mechanism of the group's reflection on itself. Disciplines are not necessarily normative. What characterised modernity, according to Foucault, was the advent of a normative age: the normalisation of disciplines, the movement from discipline as blockade to discipline as mechanism, and correlatively the formation of a disciplinary society, which is characterised not by confinement, even if one continues to use the procedure, but rather by the constitution of a *space*: supple, interchangeable, without segregation, indefinitely redundant and without exterior.

NOTES

1. *Surveiller et punir*, Paris: Gallimard, 1975, p. 211.
2. *Ibid.*
3. *Ibid.*, p. 213.
4. *Ibid.*, p. 214.
5. *Ibid.*, p. 215.

6. *Ibid.*, p. 229.
7. *Ibid.*, Part III, Chapter II, 'Les moyens du bon dressement', pp. 172 ff.
8. *Ibid.*, p. 172.
9. *Ibid.*, p. 173.
10. *Ibid.*, p. 189.
11. *Ibid.*
12. *Ibid.*, p. 183.
13. *Ibid.*, p. 189.
14. *Ibid.*, p. 194.
15. *Ibid.*, p. 189.
16. *Ibid.*, pp. 192, 195.
17. *Ibid.*, p. 195.
18. *Ibid.*, p. 182.
19. *Ibid.*

three

Towards a natural history of norms

Pierre Macherey

I

What probably most concerned Foucault was to understand how the action of norms on the lives of men determines the type of society to which they belong as subjects. Now, on this point, all his investigations turned about a fundamental question, the scope of which is both epistemological and historical: how can one move from a negative conception of the norm and the way it acts, founded on a model of juridical exclusion and related to that which is permitted and forbidden, to a positive conception, which on the contrary insists on its biological function of inclusion and regulation, in the sense not of a systematic regulation but of a regularisation, with reference to the distinction, confirmed by the so-called human sciences, between the normal and the pathological? Depending on which of these two forms is preferred, social relationships and the way individuals are inserted into the network which they constitute would have to be defined on completely different bases.

Thus – and this is the essential conclusion which comes out of *Histoire de la folie* – madness can be considered, and also, one might say, acted upon, on the basis of unreason, as with the segregative practice of confinement made real in an exemplary manner by the General Hospital: or, on the other hand, on the basis of alienation, from the moment this segregation is lifted and insane people are 'liberated', in the asylum which oversees madness in a completely different way, integrating it into what medicine claims to know about man. In the same way, *Surveiller et punir* shows how punishments can be put on as a show, acting out the opacity of major interdictions against a dark backdrop, placing those who transgress them beyond the pale of humanity, as in the public torture of regicides: or as a discipline, on the inside of the penitentiary institution which deploys a principle of transparency, reflecting what the whole of society should be, according to the exemplary function of the Panopticon.

Finally, according to *Histoire de la sexualité*, the pleasure linked with sex can be submitted to external control, tending to contain it within certain limits recognised as legitimate; or on the other hand it can be 'liberated', just as it can be said that the asylum 'liberated' the insane by treating them as sick people. This pleasure thus becomes involved in a movement of almost limitless expansion, which actually constitutes it into 'sexuality', following the positive impulse which gives it a power functioning as a 'biopower'.

The analysis of these three cases can be carried out within the framework of an apparently common orientation, since each time it encounters the same dilemma, confronting two practices opposed to the norm, which make of it a principle of exclusion or integration, revealing at the same time the way the two forms which it takes together are linked historically: the norm of knowledge [*savoir*], enunciating truth criteria the value of which can be restrictive or constitutive; and the norm of power, fixing for the subject the conditions of his (or her) liberty, according to external or internal laws. We also see how the problematic of the norm, in its relationship with society and with the subject, also makes reference to the distinction between the two possible forms of knowledge demonstrated in *Les Mots et les Choses*: that of an abstract grid of rationality, jutting over the domain of objects which it is supposed to 'represent' by enclosing them within its own framework; and that of knowledge [*savoir*] which, on the contrary, presents itself as being incorporated in the constitution of its object, which is from then on no longer only its 'object' but also its subject, knowledge [*savoir*], the form of which is given *par excellence* by the human sciences.

In any case, having stressed these correspondences between the different domains of investigation which successively held Foucault's attention, it should also be pointed out that between *Histoire de la folie* and *Histoire de la sexualité* his interest shifted, not only with regard to the corpus of objects and affirmations [*énoncés*] on which he was working, but also with regard to the point of application of the fundamental alternative out of which the main lines of his enquiry originate: and it is this shift which makes it impossible for the analyses I have just mentioned to be applied in a precise way, as if they were developing, in parallel, a type of reasoning which was formally identical. This is the shift which determines the values on either side of the norm (following the model in terms of which the norm can be traced, divided or distinguished), in view of the study of its function. The sides in question would be, on the one hand, the side to which it gives a negative connotation, which it sees as being of lesser value; and on the other hand the positive pole, which it values more highly; these two sides are the interdiction and the pathological in the case of *Histoire de la folie* and the permissible and the normal in the case of *Histoire de la sexualité*, particularly in the last two volumes to be published. Thus we see here a second dilemma surfacing, which is in some way transversal to the preceding one and suggests, regarding the action of the norm, two new possibilities of interpretation, depending on whether it is orientated towards the constitution of a pattern of abnormality – which is the essential problem in *Histoire de la folie* – or, on the contrary, towards a pattern of normality according to a point of view which finally emerged as that of *Histoire de la sexualité*.

If this is correct, one might consider the problematic which lies at the heart of Foucault's work to be situated at the intersection of these two lines of alternatives. The first of these two lines deals with the norm's relationship to its 'objects', a relationship which could be either internal or external according to whether it refers to a boundary (that is, the norm in the juridical sense) or to a limit (that is, the norm in the biological sense). The second deals with the norm's relationship to its 'subjects' which, at the same time as it excludes or integrates these latter according to the first relationship, also disqualifies or identifies them, in terms of recognition or non-recognition, in such a way as to place them on one side or another in a way which is separated or distinguished by the norm. It is by taking interest in both of these problems that we can come to understand how Foucault, whose own interest lay in just this, none the less came to modify his point of view as his investigations slowly but surely led him into new domains.

What I wish to deal with here are the philosophical implications of this question of the norm, such as I have just formulated it. Is there a 'truth' about norms and the way they act, which is related to the type of society and subject to which they correspond? And what is the nature of this truth? Do the criteria by means of which it can be evaluated arise out of a form of history or of epistemology? Or again, to what extent can the perspectives of a historical study or an epistemological study be reconciled?

II

Let us begin with an initial thesis, the scope of which is, as will be seen, directly philosophical: the affirmation of the productive character of the norm.

As has already been pointed out, depending on whether priority is given to the juridical or biological model of the norm, the way it acts can be thought of in two ways: either negatively and restrictively, like the imposition, which is by definition abusive, of a line of division, traversing and controlling, in the form of a domination, an area of spontaneous events the starting points of which are considered to pre-exist this intervention (which, after the event, orders them, by containing them in the way that a form contains a content); or positively and expansively, like an extensive movement which, progressively withdrawing the limits of its domain of action, itself effectively constitutes a field of existence in which norms find their application. And in this last case, one could say that the norm 'produces' the elements on which it acts, at the same time as it elaborates the procedures and the real means of this action – that is to say, it determines their existence by means of the very fact that it undertakes to master them.

When, for example, in a vitally important passage in *La Volonté de savoir* [*VS*] (1st edn, Paris: Gallimard, 1976, pp. 78 ff.), Foucault sets out the technology of confession – which, according to him, is the basis of our *scientia sexualis* – as a ritual for the production of truth, he means that the criteria to which representations of 'sexuality' conform are effective only to the extent that, rather than prising out this truth as though it were already present in an objective reality about sex which it makes known, this technology 'produces' the truth by itself constituting its object; this 'sexuality' which comes into being only in a certain historical type of society (one which, at the same time as it draws out or solicits confessions about sex or its practices, also manufactures that which can be confessed in a way which bears a particular relationship to the unconfessable). An analysis of this nature leads to a 'political history of truth' (*VS*, p. 80), or again to 'the political economy of a will to know' (*ibid.*, p. 98). In fact this process clarifies the notion of a will to knowledge which provides the title of the work: if there is no knowledge [*savoir*] without a 'will' which supports it – obviously this does not mean the will of a subject – this is because the truth discourse it seeks to pronounce cannot be traced back to the neutralised representation of a content of reality which could be said to pre-exist it, but, on the contrary, the same will or the same necessity which produced its object is affirmed, in a form of 'power–knowledge' in which these two aspects, power and knowledge, coincide absolutely.

I wish to open a parenthesis here which I shall in fact close only provisionally. What philosophical conception of truth is initially brought to mind by this notion of a will to knowledge which takes on the form of 'power–knowledge' [*pouvoir–savoir*]? Behind the Nietzschean reference which is too directly obvious here to be sufficient, is it not possible to see a different, more distant reference, which is in fact Spinozist? After all, Foucault is doing no more than explaining that the ideas which we can form of sexuality on the basis of materials assembled by the ritual of confession are not 'like silent paintings in a picture', the precision of which is attested to by their conformity to the object which served as a model, following the pattern of the external relationship of adaptation (Spinoza talks of *convenientia*) which binds the idea to its object [*idéat*]; he suggests that they are *adequate* to the extent that the same order of necessity which also produces the domain of reality, the 'things' which it gives to be known, is affirmed within them and in the movement which brings them into being. And when Spinoza, for his part, insisted on dynamic activity, the true idea of which is at one and the same time the result and the expression, surely he was doing nothing other than relating this truth to a 'will to knowledge' which produces it. Thus when, in an extremely famous formulation, he presented the intellect as a 'spiritual automaton', he had already suggested, through this metaphor of a machine thinking of its own accord, that it would be necessary to relate the genesis of knowledge to a 'technology', which would at the same time be that of a form of knowledge [*savoir*] and a power [*pouvoir*]. This Spinozist reference will be encountered again on a number of occasions during the course of this paper.

I now wish to return to the general aspects of this productive nature of the norm, which involve both power and knowledge in the same process, and then I wish to pursue the consequences of this. From the point of view of this productive nature, to be a subject, that is to say – since for Foucault this latter expression can have no other meaning – to be exposed to the action of a norm, as a subject of knowledge [*savoir*] or as a subject of power, is to be dependent on this action. This is the case not only regarding certain external aspects of behaviour, according to the dividing line between the legitimate and the illicit, but also regarding that which constitutes the actual nature of the thinking and acting subject, who acts only to the extent that he is acted upon, who does not think except to the extent to which he is thought of, by norms and under norms in relation to which his thought and his action can be measured – that is to say, integrated into a global system of evaluation, where they figure as a degree or as an element. Again from this point of view, being a subject is therefore literally to be 'subjected' – not, however, in the sense of submission to an order which is exterior and supposes a relationship of pure domination, but to that of an insertion of individuals, of all individuals without exception and without exclusion, into a homogeneous and continuous network, a normative apparatus, which reproduces them and transforms them into subjects.

Let us take an example which Foucault uses on a number of occasions in his later texts, and which certainly had considerable importance for him: Kant's 1784 treatise on the Enlightenment, where he discerns the first historical occurrence of an essential question which he formulates in complementary ways: 'Who am I now?' 'What is the current field of possible experiences?' These two questions can also be traced back implicitly to the thesis of the productive nature of the norm. Indeed, to situate oneself in relation to norms – to the extent that these define, for a time, a field of possible experiences – is to position oneself as a subject in the context of a normalised society which guarantees the efficacy of its laws. This does not mean in the sense of bowing subjects to the full rigour of these laws in the face of which they would be docile or rebellious according to their dispositions, or according to a principle of autonomy which in their eyes would pre-exist their exposure to the action of the law in question. On the contrary, it would mean the setting up of a domain of subjectivity which would itself be predisposed and inclined to this action. Moreover, one could extend this reading of Kant's text, seeing in it the point of departure, or indeed the effective foundation, of a doctrine of the universality of the law. For subjects produced or reproduced in this way, the law would never appear as a particular prescription, which they would encounter on their way as an indicator or as an obstacle and which would point the way to their destination without taking account of their own spontaneous intentionality; for it would be expressed in universal terms at the very core of their being, in their name, since it is also that which 'gives them a name' – that is to say, that which designates them as subjects and assigns to them norms of action which they have in this respect to recognise as their own.

It can now be said that to be a subject is to 'belong', following a striking formulation which returns in the text of a lecture to the Collège de France, specially dedicated to Kant's treatise on the Enlightenment (according to the unedited version of the lecture published in May 1984 in no. 207 of the *Magazine littéraire*). The question which has already been referred to – 'Who am I now?' – is reformulated here in these terms: 'What then is this present to which I *belong*?' It is the philosopher who asks this question and undertakes to reflect on this belonging. This is the direction followed by his thought: 'The point is to show in what way and how the speaker, as thinker, as scientist, as philosopher, himself *belongs* to this process, and (what is more) how he has a certain role to play in this process where he finds himself both an element and an actor. In short, it seems to me that we can see in Kant's text the appearance of the question of the present as a philosophical event to which the philosopher who is speaking of it *belongs*.' We should be clear about the fact that what is being enunciated here is not only that which specifies the philosopher's own position, but that which constitutes in a general way the actual condition of the subject, the being of the subject, or rather the subject-being: and it is precisely by taking upon himself to enunciate this condition that he positions himself as a philosopher. In these terms, 'being a subject' is to 'belong' – that is, to contribute simultaneously as an element and as an actor in a global process, the unfurling of which defines the current field of possible experiences, and only on the interior of which can be situated the fact of 'being a subject'.

If the subject, thus defined, has a singular aspect, it is not that of an isolated being who is determined uniquely in terms of his relationship to himself – whether this relationship is traced back to a particular concrete identity, that of a 'self' unlike any other, or whether it makes reference to a universal abstract, in the manner of the 'thing which thinks' revealed by the Cartesian Cogito (according to a rational experience which is by definition valid for all subjects which it groups together in the same primordial operation). On the contrary, it is a singularity which becomes apparent or stands out only against a background of belonging, binding the subject, not only to other subjects with whom he communicates, but to the global process which constitutes him as it normalises him, and whence he draws his own being. Later in the lecture to the Collège de France, we read again:

> And for this very reason, it can be seen that for the philosopher to ask the question about *belonging* to this present is by no means any longer to ask the question of his belonging to a doctrine or to a tradition; nor is it any longer the simple question of his belonging to a human community in general, but of his *belonging to a certain 'us'*, to an us which is related to a cultural ensemble characteristic of its own present state. It is this us which is in the process of becoming for the philosopher the object of his own reflection; and in this way is affirmed the impossibility of making the economy of the philosopher's questioning about his own belonging unique to this us. All this, philosophy as the problematisation of a present state, the philosopher questioning *this present state to which he belongs* and in relationship to which he has to situate himself, could well characterise philosophy as the discourse of modernity about modernity.

Now, reading these lines, one cannot avoid wondering if, as Foucault affirms here, this determination of the subject on the basis of the appearance of an 'us' which coincides with the conditions of a current state – that is to say, with the present field of possible experiences – begins to emerge only with Kant, especially since Kant's text which is referred to here, taken literally, seems to be talking about something quite different. Amongst other things it sketches a theory of the enlightened despot, based on the principle according to which man is a being who, in order to 'raise himself', has absolute need of a master. Foucault ignores this theory completely in his interpretation, thus revealing what might be called a symptomatic reading. If one does concede that Kant was the first to ask the question: 'Who am I now?', giving this the meaning: 'What is this us that I belong to?', how can one fail to take into account the reply which he himself gave to this question, a reply which evidently determined the formulation of the question as to whether being a subject is to define oneself in terms of belonging to a human community in general? Now the concept of the human community which appears here is constituted in part by the rationality of its law, both in the moral and juridical sense of the word: it is that which is accomplished in a state of law.

From the perspective adopted by Kant, it is possible to speak of the norm as having a productive nature: in fact the law which binds one to the human community speaks in general from the point of view of the self – one could even say, in the full meaning of this expression, that it makes *me* speak, as stated in Rousseau's formulation which Kant was particularly fond of: 'Conscience, the divine instinct', whence he drew for his own purposes the thesis of the 'moral law in me' – that is to say, within the self. Yet this productive nature remains precisely subjected to the identification of the norm and the law, which is the condition of all my actions: if the law indicates to me what I must do, even before it forbids me to do that which I must not do, the fact remains that its discourse is essentially prescriptive – that is to say, it obliges me as a pure form, and the effectiveness of this is due to the very fact that it is free from all content. Yet this is obviously not the direction in which Foucault himself wished to go. One finds here rather the premisses of the reading of Kant sketched by Lacan in his text *Kant avec Sade*, where he shows that belonging to the law and to the ideal of the community is exactly what the law prescribes, and that this directly defines the desiring subject, at the same time placing his desire under the weight of the law which gives to it alone, as a form, its whole content. It can be seen that expressing the question of the subject in a completely formal way – or, as could be said: in the category of the symbolic – is probably to make the subject the product of the law. This then situates him from the beginning in a relationship of belonging (in relationship to a rational community which is also, paradoxical though this might appear, a desiring community). Yet this is still, at the same time, to take as the unique measure of this productivity the juridical formalism of the law – that is to say, to develop a negative or negating conception of this productivity, which would tend towards nothing less than the establishment of a limit 'within' the subject himself. As such the subject would appear as necessarily thwarted by the law: a divided or split subject, a subject with this lack of being called desire – that is to say, a subject in Lacan's sense of the word. From this point of view, the subject finds his place already set out in a precisely circumscribed domain of legitimacy, from within which he has to maintain and guarantee his identity as a subject.

How can one escape this line of interpretation towards which the Kantian reference seems directly to lead? The answer is perhaps to introduce another philosophical reference to define the notion of belonging such as it constitutes the subject-being. This would be the reference to Spinoza on which I have already drawn, and which might make it possible for us to sketch an outline of modernity which is different from that which can be derived from the Kantian critique. On this point, it is possible to draw support from an indication given by Foucault himself, in *Histoire de la folie* – an indication which, it is true, was not extended to the rest of his work. It occurs in Chapter V of the first part which deals with the insane, where he evokes (1st edn, Paris: Plon, 1961, pp. 174–5) this ethical problematic which underlies all classical thought: 'Classical reason does not encounter the ethical as the outcome of truth, in the form of moral laws; the ethical as the choice against unreason is present from the beginning of all concerted thought. . . . In the classical age, it is reason which originates in the space of the ethical.' In support of this Foucault quotes the *De intellectus emendatione*: 'What then is this nature (the superior nature, the general nature of which is defined by the ethical)? We shall show that it is the knowledge of the union which the thinking soul has with the whole of nature.' Now the notion of belonging, or of union, is no longer defined here in the category of the symbolic but in that of the real. To be a subject, then, is – following a formulation which runs through the whole of Spinoza's work – to position oneself, affirm oneself and recognise oneself as a *pars naturae* – that is to say, as being submitted to the global necessity (and what Spinoza is talking of here is quite the opposite of a constraint) of a whole, of nature itself, of which each of our experiences as subjects is the more or less developed and complete expression.

One can see here, then, the appearance of a modality of belonging which is completely separate from the way belonging is seen according to the Kantian theory of rational law. For though it does make reference to an order, a reference from which it draws its own rationality, this order is not a human order but a natural order; it is not the prescriptive order of men but a necessary order of things which is expressed from the point of view of a nature in face of which there is no man who has the right, or indeed the capability, of positioning himself *tanquam imperium in imperio* – that is to say, risking a translation, 'as a power within a power'. This is why laws of this order, which are the laws of nature itself and not the laws of a human nature, are laws in the physical and not in the juridical sense of the term. Consequently, the relationship of belonging should not be determined in a limiting way, in terms of constraint, but in a positive way; or again, according to the actual terms used by Spinoza, in a causal way: for it is this relationship which constitutes and brings into being that which is affirmed by it and through it. From this point of view, to accede to a higher nature – borrowing the formulation in the *De intellectus emendatione* – is by no means to despoil oneself of one's first nature, in view of what would initially appear in terms of its finitude. It is, on the contrary, to deploy to the maximum all the power which is in it, by means of which it communicates, as a *pars naturae*, with the whole of nature of which it is tendentially the complete expression, since infinity cannot be divided. In the same way that the whole of extendability 'is' in a drop of water, and in the same way that the whole of thought is in the simplest idea, so too the whole of nature is 'in' me, so long as I learn to know myself as belonging to it, by acceding to this ethical knowledge [*savoir*], which is also an ethic of knowledge and which does away with the false alternatives of liberty and necessity.

On the basis of this last consequence it is possible to approach the formulation which is found in the introduction to *L'Usage des plaisirs* (Paris: Gallimard, 1984, p. 15), in which Foucault defines the main concern of his undertaking: 'to find out to what extent the task of thinking about one's own history can liberate thought from that which it thinks silently and make it possible for it to think differently'. To think of one's own history – that is to say, to think of oneself as belonging to a certain type of society in the conditions of an actuality – is to liberate thought from what it thinks without thinking about it, and thus to open for it the way to the only freedom which can have any meaning for it: not that of an illusory 'liberation', which would make it possible for it to experience itself as fully human, but that which allows it 'to think differently', the expression which one could also use to illustrate the *amor intellectualis Dei* of which Spinoza speaks, which, when it comes down to it, means nothing other than this.

Pursuing this reference to Spinoza still further, it is possible to arrive at a new thesis which is perhaps the most important in the thought which Foucault dedicates to the norm and to its action: after the thesis of the productivity of the norm comes the thesis of its immanence.

III

To think in terms of the immanence of the norm is indeed to refrain from considering the action of the norm in a restrictive manner, seeing it as a form of 'repression' formulated in terms of interdiction exercised against a given subject in advance of the performance of this action, thus implying that this subject could, on his own, liberate himself or be liberated from this sort of control: the history of madness, just like that of sexuality, shows that such a 'liberation', far from suppressing the action of norms, on the contrary reinforces it. But one might also wonder if it is enough to denounce the illusions of this anti-repressive discourse in order to escape from them: does one not run the risk of reproducing them on another level, where they cease to be naive but where, though of a more learned nature, they still remain out of step in relation to the content at which they seem to be aiming? Foucault seems to be moving in this direction in the debate he initiates with psychoanalysis in *La Volonté de savoir*:

> There is nothing new in the assertion that sex is not 'repressed'. Psychoanalysts have been saying just this for a long while. They challenged the simple little mechanism which comes readily to mind when there is talk of repression: the idea of a rebellious energy which would have to be strangled seemed to them to be inadequate to describe the way in which power and desire are linked; they consider them to be linked in a more complex and more fundamental way than this interplay between a wild, natural and living energy constantly rising from below and an order from above which seeks to obstruct it; there would be no need to think of desire as being repressed, for the good reason that it is the law which constitutes desire and wanting which brings it into being. The power relation would be present from the moment desire is present: it would be an illusion then to denounce it as a form of repression exercised after the event, but it would be vain also to set off in the search of desire outside power. (*VS*)

Now to present the law as that which constitutes desire is, as we have just seen, to think of the norm as having a productive nature: but it is not enough to analyse the relationship between the law and desire in terms of a causal relationship in which the desire of the subject is identified as an effect of which the order of the law is itself the cause; it is still necessary to analyse the type of causality, transitive or immanent, which is at play in this relationship. It is clear, then, that to explain how norms act effectively and efficiently it is not enough to reduce this action to a determinist model, set up as symmetrical to the discourse of 'liberation', as its mirror-image, inverted and, as a result of the process by which this inversion comes about, identical to it.

> What distinguishes the analysis made in terms of the repression of instincts from the analysis made in terms of the law of desire is certainly the way in which the nature and dynamic of compulsion is perceived; it is not the way in which power is conceived. Both have recourse to a common representation of power which, according to the use made of it and the position granted to it in relation to desire, leads to two opposite consequences: either to the promise of a 'liberation' if power is seen as having only an external hold on desire, or to affirmation if it is seen as being constitutive of desire itself: one is always trapped in advance. (*VS*, p. 109)

To move the argument forward a little faster, we could say that this last formulation, 'one is always trapped in advance' – the law, as a result of its causal nature, always anticipating possible effects – is a formulation which would result only from the affirmation of the productive nature of the norm, taking into account this other aspect of its action, which is its immanent character.

Of what would this thesis of immanence consist? It introduces the following consideration into the relationship which defines the action of the norm: this relationship is not a relationship of succession, linking together separate terms, *pars extra partes*, following the model of a mechanistic determinism; but it supposes the simultaneity, the coincidence, the reciprocal presence to one another of all the elements which it unites. From this point of view it is no longer possible to think of the norm itself in advance of the consequences of its action, as being in some way behind them and independent of them; the norm has to be considered such as it acts precisely in its effects – in such a way, not so as to limit the reality by means of simple conditioning, but in order to confer upon it the maximum amount of reality of which it is capable. In what way would this advance us in relation to preceding analyses?

Returning to the examples with which Foucault dealt, we know already that there is no such thing as sexuality in itself, no more in fact than there can be such a thing as madness in itself – even if the text of *Histoire de la folie* is not always absolutely clear on this point: there is no such thing as brute sex, the truth of which could be demonstrated by means of an originating experience, outside time and outside society, since what we call 'sexuality' is a sociohistorical phenomenon, depending on the objective conditions which 'produce' it. But in order to escape the myth of origins it is not enough to transfer the effective initiation of an action on which the practices of sexuality would depend as consequences into the domain of law and its power. It would also be necessary to understand that there is no norm in itself, there is no pure law, which could be affirmed as such in its formal relationship with itself, and could be affirmed as such in its formal relationship with itself, and could proceed out of itself only to mark its effects negatively by limiting them, or delimiting them. What we learn from the history of sexuality is that there is nothing behind the curtain: no autonomous sexual subject in relation to whom the historical forms of sexuality could be seen as phenomenal manifestations, more or less conforming to its hidden essence; nor is there any law of sexuality, which could artificially create the domain in which it intervenes, directly forcing the subject of this intervention to conform to its rules – a subject which it would thus 'possess', both in the noble and in the trivial sense of this expression. In this respect the norm can be seen to be playing the same trick as that played by reason.

In other words, sexuality is nothing more than the ensemble of historical and social experiences of sexuality, and in order to explain these experiences there is no need for them to be confronted with the reality of a thing in itself, whether this be situated in the law or in the subject to which it is applied, reality which would also be the truth of these experiences. This is the nature of Foucault's positivism: there is no truth other than the phenomenal and there is no need for reference to be made to any law which would anticipate the reality of the facts to which it is applied. This is why the history of sexuality is not a history 'of . . .', in the sense of a study of the transformations of an objective content, subject or law which would itself pre-exist these transformations such that it could be identified through the existence of a subject of sexuality or through that of a law of sexuality. Hence this methodological principle which leads the history of sexuality back to a history of affirmations [*énoncés*] about sexuality, without any subsequent need to link these affirmations to an independent content which they would be able to designate only in real or symbolic terms: in this respect it seems that Foucault definitively renounced a type of hermeneutic process aiming to interpret affirmations [*énoncés*] in order to reveal behind them a meaning – or indeed an absence of meaning – in relation to which they would be at the same time clues and masks. This, then, is a history of affirmations [*énoncés*] about sexuality, or rather affirmations [*énoncés*] of sexuality according to the formulation 'speaking sex' which Foucault takes up regarding the story of the *Bijoux indiscrets*: since there is nothing behind sex to underlie or support its assertions, sex is itself nothing more than the set of its assertions – that is to say, everything it says about itself. This is why the truth of sex is to be found nowhere except in the historical succession of affirmations [*énoncés*] which constitute, in itself alone, the domain of all its experiences.

If the norm is not exterior to its field of application, this is not only because, as we have already shown, it produces it but because it produces itself in it as it produces it. Just as it cannot be said that it acts on a content existing independently of and outside the norm, so too the norm is not in itself independent of its action, though this takes place outside itself, in a form which is necessarily that of division and separation. It is in this sense that it is necessary to talk about the immanence of the norm, in relation to what it produces and the process by which it produces it: that which 'norms' the norm is its action.

What Foucault criticises in psychoanalysis – in which, however, he recognises many other merits – is that in its way it reintroduced the grand myth of origins, relating this to the law itself, constituting it as an unalterable and separate essence: as if the norm had a value in itself, which could be measured by means of interpretation; as if its truth were independent of its effects, these latter playing only a symptomatic role in relation to it.

Thus if the action of the norm fails to meet a field of reality which pre-exists its intervention, it should also be said that it is not itself ordered in advance of this intervention but that it orders its normative function only gradually whilst this is being exercised, this exercise containing the norm at the same time for the subject and for the object. In other terms again, the norm can be thought of only historically, in relationship with the processes which bring it into being. Here, Foucault is clearly following Canguilhem who, in our time, was incontestably the initiator of a new way of looking at norms. In his introduction to the American edition of the *Essai sur quelques problèmes concernant le normal et le pathologique* (text published under the title: 'La vie et la science' in the issue of the *Revue de métaphysique et de morale* dedicated to Canguilhem which appeared in 1985), Foucault expressed his teaching very clearly:

> G. Canguilhem wishes to discover, by means of the elucidation of knowledge about life and concepts which articulate this knowledge, the nature of the concept in life, that is to say of the concept as one of the modes of the information which all living beings draw from their milieu. The fact that man lives in a milieu which has a conceptual architecture does not prove that he has turned away from life through some process of forgetting, or that a historical drama has separated him from it; but only that he sees things in a certain way. . . . Forming concepts is a way of living, not a way of killing life. (pp. 12–13)

To develop the norms of knowledge [*savoir*] – that is, to form concepts, in relationship with the norms of power – is to engage in a process which engenders, as it unfurls, the conditions by which it is authenticated and by which it becomes effective: the necessity of this process is related to nothing less than what Pascal had already referred to in an astonishing formulation as the 'force of life' (cf. the *Récit de la grande expérience de l'équilibre des liqueurs* of 1627, and this passage in the foreword to the reader which precedes it: 'Anyway it is not without regret that I depart from opinions which are so generally accepted [concerning nature's abhorrence of the void]; and I do so only because of the need to give way to the force of life by which I am constrained'). The force of life is what is being dealt with here, inasmuch as this force is not being seen in terms of essences – that is to say, it is not being mythically traced back to the status of a vital force the 'power' of which could be said to pre-exist the set of effects which it produces. If norms act, this is not by virtue of an obscure power which could be seen as being, in a virtual state, in possession of the system of all their possible effects: for the question would then inevitably be asked as to how one might know what legitimises or provides the conditions for such an action, and to reply to this question it would be necessary to have recourse to a transcendental origin of the norm, which would make it possible to anticipate everything it might produce. In opposition to the 'one is already trapped', which presupposes the norm as something which is already there, we have to see the idea according to which the norm, trapping and trapped, is itself nothing other than its trapping of itself in its own trap, which is simultaneously for it a kind of bait and a guarantee of truth. As we have said: there is nothing behind the curtain. And the trick of the norm is not to rely on any manipulative power, since it is itself completely manipulated by its own action.

The norm is therefore not a boundary already laid down, the line of which divides the destiny of man: it was Kant who saw humanity as being at a crossroads, winning liberty by choosing the right road. What is at stake here is the relationship between a nature and a culture. But does this relationship take the form of a division, passing between two orders of heterogeneous facts, or is it a relationship of constitution and exchange, which traces back to the force of life the concern to develop norms and make them recognisable? Here again, the reference to Spinoza can perhaps make things clearer.

It is well known that Spinoza developed a new conception of society, drawing on that of Hobbes but also opposing it at a crucial point. According to Hobbes, the state of society imposes norms – that is to say, laws – with a view to protecting men against themselves, and in particular against the destructive passion, a true death instinct, which haunts men and to which free rein is given in the state of nature; now this regulation of life by norms depends on a rational calculation which, restraining behaviour to within certain limits, contains and constrains men, in a way which aims to 'go beyond' the contradictions of a disordered nature; and the condition of this movement, or going beyond, is a voluntary transfer of power, accepted by all the members of the social body – a transfer which produces a new form of sovereign power, claiming for its own purposes the domination instinct which all men possess, but by turning it against them in the form of an absolute obligation. Here can be seen, in all its purity, the idea of a transcendence of the norm, with all the effects which follow from this: the interplay of divisions and contradictions which could result in Hobbes's work reading like an anticipation, in the classical age, of a sort of psychoanalysis of power.

Spinoza, unlike Hobbes, refuses to set up, between the state of nature and the state of society, this sort of relationship of discontinuity and going beyond. According to him, in society it is still nature which continues to act, exercising the same laws and the same passions, the very ones which cause spiders to fight with one another and which make little fish the food of bigger fish, with no sense of a reversal of direction of these laws, with no sense of their being turned against themselves in order to set up in their place the dialectic of an anti-power. So it is that power is not necessarily defined in terms of domination. It may be that power has historically taken the form of domination; this could well happen, but it is something which is completely accidental; and the type of society which is constituted on the basis of a power of this sort is destabilised by its own principle. To live in a society according to norms is not to substitute a rational right to that of nature – quite the contrary; but it does involve the control and regulation of the same power relations which determine, on the basis of the free and necessary interplay of dispositions, the ensemble of relationships between individuals. From this point of view, the premisses of a political theory are to be found not in the fourth part of the *Ethics* but in the third, where Spinoza sets out, even before the idea of a sovereign power is formulated, this spontaneous socialisation of dispositions which, in order to operate, requires no laws other than those of nature. The question of power is played out by definition, then, on the level of the conflicts of feeling, the development of which it espouses: it is from them that it draws its true power, *potentia*, and not from a new order, *potestas*, which would superimpose on their expression new rules and new grids of behaviour. From this point of view again one could very well read in the third part of the *Ethics* the sketch of a theory of micro-powers. To this should be added that the norms of power which are set up in this way also function, inseparably, as norms of knowledge: by multiplying the relationships between men, and weaving a network of mutual relationships between them which becomes more and more complex, they increase at the same time their ability to form common notions – that is to say, notions, necessarily commonly acquired, which express that which is common to the largest possible number of things. In this way it is the force of life which transforms the individual into a knowing and acting subject.

What is the essential difference between Hobbes and Spinoza? It is the fact that Hobbes's essential preoccupations remained to found a form of political thinking based on anthropology – that is to say, on a theory of human passion – in a way which would make possible the isolation of the fundamental motivation which directs all human actions: thus the fear of death provides a motivation which, turned in upon itself, gives to law its unique principle and provides a foundation for the juridical conception of power. According to Spinoza, to follow a process of this nature is to constitute man '*tanquam imperium in imperio*', by endowing him with a nature which is opposed to nature: that is why he himself did not attempt to base his political thought on a theory of human passions, given that these would restrict, within nature, a truly human order; but he develops, on the contrary, a natural theory of passions in general, showing how all these dispositions, and those of man in particular, are completely immersed in nature whose laws they follow, and of which they are themselves nothing more than various expressions. One might say, then, that the premisses of a political theory are in fact to be sought in the first and last parts of the *Ethics* which set out the conditions for this insertion.

It can be seen, then, how the principle of the immanence of the norm leads to its effects – to all its effects. Contrary to the common notion according to which the power of norms is artificial and arbitrary, this principle reveals the necessary and natural character of this power which is formed by its own action, which produces itself as it produces its effects, tendentially without reservation or limitation – that is, without supposing the negating intervention of transcendence or of division. This is probably what Foucault wished to express when he talked of the positive nature of the norm which is entirely manifest in its action – that is to say, in its phenomena, or again in its affirmations [*énoncés*], without being in any way held back within these, or in any way overhanging them, an absolute of power from which its effectiveness would be drawn, but the full resources of which it would never exhaust. The norm would be positive also to the extent that the way it comes into play could not be traced back to the elementary movement of dividing domains of legitimacy but would consist, on the contrary, in a progressive incorporation and a continual proliferation of its manifestation, the most general form of which would be that of integration.

The norm is seen, then, as both necessary and natural. But it is not possible to break off at this point from the *rapprochement* sketched here with certain aspects of the philosophical works of Spinoza. This hypothesis should be explored fully, and the question should be asked whether it would also lead to the affirmation of the substantiality of the norm – that is to say, to its being seen once more in the massive and global order of things, which would necessarily mean that it would have to be explained from a metaphysical point of view. For Spinoza, the law draws its force from the being of substance: and it would quite obviously be vain to seek in Foucault's work any hint of reasoning of that nature. Up to this point, Spinoza has helped us in our reading of Foucault: but we could also ask ourselves if Foucault does not perhaps help us to read Spinoza, by means of a confrontation which he himself sets up between the theme of substantiality and the nature of history; and it is clear that, in raising this last problem, we are not far either from the questions created in Marx by the status of 'historical materialism', which is a new attempt at thinking about how the historical and the substantial can be thought of together.

four

Michel Foucault and the police state

Blandine Barret-Kriegel

First of all, many thanks to François Ewald for organising this conference on Michel Foucault, whose work is of such immense scope and so much alive. This is not, however, a commemoration. We are not guardians of the temple and there was no religion, just the will to knowledge.

For my part I should like to try to recall how it was that Michel Foucault's thought opened the way to a return to the study of the State and the law. In so doing I am aware that an isolated attempt at this is bound to be at odds with a recently widespread interpretation of his work which challenges its relevance to the political field. We are told that Foucault, as a student of Heidegger and Nietszche and as a critic of the philosophy of the subject, would have been incapable of opening a way to the understanding of democratic States and incapable of reflecting on the rights of man, which are founded on the philosophy of the subject. We are told that his work is fixed at a point which society has already moved beyond, that it was caught up in the petrified schists of the minor catastrophe of the 1960s. In order to demonstrate the error implicit in this sort of interpretation, it would not be sufficient to mention empirical examples – recalling, for example, that the reintegration of law into the field of philosophical reflection was, in part, the work of his friends. It is also necessary to make clear how, in Foucault's work, the return to political law (as it is called today, referring back to the titles of the classics – the subtitle of the *Contrat social* being precisely *Principes du droit politique*) was already under way.

To be brief, I shall try to indicate that this return is signposted in three places: (1) in Foucault's method; (2) in the object which he designated as being at the centre of his theory of biopolitics – that is, the police State; (3) in the intimate relationship between his theory of man as subject and his description of the police State.

Yesterday, in his study of Foucault as a philosopher, François Wahl said – in a way which, for my part, I found convincing – that the archaeological or genealogical methodology of discursive practices is a pragmatic. It is not in fact a question of seeing one theory as being in opposition to another but of combining a view of logic with a view of history. It is not a question of thinking in thought, or positioning oneself amongst objects; but rather, as Foucault explained his position to Derrida regarding the interpretation of Descartes, of thinking in terms of the point where thoughts and their objects border on one another, thinking in terms of the knitting together, the adjunct, the intersection, the regulated interplay of words and things, and thinking of the game itself as a historical relationship. The Chair occupied by Foucault at the Collège de France was called the 'Chair of the history of thought systems'. In order to appreciate the fecundity of a methodology of this nature, and to take stock of the shifts it brought about, we should recall the philosophical weather forecast at the time he began to write. What were the main influences on the philosophical weather, which was still sheltered from the cyclones of the social? What was the wind blowing in, and what was the air pressure? – The object of study, then, was the free and thinking subject, his conscience and his liberty, his commitments and his perceptions, the philosophy of the subject and the phenomenology of his objects. Foucault's method is based on a well-known fact: the wretchedness of phenomenology. It is sometimes said, too hastily, that Foucault was the one who studied the mad, the sick and prisoners. This is what he would have done had he been a phenomenologist. Yet he wrote *Naissance de la clinique*, *Histoire de la folie* and *Surveiller et punir*. He did not collect patients' laments, nor did he capture the confessions of captives or set out to surprise the mad as they went about their tasks; he studied the mechanisms of cure and the mechanisms of punishment. He turned to institutions, he took his bearings from their buildings and their equipment, he sounded out their doctrines and disciplines, he enumerated and catalogued their practices and he published their technologies. In order to complete this shift and to deploy, in a way which goes beyond the world of representation, the epistemic field of this strange object constituting the archaeology of knowledge, he probably needed a line of resistance to oppose. Foucault found this line, and he is quite open about the fact, in the school of French epistemology which had clearly enunciated, with Cavaillès, the programme of a philosophy of the concept which would replace an epistemology of consciousness. This was the French epistemological school of Gaston Bachelard and Georges Canguilhem, which went back, as Georges Canguilhem showed, to the eighteenth century, starting with Fontenelle. It is because Foucault investigated social apparatuses and disciplines with such care and drew up in such detail the functions and the passions of the hospital and the prison that he found himself confronted, at the dark and compromised heart of biopolitics, with what he called the police State. It was the unbending nature of his pursuit of his investigations – as a result of which, instead of contemplating the insane, the prisoner or the poor person like a vase on a table, he preferred to study confinement, to understand imprisonment and to analyse assistance – which led him into the byways of research about the State where one never meets phenomenologists.

What, then, of the police State? In *Machines à guérir*, Foucault defines it as follows:

> The sum of means which need to be put into practice in order to ensure the 'public good' in a way which goes beyond the maintenance of peace and good order is, in general terms, that which in Germany and France is called the 'police'. 'The sum of laws and regulations which concern the interior of a State, which tends to strengthen and increase its power, to make good use of its strengths and to procure the happiness of its subjects' (J. Von Justi). Understood in this way, the police extend their domain beyond that of surveillance and the maintenance of order. They look to the abundance of population ... to the elementary necessities of life and its preservation ... to the activities of individuals ... to the movement of things and people. ... It can be seen that the police force is the whole management of the social body. This term 'body' should not be understood in a simply metaphorical way, for it deals with a complex and multiple materiality ... the police force, as an institutional grouping and as a modality of intervention, takes charge of the physical element of the social body. At the same period attempts were being made to find ways of thinking about the juridical status of the materiality of this civil society.[1]

Population science, public hygiene, education, it is the meeting point of all these disciplines – the point of application of which is the body, henceforth submitted to norms set up in an authoritarian way in the name of knowledge [*savoir*] about punishment and pathology – which Foucault called biopolitics.

At this point, Foucault has often been accused of overvaluing the power of norms in his actual description of the mechanisms of surveillance and punishment, education and administration, and underplaying the value of distribution; and thus to have contributed, alongside the philosophy of the social, to the general deflation of the juridical by showing how, within the police State, the law was only an expression of normalising power. This is certainly true. But his description is sufficient to deal with the reality of the police State. One will not find in Foucault – since this lay outside his field of investigation – the sort of description which one does find with other historians: of the ups and downs by which the French state successively became a State of justice, a State of finance, a police State and later a welfare State. From the observation post of the General Hospital, which was set up in the eighteenth century, Foucault placed himself directly in a position to make a clinical study of the police State; but at least he described this piece of the jigsaw of the State in its entirety, making visible the deployment of public hygiene and medicalisation, assistance and surveillance. Is the law to be seen as occupying a subordinate position? Of course. This is not to say that the police State was not in its way a State of law, yet it is still only an *approximation* to a State of law. To begin with, law in it is divided. It is parcelled into distinct crystals: public law, civil law and the penal law, each following its own destiny; on the very interior of public law and without the knowledge of political law, administrative law extends its ever-increasing influence. Then, the rights of man are challenged and marginalised. The development of the police State in fact coincided, not with a predilection for the rights of man but, as is shown by the example of Tocqueville – see his correspondence with Beaumont so marvellously edited by Michelle Perrot – with the preference for the safety of society. The nineteenth century in Europe, in which vigorous police States sprang into being, was not a good time for the rights of man but a time when the Declaration of Rights, which was not written into the texts of positive law, was the object of almost universal reprobation. Thus, in Foucault's description of law, it was not that he wanted to leave law out of consideration, but rather that he observed the exact forms into which law, as it became norm, metamorphosed.

I am now coming to the central question of the subject, and more precisely to Foucault's theory of man as subject. It seems to me that it would not be without interest to establish that the critique of the theory of man as subject has a necessary link with the description of the police State because, although we do have such theories, the philosophy of the subject is contemporary to the police State. I say deliberately: 'the theory of man as subject', because that is the definition by means of which Michel Foucault enunciated his 'theoretical anti-humanism'. In order to do this it would be necessary to establish, as I have begun to do elsewhere,[2] that the philosophy of the subject is not in any way, as is commonly held, the philosophy which made possible the founding of the doctrine of the rights of man. Given the lack of time, I hope you will excuse me if I give only a few indicators here. It is probably possible to find the Cartesian idea of man as subject, with an entrenched opposition between the *res extensa* and the *res cogitans*, between the soul and the body and, in the human mind, between will and understanding in Grotius, Pufendorf, Burlamaqui – who are considered to be founders of modern political law. This comes about in the division between the state of nature and the civic state, and the way civic life is seen as being formed by an effort of will and the way the creation of rights is seen as coming about by means of a decision of the human subject. But – and it is the criticism which Rousseau directed against them which draws our attention to this point – not the slightest trace of a doctrine of the rights of man can be found amongst the philosophers of the modern school of natural rights. There are those who form doctrines of voluntary servitude and, following on from this, of the legitimacy of slavery through the rights of war and conquest; and there have even been those – the 'black code' not being so far removed from their thinking – who saw themselves as champions of a good colonial conscience. The doctrine of the rights of man in fact supposes another theory of the rights of man than that of man as subject. In the case of the moderns who enunciated it – Hobbes, Spinoza, Locke – it was inseparable, notably in its deduction from the right to safety and the right of appropriation of one's own body, from the setting up of a relationship between man and nature; not in terms of a separation but in terms of the establishment of a relationship. This can be explained as follows: in these three authors, the deduction of the right to safety is put into practice according to the same reasoning: if life is inalienable (as Hobbes sets it out in his famous chapter in *Leviathan*), this is because it is a gift of God or of nature, because it has a transcendent or anthropological dimension, because it concerns the totality of the species even before the particular case of the subject is determined. That is why the *natural right*, which is the power of the individual, has to be distinguished from the *natural law*, which is the obligation to persevere in one's life or, as Hobbes says, 'a rule discovered by reason which forbids people from doing that which leads to the destruction of their life'. It is impossible to found the rights of man outside nature, bypassing the natural law. The theory of man as subject, with a distanced, separate nature, with the whole notion of right and laws being located in human reason and the whole principle of society being situated in an act of calculation and of will, can found a doctrine of civil rights and fit in with an administrative State, but it cannot be made to fit in with the rights of man. In the philosophy of the subject, in fact, the subject has no relationship with nature except through the intermediary of his understanding. In the first instance he is pure thought, a thing that thinks. In the same way, he is not in the first instance a nature amongst natures, a body amongst bodies. It is of less fundamental interest for the subject to appropriate his own body than to broaden his free determinations. The body is not an object of appropriation for the individual but the point of application of the management and the administration of the good police by means of the understanding of the subject.

I should like to enter a different field and point out that the long, winding destiny of the Declaration of the Rights of Man, proclaimed in 1789, finally accepted in 1946 and enforced only in 1971, and the fact that the right to security is still guaranteed only to a very poor extent on the penal level, have coexisted perfectly with the importance attached to the subject which has characterised, following on from France, a large part of continental Europe. In the nineteenth century in fact, with the growth of police States, the body was not an object of individual appropriation, not the privileged object of civil law, but the place of predilection for the mastery and possession of the 'police'. Instead of a State of justice and the constitution of a common right guaranteeing the rights of individuals and instituting safety, equality and liberty, we have come to know the police State and biopolitics.

This is why it seems to me that Michel Foucault, who thought not in terms of progress and development but in terms of identity and of different systems, none the less loosened the knot which was strangling the possibility of a return to the history of our political development, designating this relationship which is central to the history of French politics: the joint presence of the theory of man as subject and the police State.

NOTES

1. Michel Foucault *et al.*, *Les Machines à guérir (aux origines de l'hôpital moderne)*, Dossiers et documents d'architecture, Institut de l'Environnement, CERFI-DGRST, 1975.
2. Blandine Barret-Kriegel, 'Les droits de l'homme et le droit naturel', *Mélanges Maurice Duverger*, Paris: PUF, 1988.

SUMMARY OF DISCUSSIONS

Raymond Bellour pointed out that one could find in the concept of pity, such as it was formulated in Jean-Jacques Rousseau or in Roland Barthes in *La Chambre claire*, a way of thinking about human rights which would not be reducible to the norm of the subject.

Pasquale Pasquino maintained that in modern political thought, the theory of the police State is not opposed to the tradition of the rights of man (Hobbes, Locke, Rousseau). These two forms of thought are linked. Mirabeau the elder, for example, used the word 'civilisation' as a synonym for 'police'. The human-rights tradition came into being within the practice which consisted in 'policing individuals'. The police State produces disciplined individuals to whom rights can be attributed. Hobbes, in *Leviathan*, says that men are political beings. The French translation says '*par artifice*', where the Latin text is '*ex disciplina*'. This indicates that Hobbes is aware that discipline is necessary for the individual to be a subject with rights.

Blandine Barret-Kriegel confirmed that there is a link between the doctrine of the good police and civilisation such as one finds it in Voltaire's *Essai sur les mœurs* or Gibbons' *Decline and Fall of the Roman Empire*. Civilisation is opposed to barbarism in a way which takes the form of a radical split in human history. But this doctrine of policing and civilisation does not make the foundation of human rights possible, because the first human right, the right to life, can be founded only in the framework of a deduction which concerns human nature (and therefore does not tolerate a split between barbarism and civilisation).

Blandine Barret-Kriegel added that no critique of the rights of man is to be found in Foucault. Foucault produces a striking description of the proliferation of the power of the norm. This could be taken as a lowering in status of the juridical. What he is doing is describing observable positive elements, which does not amount to a critique of law. Foucault is not a critic of law, but a describer of law.

Jacques-Alain Miller wanted to see the mention of the rights of man lead to reflection on Foucault's *values*. He recalled the question which Habermas put to Foucault: Foucault refuses to accept the universal. And yet he is committed. In the name of what is he committed? He indicated that a reply to this question could be found by adding to the lines of subjectification which Deleuze speaks of as the idea of lines of valuing, which would crystallise about certain values at certain moments, in a transitory and precarious way, on certain values; or, using Pierre Macherey's Spinozism, one could talk about an ethic without ideal. But, Jacques-Alain Miller continued, in order to reply to the Frankfurt School it would be necessary to bear in mind the fact that they are Germans. Germans, having known Hitler, are sensitive to everything which attacks the philosophy of the universal. They fear, in fact, that this might make possible the re-emergence of the same sort of phenomenon. But it could be said that the cult of the universal professed by Habermas authorises no spirit of revolt. The notion of 'obedience to the King of Prussia' of which Kant speaks in *Was ist Aufklärung?* does not favour a spirit of revolt. What is at issue is the properly totalitarian value of conformism, even if this is the conformism of the universal.

Catherine von Bülow recalled that for Foucault the question of the rights of man was in the first instance that of the responsibility of one individual in the face of another. The rights of man are not so much rights to . . . as duties in the face of the suffering of others, duties which appeal directly to the subject in advance of any form of analysis.

Étienne Balibar noted (1) that as he engaged in his critique of the repressive hypothesis, Foucault attempted to stand aside from the unitary conception of the State set up by both those who resist and those who dominate. He did so by introducing the notion of the duality of the right and of the norm: the right is not the expression of norms, and norms are not the expression of rights; (2) in Foucault, it is always bodies which resist, but this resistance does not tend towards a right to life; (3) *La Volonté de savoir* criticises the idea of the originating interdependence of liberty and truth. In this, Foucault wished to deprive the spiritual of any ideal nature, though not of its intellectuality.

five

On Foucault's uses of the notion 'biopower'

Michael Donnelly

Michel Foucault came only late in his career to the notion of 'biopower'; it serves none the less as a useful rubric for assembling a number of his long-standing concerns. In *La Volonté de savoir*, he describes 'two poles of development' in the exercise of power over life, 'linked together by a whole intermediate cluster of relations':

> One of these poles ... centered on the body as a machine: its disciplining, the optimization of its capabilities, the extortion of its forces, the parallel increase of its usefulness and its docility, its integration into systems of efficient and economic controls, all this was ensured by the procedures of power that characterized the *disciplines*: an *anatomo-politics of the human body*.[1]

These are topics of which *Surveiller et punir* provides an exemplary case study, as well as a sketch of the proliferation of disciplinary power.

The second pole of biopower, Foucault continues:

> formed somewhat later, focussed on the species-body, the body imbued with the mechanics of life and serving as the basis of the biological processes: propagation, births and mortality, the level of health, life expectancy and longevity, with all the conditions that can cause these to vary. Their supervision was effected through an entire series of interventions and *regulatory controls: a biopolitics of the population.*[2]

About such regulatory controls Foucault wrote comparatively little. But the problem of population in this large sense directly informs his project for the history of sexuality (as this was originally conceived); indeed, population is 'the background that enables us to understand the importance assumed by sex as a political issue'.[3] Similarly, it is the population or species-body, emerging as a field of intervention and then as the ultimate end of government, which leads Foucault to conceptualise that new cluster of power relations, beyond the juridical framework of sovereignty, which he describes as the 'governmentalisation of the State'.[4]

I want to examine and assess here, in an appreciative but critical spirit, the role that this recurrent notion of 'biopower' plays in Foucault's arguments. My purpose is less to offer an interpretation of Foucault than to try to reformulate certain of his concepts, to make them at once more analytically adequate and more accessible to historians and social scientists. What I shall argue is that Foucault deploys the notion of biopower in an importantly ambiguous way: he is concerned first, to investigate the constitution and emergence of discrete mechanisms of biopower; but he tries at the same time, secondly, to describe long-term, or indeed *epochal*, trends to which these particular mechanisms of power may contribute, but of which they are at most individual expressions. The distinction I wish to draw here is between, on the one hand, the specific mechanisms and tactics of biopower (operating at both the poles Foucault describes, on individual bodies and on populations) and on the other hand, the long-term effects on society of the whole ensemble of those mechanisms and tactics. To put the distinction in other terms: certain formulations in Foucault's texts refer to particular targets of biopower in delimited time periods; these can be called 'genealogical'. Other formulations summarise long periods and refer to effects of biopower on 'society' – to orderly, enduring, 'programmed' consequences which follow from the application, according to strategic calculations, of biopower; these can be called 'epochal'. The ambiguity arises when Foucault (for reasons I cannot investigate here) elides these differences of focus; he seems then to conflate two distinguishable levels of analysis – to run together the genealogical and the epochal. My point is simply that these levels can and should be considered separately, and that this is a valuable way of presenting to social scientific audiences the more analytical part of Foucault's work – the genealogical part – in a clearer, more attractive light.

Surveiller et punir offers a clear illustration of the 'genealogical' and the 'epochal' styles of argumentation, and of their problematic combination. The text is ostensibly focused, as the subtitle indicates, on the 'birth of the prison' in the early nineteenth century; but in two respects it moves far away from its specifically historical burden. (1) Foucault self-consciously presents the text as an intervention into 'a field of [present-day] power relations and political struggle', what he calls 'the overall political issue around the prison'.[5] (2) The account of the birth of the prison is rapidly succeeded by a sketch of the later diffusion of disciplinary mechanisms beyond the walls of the penitentiary into society at large. The focus of the text accordingly shifts away from the historical account to what Foucault calls 'carceral society', the label he finds appropriate to describe the succeeding period. On both counts Foucault characterises these moves away from the properly historical sections of the text as 'writing the history of the present', on the understanding that 'present' refers not simply to the chronological present, but to the epoch of modernity. The claim involved here, which connects the different parts of the text, is that the historical account focused on the birth of the prison represents more broadly and more significantly a historical threshold with which the modern era begins, and whose essential character it somehow contains or announces. Hence Foucault's slide from discussing the birth of the prison to discussing 'the birth of the modern soul and of a new power to judge'.

In the design of the text it is essential that the genealogical and the epochal accounts fit together. There is none the less a remarkable difference in the procedures which carry the two streams of argument. The genealogical account is descriptive and conjunctural. It avoids large-scale causal explanation, and instead reconstructs a set of the discrete elements, developing with their different 'times' and dynamics, which come together in the conjuncture. Thus in a characteristic passage Foucault writes that:

> The 'invention' of this new political anatomy must not be seen as a sudden discovery. It is rather a multiplicity of often minor processes, of different origin and scattered location, which overlap, repeat, or imitate one another, support one another, distinguish themselves from one another according to their domain of application, converge and gradually produce the blueprint of a general method.[6]

The virtue of Foucault's genealogies is that he tries to represent the complexity and contingency of such developments; as a result the accounts are burdened with historical detail and necessarily localised in character. They evince something of how Foucault describes the approach of genealogy: grey, meticulous, patiently documentary.

By contrast, when Foucault leaves behind the historical conjuncture that was the birth of the prison, his writing becomes highly rarefied. The disciplinary techniques whose historical constitution he has tried to document are formalised into a general 'diagram' ('panopticism'), emptied of specific contents or context. Discipline thus becomes 'a figure of political technology that may and must be detached from any specific use'; 'it is a schema . . . destined to spread throughout the social body, [which] programmes, at the level of an elementary and easily transferable mechanism, the basic functioning of a society penetrated through and through with disciplinary mechanisms'.[7] The way in which these statements are phrased is a telling indication of the way the points are argued. From his historical account of the early penitentiary Foucault leaps forward to an evocation of contemporary 'carceral' society: 'Is it surprising that prisons resemble factories, schools, barracks, hospitals, which all resemble prisons?'[8]

What is striking here is the suspension of those patient and nominalist procedures which characterise genealogy, and which should guard against prematurely subsuming phenomena under overly general categories. Genealogies typically work forward in time, tracing how various practices come to be cobbled together to produce new ones. Here instead Foucault's standpoint is the chronological present; he retrospectively surveys prior decades and chooses a general label to characterise the movement and trend of history toward its fulfilment in the present. Even if 'carceral society' were serviceable or acceptable as a rough label, what was 'destined' to happen explains nothing about how it actually happened. What Foucault fails to address is how the disciplines, once constituted, were perpetuated; how particular disciplines were co-ordinated, one with another, to 'produce the blueprint of a general method'; or how the basic mechanisms and conditions of existence of carceral society were secured. These are all problems of a different order from accounting for how earlier practices were cobbled together into disciplines, or how disciplinary practices were installed in a particular institutional setting like the penitentiary.

The weakness of the 'epochal' approach is that it lapses into a crude periodisation by dichotomy, contrasting the pre-modern with the modern epoch and flattening out historical developments in the meantime. Periodisation has appropriate and necessary analytical functions; it can be wielded as an innovative and critical instrument, as Foucault demonstrated effectively in *Les Mots et les Choses*. The difficulty in *Surveiller et punir* is that Foucault circumvents a properly historical explanation as he transforms his genealogical account of disciplinary mechanisms into a 'diagram' for the functioning of carceral society. It is as if the two emblematic images (the execution of Damiens in 1757 and the timetable of a reformatory in 1837) which introduce the text could suffice, and the reformatory timetable could provide an adequate representation and model of the dynamics of disciplinary society.

I am not raising here the complaint sometimes made by historians: that Foucault oversimplifies history and hastily reduces its empirical complexity and variety to idealised schemata. Foucault was not a social historian; and *Surveiller et punir* is plainly not intended as a monograph on the early period of the penitentiary. His purposes were different. For the genealogical project the notion of panopticism is a legitimate and useful conception – in so far as Foucault deploys it to make intelligible actual practices. The difficulty arises, in my view, when he generalises the notion and empties it of all specific context. Panopticism may usefully suggest something of the general character of the 'new political anatomy of the body social'; but as it emerges from Foucault's historical reconstruction it can at most prefigure what that new political anatomy has actually come to be. The diagram of generalised discipline can in itself indicate nothing of the conditions of existence of the modern epoch; nor can it in any determinate sense be considered constitutive of that epoch.

The problem which these remarks in sum signal is an unbridged gap between Foucault's genealogical and epochal arguments; hence the ambiguity which arises from his sliding from one to the other. The genealogical investigations are by their nature historically specific, localised, detailed. The epochal conception describes global results of the disciplines, once they are assumed, as Foucault says, to programme 'the basic functioning of a society penetrated through and through with disciplinary mechanisms'. Between the historical emergence of disciplinary techniques and their eventual concatenated effects in carceral society, Foucault establishes no compelling connection. He does not successfully address the question of how carceral society emerged; he does not successfully carry through his genealogical-style arguments into the present, but allows weaker, epochal arguments to take their place. My point, in conclusion, is to endorse Foucault's genealogical approach as better fitted to broach the problem he has so tellingly laid out.

NOTES

1. Michel Foucault, *'Histoire de la sexualité*, I, *La Volonté de savoir*, Paris: Gallimard, 1976, pp. 182–3 (English translation (ET): *The History of Sexuality I: An introduction*, transl. Robert Hurley, New York: Pantheon, 1978, p. 139).
2. *Ibid*., p. 183 (ET: p. 139).
3. *Ibid*., p. 191 (ET: p. 145).
4. Michel Foucault, 'Governmentality', transcript of a lecture published in *Ideology and Consciousness*, no. 6, 1979.
5. Michel Foucault, *Surveiller et punir*, Paris: Gallimard, 1975, p. 313 (ET: *Discipline and Punish: The birth of the prison*, transl. A. Sheridan, London: Allen Lane, 1977, pp. 31, 306).
6. *Ibid*., p. 140 (ET: p. 138).
7. *Ibid*., p. 210 (ET: pp. 205–7).
8. *Ibid*., p. 229 (ET: p. 228).

six

Foucault and the liberal view of the individual

Alessandro Pizzorno

The liberal view opposes power to freedom. The nature of power is assumed to be potentially absolute and potentially arbitrary. Political and legal institutions are here to limit it and protect the individual members of a political community against the dangers of absoluteness and arbitrariness – that is, against the danger that one or more individuals might be able to use power for their own ends in an unlimited and unpredictable way. It follows that power is essentially conceived of as exercised by individuals over other individuals.

'Individual', in the liberal view, is a primitive term. It is, indeed, posed as the only observable reality we can refer to when we describe society. Individuals are there all the time, each identical to himself in time, with their wills and their decisions. Power can be applied to constrain their decisions. When such a constraint is not applied, the individual is socially free. He can then choose according to the judgement he gives of what the outcome of his action will be. The judgement he gives now about the advantages or disadvantages of pursuing certain ends is considered to hold when those ends are attained because the individual, in the liberal view, is assumed to be a durable unit of action, holding the same criteria of judgement, the same preferences – or, at least, some general metapreference – over time. Similarly, the individual bears the consequences of his past actions, for which he can be punished or rewarded. This makes him a *responsible* subject of rights and duties.

The individual in the liberal view is therefore a unit, continuous in time, possessing a personal identity that nobody normally questions (i.e. everybody takes for granted) and through which past and future actions appear to be linked together. These actions receive meaning by being imputed, logically as well as morally and legally, to that particular subject. In other words, being willed by a particular subject makes those actions comprehensible to an external observer, who will link them to some intention, or other process of choice; and makes them also possible objects of sanction. As a consequence, society must be conceived of as a population of preconstructed, prelabelled individuals, each a bearer of interests that he will seek to enhance. It is to such a 'will' to enhance interests that freedom or constraint can then be applied.

Foucault defines slightly differently the view of power that he makes the target of his polemics. He calls it the 'juridico-discursive' view, and sees it constituted by two main ideas: one, that power expresses itself only through constraints and operates by preventing rather than enacting; the other, that the 'truth of discourse' can gain us freedom from power. It is true that both these ideas are typically associated with the liberal view, but they are linked only tortuously to that idea of the nature of the individual with whom the liberal conception of power and of freedom is called to stand or fall.

As such, the conception that power is merely negative, a force which operates only by coercing, is therefore not held so universally as Foucault's polemics makes it out to be. Indeed, no one in his right mind would deny that the exercise of power can determine people to act, induce them to act – promote, rather than simply prevent, action. One would consider similarly uncontentious the views that power is what allows the *stabilisation of the superiority* of certain individuals over others, and that this process is to be found at work in every knot and tie of the social network, not just in some central place from which it would then descend by hierarchy.

Much more distant from the notions of the usual intellectual and political debate about power and freedom, much more apt at taking the reader by surprise, is instead the idea that power *makes, produces the individual* (*Surveiller et punir*, p. 172).

> The individual is not to be conceived as a sort of elementary nucleus, a primitive atom, a multiple and inert material on which power comes to fasten or against which it happens to strike. . . . In fact, it is already one of the prime effects of power that certain bodies, certain gestures, certain discourses, certain desires, come to be identified and constituted as individuals. The individual, that is, is not the *vis-à-vis* of power; it is, I believe, one of its prime effects. (*Power/Knowledge*, p. 98)

This is the essential and original point in Foucault's conception of power. More importantly, it is the point in Foucault's conception of the individual from which the main interpretative applications derive. How can one proceed to make sense of it? First, the idea that the individual is a subject of action, continuous and identical to himself, has to be abandoned, together with the idea that the individual is a primitive term, a 'given', that both the actors dealing with him and the scientific observer studying him should take for granted. Instead the individual must be conceived of as a construction power makes up out of a series of acts and events that would not necessarily possess any unity of meaning were it not for the meaning power introduces into them. This I propose to discuss as the radical view behind Foucault's analysis of situations of power. It represents, I think, a more fundamental challenge to the liberal view than the Marxian and Weberian conceptions. True, for both Marx and Weber power has structural foundations and is seen as emanating not from the will of some individual but from the logic of the relations of production, or from the functional needs of organisations in general. But the 'sufferer' of power, for Marx and for Weber, is the individual as such, who is prevented by the working of such structural power from developing in ways that would otherwise have been open to him. Even if they do not define the object of constraint as being some 'free will' of the individual, or imagine any pre-constructed individual to exist before or outside the relations of production or the iron cage of bureaucracy, both Marx and Weber (the latter perhaps less clearly so) need to posit the image of an individual who is endowed with clearly identifiable 'true' interests – that is, interests, valid and understandable only in the long run. If the notion of 'false consciousness' can be used to explain the actual behaviour of the worker within the capitalist system, this is because a 'true consciousness', some true interest, can be assumed to constitute the real identity of the individual who is subjected to power. Similarly, if the individual can be described as caged within the bars of bureaucracy, this is because some 'authentic' nature can be attributed to him which, were it not for those bars, would lead him somewhere in freedom.

I have shown that Foucault is able to draw a different picture of the operations of power because he works with a different concept of the individual. To understand how he proceeds, we need to go back to a principle of the 'archaeological' method according to which the original material of historical and social analysis is nothing but a population of acts and events. These events are put on the table, as it were, in their naked form, without accepting the forms within which they have been structured by the observers seeking to establish some *'continuité irréfléchie'* (*Power/Knowledge*, p. 36).

> We should question these ready-made syntheses, these groupings which we normally allow without looking closely at them, these connections whose validity is accepted before in advance . . . and rather . . . accept that, in the first instance, we are dealing with nothing more than a population of dispersed events. (*Power/Knowledge*, p. 32)

Here Foucault is not referring explicitly to the notion of the individual. He is dealing with the more general methodological problem of how to describe in a meaningful way the patterns and regularities emerging out of a population of observations or, more precisely, out of a population of documents, accounts, interpretations. But surely the concept of the individual is one of those *continuités irréfléchies* that need to be dissolved if sense is to be made of a certain population of events. 'Making historical analysis the discourse of the continuous and making human consciousness the original subject of all historical development and all action are the two sides of the same system of thought.' (*L'Archéologie du Savoir*, p. 22) The answer to the crucial question 'how is it that one particular affirmation [*énoncé*] comes into being rather than another which could have stood in its place?' cannot therefore be found in merely identifying the individual and his intention behind the statement or the act. It has to be found in the network of links with other statements and events in which that particular statement can be placed.

The notion of the individual human being therefore loses its privileged epistemological status. It is a construct like the others that are needed to make sense of acts and events that reach us like atoms and are to be pieced together and assigned to meaningful series. Personal identities are one among other series. They emerge in a battlefield, which means that differentiation and opposition are the main features of the process through which they receive a recognisable form. Without something or somebody opposing us, we would not be able to trace the boundaries of ourselves.

Some rather heavy consequences follow from this methodological view. One of these bears on the notion of freedom. The subject of freedom can no longer be identified with the individual bearer of interests and pursuer of ends; the 'responsible' individual of the liberal view. Rather, what stands opposed to power and ends up either free or subjected (normalised) are acts, gestures, states of mind and of body. Among them is to be found the recalcitrant, resistant, unyielding material that normalising power may fail to reduce. One will know that freedom is alive not when the interests emerging in a society are allowed to express themselves, be represented and be pursued; not even when dissent and heresy are allowed to manifest themselves; not merely when arbitrary decisions are solidly checked; but, rather, when contestation, unruliness, indocility, intractability are not yet abolished, when the recalcitrant is not transformed into the dutiful.

A second consequence is that the 'self' can become an instrument of power, a tool actively working at reducing its own recalcitrance, resistance, unpredictability, and at obtaining its own docility. Indeed, *self-discipline* seems to be the most efficacious technique of power in modern society.

I have reduced Foucault's positions on freedom and power to their extreme consequences. Foucault himself was not so much interested in making these logic passages explicit as in describing the genealogy of power and its manifestations. As for freedom, he never completely gauged the distance which separated his own notion from the one expounded in the liberal and commonsense view; so that his critics felt justified in criticising the former with arguments that should have been trusted only if applied to the latter. But since one cannot escape now, after so much criticism and misunderstanding, from making the opposition clear, let us look at it again sharply, in order to draw from it both its epistemological and ethical consequences.

On the one side, the liberal view. The individual counts for one and constitutes the ultimate observable reality. He can be free from or subject to power according to whether or not access to the representation and pursuit of his interests is possible. Self-discipline does not make the individual subject to anything – on the contrary, it strengthens his interior resources which can make his freedom real. Moreover, the search for truth operates to expand freedom, because the critique of power helps to limit it.

On the other side is the view that the individual as such, as a durable identifiable reality with his own interests and values, is merely a product of the power relations that happen to be dominant in a certain society, in a certain period. The institutions of society operate by forming individuals – that is, series of acts and gestures linked together in personal identies for the convenience of social life. Power is the force, within social institutions, which operates to this effect. Discipline is a particular technique of power whose effect is to help make it durable, diffuse and reproducible. Self-discipline is one instance of these techniques of power.

Taken in its naked coherence, this last position appears totally alien to the way the concepts of power and freedom have been used in the European political and ideological languages for a long time. It also appears self-defeating – if not logically, at least morally and politically. Freedom, in fact, comes out merely as a temporary possibility, the forces struggling in its name either doomed to be defeated or, should they finally succeed, bound to abolish freedom in the very construction of what was meant to be a new free order. And indeed, a free social order cannot in this view be easily conceived, since by definition order will be achieved only as an effect of the good working of the forces of normalisation and reduction of unruliness – i.e. of the working of power. Individuals or movements, it seems, can be free only 'against'.

Even if Foucault had not set down his position so openly, we are entitled to perform this operation ourselves because all its premisses are contained in his work. And the meaning of so doing, paradoxically, is not to criticise Foucault, in spite of the apparently absurd conclusion to which his position has been brought, but rather to lay the ground for a keener understanding of phenomena that the traditional liberal conception leaves completely unexplored and substantially uninterpretable.

The fighters for freedom, from the times of the absolute State to the times of the totalitarian State, needed to live in a situation of theoretical naivety as to humankind's real relations to power. Unfortunately, we know better. We know that human beings can willingly submit to power, even to absolute or totalitarian power. They can even be made to love the hand that subjugates them. We know that ever-new techniques are devised and applied which lead unwary individuals to modify their preferences and their values so that these may accommodate the needs of the State, of some organisation, of some social institution, or of other sources of social and political power. We know that such types of process start within the family and somehow never cease during the life of the individual. We know that the administrations of liberal-democratic regimes multiply the instructions and prescriptions that render their citizens more reliable, controllable, predictable. This does not mean that, as a consequence, they have become more equal, but simply that they are better prepared to find it convenient to trade private idiosyncrasy for public normality.

Traditionally, democratic theory concentrates on questions like freedom of expression, representation of interests, balance of power. All these, in a liberal-democratic regime, seem well-established acquisitions. The constitutional debate is circumscribed to questions of application, efficiency, consistency. But consider the current state of the freedom of expression. The noise of everything that is freely expressed is such that the expression of any single voice is completely stifled. One does not need to follow Foucault in his demonstrations that the very terms and categories in which the free expression of opinions takes shape are patterned according to the needs of some pre-existing powerful social requirements. It suffices to be aware of the disheartening circumstance that the efficacy of the communication of the opinions that could be voiced tends to fall close to zero with the expansion of the number of voices. This is a category of events of which a more articulated analysis should be attempted, with conceptual tools different from those Foucault provides and this is not the right place. But this mention is just to note the irrelevance, once more, of the traditional liberal notions of power and freedom.

Free access to representation of interests, also, becomes an irrelevant notion when one crosses the limited boundaries of the political market and enters into the more densely populated territory of the daily pursuit of happiness and recognition. Here the paths of everyone's freedom are tightly defined by the dutiful accomplishment of those administrative, fiscal, financial, consumption requirements whose observance allows the big social machine of co-operation and the small social machines of mutual recognition to run smoothly and reproduce themselves.

As for the constitutional mechanisms of checks and balances, they apply to the interaction of institutional powers between them, not to the conditions that make individuals adapt to institutions.

It will be easy to conclude that the liberal notion of the free individual fails to address the questions whose weight members of contemporary societies dimly or clearly seem to have become aware of. We know that in liberal-democratic regimes power as defined by the liberals is, by and large, checked;

that freedom according to the liberal is, by and large, secured. But when we unexpectedly discover some source of powerlessness of the individual within contemporary institutions – or some voice, like Foucault's, spells it out for us – we find ourselves with a deficiency of shared concepts and intellectual tools to illuminate our condition.

Foucault's voice was interrupted before he could complete the discourse on the modern meaning of power and freedom. It can even be argued that he did not wish to complete the last part of the story. Like so many social thinkers before him, when he came too close to an explicit definition of the condition of his contemporaries, he turned to the social analysis of a distant epoch. After the *Division of Labour* and *Suicide*, Durkheim preferred the analysis of primitive religion. After the *Protestant Ethic*, Weber started his *tour de force* around the religions of the world. Foucault not only shifted the epoch, but somehow reversed the object of analysis. In the Greeks he sought to uncover the techniques that make self-discipline an autonomous mechanism, that allow the subjective constitution of the subject. He probably felt the need to turn away from the too-close targets which had haunted him during his research on the genealogy of the modern system of power. The idea that the central authority of the modern State was the essential force behind the working of power was one of these targets. Another was to be found in the idea that everything could be derived from some model of class domination. He hit both these targets, despite lacunae and deficiencies in his analysis. His research was more easily and definitely successful in discrediting the humanitarian and reformist interpretations of the modern changes in the modes of punishment, and of social control in general. But Foucault kept all these targets – Marxist, neo-liberal, reformist – too close when he was interpreting the meaning of his discoveries. He was probably distracted by a Parisian environment where ideologico-scientific myths tend to survive when they have long since been dismissed elsewhere, and those who do not accept them feel obliged to struggle with them.

He was distracted, for instance, from a theme which could emerge neatly from his research if only he had focused more on it: the hypothesis that modern liberal-democratic regimes are made possible only by a previous long-lasting process of 'disciplining' their citizens. The notions of hypothesis, causal explanation, research theory, were certainly alien to Foucault's method, which aimed exclusively at describing theoretical emergences. On the other side, we cannot avoid the feeling that if one outstanding contribution should be singled out in Foucault's research, on which further research can be continued, this is constituted by a new understanding of the formation of the *modern disciplined man*.

Consider Foucault for a moment against the background of Weber, whose work can also be seen, in its central core, as being devoted to an understanding of the constitution of the modern disciplined man. For both Weber and Foucault, discipline operates as an inner force, a mechanism of the soul. But by placing all its emphasis on the initial step of the emergence of a vocation, Weber finds himself deprived of specific concepts to deal with the expansion of all the disciplined behaviour outside the effects of some vocation. His insight is good for a (partial) understanding of the self-disciplined behaviour that can be placed at the origin of capitalist accumulation. But there is no explicit micro-theory to understand the process creating the conditions for the disciplined behaviour typical of the bureaucratic society – except, maybe, the rather undeveloped and generic concept of routinisation. The idea of the separation of the person from the office was a good beginning. Weber could have understood it as a case of the more general analytical procedures that characterise modern forms of power. He would then have made a first step on to a path along which Foucault has more daringly advanced.

Another question that is raised by interpreting Foucault's work as centred on the formation of the modern disciplined individual relates to the connection established between population density and analytical techniques of power. Here Foucault is rather to be located on some line originating with Durkheim, who had posited what he called 'moral density' as the prime mover in the mechanism leading to the division of labour. Here again Foucault daringly advances on what Durkheim only sketchily anticipated. The division of labour is an analytical mechanism applied to a population of individuals. Foucault sees the analytical mechanisms of power operating, as it were, 'intra-individually', on a population of acts, gestures, bodily articulation and mental classifications. The effect is not only to reabsorb within a general interpretative scheme the demographic phenomenon – and, in particular, the unprecedented population growths of the classical European age – but to gain a series of interpreting devices linking macro- with micro-explanations.

Foucault's advances in traditional domain therefore appear mainly linked to his working with the notion of an individual taken not as a primitive term but as the product of social techniques of power. And his interpretations of the nature of the modern transformation show how this analytical constitution of the individual could become transparent to us as an effect of the analytical re-ordering being continuously performed by the power-knowledge institutions of modern society.

4 ETHICS AND THE SUBJECT

one

Foucault: the ethic and the work

John Rajchman

A PHILOSOPHER IN SPITE OF HIMSELF

I am not convinced that Foucault always wanted to see himself as a philospher. In 1976, in an interview with Marxist geographers, he declared: '... philosophy, since Descartes in any case, has always been linked in the Western world with the problem of knowledge. There is no getting away from it. ... It is no good my saying that I am not a philosopher; if, when it comes down to it, I am dealing with truth, I am a philosopher whether I like it or not.'[1] Hence the question: is Foucault a philosopher in spite of himself?

I think that Foucault's desire not to call himself a philosopher, to maintain this distance from himself as a philosopher, was part of the way he practised thought. In other words, his relationship with 'tradition' was not a relationship of identification but was always an open question, a question of *practice*. He did not conceive of his own work, nor of that of his predecessors, as a homogeneous whole with eternal or fixed boundaries; rather he sought discontinuities, fissures, contingencies and re-elaborations in what presented itself as tradition. The 'problem of knowledge' [*connaissance*] was not always put in the same way; and the various ways of posing this problem also have a history. The point is not so much to give a definitive reply to this question as to reshape and constantly reinvent it. As Blanchot says, Foucault was always a 'man on the march'.[2]

The diversity of the 'we', of those of us who are discussing him together, indicates the diverse nature of Foucault's relationship with philosophy. We each have different readings not only of Foucault but also of philosophy. There is no *one* Michel Foucault the philosopher. Yet perhaps this diversity itself arises out of a double-edged philosophical practice: on the one hand a relationship with that which presents itself as 'philosophical'; on the other hand with that which is not or that which is not yet 'philosophical'.

Practice 1: One should not suppose that there is such a thing as a general history of 'Western philosophy', nor should any attempt be made to construct one or to find a place in it. One should rather start from the idea that tradition is not monolithic, and that the map of ways of thinking can always be redrawn. The general schemata of history should be questioned, broken down and opened up to other questions. 'I prefer to utilise [the thought of] the writers I like . . . to use it, to deform it, to make it groan and protest'.[3]

Practice 2: One should go *outside* philosophy – to use Deleuze's phrase – and test philosophy against questions which seem alien or external to it. The art of thinking should be made into the art of delimiting new problems, about which groupings will form which did not pre-exist them.

Thus, in accordance with practice (1) (in his remarks on the beginnings of contemporary philosophy in France in the 1930s), Foucault distinguished the philosophy of formal rationality from the philosophy of subjective consciousness,[4] thus distinguishing Cavaillès's tradition from that of Sartre. He was particularly struck by the fact that Cavaillès, who had given his life to the Resistance, had found commitment [*engagement*] somewhat easier than the philosophers of commitment had done.

This distinction could seem banal to English-speaking philosophers who are used to accepting Frege's criticism of the psychologism of Husserl and its Wittgensteinian radicalisation. Cavaillès became interested in Wittgenstein, Frege and Carnap as early as 1935 and, repudiating the philosophers of consciousness, studied the foundations of mathematics and set theory. English-speaking philosophers, then, could only admire the fact that Foucault sided with Cavaillès against Sartre, and that he looked for a way out of phenomenology.

On the other hand, these same philosophers learnt with astonishment, from Foucault's writings in the 1960s, that in spite of their well-known antagonism, phenomenology and positivism derived from a common archaeological foundation; and the least one can say is that they were surprised at the 'fork' described in *Les Mots et les Choses*, where the 'being of language' leads in one direction to Russell and in the other to Freud.[5]

As is well known, Foucault suggested new ways of reading Freud and Nietzche: no one before him had located the central event in Freud's thought in his break with the theory of degeneration. No one before him had read Nietzsche in relation to the Bachelard–Canguilhem tradition, the 'new history' of the '*Annales*' school, the question of ideology in the struggles of the 1960s, or the history of madness. Yet for all that, Foucault was not a 'Nietzschean': for him the point was to reread Nietzsche on the basis of new questions, and not only on the basis of those of the 1930s. In short, Foucault wanted to break down the boundaries which segmentalised philosophical understanding by introducing new questions and rethinking those which history has left us.

In accordance with practice (2), Foucault found new questions in fields traditionally seen as being external to philosophy, in which the methods for treating the insane belong to the history of reason, and the art of constructing buildings belongs to ethics. How can one write at one and the same time for prisoners and for philosophers? 'For me,' he explained in 1975, 'Nietzsche, Bataille, Blanchot and Klossowski were ways of getting out of philosophy', of making 'permeable – and therefore finally derisory – the barrier between the philosophical and the non-philosophical'.[6] But for him, that which is external to philosophy is not constituted only by 'literary' discourse but comprised equally of the medical treatment of deviance in the nineteenth century and the science of policing in the eighteenth. Was it not John Searle, who wanted to transcribe the archaeology of affirmations [*énoncés*] into a theory of speech acts, who said that he took it from Foucault that masturbation could be an object of philosophical interest?

THE *ETHOS* OF PHILOSOPHY

In his preface to *L'Usage des plaisirs*, Foucault tried to thematise his attitude towards himself as a philosopher and towards philosophical traditions as an *ethos*, as a way of being a philosopher. Here he maintains that philosophical discourse is always derisory when it attempts to establish itself as a meta-discipline, fixing the boundaries of legitimacy and providing for the unity of all other disciplines. What is 'alive' in philosophy is rather its attempts to change in relation to that which seems alien to it.

As such, Foucault's work cannot be set out as a theory or as a system; it is punctuated by periodic attempts to go *back to the drawing board*, where the point is to '... think differently about what one thought previously and to perceive what one has done from a different angle and in a clearer light'.[7] His relationship with himself such as can be glimpsed in his work, then, could be said to take the form of an exercise by means of which one becomes what one is by releasing oneself from oneself. Those who partake of this *ethos* of releasing oneself from oneself live on 'a different planet' from those who seek a fixed point of certainty, an authentic way or choice. And it is for this reason that, in the history of philosophy, Foucault does not attach himself to a tradition or to an 'us', but seeks out events – the sort of event from which there is no return and which transforms us for ever. It is this conception of relationship to self as *ethos*, or as a philosophical mode of being, which is the main concern of Foucault's attempt to rethink traditions which we call ethical.

ETHICS IS NOT MORALITY

Philosophical traditions do not present themselves to us as a unified whole. Even what we call Judaeo-Christian morality is formed out of a sort of collage of pagan sources. Multiple changes have affected not only the codes which regulate conduct but the very conception of ethics: they affect its central questions, what it supposes to be true about us and the types of relationships it is supposed to have with religion, science, politics and law.

Foucault thought that insufficient study or thought had been devoted to the formative practices of modes of being in the history of origins and the transformations of the ethical. He thought it was appropriate, therefore, to study the history not of morality but of ethics. This is a theme which runs through the whole of Foucault's work. In *Les Mots et les Choses*, he wondered if it was still possible for philosophy to guarantee moral codes in the same way that ancient cosmologies had done (with a theory of the Republic, juridical or civic subject): 'For modern thought, there is no possible morality . . . thought . . . is itself an action – a perilous action.'[8]

This relationship between thought and modes of being was already at the centre of his study of the anthropological theme in Kant's critical philosophy. This was also the question which led him to try to analyse the penal system on the basis of new techniques of the 'governance' of individuals – techniques which made criminality as much an object of knowledge [*savoir*] as a way of being. Foucault wondered if an exercise in effective power might not be hidden beneath the traditional juridical order. Instead of analysing sovereignty taking positive or natural legal subjects as his starting point, he attempted to analyse the historical or material constitution of subjects. Instead of conceiving of the individual on the basis of his political status, he tried to question this status and to envisage the 'manufacture' of the very being of individuals.

As such, his way of conceiving the distinction between the ethical and the moral was different from the neo-Kantian opposition between *Moralität* and *Sittlichkeit* upon which a certain 'philosophical discourse of modernity' has been constructed. For Foucault the point was not to insert oneself in some fine natural or essential totality, nor to raise oneself into some transcendental rational and normative republic. Nor is there any point in deriving a solid foundation for rationality, nor in getting back a lost feeling of community within the context of some modern Reason. The point was rather to study the practices of self in their own sphere and to question, on this basis, their place in a given society. This is how Foucault's practices of self are similar to Wittgenstein's ordinary forms of life, in which that which presents itself as subjective arises out of common (public) transformable practices.

Foucault, then, asked not how practices of the self acted as vehicles for the decisions of a culture, but how it could come about that a culture should have assigned a particular position to them. It is because he also wanted once again to question the ethical being of the individual that in *Le Souci de soi* he took up the fluid idea of individualism, which is invoked to explain very different phenomena at different periods.[9] It is appropriate, he says, to distinguish the practices of self which take the individual as an object of knowledge [*savoir*] and action (as in Christian asceticism) from the value which is accorded to the individual in certain groups of which he is a member (as in the military aristocracy), and from the value accorded to private or family life by the middle classes in the nineteenth century. Thus he wanted to distinguish the individual liberty of the Greeks from the 'platitude, derived more or less from Hegel, according to which the freedom of the individual was of no importance in face of the noble totality of the city'.[10]

Conceiving of ethics on the basis of the practice of the self made it possible for Foucault to construct a historical approach which was different from that of idealist Romantic thought, in which the constitution of the individual makes its way from the Augustinian will to the 'rebirth' of the idea of life as work of art (described by Burckhardt) and then carries on from the Cartesian Cogito to Baudelaire's dandyism and to analytic confession. To emphasise ethics rather than morality was to raise the question of the practices which form the individual in relation to knowledge [*savoir*], politics and modern law.

THOUGHT AS ETHICS

If we accept the distinction between the ethical and the moral, at least in terms of a historical hypothesis, can we go on to apply this to Foucault's own thought? More precisely, can his own thought be conceived in terms of the four elements which he isolated when he undertook to study ethics as a practice of the self?

1. Substance

'The subject is not a substance. The subject is a form, and this form is not at all times and in all places self-identical . . . what interests me is precisely the historical constitution of different forms of the subject in relation to truth games.'[11] What is to be transformed, in this practice of the self, is the way history makes evident and presents forms through which the subject thinks he can identify himself in truth; it is not the nature of the subject which is at stake here but his 'second nature'; not that which is given, but that which makes it possible for him to give himself. The substance is that which, in the being of the subject, is open to historical transformation.

2. The mode of being made into a subject

It is the invitation to a practical freedom which incites this transformation. It is the chance of giving 'a new boost, as vast as possible, to the still unfinished work of liberty'.[12] This is the possibility of making freedom into a practical and not simply a formal question; a freedom not of action, nor of intentions or desires, but of a choice of a mode of being.

3. The ethical task
The means of transformation will be that of a critical analysis which reconstitutes the forms of the subject into 'transformable singularities'.[13] The point is to determine exactly what we have to struggle against in order to free ourselves from ourselves. This is the analysis of the problematisation of 'the evidence on which our knowledge [*savoir*], our consent and our practices are based',[14] from which is derived a 'we' who are always temporary'.[15]

4. The telos
The aim of this open transformation is the practice of truth-telling, which a society can neither control nor silence; the beauty of the risk of self, a critical attitude in relation to what happens to us and 'a defiance of all phenomena tending towards domination'.[16]

Foucault's work – to the extent that all philosophical work implies an exercise of the self, in other words an ethic – could therefore be summed up as follows: in the name of a practical form of liberty, in which possible forms of experience become apparent, a nominalist critique is to be developed as a means of resisting domination.

PROBLEMATISATION

In the preface to *L'Usage des plaisirs*, Foucault, as we saw, wanted to rethink his previous research in a different light – that of problematisation. There is a history of thought because of the existence of a history of specific problems which thought had to confront. What was it, in the experience of criminality, illness, madness or sexuality, that presented itself in such a problematic way that this experience became something which had to be and could be thought about?

The Foucauldian history of ethics is a history not of principles and their mode of legitimation, but of ways of replying to specific or individual problems. What was the conception of the obstacles which had to be surmounted in order to be good, or to do what one ought to do? How does one rationalise what should be done with regard to what one considers bad or wrong? And, more precisely, how can one rethink the task of thought in relation to forms of knowledge [*savoirs*], to strategies of doing, to the law and to politics?

1. Knowledge–power [savoir–pouvoir]
How did problems or the dangers specific to self, and to society, become objects of a possible form of knowledge [*savoir*] and strategy? This is the question posed by his analyses of systems of thought, the great metaconcept which is that of 'normality' – a normality which would be absent from the

problematisation of Greek pleasures, and specific to racism 'in its modern, state-linked, and biologising form'.[17] How could these former practices of the self be colonised by this normalising apparatus?

2. The law

How is it that new problems, like accident insurance, become not only the object of new legislation, but also a new way of conceiving of the law? Law must be analysed at the point where its application poses problems. It is necessary to trace the history of the styles of juridical reasoning which determine which sort of objects can fall under jurisdiction, who makes use of them and how. This is the critical juridical nominalism proposed by François Ewald: not a philosophy of the essence or the nature of law, but a history of events or problematisations through which an individual 'juridical experience' is constructed.

3. Politics

In what way and through what means of conception do certain problematic events become 'political'? For example that event whose name is a date, '68?

For Foucault, politics is not a constitutive element of these problematisations; on the contrary, it is the problematisations which raise questions about politics and transform the way it is conceived. In this sense, the point is not so much to find definitive solutions as to find out how to bring about their entry into that which presents itself as the political field.

This is illustrated by the question posed by his analysis of the problematisations of the 'welfare–warfare state'. How should it be that a new problematisation of life and death, a new way of governing changed not only the functioning but also the concept of the State? How is it that 'liberal' thought (the categories of civic society/State) emerged as a way of thinking about this new biopolitics, and how was this problematised in turn?: '. . . my way of looking at political questions . . . is by way of problematisation; that implies the development of a domain of actions, of practices and of thought which seem to me to raise problems for politics.'[18]

But the analysis of these dangers is itself dangerous, for it takes place in situations which lie outside deducto-normative reasoning. As when one sees that something needs to be done, though one does not yet know exactly what. It is then that I open a space not of deduction, but of analysis and questioning in which one might seek to determine a danger which still remains to be identified and to which it will be necessary to react. The 'ethico-political choice' consists in 'determining what the true danger is': 'I should like to trace the genealogy of problems, of problematics. I do not mean that everything is bad, but that everything is dangerous, which is not the same thing. If everything is dangerous, then there is still something we can do.'[19]

POSSIBILITIES

Foucault's philosophy bears on what we can think and what can be changed in what we can think. The link between the possible and the thinkable goes back to Kant. Foucault wanted to introduce the event into critical philosophy, and advance a critical history of thought. For if experience is made possible by categories, and if categories change, then possibilities also change.

The task of criticism becomes that of inserting the event into that which presents itself as evidence. These events are what makes things conceivable. This is why, in *L'Archéologie du savoir*, Foucault talks of a historical *a priori* – an *a priori* not of legitimate boundaries but of historical possibilities of experience. For Foucault, as for Kant, freedom is not one ethical possibility amongst others; it is the actual possibility of ethics: 'Ethics is the deliberate form assumed by freedom'.[20] However, for Foucault, in a way which is contrary to Kant, this freedom is not supra-sensible but historical. It arises not out of a rational Republic of autonomous subjects but out of an unceasing questioning of historical bestowals of identity. Foucault wanted to write a history not of that which is true or false but of that which can be true or false; not of that which must be done but of that which can be done; not of ways of life but of possibilities of life. It is in this perspective of the historical possibilities of knowledge [*savoir*], action and subjective identity that knowledge [*savoir*] is, for Foucault, marked off from science, power is marked off from politics, ethics is marked off from morality; and that the relationships between forms of knowledge [*savoirs*], powers and modes of being are never given but always to be sought after, since they are never essential or necessary but always historical and transformable.

By making the question of criticism a historical one, Foucault discovered a sort of impossibility which is not logical but historical. It is not the impossibility of a square circle or of a non-existent God, but the impossibility of that which it is no longer, or not yet, possible to think. Not that which has no meaning but that which does not yet have meaning, or no longer has meaning. It is this historical constraint or exclusion which it is the job of thought to make visible. It would even be possible to think that the impossibility in question here was already present in seminal form in what Foucault called, in *L'Histoire de la folie*, 'the absence of work'.

Yet, on a deeper level, Foucault's critical work relating to the field of individual historical possibilities itself opens up new philosophical possibilities, and sketches a new way of conceiving the relationship between history and philosophy, a new way of envisaging the relationships between philosophical strivings and modes of being – in short, a new way of doing philosophy.

NOTES

1. 'Question à Michel Foucault', *Hérodote*, no. 1, January 1976, p. 74.
2. *Foucault tel que je l'imagine*, Montpellier: Fata Morgana, 1986, p. 17.
3. 'Quel corps?', translated from the English, *Power/Knowledge*, pp. 53–4. [Original given here – Translator.]
4. 'La vie: l'expérience et la science', *Revue de métaphysique et de morale*, January 1985.
5. *Les Mots et les Choses*, Paris: Gallimard, 1966, p. 312.
6. 'Passe-frontières de la philosophie', *Le Monde*, 6 September 1986.
7. *L'Usage des plaisirs*, Paris: Gallimard, 1984, p. 56.
8. *Les Mots et les Choses*, p. 339.
9. *Le Souci de soi*, Paris: Gallimard, 1984, p. 56.
10. 'L'éthique de soi comme une pratique de liberté', *Concordia: Internationale Zeitschrift für Philosophie*, no. 6, 1984 (translated from the English) [and back again from the French – Translator].
11. *Ibid.*
12. 'What is Enlightenment?' in *The Foucault Reader*, ed. Rabinow, New York: Pantheon, 1984, p. 46 (retranslated from the English) [and back again from the French – Translator].
13. 'Première préface à *L'Usage des plaisirs*', *The Foucault Reader*, p. 334 (retranslated from the English) [and back again from the French – Translator].
14. *L'impossible prison* ed. Michelle Perrot, Paris: Éditions du Seuil, 1980, p. 44.
15. 'Interview', *The Foucault Reader*, p. 385.
16. 'L'éthique de soi comme une pratique de liberté'.
17. *La Volonté de savoir*, Paris: Gallimard, 1976, p. 197.
18. 'Interview', *The Foucault Reader*, p. 384. [Retranslated from the French – Translator.]
19. *Ibid.*, p. 343.
20. 'L'éthique de soi comme une pratique de liberté'.

SUMMARY OF DISCUSSIONS

John Rajchman stressed, in response to a question about problematisation, that this was a term which Foucault came to use only later in his writing career. It was the way in which, at the end of his life, Foucault was thinking about his own work. Problematisations were not only the object of Foucault's work but their point of departure. Thus it was that Foucault discovered that the treatment of prisoners was intolerable at the same time as he discovered the gap between the concrete life of prisoners and the legal and economic evidence of the conception of prison.

Christian Jambet noted that the treatment which Foucault reserves for Plato's *Symposium* and *Phaedra* in *L'Usage des plaisirs* bears witness to a different genealogy of Platonism from that of Nietzsche. How can one situate the distance which Foucault establishes between himself and Nietzsche? And how can one situate the moment where the problematisation of Greece moved towards a theory of liberty rather than the beginnings of a process of decadence?

Manfred Frank maintained that writing *Naissance de la clinique* or *Surveiller et punir* presupposed a certain ethical decision. In order to judge the situation regarding prisons and to find this significant for society as a whole, it is necessary to take up a position. We find a situation 'intolerable' only when an alternative comes into being. In this there is something ethical because it is normative, 'counter-factual'. This ethical dimension underlies Foucault's ethical practice. Can an ethic be founded simply on the opening up of possibilities? German fascism was also a possibility, and that is not enough to satisfy our ethical requirements. Can an argument be found in Foucault which would be capable of showing that fascism is less likely to satisfy our ethical needs than his own commitment?

John Rajchman argued that one cannot consider a situation intolerable unless one is capable of imagining an alternative which one is sure would be better. For Foucault, people struggle in concrete situations; there is no need to see their struggles as idealist.

two

Reflections on the notion of 'the cultivation of the self'

Pierre Hadot

In the preface to *L'Usage des plaisirs* and in a chapter of *Souci du soi* [*SS*], Foucault refers to my article 'Exercices spirituels' which appeared in *Annuaire de la 5ᵉ Section de l'École pratique des hautes études* for the year 1975–6, and was reproduced in my book *Exercices spirituels et Philosophie antique* which first appeared in 1981, with a new edition in 1987. It seems that Foucault's attention was drawn to the description I made in it of ancient philosophy as an art of living, as a style of life, as a way of life, and by my attempt, in this book, to explain why it was that modern philosophy had forgotten this tradition and had become almost exclusively a theoretical discourse; also by the idea I sketched in the article, and later developed in my book *Exercices spirituels*, that Christianity took over certain spiritual exercises practised in Antiquity for its own purposes.

I should like here to make some remarks to clarify further this encounter between us, the differences in interpretation and finally the philosophical choice which separated us and could have provided the substance of a dialogue which, unfortunately, Foucault's premature death interrupted all too soon.

Foucault describes with precision in *Le Souci de soi* what he calls the 'practices of the self' preached by the Stoic philosophers in Antiquity: the care of the self which can, moreover, be realised only under the direction of a spiritual guide, attention to the body and to the soul which implies care for the self, the exercises of abstinence, the examination of the conscience, the filtering of representations and finally the conversion towards the self, the possession of the self. Foucault conceives of these practices as 'arts of existence', as 'techniques of the self'. Yet it seems to me that the way Foucault describes what I had called 'spiritual exercises', and he prefers to call 'techniques of the self', is too much centred on the 'self', or at least on a certain conception of the self.

We should note that Foucault presents the ethic of the Graeco-Roman world as an ethic of pleasure which is taken in the self (*SS*, p. 83): 'In place of this sort of violent, uncertain and provisional pleasure, access to the self is capable of substituting a form of pleasure which one can take in oneself in serenity and for all time.' To illustrate this idea he quotes Seneca's twenty-third letter, which deals with the joy which can be discovered in oneself, precisely in the best part of oneself. But in fact I have to say that there is some inexactitude in his presentation of this. In the twenty-third letter, Seneca is in fact explicitly contrasting *voluptas* and *gaudium*, pleasure and joy; and one cannot therefore speak, as Foucault does (p. 83) on the subject of joy, of 'another form of pleasure'. It is not just a question of words, although the Stoics attached a great deal of importance to them and distinguished carefully between *hēdonē* and *eupatheia*, precisely between pleasure and joy (this distinction crops up again in Plotinus and in Bergson, the latter linking joy with creation). No, it is not just a question of vocabulary: if the Stoics set store by the word *gaudium*, the word 'joy', this was precisely because they refused to introduce the principle of pleasure into moral life. For them happiness did not consist in pleasure but in virtue itself, which is seen as being its own reward. Well before Kant, the Stoics wanted jealously to preserve the purity of intention of the moral conscience.

Secondly, and most importantly, the Stoics did not find joy in the 'self' but, as Seneca says, 'in the best part of the self', in the 'true good' (Seneca, letter XXIII, 6); that is to say (XXIII, 7), 'in the turning of the consciousness towards the good intentions which have no object other than virtue, right actions' – in what Seneca calls (CXXIV, 23) perfect reason, which finally means divine reason (XCII, 27), since for him, human reason is only perfectible reason. The 'best part' of the self is ultimately a transcendental self. Seneca does not find joy just in 'Seneca', but by transcending Seneca, by discovering that he has a reason in himself, a part of the universal Reason which is within all men and the cosmos itself.

The Stoic exercise aims in fact at going beyond the self, at thinking and acting in union with universal Reason. The three exercises described by Marcus Aurelius (VII, 54; IX, 6; VIII, 7), following on from Epictetus, are very significant in this respect: to make judgements objectively in accordance with internal reason, to act in accordance with reason which is common to all men, and to accept the destiny which is imposed on us by cosmic reason. For the Stoics there is only one reason here, and this is the reason which is the real self of man.

I understand Foucault's motive in glossing over these aspects very well, though he was well aware of them. His description of practices of the self (like, moreover, my description of spiritual exercises) is not only a historical study; it was meant also to offer contemporary man a model of life (which Foucault calls the 'aesthetic of existence'). Now, according to a very general tendency in modern thought – a tendency which is perhaps rather more instinctive than considered – the notions of 'universal Reason' and 'universal Nature' are no longer seen as having much meaning. It was therefore expedient to parenthesise them.

For the moment, I should like to say that it seems difficult from a historical point of view to concede that the philosophical practice of the Stoics and the Platonists was related only to the self, to the cultivation of the self and to the pleasure taken in the self. The psychic content of these exercises seems to me to be something quite different. The feeling of belonging to a Whole seems to me to be the essential element: belonging to the Whole of the human community, belonging to the cosmic Whole. Seneca sums this up in four words (letter LXVI, 6): '*Toti se inserens mundo*': 'plunging oneself into the totality of the world'. Groethuysen, in his admirable *Anthropologie philosophique* (p. 80), recognised this fundamental characteristic well. Now, a cosmic perspective of this nature radically transforms the feelings one might have about oneself.

Curiously, Foucault has little to say about the Epicureans. This is all the more unexpected since, in a certain sense, the Epicurean ethic is an ethic without norms, an autonomous ethic, which cannot be founded on Nature; an ethic based on chance which would, as such, appear to suit the modern mentality perfectly. The reason for this silence can perhaps be found in the fact that it is difficult to integrate Epicurean hedonism into the general schema of the use of pleasures put forward by Foucault. However this might be, the Epicureans also have their spiritual practices, for example the examination of the conscience. But as I said, these practices are not founded on the norms of Nature and universal Reason, since for the Epicureans the world is formed only as a result of chance. And yet, here again, this spiritual practice cannot be defined only as a cultivation of the self, as a simple relationship of the self to the self or as a pleasure which can be found in one's own self. The Epicurean is not afraid to confess that he needs something other than himself in order to satisfy his desires and to find his pleasure: he needs bodily food, the pleasures of love, but also a physical theory of the universe in order to suppress the fear of the gods and of death. He needs the companionship of other members of the Epicurean school in order to find happiness in mutual affection. Finally, he needs imaginative contemplation of the infinity of the universe in order to feel what Lucretius calls *divina voluptas et horror*. This immersion of the Epicurean sage in the cosmos is well expressed by Epicurus' disciple, Metrodorus: 'Remember that, being born mortal, with a limited life, you have raised yourself through thinking about nature to the eternity and infinity of things, and you have seen everything which has been and everything that will be.' There is, in Epicureanism, an extraordinary reversal of perspective: it is precisely because existence appears to the Epicurean as pure chance, inexorably unique, that he welcomes life as a kind of miracle, as a free and unhoped-for gift from Nature, and considers existence to be a marvellous festival.

I should now like to take another example in order to illustrate the difference in our interpretations of 'concern for the self'. Foucault wrote an interesting article entitled 'Écriture de soi' ('Writing about the self') which, moreover, takes as its starting point a remarkable text concerning the therapeutic value of writing which I studied in my *Exercices spirituels* (p. 69) and according to which the famous monk Anthony was supposed to have counselled his disciples to note in writing the actions and movements of their souls, as if they were going to make these known to others: 'Let writing take the place of the eyes of others,' he said. This anecdote led Foucault to reflect on the forms taken by what he calls 'writing about the self' in Antiquity, and notably the literary genre of the *hypomnēmata*, which could be called spiritual 'notebooks', where thoughts of others are written which could contribute to the edification of the writer. Foucault defines the purpose of this as follows (p. 8): the point is to 'capture that which has already been said', to 'collect together that which one might have heard or read, and this for a purpose which is nothing less than the constitution of the self'. He then wonders: 'How can one be placed in the presence of oneself with the aid of discourse which is without age and which comes from just about all over the place?' And this is his reply: 'This exercise was to make possible a return to the past: the contribution of the *hypomnēmata* was to be a means of detaching the soul from concern about the future and inclining it towards a meditation on the past.' He thinks that he has discovered, both in Stoic and in Epicurean morality, the refusal to accept an attitude of mind which looks to the future and the tendency to attribute a positive value to the possession of a past which can be enjoyed sovereignly and without care. It seems to me that there is an error in this interpretation. It is true that the Epicureans, and they alone, considered one of the principal sources of pleasure to be the memory of pleasant moments in the past. This, though, has nothing to do with the meditation on the 'already said' practised in the *hypomnēmata*. Yet the fact still remains, as I showed in an article which appeared in *Diogène* in 1986 (no. 133) that Stoics and Epicureans agree in affirming an attitude which consists in liberating oneself both from concern about the future and from the weight of the past in order to be able to concentrate on the present moment – either to enjoy it, or to act in it. And from this point of view, neither the Stoics nor even the Epicureans attributed a positive value to the past: the fundamental philosophical attitude consisted in living in the present, possessing the present and not the past. The fact that they did, moreover, attach great importance to thoughts formulated by their predecessors is a different matter. But if the *hypomnēmata* bear on what has already been said, it is not just on anything that has been 'already said', which would have no merit other than belonging to the past, but because in these things which have already been said (in general, the dogmas of the founders of the school) can be recognised that which reason itself would say *in the present*; that is, because in these dogmas of Epicurus or Chrisippus a value can be recognised which is *always present*, precisely because these dogmas are the expression of reason. In other words, by writing, by noting these things down, it is not alien thought that one is making one's own; rather, one is using formulations which one considers to be well made in order to make present, to bring alive, that which is already present within the reason of the writer.

According to Foucault, this exercise is supposed to be entirely eclectic and would therefore imply an element of personal choice, which would thus explain the notion of the 'constitution of self'. 'Writing as a personal experience made through the self and for the self is an art of disparate truth or, more precisely, a considered way of combining the traditional authority of that which has already been said with the uniqueness of the truth which is affirmed in it, and the particular nature of the circumstances which determine its usage.' But in fact, at least for the Stoics and the Epicureans, personal choice is not situated in eclecticism. Eclecticism is used only for the purpose of converting beginners. Thus Foucault finds an example of eclecticism in Lucilius' *Letters*, in which the Stoic Seneca quotes sentences from Epicurus. But the point here was to convert Lucilius, to begin to make him practise a moral life. This usage of Epicurus appears only in the first *Letters* and rapidly disappears. On the contrary, personal choice is in fact situated exclusively in adhesion to a precise form of life, Stoicism or Epicureanism, which is considered to conform to reason. It is only with the new Academy – in Cicero, for example – that personal choice is made according to what reason considers likely at a particular moment.

It is not, then, as Foucault thought (pp. 11–13), by writing and reading disparate thoughts that the individual forges his spiritual identity. First, as we have seen, these thoughts are not disparate, but chosen for their coherence. Secondly – and most importantly – the point was not to forge a spiritual identity by writing but to free oneself from one's individuality, to raise oneself to universality. It is therefore inaccurate to talk of 'writing about the self'; not only is it not oneself that one is writing about, but also the writing does not constitute the self: as in other spiritual exercises, it changes the level of the self; it universalises it. The miracle of this exercise, practised in solitude, is that it makes access to the universality of reason possible in time and space. For Saint Anthony the therapeutic value of writing consisted precisely in this universalising power. Writing, Anthony said, takes the place of the eye of the other. The writer feels in some way looked at; he is no longer alone, but part of a human community which is silently present. By formulating one's personal acts in writing, one becomes part of the link between reason, logic and universality. One is making objective that which is confused and subjective.

To sum up: What Foucault calls the 'practices of self' in the Stoics, and also in the Platonists, does correspond, it is true, to a movement of conversion towards the self: one liberates oneself from externals, from sensual attachment to external objects and to the pleasures which these can procure; one observes oneself, in order to see if one has progressed in this exercise; one seeks to be one's own master, to possess oneself, to find one's happiness in internal freedom and independence. I agree with all these points. But I think that this movement of interiorisation is inseparably linked to another movement in which one raises oneself to a higher psychic level; in which one rediscovers another type of exteriorisation, another relationship with the exterior, another way of being-in-the world which consists in being aware of oneself as a part of Nature, as a particle of universal Reason. One lives, then, no longer in the conventional and usual human world but in the world of Nature. As I said elsewhere, one is practising 'physics' as a spiritual exercise.

As such one identifies oneself with an 'other' which is Nature, universal Reason, which is present in each individual. In this there is a radical transformation of perspective, a universalist and cosmic dimension which Foucault, it seems to me, did not sufficiently stress: interiorisation is going beyond the self in a way which leads to universalisation.

All these observations which I have just made are not to be situated only in the framework of a historical analysis of ancient philosophy; they are aimed also at the definition of the ethical model which modern man might discover in Antiquity. To be precise: what I rather fear is that, by concentrating his interpretation to such a great extent exclusively on the interpretation of the cultivation of the self, on concern for the self and on conversion towards the self and, in a general way, by defining his ethical model as an ethic of existence, Foucault might have been advancing a cultivation of the self which was too purely aesthetic – that is to say, I fear, a new form of dandyism, a late-twentieth-century version. But this would have to be studied more closely that I am able to do here. For my part, I believe firmly – naively, perhaps – in the opportunity for modern man to live out, not the wisdom (the majority of the Ancients did not believe in this opportunity) but an exercise, still fragile, of wisdom, in the triple form which was defined, as we saw, by Marcus Aurelius: attempting to practise objectivity of judgement, attempting to live according to justice in the service of the human community, and attempting to become aware of our situation as belonging to the universe (that is, acting on the basis of the lived experience of ourselves as concrete, living and perceiving subjects). This exercise in wisdom will therefore be an attempt to open ourselves up to the universal.

More precisely again, I think that modern man is able to practise the philosophical exercises of Antiquity, whilst separating them from the philosophical or mythical discourses which accompany them. This same spiritual exercise can in fact be justified in a concrete way in terms of extremely different forms of philosophical discourse, which are only clumsy attempts, which come about in retrospect in order to justify internal experiences, the existential density of which finally escapes all attempts at theorisation and systematisation. For example, the Stoics and the Epicureans invited their disciples, for totally different reasons, to concentrate their attention on the present moment whilst freeing themselves from concern about the future or the past. Yet whoever practises this exercise sees the world with new eyes, as if he were seeing it for the first time. He discovers, in the enjoyment of the pure present, the mystery and splendour of existence; and, as Nietzsche said, we can then say yes 'not only to ourselves but to existence'. It is not necessary, therefore, to believe in the Stoic's Nature and universal Reason to practise these exercises, but in practising them one lives concretely according to reason ('even if everything tends towards chance, you, yourself, should not tend towards chance', said Marcus Aurelius (X, 28, 3); one accedes concretely to the universality of the cosmic perspective, to the marvellous and mysterious presence of the universe.

NOTES

Bergson, J., *L'Énergie spirituelle*, Paris: PUF, 14th edn, p. 24 (on pleasure and joy).

Foucault, M., 'L'Écriture de soi', *Corps écrit*, no. 5, 1983, pp. 3–23.

Foucault, M., *Histoire de la sexualité*, vol. II, *L'Usage des plaisirs*; vol. III, *Le Souci de soi*, Paris: Gallimard, 1984.

Groethuysen, B., *Anthropologie philosophique*, Paris: Gallimard, 1952.

Hadot, Ilsetraut, 'Épicure et l'eseignement philosophique hellénistique et romain', in *Actes du VIIIe Congrès de l'Association Guillaume Budé*, Paris: Les Belles Lettres, 1970, p. 351 (on the provisional and therapeutic character of quotations from Epicurus by Seneca).

Hadot, Ilsetraut, *Seneca und die griechisch-römische Tradition der Seelenleitung*, Berlin, 1969.

Hadot, Pierre, *Exercices spirituels et Philosophie antique*, Paris, 2nd edn., 1987.

Hadot, Pierre, 'Le présent seul est notre bonheur. La valeur de l'instant présent chez Goethe et dans la philosophie antique', *Diogène*, no. 133, Paris, 1986, pp. 58–81 (quotation from Nietzsche, p. 80).

Schmid, W., *Die Geburt der Philosophie im Garten der Lüste*, Frankfurt-am-Main: Athenäum, 1987.

SUMMARY OF DISCUSSIONS

Jean-Pierre Vernant returned to the theme of problematisation in order to indicate that this means that certain conditions, at a certain moment, cause a field to modify itself and an object which until that point had not been noticed to appear. 'Problematisation' designates simultaneously a modification of history in general and a way of being for the self for all persons.

Foucault put his finger on two points: the difference between what the Greeks called 'pleasures' and that which we ourselves call 'sexuality'. Sexuality is a modern invention, the conditions necessary for the emergence of an experience of this nature having come together only relatively recently. Foucault, moreover, was seeking to find out at which moment the category of the individual emerged. Not the self in the first-personal sense [*le moi*], which was a non-existent category for the Greeks, but in the third-personal sense [*le soi-même*]. Socrates' soul is not the psychological individual, but an impersonal or supra-personal *daimōn* in Socrates. Foucault shows how, in certain cultural and social conditions, the individual becomes the object of concern for the self by means of work on the self; of a fabrication of the self by means of techniques which are spiritual exercises, examinations of conscience, attempts at recall, and so on. Foucault saw that there was a fundamental question here. Even if, in Antiquity, wisdom was more orientated towards an integration of the self into the cosmos than towards the exploration of the self by the self, that did not make it impermissible for him to transpose this experience into something which could today be seen as an aesthetic of existence.

Jean-Pierre Vernant noted the parallels and the differences of orientation between the enquiry carried out by Foucault in order to understand how the individual, in Western culture, came to adopt the characteristics which we recognise and, on the other hand, the enquiries pursued by Meyerson on the history of the person.

Pierre Hadot confirmed that, for the Ancients, the self is an interior *daimōn*: it is not a question of a subject, but of an internal object. It is very difficult to use the terms self and subject in the context of Antiquity.

Moreover, **Pierre Hadot** stressed that there is an abyss between Antiquity and the modern world. It is possible to extract, as Foucault did, from Marcus Aurelius, Plutarch or Seneca, 'a detail of this morality' (Paul Veyne) and give it a present-day meaning. Foucault did find a morality in the ethics of ancient philosophy, but the way he presented this philosophy was not, perhaps, totally accurate.

three

The constitution of the subject and spiritual practice

Observations on *L'Histoire de la sexualité*

Christian Jambet

It might seem strange to read Foucault with problems in mind other than those of the West. The objects of his analyses belong strictly to the space of Western culture: the whole of this space is involved, but only this space. None the less, the East is not entirely absent from Foucault's work, and two illustrations of this, at least, have attracted my attention.

In the preface to the first edition of *Histoire de la folie* we read:

> In the universality of the Western *ratio*, there is this divide which is the East: the East thought of as the origin, dreamt of as the giddying point which is the place of birth, of nostalgia and promises of return, the East which offers itself to the colonising reason of the West but is indefinitely inaccessible, for it remains always as a boundary: the night of beginning in which the West was formed but where it drew a dividing line, the East is for the West everything which the West is not, yet it is here that it has to seek whatever might be its originating truth. The history of this great divide is something which should be traced, throughout the whole of the West's process of becoming, it should be followed in its continuities and shifts, whilst at the same time its tragically hieratical nature should be allowed to appear.

'Orientals' are to be seen in terms of their pure otherness: it is on this that their ever-present prestige is based, as well as their totally alien nature. They determine the external limit to our way of thinking, but in so doing they suggest the pattern of its lost origin: cannot an analogy be drawn here between the experience of the East and that of insanity? This is not to suggest that both truths would be of the same nature, that the Oriental should be seen as something of a madman and the madman as a substitute Oriental, but rather that our ways of thinking [*savoirs*] are such that we have to treat them as objects of similar procedures. That is to say, from the point of view which then became his own, Foucault was sketching a research programme which could be set out as follows:

- to study ways in which this notion of the Other was constituted, from the Renaissance up to the appearance of Orientalism;
- to show how Orientalism was able to modify this notion at the same time as magnifying it, and how it transformed the quest for the lost origin into that of a 'different history', by means of which ours could be at one and the same time disputed and clarified;
- to clarify that which seems in the East to insist, in a way which is perhaps misrepresented by our ways of thinking [*savoirs*], on a 'tragic' experience, which makes sense to us alone but which necessarily had to take place outside us.

The East is probably only one of the names in our culture by means of which it creates a space outside itself, yet this name is not pure appearance. No more than the 'lightning-like decision, heterogeneous to the nature of historical time, yet incomprehensible outside it, which separates the dark murmuring of insects from the language of reason and the promises of time.'

The second illustration of which I am thinking comes at a distance of twenty years from the first. It is of a quite different nature: it is the interest which Foucault took in the events in Iran. How would it be possible to make sense of this in terms of a political commitment made at a point in time and subject to whatever the consequences of the revolution turned out to be? This would be to reduce its scope to mere empirical determination: would it be wise to encourage uprisings leading to the fall of a monarch?

What Foucault's texts say, in fact, is something quite different: the point is not the politics of a future state but the essence of an uprising, of the 'spiritual' politics which makes it possible; and it is in consequence a form of 'transcendental' enquiry: what are the conditions which make it possible for a culture to decide on a revolt, on the basis of hope and an experience seen in terms of 'events in heaven'? Here, the East is no longer looked at in terms of names forged by the West but as the locus of a problematisation of power and liberty which is different but real, alien but autonomous. Foucault sees immediately that here history is the expression of a metahistory, or again of a hiero-history, and that the temporalisation of time is suspended in favour of messianic events whose place is not the world of phenomena understood by science. He also sees that from this point a certain way of being a subject becomes possible – quite different from the scientific, legal and moral subject which the Galilean and Cartesian shifts definitively set up in the West. At the time Michel Foucault was the only Western philosopher to show an interest in questions of this nature; so we should be careful not to speak thoughtlessly about what his ultimate position was.

I should like to show that in these last two books, as he was describing a certain type of problematisation of liberty in the Western world of Greece and Rome, Michel Foucault none the less opened routes which are of essential interest to the research of Iranian Islam; that it is possible, in the light of these, to overcome several apparent antimonies and that certain consequences follow for our perception of the history of freedom.

1 THE CRITIQUE OF NATURALISM AND THE STRUGGLE AGAINST HISTORICISM

I should like first to show how the historicism of which the science of religion had to rid itself in order to deal appropriately with spiritual events (here Iranian spiritual events) is of the same essence as the naturalism which Michel Foucault criticises under the heading of the 'repressive hypothesis'. It is well known that Iranian studies, notably those dealing with Islamic Iran, have been significantly advanced thanks to the work of Henry Corbin. The major difficulty he encountered as he read texts on Sufi or Shi'ite spirituality can be set out as follows: the authors of these texts – whether they were the disciples of Sohravardi, the 'Persian Platonists', the philosophers of the School of Isfahan who were followers of Avicenna, or the theoreticians of 'Twelver' Shi'ism – order their thought around the idea of the existence of a hierarchical universe which comprises, beyond the sensible world of the earth and the spheres, the various degrees of an 'intelligible' world and, between these two sides of reality, an in-between world 'where spirits become corporeal and bodies become spirits'; this is the world of 'archetype-images' visible to the imagination of the sage or of the proven faithful. Henry Corbin suggests calling this the 'imaginal world'.

To the Iranian religious consciousness, this world is the threshold of spiritual universes. It therefore determines sets of conduct, obligations and practices, which here could be called moralities or politics: it is in this imaginal world that prophetic events take place, that the cycles of the Imat succeed one another, that the divine secrets are revealed and that the resurrection body develops. All this *takes bodily form* in the spiritual matter of the active imagination according to the laws of a time and the proportions of a space which lead to the desire for release from this world and justify the symbols of faith and the promises of eschatology.

Should this conceptual edifice be treated as a 'mode of representation'?

Should one see in it secondary expressions of historical, political or institutional struggles? Should one say, for example, that Ismailiyan Shi'ism is 'in the first instance' a religious and political party, grouped round the concrete and feudal interests of Northern Iran, or, on the contrary, the masses of poor peasants and newly converted non-Arab Muslims? Should one say, then, that the deployment of the series of imams in the subtle time of the soul according to its own cyclical rhythm is nothing more than an ideological veneer required by this concrete history? This hypothesis, which one could refer to as historicist, is in reality ahistorical and incapable of treating its object. It was by renouncing this approach that Corbin was able really to show that what constituted and gave coherence to concrete history was this metahistory 'in heaven', and that this was not a simple means of justification in which at a given time the eternal division between oppressors and oppressed would be enveloped, but that it was, in the first instance, an original and irreducible production – the 'problematisation', as Foucault would say – of a certain type of relationship between oneself and others – a concrete, practical and theoretical form of liberty.

It seems to me that this movement which Corbin makes – which opens the way for Shi'ite studies, by making it possible to 'see like those who see in that way', by studying the modes of being and modes of consciousness as indissociable elements of the same type of subjectivity – is not far from the movement by which Foucault, in his study of Graeco-Latin philosophies and spiritualities, puts an end to the naturalist hypothesis.

If there is such a thing as a theme which continues explicitly through the modifications brought to the project of the 'history of sexuality', it seems to be this. In *La Volonté de savoir*, the point is to show that the attention paid to sex cannot be analysed in terms of categories of transgression or interdiction. The fact that Foucault is attacking here a form of Freudo–Marxism is not the most important point. He wants above all to make us wary of a belief in an eternal essence in the sexual relationship, the effects of which practice and theory would have to translate or combat, and of the idea that ethics could have had as its function only a purely negative task: to repress a threat coming from the depths, to express universally respectable interdictions, and to stop or filter out certain possible but inadmissible forms of behaviour. He writes, on the contrary, in *L'Usage des plaisirs*: 'These notions of sexual austerity have to be understood not as a translation or commentary of profound and essential prohibitions but as developments and stylisations of an activity in the exercise of its power and the practice of its liberty.'

It can be seen that the 'repressive hypothesis' sets up a *nature of sex*, good or dangerous, in opposition to the structures which oppress and temper it. But this antagonism is also doubled up with another opposition: on the one hand there would be the weighty, institutional and historical *powers* whose job it is to enforce this temperance and this domination; and then, on the other hand, we would have the forms of discourse which would enunciate it, in the modality of illusion, mystification and obligation. There is a great deal in common between the historicist model which treats discourse as an ideological superstructure, and the naturalist model which supposes that sex has an essential and eternal nature, since it is this nature which founds the distinction between the structures which are supposed to have historical power over it, and the words whose job is to do no more than translate – albeit in a confused way – its effects. The consequence of this would be that the 'real' history of means of constraint would be based on the foundation of an eternal nature of sexuality whilst, according to the famous formulation, ideology would not have a history.

Michel Foucault starts from the opposite hypothesis: what history does have, that which truly *makes* the history of sexuality, is the grouping of 'problematisations through which being presents itself as potentially and necessarily thinkable, and the practices on the basis of which these problematisations are formed'. Sexuality, then, comes into being thanks to the practices and discourse in which it *becomes* the object of attention and concern. In the immanence of one and the same level of analysis, institutions, powers and forms of knowledge [*savoirs*] knot together into 'forms of recognition' – that is to say, a certain type of subjectification. To proceed from systems of morality and to suppose that these surround the hard core of an eternal problem appears to consign them to history. Yet in fact it reduces them to a natural and eternal essence. To substitute for this 'a history of ethical problematisations made on the basis of the practices of the self' is to assign, to that which seemed inessential, the importance of that which is most serious and most material. That is not to say that *consciousness* determines concrete *being*, the material. This suppresses, by means of these two concepts, the fundamentally naturalistic hypothesis which sustains them: discourse is not 'consciousness' but the constitution of the self, the determination which has a relationship of solidarity with a certain object, with the world in which it exists, and with the subject for which it exists.

In the science of religion, Henry Corbin was able to free himself from historicism by means of a phenomenological hypothesis: that is, the founding act of the imaginal world which makes it possible for the Shi'ite subject to establish the ensemble of this practice and discourse. Following the concepts which belong to the archaeology of knowledge, Foucault is able to obtain a parallel result. I should like to show how, in detail, he develops his theory of 'constitution'.

2 CONSTITUTION AND SUBJECTIFICATION

On the subject of pleasure in the *Philebus*, Foucault writes that 'the ontology to which this ethic refers is not an ontology of lack and of desire'. This is to insist on the independent nature of what is to be the Christian history of the flesh; to say also that what we, along with Hegel and Freud, take as the essence of pleasure (the fulfilling of an absence by means of an object over which another has power) does not exist for Plato. Or rather, it *is* not in the reality which Plato determines to be true. This is one of the major lessons of Foucault's work: that ontology is susceptible to history. It should be stated not only that there is a multiplicity in the doctrines of being but, more radically, that being *constitutes itself*. It is the effect of real experiences which gives substance to this, and this 'constitution' depends also on a formal aspect, the form taken by the 'truth game' at a given time. *L'Ordre du discours* spoke, in a Nietzschean way, of the division which arose out of the 'will to truth'. This claims to determine in particular what makes truth and falsehood possible, what grants authentic status to behaviour and to assertions. We would be wrong to deduce from this that all truth is nothing but appearance, the effect of a discourse which imposes it, and that all knowledge [*savoir*] is vain. We do not progress in the direction of scepticism if we see the will to truth in the experiences which sustain it, but in the direction of the limitless extension of truth itself. It belongs to everything that is, everything that is *true*. We are as far as we can be from the lessons of logicalism, since we are not referring the true to an experience nor to a coherence which is supposed to be eternally valid, but we are considering to be true everything which comes into being in truth discourse.

Now it is exactly such an extension and multiplication of the true that the sciences of religion need. This result is no doubt explained by the proximity of *Histoire de la sexualité* to ethical discourse and therefore to spiritual discourse; we are able to infer from it rules of verification for the status of 'religious' discourse. It will not be necessary for us to ask if the universes built by knowledge [*savoir*], and set out according to the experience of the religious, contradict the nature of things; instead we shall have to ask what sort of truth is deployed in them.

This line of truth between practices and theoretical knowledge would not hold unless it were valid for a subject. For the subject, it would have the virtue of naming the real, and through this truth the subject would experience it. This link between truth, the subject and experience would be total.

Now this concept of the subject is not self-evident. Michel Foucault tells us that it is in itself one of the effects of the truth procedures by means of which it is made necessary. One might say that *there is a subject* because a certain type of 'relationship with the self' comes into being in a culture. It is because individuals grant one another a certain form of attention that they recognise one another as subjects. Contrary to consciousness, which requires the recognition of the other, the subject needs only recognition of the self: such is the lesson of the ethical discourses studied by Michel Foucault. The consequence of this is, first, a historical reinterpretation. From the time of Hegel, Stoicism has been understood, essentially, as that form of consciousness of the self which is pure liberty 'in thought': the other, the 'things which do not depend on the self', are denied in the face of that which alone counts. It is therefore through a certain type of relationship to others (a negative relationship) that I am constituted as a subject, and as a free subject. According to Foucault, who follows here the analysis of Pierre Hadot, the subject is in the first instance his relationship to himself. Rather than the illusory negation of the other, he is the constitution of the ethical *substance* on the basis of a material, the 'individual', according to a form of subjectification which brings the Stoic subject into being. The consequences of this are clear. The history of the subject will no longer be seen to depend on a phenomenology of consciousness, itself linked to dialectical relationships between one person and another, but on the multiple forms which the 'self' can take. And these latter depend, not on the play of intersubjectivity but on the conditions by means of which a freedom which is supposed to be sustained by the subject can be problematised. Sexual austerity, practices of asceticism, techniques of self, access to the 'true love', 'the antagonism of the self to the self', 'the autocratic structure' of the subject: liberty becomes 'a certain form of relationship of the individual to himself'. It is certainly true that this has decisive effects on one's conduct towards others, that this conduct can be studied and controlled in order that the relationship with the self should be true and honorable; but the important point is that in the experience where a being presents itself as true and real, we are constrained to recognise a configuration that is at the same time constituting and constituted: the subject.

This is how a certain type of 'transcendental–historical' element is affirmed. The notion of the subject being, in its own way, 'transcendental' is the condition of possibility of experience and the practice of the true. Yet for all that the subject is still constituted, and again he is not universal. Michel Foucault subverts the Kantian distinction between the subject of understanding and the moral subject. But he also considerably weakens the universality of the transcendental subject. Now this weakening is absolutely essential if we want to progress in the knowledge of the spiritual: we shall be able to understand then how a *subject* of visionary experience is possible, in the conditions which make it at the same time a constituting and a constituted subject.

3 MATERIAL AND FORM OF EXPERIENCE

A subject at the same time constituted and constituting: the contradiction which seems inherent in this notion may well seem similar to that which animates the Aristotelian substance, in which it can be said that matter is determining since matter is the principle of the singularisation of the substance. But it can also be said that form is determining, since without form, matter, absolutely undetermined, is only, Aristotle says, a 'quasi-being', a sham existent halfway between being and non-being. According to Foucault the subject is the locus of experience in the sense that the Aristotelian substance is the substrata of a mode of becoming internal to the power to act. What we find here on the side of power is the individual, and on the side of action the form in which the ethical subject is problematised by the working on the self. Corresponding to this pairing would be that of practice and knowledge [*savoir*], history and discourse: without this Aristotelian model archaeology would be a pure theory of forms 'suspended' outside any substratem; without this it would probably succumb to a doctrine of matter without form, to a physics of singularities which would not permit the precise understanding of how discourse and practice can be said to have a common origin.

Individuals are therefore the matter on which the work of subjectification is to be carried out. They do not really have any being outside this work, previous to it, or in the absence of the form in which ethical or spiritual experience shapes them. But these forms of truth would in turn have no substantial existence beyond their insertion into the concrete matter of practices, behaviour and morals. This circle – of form and matter – orders a second circle: forms of knowledge [*savoir*] are the effective content of a particular problematisation. By this, Michel Foucault means to designate the process by which a certain material domain is invested with values, imperatives, requirements, rules and exhortations. It should be noted that the investment is more a process of granting than the simple 'attribution of value' to an empirical domain. It is in a sense strategic, the encircling and methodical reconnaissance of a place with a view to its conquest. Something becomes an object of knowledge [*savoir*], and at the same time an object of governance. The union of form and matter is both domination and 'guiding'. Through his discovery of the link between the governance of self (the treatment of the self by the forms of a certain ethical problematisation) and the governance of others, Michel Foucault was able to reduce micro-powers and massive institutions to the same model, that of the dominating union of a form and a substance. Ethics and politics are henceforth no longer separate domains which it is the mission of a philosophy of history to reconcile; and the same can be said of the various domains of spiritual life.

Hence the ceaselessly repeated question of the link between religion and politics, between mysticism and power, between the spiritual and material world, disappears.

Investment of value in a material domain of this nature, and attention given to this sort of care for the soul or the body, are never particular cases of a sort of uniform or universal attitude. Foucault says that there are 'thresholds of reflection' which are more or less intense. That is to say, there is no 'reality' which pre-exists the coming into being of these thresholds of questioning, but it varies, on the contrary, with their coming into being or their disappearance.

Certain states of being, certain acts, arise out of the lack of material distinction where they were vegetating before calling forth or giving rise to this sort of questioning. They come to life as they become ethical problems, requiring theoretical and practical treatment. Whereas other modes of existence remain in a state of indifference where they are of no interest to the search for the true: they do not disturb knowledge [*savoir*] and they do not require of it that it should be the material of its analyses and maxims. In Aristotelian terms, they remain pure possibilities.

Why should a particular investment of value take place or not, and why should this affect a particular object, the aspect of a certain degree of reality? The answer to this lies in the practice. The practice creates the 'threshold of reflection'. Yet this practice would not itself come into being if it were not informed by a coherent problematisation. Thus the practice provides the ethical or spiritual substance of investment and as such creates a 'threshold' of interrogation. Yet this is only on the condition that it receives a form to bring it to life, the form of a certain problematisation, the form of interrogation the localisation of which it provides. In this circle of form and matter, practice and problematisation, the substance of ethical life comes into being: experience.

The subject is to be situated on the side of the form – that is to say, of the categories according to which a certain problematisation takes place. He then becomes a constituting subject. Yet he is also to be located on the side of material practices, elected and transformed into thresholds of interrogation. He is constituted as the blind spot of this focalisation.

We learn from Michel Foucault that in the 'aesthetic morality' from which the fourth-century Greeks drew counsel for their existence as beings of pleasure, the most intense threshold is 'in its entirety a blind spot and a point of hypervaluation'. It is on this point, one might say, that rules and questions run riot and multiply, and it is here that the substance of the moral subject lies. It is in this point that the lines and perspectives which determine the form of its activity come together. But this point cannot be grasped. Not only by us, but by those who, in their living experience, ceaselessly question it. It is obviously not inconsequential that one point to which the subject attaches particular importance – although this disappears the moment he attempts to see himself in it – is the sex act. Yet perhaps this is not the only act which can absorb attention in this way, which can be 'hypervalued' and yet remain intractable to all attempts to grasp it instinctively. We shall see that it is precisely such thresholds of spiritual hyperinvestment which one meets in the analysis of religious events, and notably (but not exclusively) in Islamic spiritual events. The more these thresholds are laden with meaning and interest, the more they manifest themselves as enigmas. To call them by name: ecstasy, messianic events, apparitional vision, and in general everything which becomes simultaneously the object of intensely multiplied discourse and strict secretiveness; not that there is a secret to be given away, but that nothing can be said about it – in short, because there is embarrassment.

We find this combination of 'hypervaluation' and non-knowledge which characterises the subject of the ethical 'concern for self' again at the heart of the 'spiritual subject'. The forms of knowledge [*savoir*] can multiply the experience of what the subject is supposed to be; the more he is exalted, the more indiscernible he is. The practices which one would expect to isolate and define him only make him more anonymous. As I was saying, there is no shortage of examples amongst the objects dealt with by historians of spirituality. To begin with I shall just mention that there exists in certain forms of Sufism a 'hypervaluation' of the organs of the body. They are invested with a whole mystical prophetology; to each organ there corresponds a figure from amongst the prophets. Thus there is a hierarchy of organs, just as there is a succession of prophets up to the time of Muhammad, the seal of universal prophecy. To each organ corresponds a certain degree of realisation of mystical or spiritual states. Realising the state, transforming the material corporeal organ into an organ of the subtle body of light, means acceding to a certain degree of contemplation, progressing to the annihilation of the self in God, which leads to hyperexistence in God. This obviously assumes the appropriate techniques which make it possible, under the guidance of a master, to modify, guide and finally metamorphose one's body. Now if there is something about which the discourses are silent, something obscure, indefinite, this is the concrete content of what this state of corporeal and spiritual hyperexistence actually is. This is not only because the uninitiated are to be kept away from this sort of knowledge by secrecy; but because the texts which in their intrepid way most insist on these states and do not hesitate to reveal the way which leads to them become vague, halting and indecisive when they are dealing with their central object (the form of the spiritual object). Everything then becomes very general, very monotonous, as if the discourse were failing; not that the experience is too strong, but that it can no longer properly be sustained as an experience. The matter and the form of the experience intersect at the point where a subject exists; yet this subject can only be the 'blind spot' of the forms of knowledge [*savoirs*] which validate it.

I have now in fact moved away from Michel Foucault's own domain of studies to that which, for want of better words, one might call 'the science of religions'. And in consequence I have reached the point I wished to make: this doctrine of the experience and constitution of the moral subject can be properly used in the elucidation of a number of events in spirituality, and particularly in the domain of Iranian Islamic spirituality. I have already mentioned one of these. I should like to show briefly, and to clarify briefly, the way in which the 'thematic' of the concern for self is found in this spirituality; then I should like to suggest, drawing on several observations already made, how our actual approach to such matters can profit in the light of Foucault's problematisation.

4 MYSTICAL SUBJECTIFICATION AND MORAL SUBJECTIFICATION

Foucault's work insists on the break between the moralities of Ancient Greece and Rome and that of Christianity. There are communications and exchanges, transmissions and intermingling, but on the actual question of sexual ethics, Michel Foucault conceives of the movement between late Antiquity and the triumphant Christian world very precisely as a discontinuity. The concern for self which made it possible for the subject to 'make himself empty for himself' was replaced by the extortion of 'confessions of the flesh'. Stoical asceticism aimed to reduce forces acting on the self by a certain art of self, and the Christian pastoral structure exorcised evil by the fulfilment of a law. On the subject of the medical governance of the *aphrodisia*, Foucault writes: 'In this regime the point was not to set up a struggle between soul and body, nor even to establish means by which the soul could defend itself against the body; the point was rather that the soul should correct itself in order to be able to direct the body according to a law which was that of the body itself.' It would hardly be possible to stress more strongly what it is that makes the two problematisations incompatible.

Now with regard to the 'relationship to the self', what we discover in the study of spirituality in classical Islam is rather a continuity. It seems that, if we were to adopt the perspective outlined by Foucault, the following result would be obtained: corresponding with the clear break brought about by Christianity, we would find later (between the ninth and thirteenth centuries AD), a reinstatement, a reactivation of the themes of neo-Platonic and Stoical ethics. This is in the ethics of Sufism and the illuminative philosophies at the heart of Islam. Here the 'mystical subject' takes up for its own account the problematisation of the 'ethical subject', submitting it to its own new imperatives.

My first example of this is taken from the biography of the 'master of oriental wisdom', Shihāboddīn Yahya Sohravardī (1155–91). It was edited by one of his first disciples, Shahrazūrī. In it we read that in order to attain the mystic 'stations' of the sages and perfect contemplation, Sohravardī practised certain classical exercises of Sufi ethics: silence, rigorous fasting, solitude, sleep deprivation. This ethic might seem close to the asceticism of the Christian monks, and indeed it probably took some of its characteristics from this asceticism. Yet Shahrazūrī tells us that his master practised 'care of the self': this is the literal meaning of the Arab expression '*ishtighāl bi naīsi-hi*'. It does not just mean that Sohravardī 'was concerned about himself' but that he *practised* this concern, which can therefore be placed on the level of the techniques of ecstasy and spiritual advancement. Of course he modifies the overall colouring of this. Elsewhere, Sohravardī says: 'We ourselves are the oppressors of our souls' (which could also be translated: 'of ourselves'). In the ignorance into which we fall regarding divine worlds, we are not in a state of sin but in a situation of exile. This is expressed in terms of a forgetting of self which is a form not of transgression but of abandonment. Returning to God, and going towards the Emerald Cities beyond the montain of Qāf, in the imaginal world, is to return to oneself. The severest forms of asceticism are not punitive macerations which are supposed to efface any remnant of the 'self' but techniques of awakening, which reveal in the 'self' the unique, angelic Face which corresponds to what the angel expects from our soul. Sohravardī is thus preserving the problematisation received from neo-Platonism, although he modifies it.

A second example is the 'struggle against the self' of the master of Sufism Sahl al-Tustarī (who died in 896). Here again we are dealing with a master of the greatest importance for the history of Sufism (he figures in the life of al-Hallāj). We see how, thanks to him, 'concern for self' was to become a central theme much later on in Sohravardī: he refers to a whole series of pronouncements: 'fighting against oneself' [*jahada nafsahu*], 'mortifying' oneself. This mortification is not humiliation in the Christian sense. It refers to the interpretation, present in a famous *hadith* of Muhammad, of the 'war' [*jihad*] which the Koran (29, 69) proposes to the faithful. The Prophet of Islam distinguishes between the minor *jihad* and the major *jihad*, and the latter is the 'fight with oneself'. It is better than the struggle against the infidels. One would be mistaken to make this working on the soul into a form of compensation, the payment of a debt. It is rather a relationship with the self which mediates a relationship with God. It takes, for the Ismailiyans, the form of a rising of the soul to the degrees of the primordial archangelic world. For Sahl al-Tustarī it is the condition of contemplation. The lightning of divine beauty illuminates the soul, which then engages in a 'fight against the self' which opens the way to contemplation. This, in return, intensifies divine aid, the 'guidance' [*hidāya*] which was at the origin of the awakening. What, then, is the great difference between this 'concern for self' and what we learn from Foucault to recognise in the theoreticians of Graeco-Latin ethics? Going back to its essential elements, it seems to come down to this: for Plato, or for the Stoics, even if the soul is guided by a principle exterior to itself – universal Reason, or the ineffable One – it is still in the soul itself that the principles necessary for its progress are contained. Better still, it is the subject which is integrally sufficient for this progress. At its own level it finds the guide of its own liberty: the 'hegemonic' according to the Stoics, or that good part of the soul which could not deliberately desire evil. For the masters of Sufism, on the other hand, it is the Other which is the principle by means of which the soul is torn from its passions: the subject of the work of the self on the self is divine beauty, the divine unity, which is still in a position of radical otherness. This is why the first result which the spiritual apprentice has to achieve is, paradoxically, not a return to the self but the forgetting of self-love. The fact remains, however, that this forgetting of the self, the forgetting of the oppressive soul, leads back to the possession of the pacified soul: finally, then, there is a return to the self. The pure *other*, the divine unity, is overcome only by contemplation in the unity of oneself where the soul experiences at the same time both its own disappearance and its own hyper-existence.

In order to sustain such a conception of the asceticism, Sahl al-Tustarī constructed a remarkable theory of the soul. This rests on the notion of the 'secret of the soul' [*sirr al-nafs*]. God desires to realise His own sovereignty [*rubūbīya*] in the soul. He therefore made the soul a place of internal dialogue. In truth, God is speaking only to Himself there, He soliloquises in the soul. Eternally, He pronounces in it: 'I am your Lord, the Most High' (Koran, 79, 24).

The intimate recess of the heart, the 'secret of the heart' which has to be discovered and experienced more and more, is nothing other than this Lordliness, this divine immanence at the centre of the soul. This is why all the techniques which make it possible to go directly to God are in fact practices opening the way to the soul and leading the self back to the self. The way of the soul is also that of the body: for contemplation is accorded only to the person who masters these two essential practices, engaging body and soul together: prayer [*salāh*] and memorisation–recitation [*dhikr*]. Sahl al-Tustarī typifies these two dangers which lie in wait for us in the figure of Fir'awn (Pharaoh) and Balaam: the first fails to recognise what true attention to self is. He does not know the proper way to practise concern for self, which he confuses with the glorification of his own 'ego'. The second is unaware of the extent of the self: he stops the spiritual ascent too early and remains chained to the lowest degrees of his being. If one avoids these two traps one can, by *listening* to the divine Word, obtain the illumination of the soul, and the body begins to shine forth with its own innate beauty. (For more details on this see Hujwīrī, *Kashf al-Mahjūb*, transl. Nicholson, pp. 200 ff., and Gerhard Böwering, *The Mystical*

Vision of Existence in Classical Islam, Berlin/New York, 1980, pp. 185–207; Sohravardī, *Le Livre de la Sagesse orientale*, Paris, 1987, p. 51.)

5 THE HISTORY OF TRUTH AND THE HISTORY OF RELIGIONS

Let me conclude, then, with some of the results obtained by Foucault in his last books – results which, it seems to me, could well be of interest to studies in Islamic spirituality:

To begin with, as I said, Foucault makes it possible for us to reinforce what the 'phenomenological' process achieved. This had the merit of returning to the spiritual universes of Sufi ethics, or Shi'ite hope, their irreducible truth. We no longer need to reduce them to the status of ideologies, seeing their reason for being in terms of a particular material basis. It is true, though, that the phenomenology of religion proceeded to a curious form of 'parenthesising'. Far from taking it that spiritual universes could not be affected by any kind of reality, so that they could be interpreted as the effects of a subjective activity, phenomenology reversed this universal suspension of belief into its opposite and *affirmed* the truth of essences intuited by whoever sets them up in the reality of his visionary world. According to Corbin, the set of objects of discourse and experience which are correlative to subjective foundation is *true*, because of the very fact that it determines this possible experience. Sweeping historicism aside, this phenomenology of the spiritual is in full accordance, as I see it, with Foucault's problematic, with the following important differences: first, in that it is necessary, according to the phenomenology of religions, to trace the truth of discourse back to the founding origin of a subject. Whereas according to Foucault, as we saw, the experience has to be traced back to a subjectification, to a complex constitution, to a problematisation which at one and the same time produces the subject and is sustained by this subject. Corbin's Platonic style of model is paralleled by Foucault's Aristotelian style of model. Next, it is clear that according to phenomenology the recurrence of founding acts is possible: repetition in time. For Foucault there is no recurrence, only modifications without return. For Henry Corbin the elucidation of subjective and objective universes leads back to self-recognition; for Michel Foucault they are an exercise which aims at 'release from the self': the history of forms of truth is then – according to the quotation from Char on the back cover of the book – to 'contradict' a 'long succession of synonyms'. In Henry Corbin's phenomenology the point was rather to assent to a recurrent and cyclical history, it being understood that this history was the 'other history', the one we hid or misunderstood: the history of the 'Orientals'.

The second point is that of subjectification. If, as I think, the thematic of 'concern for self' is a fertile one in the study of Islamic spirituality, we should recognise that alongside the particular trajectory which led the West to the thematic of moral awareness, by route of Christianity, the maintenance and the modification of the ethic of the 'concern for self' in Islamic spirituality explains how a different ethic, and therefore a different form of free subject, could have come to light in that neighbouring yet infinitely alien culture. What, then, is the significance for us today of this separation in the history of truth-functions? Our present history takes the form of the setting up of an opposition of the culture which invented freedom (ours) and a way of feeling and living which is supposed to be unaware of everything about freedom (Islam), and is based entirely on the politics of Law. What if we saw this in a different way? What if we were to renounce this old opposition between Enlightenment and despotism, to learn of the effects, fortunate or otherwise, that can be produced by the conflict between liberties, neither of which can be regarded as totalities but each of which is worthy in its way to act as modes of existence of the subject?

SUMMARY OF DISCUSSIONS

Fati Triki was of the opinion that the awakening of Islam was not an exclusively spiritual phenomenon but a political one: it expressed the desire to break with the domination of Western reason as it materialised in the establishment of nation-states after colonisation. This desire sought support in the legitimacy residing in the fundamental elements in Islam. But on the other hand, this desire to break away and return to Islam is used to justify a policy of terror which Foucault would have condemned.

Christian Jambet pointed out that there is a conflict going on inside Islamic culture, and that this conflict has allowed forces to come into being which are too often confused. The problematisation of freedom appears in Islam in very different literary genres. To understand these makes it possible to see in Islam what amounts to a real possibility of being a free subject. One is not condemned to export the theory of the rights of man in order to save Islamic territories from the bloody politics which assail them.

Walter Seitter wondered if it would be possible (and desirable) for Foucault's last works to serve as a means of return to Christian spirituality.

Christian Jambet answered that the study of the phenomena of subjectification did not call for any 'return' but for progress in the science of religions, to the extent that this would permit one to escape from the opposition between materiality and mystical phenomena. Visions are material; they should be studied as material elements in a relationship between practice and subject. This would make it possible, in the domain of Iranology, to move from a religious science to a science of religion.

four

The aesthetics of existence

Post-conventional morality and the theory of power in Michel Foucault

Rainer Rochlitz

In 1975 and in 1976, Foucault published two books which announced a grand theory of power.[1] His point of departure was on each occasion events taking place at the time: prison revolts and the triumph of psychoanalysis (particularly Lacanian psychoanalysis) amongst intellectuals, replacing the 'political' notion of power with the notion of juridical, or moral, law. The procedure Foucault adopted to analyse history as we live it consisted, from *Histoire de la folie* onwards, in stepping back and reconstituting the genealogy of present constellations. But to what extent does history, even if this history is articulated in a philosophical way, allow us to step backwards? By making himself a historian of the present time, Foucault was casting an ethnological eye on our present life; he was destroying that which we take for granted and causing us to ask questions about our certainties. In so doing he was fulfilling the authentic role of an intellectual and was happy to claim this role for himself.

At the same time, however, it seems that Foucault's vigilance stopped at the point of the conditions of possibility of his own questions. His projects, while they inaugurated new domains of research, were so much a tributary to their own historical context that it was impossible for him to pursue them according to the initial meaning he attributed to them: in *L'Ordre du discours*, sexuality still arose out of interdiction and exclusion (p. 11); six years later it became rather the object of a 'placing in discourse' organised by 'biopower'; eight years later, the threat of this power passed on to a second level to give way to a reflection on a style of life not regulated by social norms: to a 'post-conventional' mode of life. It is not enough to denounce these inconsistencies: rather, one should try to see the logic in them.

The historian recounts, on the basis of a point he has arrived at but did not choose, the beginning and the end of a history which offers a certain meaningful unity; but history alone does not provide the conceptual instruments which would make it possible for him to decipher this. From the point of view of history, a shift in perspective does not lead to another theory about theory, nor to another theory of truth, language, power or society, but to another outline of history which implies a different 'problematisation'. In *La Volonté de savoir* [*VS*], Foucault wonders why we seek our truth in sexuality and discovers in it an 'apparatus' [*dispositif*] of power which leads us to ask such questions; illustrating this discovery in historical detail, regarding children, women, perverts, populations and races, would present only little theoretical interest; Foucault probably tired rather quickly of this erudite work for, more than a historian, he is an 'essayist', in the sense that he finally comes to claim for himself.

In *L'Usage des plaisirs* [*UP*] he wonders how it was that Western man was 'led to see himself as a subject of desire' (p. 12). The transition from the question of the 'apparatus of sexuality' (in which are rooted the modern technologies of the 'discipline of the body' in schools, barracks, workshops and prisons, and those of the 'regulation of populations' – from State racism to policies to increase the birth rate to the question of the relationship to the self defined by aesthetic style or the hermeneutic of desire, is not a self-evident one. In vain does Foucault try to explain the change in subject; he is not convincing[2] – the enormous value attached to 'biopower' seems suddenly to have disappeared. What has most probably happened is that the essayist has become interested in something different, a different pressing matter of the present – which is his right. But his unsatisfactory explanations draw our attention to a weak point in his procedure: he who tries to 'release himself' from the history in which he is living becomes more a prisoner of it than anyone else; his questions are dependent on their context, to an extent which eludes all theoretical control and obliges him to go so far as to reconstruct his whole theoretical framework because of his extreme historical sensibility. Two things, however, distinguish Foucault from the philosopher-journalists who drew inspiration from him: a global scheme of history borrowed from Nietzsche, linking the original will to power and reason; and a scientific rigour which he inherits from his masters, Dumézil annd Canguilhem.

According to one of the definitions which he gives to the totality of his work, Foucault is asking questions about the 'history of the truth' – about the 'truth games' which the historian is able to describe; yet he barely asks any questions about the truth of the history he is writing; at most he concedes that the task of 'telling the truth' is infinite. The truth for him is not, in the first place, a 'performative' concept; it is, in the first instance, the object of a 'game' or of an 'apparatus' [*dispositif*], each of these objects being closed off from one another by rules defined in an authoritarian way, rules out of which his own discourse does not arise: this is illustrated again by one of his last texts, the conference on

Kant's essay 'What is Enlightenment?' (*Magazine littéraire*, May 1984, p. 39), which established an opposition between the 'ontology of the present' which Foucault requires and the 'analytic of truth' which he thinks he will be able to do without. To escape the apparatus [*dispositif*] is to 'think differently' (*UP*, p. 15), a rather vague expression for which Foucault requires the exploratory form of the 'essay' (*ibid.*[3]). His object is to write the history of 'problematisations' (*ibid.*, pp. 16–17); and there again, Foucault does not ask what it is that makes the problematisations of the past 'problematical'. Narrowly dependent on the present, his critical theory is neither willing nor able to explain criteria in the name of which it attacks certain historical forms of power, knowledge [*savoir*] or subjectivity. It is not willing, because of the fear that this will result in the building of a new system of legitimation; it is not able, to the extent that it has no distance *vis-à-vis* the subversive act of its own questioning.

What is none the less striking is that Foucault's critical contributions – whether they take the form of writing or political practices – contain a normative content, even a virtually universalist normativity: referring to a requirement for the autonomy of the person and opposition to unjust suffering. Nothing, in the explicit statement of his thought – which above all lays claim to the Nietzschean heritage of extreme anti-normativism and anti-universalism – can make possible the justification of such requirements. Foucault receives this implicitly from modern culture; a Christian and secular humanist heritage which he elsewhere denounces as illusory and pernicious. At the same time, Foucault depends on a latent consensus of engaged intellectuals; he addresses himself to a general feeling which experiences the scandal denounced by his minutely detailed and apparently objective, quasi-positivist descriptions. Hence the risk of participating in the intellectual 'sensibilities' of the moment or instinctive reactions (the new philosophy, events in Iran). But because this feeling remains implicit, Foucault as thinker is able to present himself as a solitary spirit advancing hesitantly amongst historically constituted systems of thought, narrowly linked with practices and power relations. The context of the discussion and the research in which he is situated – and which breaks this questioning solitude – is reduced to the names of a few friends, almost conjured up in the effort to escape from the apparatus which he has established. Hence the fact that there is a certain heroism in Foucault's writing, notably in the years 1975 and 1976, the tone of a dramatic release regarding prejudices which are the more tenacious and powerful inasmuch as they are part of networks of interest and anonymous powers.

In *L'Usage des plaisirs* and in *Le Souci de soi*, the tone is no longer the same. In the middle of the 1970s his writings on the subject of a theory of power had an extreme critical vehemence and were engaged in a way which was almost militant, far from the refined, academic style of the 1960s. Volumes II and III of *Histoire de la sexualité* are completely different: after the committed criticism we now have a model to follow, or at least to meditate on; the theory of biopower disappears in favour of the exemplary management of one's personal existence. *L'Histoire de la vie privée* was a project which was to be undertaken at this time by some of his friends. Had the threat of the sexual apparatus – 'Genocide is the dream of modern powers' (*VS*, p. 180) – disappeared? Or had Foucault gone back on his feelings of commitment? In a tone of regret and admiration he paints for us 'the art of existence' such as it was wisely enacted by the ruling elites of classical Greece. This picture is of course still seen in opposition to that of the Christian pastoral practice – which is characterised drily in exactly the same terms as before – and to the apparatus this set in motion which was so laden with consequences for the future. Yet there is no further question of struggling against the biopower which is seen as its latest development; the point is to reflect on a new way of conducting one's life, on the use which one makes of pleasure and on the care which one takes of oneself, in a way which is unrelated to any norm or social control, but has the sole purpose of leading a beautiful life and finding in it the ideal form of hygiene, avoiding excess but paying no attention to what is meant by perversion.

Foucault does not hide the fact that this is a morality destined for a small elite of masters, and that the mastery of self which he sympathetically describes is an exercise which prepares one for the mastery of others, an exercise which is very distant from any critique of domination. Nor does he hide the fact that it is a 'morality of men for men' (*UP*, p. 96); a sexual morality which pays no attention to the reciprocity of pleasure, recognising only a relationship between the dominator and the dominated, the central problem of which is therefore the conversion of the 'boy' – dominated in the love relationship and on a par with women and slaves – into a future master and citizen. However, Foucault does not hesitate to put forward the Greek model for the consideration of the 'liberation movements' in the Western world of the 1980s.[4]

This is linked with the fact that Foucault establishes a rigorous continuity between the 'juridical-moral codification' of Christianity and psychoanalysis as the ultimate stage of a 'power of truth' exercised on the body and pleasures. Like Nietzsche, Heidegger and Bataille, Foucault proceeds to an enormous simplification of modern and medieval history;[5] this may be called 'pastoral power'. This simplification explains why Foucault – following on from Nietzsche and from Heidegger – relies on Ancient Greece and discovers in it a source which has dried up since the Christian era: that of an art of life which Christianity extirpated in the name of the struggle against sin, through its normalising tendency and through a concept of truth which makes desire into an object of knowledge [*connaissance*] so that this can be better controlled and normalised.

Foucault's originality, given the closeness of his perspective to that of

Nietzsche, is that his genealogy does not seek the origin of 'the power of truth' and the 'hermeneutic of desire' in resentment, in the morality of slaves and in a universality which masks a perverted will to power, but in a problematisation which appeared at the very heart of classical Greece, notably with Plato. Nietzsche had suspected that Socrates 'was not a Greek'; Heidegger had discovered in Plato the origin of an objectivist concept of truth out of which the modern idea of science and technology came into being, the break in our belonging to nature as *physis*. Foucault interprets the objectification of love in Plato as a hermeneutic of desire; in terms of an attempt to solve the problem presented by homosexuality, seeing the love relationship as a relationship of domination: Platonic eroticism 'is a way of responding to an inherent difficulty in Greek culture, created by the relationship between men and boys: the status which should be accorded to the latter as objects of desire' (*UP*, p. 266), inasmuch as there was also a need to transform them into subjects and future masters of the city. 'Plato resolves the difficulty of the object of pleasure by tracing back the question of the loved individual to the nature of love itself; structuring the love relationship as a truth relationship; . . . and inverting the role of the loved young man in order to make him a lover of the master of truth' (*ibid.*). Thus, homosexuality is seen as being at the origin of a problematisation which the Western world cannot thereafter escape.

Foucault does not, however, explain what it is that makes it possible for him to discover this origin of the hermeneutic of desire which is taken up, for different ends, by Christianity; nor does he explain what it is that makes it possible for him to envisage love relationships exempt from domination. Being a prisoner of his own theory of power, he cannot admit that it is only modern reflection on sexuality which makes it possible for him freely to pronounce such a hypothesis about the origins of the objectification of desire; and he is not able to realise the extent to which the idea of pleasure shared without domination depends on modern ideas about equality, reciprocity and non-violence, which developed *at the same time* as biopower.

It is also true that Foucault, unlike Nietzsche and Heidegger, does not attribute responsibility for the historical turning point directly to Plato. Stoical thought, while it sharpens the attention which it would be necessary to bring to bear on sexual life, does not see it in terms of an absolute evil and has no sense of finitude, sin and fall any more than it has a notion of a general law to which one should submit oneself. Christian thought, therefore, has sources *other* than those which come from Greek thought, sources about which Foucault has nothing to say. In Nietzsche's *The Genealogy of Morality* one finds anti-Semitic and anti-democratic outbursts[6] which Foucault never quotes, yet which he replaces with no other theory.

In fact there is a concept which is totally absent from Foucault's morality; this is precisely the concept which, according to Nietzsche, has its origins in

Judaeo-Christian resentment: the concept of universality. The fact that everyone can claim to be treated in the same way and claim the same fundamental rights counts less for Nietzsche and Foucault than the consequences of this sort of claim for the aristocratic culture of the art of life. Yet is it really necessary to choose between an elite's art of life and the universality of rights? And again: does the art of life constitute a defence against 'biopower'? Foucault would not go so far as to make formulations of this nature, yet he has nothing to say which might oppose conclusions of this nature.

According to Foucault, Christianity is therefore principally responsible for this 'sexual apparatus' which in his eyes constitutes the key to modern 'biopower'. Amongst the texts promised by Foucault there are two notable absences: *La Chair et le Corps*, the second volume of the original plan for *Histoire de la sexualité*, and *Les Aveux de la chair*, a book which was apparently almost complete. Whilst we await its publication it will be necessary to draw on remarks scattered in the works and articles available to the public, which say: 'It is often said that Christianity brought into being an ethical code quite different from that of the ancient world. Less emphasis is usually placed on the fact that it proposed and spread new power relations through the ancient world' (Dreyfus and Rabinow, p. 214).

Disregarding the historical abridgement concerning the Christian era and the whole evolution since the Renaissance, the Reformation and the French Revolution, at this point three critical observations could be made about Foucault's writings: (1) he only ever saw the negative side of Christianity and, in a general way, of the idea of universality which it bears within itself (which is why he minimises the elitist characteristic of the Greek model); (2) he sets up a short circuit between morality and power, according no autonomy and no internal logic to moral development; he therefore treats Christianity and Christian morality somehow as a simple 'superstructure' of a power apparatus; (3) as a result of this one-sided view he seems unable to realise what creates the ambiguity of modern society – that is, the fact that it makes possible at one and the same time the power structure which Foucault pertinently analyses and theories like those of Foucault, and all those who develop critical ideas of the same type.

Foucault locates the birth of modern biopower in a continuation of the 'religious crises' of the sixteenth and seventeenth centuries and notably at the end of the eighteenth, following a break already set out in his preceding works; it is at this time that an intense 'putting into discourse' of sexuality is supposed to have started, linked with a new type of power which takes charge of 'men as living bodies' (*VS*, p. 117) and places the human sciences at the service of social control. The French Revolution is therefore, without further ado, taken as a hinge point between two types of power, the first of which, when it comes down to it, seems the least dangerous: the power of aristocratic 'blood' which is succeeded by bourgeois power, founded on 'sex' as concern for a disciplined body and the health of the race. The notion of sexuality provides Foucault with an opportunity for a ruthless indictment of the bourgeois era. The difference between bourgeois and democratic society and totalitarian and racist regimes seems thus to be relative, according to a schema of argumentation which puts one in mind of Horkheimer and Adorno's *La Dialectique de la raison*.[7] As a result of his desire to demystify bourgeois ideals, Foucault sees all the progressive conquests made by the State of law, democracy, and the guarantees and forms of protection from which the members of a developed society benefit – in spite of all the inadequacies of the way these are applied and all the structural vices of the social State – as the development of a power structure of growing cynicism. Because of his desire to 'demystify' all discourse about 'sexual liberation', Foucault can no longer see what modern society owes to, amongst other things, psychoanalysis, except in terms of the political context in which it opposed, as Foucault concedes, biologism and theses regarding 'degeneration'. Foucault does not show that the 'truth of desire' sought by psychoanalysis has no end other than social normalisation. 'Truth' is for him a synonym of objectification with a view to domination; otherwise he would not have been able to reduce the 'human sciences' – out of which, after all, his own writings arise, if we take the term in the broadest sense, without which it loses interest – to an element of the apparatus of power: 'The carceral network constitutes one of the formations of this power–knowledge which made the human sciences possible. Knowable man (soul, individuality, conscience and behaviour matter little here) is the effect–object of this analytic investment, this domination–observation' (*Surveiller et punir*, p. 312). Since the 1960s at least – and for a lot of researchers, well before this period – the methodology of human sciences established the symbolic character of the object of these sciences, and therefore the fact that this commits us to an intersubjective relationship of recognition which is irreducible to an object in the strict sense. Foucault does not take account of this evolution, though he himself participates in it; he seems to take it that the totality of human science could be traced back to the stream of objectivism, behaviourism or functionalism, the existence of which there is no point in denying, in a way which thus places them effectively at the service of 'social technology' or technocratic management. The benefit of this simplification is twofold: it makes possible the reduction of modern power to a structure of uniform strategies which is relatively lacking in complexity, aiming to extend their sphere of influence and the intensity of their domination; and it confers on the person analysing them the status of an exception, as having a sharpened sensitivity for the usurpative character of this power which besieges minds, thus as being capable of an extreme vigilance which goes beyond the naivety of most people.

There is, therefore, a naivety in his suspicions, a naivety as to the identity of the entity under consideration and a naivety as to the foundation of the nature of the thought under suspicion. Having objectivised truth into a 'truth game', to the 'history of truth', and having objectivised language and society into an 'apparatus' of discourse and power, Foucault cannot grant an objective status to his own aesthetic sensitivity, or to his style, or to the acuity of his thought, where a form of critical power is concentrated which is quite alien to 'games' and 'apparatus', this being analogous rather to a sort of Cartesian doubt. This is why he cannot admit that the qualities which make it possible for him to escape from the powers he talks about might have an existence independent of himself, since they are inscribed in the very structure of modern society as a form of institutionalised critique, and as a space of liberty and discussion which is irreducible to the system of power.

The analysis in terms of the play of strategies is of a formalist type.[8] Yet the coldness and neutrality of Foucault's functionalism are purely and simply apparent; it is a dramatic and ironic functionalism, the grinding style taking the place of the normative base of the criticism. When he denounces the dream of genocide and the training of the body in modern society, Foucault demonstrates the critical character of his functionalism.

Foucault's criticism bears within it a secret universalism which he himself cannot explain for fear of contradicting himself; the point in question is the project of a post-conventional morality. It is expressed first in terms of an 'aesthetic' demand for pleasure and knowledge which could never be reconcilable with a functionalist system of gratuitous power, pleasure and knowledge which have no 'purpose' other than their intrinsic ends: 'It would be necessary to free oneself from the insistency of sex if one wanted, by means of a tactical reversal of the diverse mechanisms of sexuality, to maintain bodies, pleasure and knowledge [*savoir*] in their multiplicity and their potential for resistance against the appropriations of power' (*VS*, p. 208). What Foucault opposes to the biopower which trains bodies and regulates populations is neither the Nietzschean cult of strength nor a form of democratic life, but a ludic universe of pleasure and knowledge [*savoir*] which disregards all social activity and all economic and administrative constraints; he cannot therefore question the existing social system in any real way, since he has no form of organisation to substitute for it. Foucault's criticism is in the first instance purely 'aesthetic'; it has no rational foundation, since it has located reason on the side of the apparatus which is to be fought against. Yet the aesthetic background to his criticism is charged with an ethical universality which remains implicit. 'Making a work [of art] of one's life' (*UP*, p. 16) is a project for privileged minorities, liberated from all functions in the material reproduction of society, who can use all their strength to perfect the refinement of their lifestyle. The art of life preached by Foucault is none the less the anarchistic equivalent of a post-conventional ethic:

> The conclusion would be that the political, ethical, social, philosophical problem of our time is not to try to liberate the individual from the State, and from the State's institutions, but to liberate us both from the State and from the type of individualisation which is linked to the State. We have to promote new forms of subjectivity through the refusal of this kind of individuality which has been imposed on us for several centuries. (Dreyfus and Rabinow, p. 308)

Yet is the individualisation which Foucault rejects along with the State and conventional normal ethics really reducible to the apparatus of power which arises out of Christianity? Could it not also be seen as a counterbalance to the imposed socialisation and a way of training the mind to be critical regarding institutions and their levelling tendency? What Foucault in particular refuses to admit of in Christianity, in modern society and in psychoananlysis is the demand for *interiorisation*. He suggests the possibility of liberating us from Christianity, from 'pastoral power', without our having in advance to integrate the system of conventional norms. He seems to believe that all we have to do is to understand the mechanisms of power, its conventional and historical character, in order to bring to light its illusory nature and to free ourselves from its influence; this process of becoming aware would be the equivalent of a 'genealogy of morality' which would demystify values. Foucault would have been able to avoid such a break with his own moral institutions – the nature of which are clear from his political activities – only by proceeding to an interiorisation – and thus to a critical examination – of the norm which he denounces as an element of the apparatus of power.[9] In spite of himself, Foucault is here placing himself in a religious tradition which refuses to accept interiorisation. Unable to found his criticism of the actual structure of modern society as an institutionalisation of the right to criticise, he refers to the potential of 'resistance' which gives rise, almost mechanically, to the exercise of all power: a community united not by common convictions but by the oppression they experience together. Yet what can be said of the oppressed who 'take' power, after a 'strategic coding of points of resistance which make a revolution possible' (*VS*, p. 127)? There is nothing to guarantee that this new power would not, in turn, be repressive.

This refusal to interiorise, and the implicit reference to a presupposed community, could equally explain Foucault's commitment to an 'aesthetics of existence'. The art of living in classical Greece was founded on a metaphysical dogmatism which admitted scepticism but no 'transcendental' foundation of criticism; it is in the name of this dogmatism that Socrates, the subversive questioner, agreed to be condemned. In the same way, the splendour of the Renaissance – which Foucault evoked following on from Burckhardt, and which Nietzsche continued to regard with nostalgia – also illustrates an art of life founded on religious and metaphysical dogmatism; here again, the emancipation of the individual is essentially limited to the domain of aesthetics, where an audacity is permissible; whilst science remains under surveillance and the strictest morality coexists alongside cynicism. The metaphysical certainties – later upset by Descartes, Kant and their successors – are not yet called into question. Perhaps the audacity and the dilemma in Foucault's thought should be understood in the same way. Foucault, the vehement questioner, was after all a professor at the Collège de France: this position went almost unchallenged during his lifetime; after the death of Sartre, Foucault, the genealogist of morality, became a sort of moral authority. What, then, is the biopower which leads to nominations of this nature? Is it all just some kind of trick?

The aesthetics of existence brings this dilemma to light. There is something laughable about Foucault's proposing a new art of living if we continue to bear in mind the threats of genocide which he had brandished some years earlier. If some social minority decided to set about making its life a work of art, this would hardly be a matter of concern for a power apparatus of this nature. Foucault's greatness lies in the fact that he did not hide these contradictions.

NOTES

1. 'I shall interrupt this book which is to serve as a historical background to the power of normalisation and the formation of knowledge in modern society' (*Surveiller et punir*, p. 315). 'Greek law had already coupled torture and confession, at least for slaves. Roman imperial law had broadened the practice. These questions will be taken up again in *Le Pouvoir de la vérité*' (*La Volonté de savoir*, p. 79).
2. *L'Usage des plaisirs*, p. 11: 'It seemed difficult to analyse the formation and the development of the experience of sexuality starting with the eighteenth century, without carrying out historical work and criticism on desire and the desiring subject, that is without undertaking a "genealogy". . . . Yet it was clear that undertaking this genealogy would lead me a long way from my original project. I had to choose. . . . I chose the latter option, reflecting that after all, what I was aiming at – what I had wanted to aim at for a number of years – was an undertaking to bring to light some of the elements which could serve towards a history of truth' (p. 12).
3. This is why the 'system' constituted retrospectively by Gilles Deleuze (*Foucault*, Paris: Éditions de Minuit, 1986) disregards the topical value of the aspects on each occasion highlighted by Foucault.
4. 'Their major theme was the constitution of a sort of morality which would be an aesthetics of existence. Well, I wonder if our problem today is not in a certain way the same, since for the most part we do not believe that a morality can be founded on religion and we do not want a legal system that would intervene in our private, personal and intimate life. Recent liberation movements suffer from not being able to find a legal system on which the development of a new morality could be founded. They need a morality, but they cannot manage to find any other than that which is founded on what is claimed to be scientific knowledge of the self, desire, the

unconscious, and so on' (in Hubert L. Dreyfus and Paul Rabinow, *Michel Foucault. Un parcours philosophique*, Paris: Gallimard, 1984, p. 325). [Not present in the English version: Translator.]

5. Cf. Jürgen Habermas, *Der philosophische Diskurs der Moderne*, Frankfurt: Suhrkamp, 1985.
6. Friedrich Nietzsche, *Œuvres philosophiques complètes*, vol. VII, *Par-delà bien et mal. La Généalogie de la morale*, Paris: Gallimard, 1971, pp. 231 ff.
7. 'Anyway, for us it is not only a theoretical question, but a part of our experience. I'd like to mention only two "pathological forms" – those two "diseases of power" – fascism and Stalinism. One of the numerous reasons why they are, for us, so puzzling is that in spite of their historical uniqueness they are not quite original. They used and extended mechanisms already present in most other societies. More than that: in spite of their own internal madness, they used to a large extent the ideas and the devices of our political rationality' (Dreyfus and Rabinow [English version], p. 299).
8. Cf. A. Honneth, *Kritik der Macht*, Frankfurt: Suhrkamp, 1985.
9. Cf. Habermas, *Morale et Communication*, French transl. C. Boudindhomme, Paris, Éditions du Cerf, 1987, pp. 170 ff. First interiorisation: 'It is known that Freud and Mead admitted, in ways which were compatible, that particular models of behaviour arise out of speech acts and intentions linked to the context, uttered by particular persons, and acquire the external form of social norms to the extent that the sanctions which are attached to these norms are *interiorised* [through the adoption of the attitude of others] – that is to say, integrated into the personality of the adolescent and caused to be independent from the power sanction of the reference person [parent or educator].' The subject is thus submitted to the *generalised arbitrariness* of a socially established expectation. It is this 'generalised arbitrariness' which Foucault demystifies in the name of power, instead of proceeding to a second interiorisation: 'The power of sanction which is found behind social roles loses its transcendental imperative character, it is true, only to the extent that the adolescent, here again, interiorises the coercive strength of the institutions which begins to have real effects on him and to the extent that he anchors this strength in himself in order to cause it to come into play as an internal system of control. From the moment that A considers the group sanctions to be his own, directed by *himself* and against *himself*, it is necessary for him to *presuppose* his belonging to a norm through which he, in this way, punishes transgression.' This necessity to be able to accept the norm to which one submits leads the subject to criticise existing norms without abandoning the ethical requirement.

SUMMARY OF DISCUSSIONS

Jacques Alain-Miller: Rainer Rochlitz is asking, not why Foucault was so wicked, but why it was that whilst being so wicked in theory (being so anti-universalist, so relativist, so opportunist), he was so good in practice (militating on behalf of prisoners, the mad, and so on). As such he is led to suspect in Foucault a universal ethic which remains implicit. He has this suspicion because he thinks of ethics in accordance with a Kantian regime. Now Foucault's ethic is not Kantian. Foucault has a particular predilection for a pre-Kantian position of morality where ethics is not linked with the universal, in which it is not cut off from the pathological. The 'intolerable', for example, is a category of sensibility. There is a lot of danger in separating the ethical from the pathological, since the pathological constitutes a defence against terror and the horrible.

Foucault gives the example of an ethic which does not have to be an ethic, of an ethic which does not have sacrifice at its core. It is quite comparable with that of Spinoza. There are ethics which are founded not on absence but on the more or less and which, rather than encouraging sacrifice, invite to fuller being. Their aim is wisdom. Pierre Hadot thinks this is still possible in practice; Foucault is putting it forward as a possibility. He is not sure if it is practicable today. First of all there is the fact that this is an ethic for a ruling class, though this can be modified by the fact that Foucault would have liked everyone to be in minorities; he would have preferred only minorities, no majority. Wisdom in particular supposes an integration in the cosmos which is no longer possible in a world which is constantly being reshaped by discourse and by science. Modern pleasures can no longer be regimented by the usage of pleasures in Ancient Greece.

Rainer Rochlitz stressed that if the universal of which he talked did bear any relation to Kant, it would be to a post-Kantian morality; it did not refer to an imperative, but to a requirement inherent in morality such as it exists socially. There would be no question of cutting off the ethical from the pathological. The universal can result only from a debate that no one can finish, in which any harmed interest would always eventually emerge. This universality would take account of the divergence of other people's interests and would impose no imperative on them. The idea of wisdom does not enable us to make a response to the modern question of morality. How can conflicts which arise between us be settled?

five

Beyond life and death

On Foucault's post-Auschwitz ethic

James W. Bernauer

Amid the many photographs contained in the beautiful volume of tributes published by Syros as *Michel Foucault: Une histoire de la vérité*, there is one which has especially stayed in my memory.[1] It was taken in 1982 during one of Foucault's trips to Poland, and it shows him walking between two rows of electrified barbed wire, a watchtower in the background. A visit to another prison? Only after consulting the information at the back of the book did I realise it was Auschwitz. Of course. It was only to be expected that he would have wanted to see Auschwitz with his own eyes, the eyes which stare sternly out at the photographer. If Claude Lanzmann's *Shoah* has permitted us to hear the voices of that distant hell, I believe Foucault has enabled us to see its nearness, to feel its intimacy, and to challenge its logic.

The title of this paper alludes less to Nietzsche than it does to a desire and a problematic. Mine, but also, I would claim, Foucault's in the last stage of his thought. Michel Foucault was often disappointed with the philosophical community's reception of his works, its misunderstanding of their aims and its neglect of their problematics. Although Foucault would occasionally express his frustration with this reception, far more frequently he would merely pass it over in silence and move on to the new project which had excited his insatiable curiosity. His refusal to force commentators to deal with specific issues which his writings raised certainly did not affect his own creativity. Nevertheless, in one case at least, I think that his reluctance has seriously limited our appreciation of his contribution to a discussion into which he wished to enter explicitly, and has occasioned some major misinterpretations of his last published works. In an important 1977 conversation, Foucault was asked about the concluding part of *La Volonté de savoir*, the section entitled 'Right of death and power over life', where he treated such topics as biopower, racism, Nazism, and what he described as society's 'threshold of biological modernity'. This is the point at which politics places man's 'existence as a living being in question' because the 'life of the species is wagered on its own political strategies'.[2] Foucault sees our recent world wars and our current atomic situation, in which entire populations are exposed to death in the interest of preserving a nation's life, as the outcome of a power–knowledge regime that is committed to the administration of life itself. In reply to his interviewer's interest in this section, Foucault uncharacteristically voiced his frustration: 'Yes, no one wants to talk about that last part. Even though the book is a short one, but I suspect people never got as far as that last chapter. All the same, it's the fundamental part of the book.'[3] And, I would add, the fundamental key to the entire history of sexuality project. In the ten years since that interview, the silence which initially met that last section of *La Volonté de savoir* has rarely been broken.[4] If 'Right of death and power over life' provides the horizon for my own consideration of Foucault's last writings, it is because I think that his later work on the history of sexuality is fully appreciated only within that horizon. Indeed, that work should be viewed as Foucault's own continuation of the discussion which failed to attract other participants in 1976.

As we know, Foucault's last works have met with a very mixed critical reaction. The reviewer in my local Boston newspaper expressed a benevolent confusion. He described his reading of *L'Usage des plaisirs* as a 'rare pleasure, like watching fireworks of the mind', but then went on to confess that he remained 'unsure about what the book is discussing'.[5] This refreshing honesty was almost inaudible amid the chorus of American criticism. Typical of the latter was the charge that Foucault had elevated the quest for beauty in life over all other intellectual and moral virtues, with the result that the 'self rather than the world and its inhabitants becomes the central focus of aesthetic enhancement'.[6] The charge is representative inasmuch as the common target of criticism has been Foucault's 'aesthetics of existence', which has been taken as a sign of his allegiance to a Greek morality or to an amoral aestheticism. Despite Foucault's effort to avoid such misinterpretation, his late shift to a consideration of the subjective axis and his emphasis on the desire to think differently have led many to see an unrecognisable Foucault. Thus, even a careful and admiring critic could lament that his last works were both disappointing and a retreat from the principles that defined the valuable legacy of his earlier studies.[7] It seems clear that Foucault did not wish his aesthetics of existence to be understood as an echo of that Greek morality which he found neither exemplary nor admirable.[8] In general, he used it in criticism of those models which would confine human creativity to the realm of art and replace the task of self-elaboration with the duty of a self-discovery governed by a hermeneutics of desire. Far more may be said. I wish to claim that the Foucault who asserts the need for an aesthetics of existence is best recognisable if that need is considered from within the perspective of the approach to life in *La Volonté de savoir*'s last part. An 'aesthetics of existence' is in contrast and resistance to a 'science of life'. To speak of human existence as a work of art is to take it out of the domain of the scientifically knowable and to free us from the obligation of deciphering ourselves as a system of timeless functions which are subjected to corresponding norms. As Foucault indicated earlier, such deciphering would be a psychological approach.[9] But psychology itself emerges from biological science and the determination of human existence as an organism, as life. If human being is under the obligation to discover its true self as a sexual reality, it is because, in our age's Faustian pact', sexuality is identified with the natural force of life itself.[10] But not only with life. The binding of personal identity and organic life immerses that identity within the flow of blood, which is a sign of life but also an index of that life's fragility. Life bleeds; and thus the confession of sexual identity avows not only life but its permanent war with death.

If the key to the character of Foucault's last concerns is his fascination with the question of why our culture made sexuality into a moral experience, I would like to suggest how this question had itself become so problematic for him.[11] His history of sexuality's genealogy of the man of desire may be viewed as an additional fragment in Foucault's examination of pyschoanalysis. But behind his probing of that hermeneutics of desire, which rests upon the triad truth–sexuality–subjectivity, is the spectre that human existence will continue to understand itself as a struggle of life versus death, Eros against Thanatos. Our souls have been fashioned as a mirror of that contemporary political landscape in which massacres are vital, in which there is a right to kill those who are perceived as representing a biological danger, in which political choice is governed by the sole option between survival or suicide. If *Surveillir et punir* showed that philosophical thought must struggle with the power–knowledge relations which would transform the human soul and existence into a mechanism, Foucault's history of sexuality points to the ethical task of detaching ourselves from those forces which would subordinate human existence [*bios*] to biological life [*zoë*]. In the first part of this paper, 'Our political selves', I shall place Foucault's genealogy of the man of desire within the context of his ambition to subvert the scenario of the soul as a struggle between life and death. Although Foucault acknowledges its general opposition to fascism, his criticism of psychoanalysis as a form discloses his own understanding of the role it plays in supporting that specific story of the soul which dominates our contemporary culture of the self. His subversion of this story was for the sake of making another ethos available, a 'use of philosophy which may enable us to limit the areas of knowledge'.[12] The practice of such limitation is the meaning of the general ethic for thought which is the legacy of Foucault's entire project. His explicit turn to ethics at the end of his life was not, however, an abandonment of his political concerns. It is precisely because he recognised that our political culture of life versus death involved a particular mode of political relationship to the self that the practice of ethics became central to his last works; it is, as he said, 'politics as an ethics'.[13] This paper's second part will present a sketch of this general ethic for thought. Although there are many directions in which that ethic might be employed, the paper's concluding section, 'A journey to Auschwitz', will indicate but one possible way in which Foucault's own schema for ethical interrogation may illumine a dark corner on the Nazi stage of our present history.

1 OUR POLITICAL SELVES

The battle between life and death which forms our actual political terrain also furnishes the map for our epistemological and imaginative landscapes. The replacement of a natural history by a science of biology pledged our lives to history and struggle. In place of the priority given by classical nature to the stable kingdom of discrete plants, knowledge and imagination are captured by the energy of animality. Life escaped the space of order and became 'wild once more', dwelling on the frontiers of life and death. Life is besieged by death on all sides: it is 'from the depths of their lives that death overtakes living beings'. This fraternity with death reveals life as a murderous evolutionary force: 'It kills because it lives'.[14] But this morbid law of life is also ours, as Freud came to discover. The existence of man and civilisation is the contest between the drives of life and death [*Eros und Tod, Lebenstrieb und Destruktionstrieb*]. 'And it is this battle of the giants that our nursemaids try to appease with their lullaby about Heaven'.[15] For Foucault, the silencing of this combat was not a temptation only for nursemaids. 'We know that psychologists and philosophers have dismissed all this as Freudian mythology.' While dismissals may win independence from mythologies, only a 'politics of our selves' will liberate us from a soul and a self-relationship which have been created and defined by very specific historical forces of knowledge, power and subjectivisation.[16] This Foucauldian politics of ourselves is in resistance to a form of power which 'categorizes the individual, marks him by his own individuality, attaches him to his own identity, imposes a law of truth on him which he must recognise', and makes individuals subjects.[17] The suicidal life of Herculine Barbin bears witness to the force of such power–knowledge–subjectivity relations.[18] As a result of such relations, present political struggles must 'revolve around the question: Who are we? They are a refusal of these abstractions, of economic and ideological state violence which ignores who we are individually, and also a refusal of a scientific or administrative inquisition which determines who one is.' If one side of this resistance is to 'refuse what we are', the other side is to invent, not discover, who we are by promoting 'new forms of subjectivity'.[19]

If Freud became the principal concern lurking in Foucault's genealogy of desiring man, it is because Freud's delineation of the soul as Eros and Thanatos re-enacts that special relationship with the self which is the bequest of Western culture – namely, that sexuality is the index of one's true self. Foucault's journey to this anti-Freudian politics of the self followed a very circuitous route. In the years immediately after the publication of *Histoire de la sexualité*'s introductory volume, Foucault's research roamed across a field of topics closely related to the issues of the projected last volume, *Population et Races*. In 1976, he taught a course on the appearance of a discourse on war and how it functioned as an analysis of social relations; in 1978 and 1979, he presented courses on the genesis of a political rationality which placed the notion of population and the mechanisms to assure its regulation at the centre of its concern, and conducted seminars on the theory of police science and on nineteenth-century juridical thought.[20] *Population et Races* would have examined how the sexual domain became an object for ever-increasing state intervention, as well as the emergence of eugenics and theories of race in the contemporary configuration of knowledge. Despite the variety of his interests in these years, a special concern did take shape and directed Foucault to a study of Christianity and a hermeneutics of desire. This was the problematic of governance as it appeared in sixteenth-century Christianity. The first major statement of his approach to the problematic came with his 1980 course, which he entitled 'De l'administration du vivant' (On the governance of the living'.[21]

He presented the Christian regime of governance against the background of an opening meditation on Sophocles' *Oedipus*. Freud's interpretation of the play is familiar. For him, Oedipus's search for the truth 'can be likened to the work of a psychoanalysis'. One relentlessly pursues the truth of one's identity, which is hidden far from one's conscious awareness and shows itself as linked to the dimension of desire and sexuality. The story possesses perennial appeal because we recognise ourselves in Oedipus. As Freud points out: 'His destiny moves us – because the oracle laid the same curse upon us before our birth as upon him'.[22] Perhaps the myth attracted Foucault because it portrays so well the major domains of his own work: an analysis of the knowledges [*savoirs*] through which we are constructed as knowable and from which we derive the paths for fleeing self-ignorance; an examination of the power relations generated with those knowledges [*savoirs*] and of the systems of dependence to which we become subject in seeking our truth; finally, a study of how subjectivity became intimately associated with both truth and sexuality, how the discovery of one's sex is the discovery of one's true self. In Foucault's earlier writing, his archaeology of psychoanalysis involved an identification of its general power–knowledge relations, especially its relationship to a medical model and its notion of the unconscious; in the the first volume of *Histoire de la sexualité* it entailed a critique of the place psychoanalysis occupies in the modern deployment of sexuality; finally, his history of the man of desire excavates the relationship of the self to the self which operates in Freudian thought. All these encounters estrange us from Freud's story of the soul and, thus, from the destiny of our politics. I would like to touch briefly on each of these moments of estrangement.

While Freud admitted that psychoanalysis 'had its origin on medical soil', he had hoped that it could be transplanted.[23] Foucault's *Naissance de la clinique* indicated, however, that modern readings of the person are tied to a medical perception. The work argued that clinical medicine was the first science of the individual. Integral to this science was the role of death as constitutive of one's individuality and unique intelligibility, a status which was the precondition for the extraordinary importance given by historians to pathological anatomy in the development of a science of medicine. Death and disease broke from metaphysical understandings and became essential elements in the identity of the person. The idea of a disease attacking and destroying life is replaced by the conception that death is embodied in the living bodies of individuals. It is not because diseases attack him that man dies; it is because he will die that he is susceptible to disease. Created here was the crucially significant notion of a 'pathological life' which can be carefully charted and analysed in terms of an *individual's* existence. But death is the essential truth of human life, and any enquiry into the meaning of individual life is guaranteed to meet that medical perception which holds up to man the 'face of his finitude', but also promises to exorcise it through certain techniques.[24] The medical component is clear in questions of sexuality, but if Foucault is correct, all knowledge of the modern finite, bound-to-death self is orientated, by its very object, to aim at a truth which aspires to function as cure. This would account for the fact that Freud, who could demystify so many of the asylum's major structures – its constant silence, observation, condemnation – could not eliminate the place occupied by the doctor, upon whom these transformed structures were concentrated: the trained observer whose silence is judgement. It is the very knowledge of our finite, individual selves which invites a medical paradigm and accounts for the fact that, in our culture, Freud and medical thought have come to take on philosophical significance.[25] The controversies which swirl around the relationship between medicine and psychoanalysis are native and permanent to Freudian thought to the extent of its modernity. Foucault's *Les Mots et les Choses* extended his archaeology of psychoanalysis by indicating the foundations for the specific character of the unconscious which is at the core of psychoanalytic self-knowledge. Psychoanalysis occupies a central position in modern thought because it explores, but is also defined by, an opaqueness or unconsciousness generated by modern knowledge's dispersion of man within processes of life, labour and language. All these possess histories alien to and independent of man. The themes of Death, Desire and Law, in which one's psychoanalytic search for intelligibility takes place, are born together with and remain dependent upon modern knowledge's drawing of man in those great colours of life, labour, speech. In exploring these psychoanalytic themes, Western culture is brought back to the foundations for its anthropological knowledge and thus, as Foucault points out, 'pivots on the work of Freud, though without, for all that, leaving its fundamental arrangement'.[26]

The central role which sexuality plays in the psychoanalytic image of the person is the next major element which indicates Freudian thought's coherence with the modern network of power–knowledge. Psychoanalysis is in alliance with the modern period's threefold sexual production: the creation of sexuality as a reality, especially the sexualisation of children's experience; the constitution of a *scientia sexualis* based on global study of the population and analytic study of the individual; the privileging of sexuality as the access to the truth of human identity. The 'cultural vigor' of psychoanalysis is at the 'junction of these two ideas – that we must not deceive ourselves concerning our sex, and that our sex harbors what is most true in ourselves'.[27] Despite its greater subtlety, psychoanalysis operates within the modern regime of sexuality and even intensifies it. It gives support to the conception of sex as a stubborn drive, constantly at war with repressive powers; psychoanalysis, therefore, obscures the positive function of power as productive of what we take the sexual realm and its themes to be. And, for Foucault, this is the case whether the psychoanalytic approach is according to a theory of instincts or in terms of how the law itself constitutes the nature of sexual desire. In addition, psychoanalysis unifies the system of the family with the modern sphere of sexuality by placing the incest desire at the centre of the individual's sexual life. Freud co-operates in constituting the family as a privileged target for political governance in that it is transformed into the 'germ of all the misfortunes of sex'. Finally, psychoanalysis provides one of the most striking examples in the modern transformation of Christianity's pastoral power. It has taken over the techniques of confessional practice and thus places the individual under the obligation to manifest truth to another in a situation of dependence and through the action of speech, which is invested with a special virtue of verification.[28]

The greatest support for the psychoanalytic project is provided by a special relationship which the self takes up with itself – namely, that sexuality is the index of one's subjectivity, of one's true self. The kinship of subjectivity–truth–sexuality is the linchpin of Freudian thought. The capacity of sexual desires and deeds to become the most revealing signs of our truest, deepest selves is dependent upon a long historical formation through which we were created as subjects in a special relationship to both truth and sex. I shall not repeat here Foucault's tracing of either Plato's initial interrogation of the 'man of desire' in *L'Usage des plaisirs* or the emergence of the Roman culture of the self in *Le*

Souci de soi. The Platonic desire to know oneself, united with the practices of such groups as the Epicureans and the Stoics, established a governance of the self that Foucault regarded as a sort of 'permanent political relationship between self and self' or a 'politics of themselves'.[29] This ancient concern with the self was the prelude to the development of a Christian hermeneutics of the self which reflected novel forms of power, knowledge and relationship to the self. The exercise of Christian pastoral power focused especially on sexuality, for its seditiousness was a sign of man's fallen state. The obedience to pastoral authority which overcame that state involved a search for truth – not just the general truths of faith but the specific truths of each person's soul. This excavation of personal truth gave birth to a technology for self-discovery. It entailed a permanent struggle with the Evil One who 'hides behind seeming likenesses of oneself' and whose mode of action in the person is error.[30] The endless task of self-scrutiny is accompanied by regular confessions to another, for verbalisation of thoughts is another level of sorting out the good thoughts from those which are evil – namely, those which seek to hide from the light of public expression.[31] The principal product of this technology was a unique form of subjectivity. One is related to oneself as an obscure text demanding permanent interpretation through ever more sophisticated practices of attentiveness, concern, decipherment and verbalisation. The soul is a house of truth, and true discourses are able to be articulated concerning it.

This Christian regime of pastoral power and self-discovery was not left behind by the modern age. Indeed, the sixteenth century opened a 'period which is characterised not by the beginning of a deChristianisation but by the beginning of a Christianisation-in-depth'.[32] Freud's interpretation of *Oedipus* bears witness to that transformed spiritual struggle in Christian practice. And it is indeed transformed. While the continual conflict within the soul between the grace of God and the lures of the Evil One anticipates the modern struggle between life and death, Christian immortality is superseded by participation within a life process whose last judgement on individuals is always death. An equally significant transformation was modernity's rejection of the specific Christian asceticism that was integral to its mode of relating to the self. Christian practices involved a renunciation of the self who was articulated. For the Christian, the truths of the self were always precarious, for they always related to the soul's conflict with the evil within oneself. There could be no firm allegiance to a positive self, for there was no truth about the self which could not be utlilised by the False One as a device for misleading and ensnaring the soul. The individual's relationship to the self imitates both the baptismal turning from the old self whom one was to a newly found otherness, and the ceremony of public penance that was depicted as a form of martyrdom which proclaimed the symbolic death of the person one had been. The continual mortification entailed by a permanent hermeneutic and renunciation of the self makes of that symbolic death an everyday event. All truth about the self is tied to the sacrifice of that same self, and the Christian experience of subjectivity declares itself most clearly in the sounds of a rupture with oneself, of an admission that 'I am not who I am'.[33] Modern technologies of the self promoted the emergence of a positive self; one recognises and attaches oneself to a self made available through the categories of psychological and psychoanalytic science, and through the normative disciplines consistent with them. Thus, like Oedipus, we become victims of our own self-knowledge. For Foucault, this is an event of supreme political importance because the positive modern subject is fashioned in isolation from ethical and aesthetic concerns. If a critical distance from the modern power–knowledge–subjectivity formation is the precondition for a new politics of ourselves, the key campaign in that politics will be new efforts to fashion an ethical way of being a subject. In the current epoch, that will especially entail new relationships between ourselves and modern knowledge.

2 FOUCAULT'S ETHIC

Foucault's proposed philosophical ethos, his aesthetics of existence [*bios*], is his form of resistance to that regime of knowledge–power–subjectivity relations which establishes itself in concert with the hermeneutic of a self who is regarded as a struggle between life [*zoë*] and death. As Foucault's final course in the Greek virtue of truth-telling [*parrhesia*] suggested, the beauty of this existence is to be located in a personal harmony of word and deed.[34] As for the Cynics whom Foucault so admired, it is the creation of an 'other life' which is worthy of remembrance – not because it conforms to an ideal necessary order but because it shapes a presence from a multiplicity of truths personally confronted. The centre of this philosophical ethos, of this parrhesiastic engagement within history, is not the articulation of philosophical doctrines; responding to the crisis of a politics of life versus death, it is the practice of an ethical interrogation and self-formation which generates a host of new options for moral and political choice. Just as he had earlier undermined the simple alternatives of reason versus madness and liberation against repression, so now he undercuts the reduction of experience to a struggle between life and death.

Although it was only in his last writings that Foucault dealt at length with ethics, the moral interest was decisive throughout his work. Pulsating through his thought is the insight which he first formulated in 1962: in modernity 'reason ceased to be for man an ethic and became a nature'. As he pointed out in *Les Mots et les Choses*, modern thought has never been able to propose a morality.[35] Foucault's final work confronts this failure by constituting thought and knowledge as activities which must be ethically interviewed, both to grasp their own process of formation as well as to enable us to pass beyond their specific knowledge configuration. It is precisely this ethical perspective which enables him to 'resituate the production of true and false at the heart of historical analysis and political critique'.[36] Foucault's effort to liberate ethical reflection from its modern dependence upon knowledge makes his work a counter-ethic to that 'ethic of knowledge' [*connaissance*] which promised 'truth only to the desire for truth itself and the power to think it'. His ethical interrogation is not only an analysis of the truths that shape our moral conditions and of our desire for them but a mode of self-formation, the 'process in which the individual delimits that part of himself that will form the object of his moral practice, defines his position relative to the precept he will follow, and decides on a certain mode of being that will serve as his moral goal. And this requires him to act upon himself, to monitor, test, improve, and transform himself.'[37]

This schema for ethical interrogation had a long gestation period and represents Foucault's fashioning of his personal relationship to his entire work and to the desire which inhabited it. Foucault's 1963 examination of the novelist Raymond Roussel was stimulated by a fascination with Roussel's last gesture, the release of a posthumous volume in which he supposedly explained the techniques and aims of his obscure prose. In fact, Foucault claimed, Roussel's last work was far less the unveiling of a secret than it was the disclosure of the 'underground force from which his language springs'.[38] Foucault's final work imparts an analogous lesson. Foucault came to the project and categories of that last stage only by way of his previous efforts. The underground force which they disclose is a movement towards an ethic for thought. Foucault's distinct experiments with thought were not random but join together to effect a common dynamism. The elements in his ethical schema mirror the four arts of interrogation which he practised throughout his writings: (1) What was it necessary to think today in contrast to the traditional domain of the thoughtworthy? What should the substance of thought be? (2) In examining this domain, what sort of understanding should be sought? What mode of subjectivation should the thinker take up? (3) How should the search for such understanding find its methodological way? What ascetic practices must it perform on itself in order to be enabled to think differently? (4) What goal is pursued through the definition of substance, mode of subjectivation, and practice of asceticism? Foucault's exploration of these questions throughout his works succeeded in creating a broad ethical enquiry on the activity of thought itself. It may be described as an ethical treatise, but it is not a general statement of a code for thinking, nor even primarily an exemplary model for enquiry. Foucault's treatise, as it is encountered in his writings, constitutes a practice which educates his readers into an ethical responsibility for intellectual enquiry. It provides not an obligatory conduct but a possible escape from an intellectual milieu unnourished by ethical interrogation. Foucault's practice of his ethic marks paths for a collaborative assumption of new responsibilities.

The domain or substance of Foucault's ethic is made up of the practices which give rise to those issues that entail, implicitly or explicitly, the exercise of moral-political discernment and decision. Rejecting moral experience as a matter of either response to religious revelation or commitment to an aesthetic task, the modern period articulated moral conduct in the context of true knowledges [*savoirs*]. Foucault problematises this modern statement by examining such crucial knowledges [*savoirs*] for moral reflection as biology, psychology and medicine, sciences which direct both the cognitive enterprise and the technologies for human self-relation. At the source of his delimitation of a substance to be ethically interrogated is the realisation that the formation of a domain in terms of true and false values is no less significant and dangerous than was the appearance of discourses which defined the holy and the profane, the saved and the damned, the good and the wicked. The ethical substance of his treatise creates a field for analysis which overcomes the theory–practice dualism. It is composed not of institutions, theories or ideologies but of practices, the discursive and extra-discursive relations which are operative in a culture's programme for the conduct of intellectual pursuit, of practical action, and of self-constitution. Foucault's ethical perspective was signalled in his concern with the action of the axes: what knowledge does (and not reads), how power constructs (and not represents), how a relationship to the self is invented (and not discovered). Philosophical enquiry becomes substantially ethical, in a Foucauldian sense, when it is concerned with the problematisations which pose themselves to a culture as a result of the interplay of its practices: its types of knowledge, its political strategies, and its styles of personal life. The focus for an analysis of the ethical substance is the thought which responds to these problematisations or inhabits these practices, if thought is understood as the 'way people begin to take care of something, of the way they become anxious about this or that – for example, about madness, about crime, about sex, about themselves, or about truth'.[39]

The second element in Foucault's ethical interrogation, its mode of subjection, is the type of enlightenment pursued by this interrogation. Foucault's debate with Kant was central here, for his work denatures or historicises Kant's great questions on knowledge, obligation and hope. Not 'What can I know?' but, rather, 'How have my questions been produced? How has the path of my knowing been determined?' Not 'What ought I to do?' but rather, 'How have I been situated to experience the real? How have exclusions operated in delineating the realm of obligation for me?' Not 'What may I hope for?' but rather, 'What are the struggles in which I am engaged? How have the parameters for my aspirations been defined? The point of such shifts is to free thought from formal structures and place it in a historical field where it must confront the singular, contingent and arbitrary which operate in what is put forward as universal, necessary and obligatory. 'The point, in brief, is to transform the critique conducted in the form of necessary limitation into a practical critique that takes the form of a possible transgression.'[40] The asceticism of his treatise is contained in the exacting arts of questioning which he developed in the archaeological-genealogical methods for analyses of discursive formations, power–knowledge apparatuses [*dispositifs*], and ethical systems. Foucault's methods stress our responsibility for the support we lend to the dominance of specific discourses. Foucault redefines the field of critique: from an arena that is already enunciated in terms of identifiable repressions and specific programmes of liberation to an ever-changing historical space in which power is capable of colonising the most noble knowledges [*savoirs*] and projects. Foucault's ethic is permanent critique in the interest of an endless practice of freedom. This freedom is the goal of his ethic. Foucault realised that there was never to be a definitive escape from configurations of knowledge–power–self relations, yet he was unyielding in his conviction that no specific configuration was necessary and unchangeable. His earlier declaration of the death of man was complemented in his last years by a counsel to get free of those relationships to self which we have inherited as children of Western technologies for self-development. Inherent in that counsel is a new style of relating to our modern knowledges [*savoirs*]. On the landscape of vast projects of research and evaluation, Foucault pressed an ethic of responsibility for the truths one speaks, for the political strategies into which these truths enter, and for those ways of relating to ourselves that make us either conformists or resisters to those relations. It is a timely ethic which assists in reclaiming thought's moral responsibilities. I believe that Foucault's ethical practice of thought largely accounts for his widespread appeal today. Although his commentators disagree with one another, their interest in his work shows a common appetite for a practice of thinking which exhibits the ethical dimension of reason.

Foucault's ethic proposes the wisdom of a dispossession, not only of certain systems of thought and action but also of a muteness before our age's indigenous suffering. If archaeology became a provocative image for thought, it was in part because there was the feeling that such a vision at least attempted to deal with the subterranean forces which erupted in our time. Our modern era's claim to knowledge of and its will to perfect the human reality have had tragic consequences – consequences which have mocked that claim and will. In their justification of immense technologies for producing a new man, human sciences seemed to turn against human beings. And perhaps philosophy did the same. Whereas the philosopher had once taught, through his own life, how death could be borne, he had come too often to teach in our age the superior wisdom of how to accept the massacre of others: in the name of truth.[41] It is the inexcusable service which professional thinkers have rendered to our period's diminishment, confinement and, indeed, murder of innocent people that stirs a horror in Foucault which occasionally surfaces in the violence of an image or the shrill tone of a formulation. The strategy of Foucault's resistance to this evil is an ethics for thought which consists in a series of questions whose pursuit manifests the assumption of an ethical responsibility. The practice of this ethic disputes the solidity of our world and history, much as a dream or a work of surrealist literature might.

3 A JOURNEY TO AUSCHWITZ

However Foucault's legacy is judged by future generations of readers, his thought certainly made it more difficult for his contemporaries to think unhistorically, non-politically, a-ethically – that is, irresponsibly. In concluding this paper, I would like to pass beyond my very general formulation of Foucault's ethic and suggest but one direction in which his work might be employed to continue his history of the present in the direction which *La Volonté de savoir*'s last section proposed – namely, an analysis of the Nazi epoch. On the level of both common opinion and elaborate examination, there has been the tendency to perceive the brutality of Nazi thought and deed as an abandonment of morality itself. Perhaps George Steiner is the most forceful advocate of this viewpoint. Taking his cue from a remark of Hitler, who once asserted that 'conscience is a Jewish invention', Steiner explains the *Shoah* as a murderous revolt against the threefold Jewish embodiment of conscience for Western culture: biblical monotheism, the ethical teaching of Jesus, and Marx's messianic socialism.[42] This interpretation asserts that Nazism embraced immorality itself as a new code of conduct. The effect of this type of analysis is to shelter us from any anxiety that we ourselves might share a moral kinship in the Nazi kingdom of death. If that kingdom's bloody deeds exhibit its evil, our proclaimed allegiance to moral values must show that we are citizens of some republic of good. It is more comforting to be told what the concentration camp prisoner heard from his guard – 'Hier ist kein warum' (Here there is no why) – than it is to interrogate the intelligibility of Nazism as itself an ethic. And yet the duty of such an interrogation is one of the places where Foucault's work leaves contemporary thought.

Foucault's approach to ethics enables us to take seriously the distressing fact that so many who were involved in such evil thought felt themselves to be paradigms of virtue. Hitler spoke for vast numbers when he claimed that 'only the German people has made moral law the governing principle of action'.[43] Perhaps the most infamous example of this self-proclaimed moral stature is Heinrich Himmler's 4 October 1943 speech to leaders of the SS in Posen, Poland. He speaks without any circumlocution about the horror of genocide: 'Most of you know what it means to see a hundred corpses lie side by side, or five hundred or a thousand.' But then he adds: 'To have stuck this out and – excepting cases of human weakness – to have remained decent [*anständig geblieben zu sein*], this is what has made us hard.'[44] He elaborates on this decency by praising the virtues of SS men: their loyalty [*die Treue*], their ability to obey [*der Gehorsam*], their bravery [*die Tapferkeit*], their truthfulness [*die Wahrhaftigkeit*]. Despite the annihilation of millions, Himmler could assert that 'our inward being, our soul, our character, has not suffered injury from it'.[45] A common reaction to such a proclamation of moral strength would be to see it as hypocrisy or as a defence mechanism needed to camouflage psychologically from the speaker the full horror of the facts which he reveals.[46] Foucault's work implicitly criticises such an explanation and indicates a promising reversal of perspectives for future research and understanding: an examination of Nazism not as a nihilism but as an intelligible ethic. I shall mention but a single possible approach, emerging from Foucault's work, to an examination of this ethic.

One of the most perplexing difficulties for an understanding of the Nazi period has been the relationship of its violent acts to the moral and religious traditions of pre-Hitler German culture. I shall avoid rehearsing the analyses which either argue for radical discontinuity or stress some measure of continuity in this relationship. I believe that Foucault's schema for an ethical analysis may be of fundamental assistance to the task of uncovering some of the concrete features in the transformation of an earlier religiously rooted ethic into a post-Christian Nazi ethic. I shall stay with the case of Himmler as an example, but with no intention of limiting its application to him. We know that the substance of Himmler's ethic was constituted by the battle of life and death [*der Kampf auf Leben und Tod*] which juxtaposed the vitality of Nordic blood with the deadly degeneration represented by inferior races. What was at stake was the advancement of life or the death of the people [*Volkstod*]. 'We had the moral right, we had the duty towards our people, to kill this people which wanted to kill us.'[47] Reflecting Hitler's demand that National Socialism must be a 'homage to reason', and that for it 'reason alone must have the last word', Himmler's mode of subjection was to those natural historical laws which were revealed through a science of race.[48] The ethic of National Socialism is regarded as a form of applied biology. The asceticism of Himmler's ethic was not just the rigorous discipline of the SS man's formation, with its stress on duty and obedience, but the practice of killing as a moral imperative to enhance biological life. A eugenics for one racial body which entailed a 'euthanasia' for others. And the goal of all of this – to which Nazi anti-Semitism was itself subordinated – was a definitive biological purification for history, a revitalisation of life itself, its triumph over death.[49]

While elements of pre-Nazi religious and humanistic values could be traced in each of these levels of the Nazi ethic, I would like to mention just one: the *telos* of this ethic, its aspiration for a purification of life. This aspiration certainly has broad religious sources.[50] As a result of the diary which Himmler kept in his early years, we are enabled to watch a personal transformation from an ideal of religious purity to the Nazi mission for racial purification. Not surprisingly in the light of Foucault's studies, it was his struggle with sexuality which effected the transition.[51] In relocating our questions from the dimension of moral codes to that of ethical formation, Foucault allows us to see the construction of ways of relating to the self and to perceive moral tasks which survived in Himmler's character even if there seems to be a total inversion on the level of stated moral principle. Certainly, Himmler's loss of religious conviction closed his long struggle with Catholic standards of sexual purity. That ending was only the beginning of a transfer both of that moral ideal to a racial programme and of a mode of ethical problematisation which perdured even when explicit principles changed beyond recognition. If the alternative of salvation or damnation had once been the story of Himmler's contest with sexuality, it was to be racial purity or degeneration which was to govern his maturity. Jews came to embody for him the sensuality against which he had waged his earlier struggle. This metamorphosis of Himmler's moral career was to have an impact of unprecedented pain upon history. Of course, the formation of Himmler's ethic was but one aspect of much broader historical transformations. Foucault's work, especially his treatment of biopolitics and the history of sexuality, has suggested new routes for their investigation, pathways that must now be trodden by others. Foucault's exploratory steps have recently been confirmed by Robert Lifton's important study of Nazi medical doctors and researchers. Lifton does not draw out the ethical implications of his conclusion that the Nazi state was a 'biocracy', which was driven by a 'sweeping version of biological – one might say evolutionary – purification'.[52] Within this biocracy, biological and medical research became the vanguard of a new politics of life and death. Thus, it is easy to understand the former Nazi doctor who explained that 'National Socialism failed because we could not develop enough biological teaching – it was not possible to educate people sufficiently in biology'.[53] Foucault's ethic for thought will help to ensure continued failure for such enterprises of reason.

In his memoirs, Albert Speer identified the state of mind which permitted the monstrous evils our age has endured: 'It never occurred to us to doubt the order of things.'[54] Perhaps one of the greatest contributions of Foucault's work to contemporary culture is its encouragement to doubt the dramatic, comprehensive scenarios upon which we have been nurtured: history and politics as a contest between life and death; the appeal of revolutionary programmes for human liberation; the birth of scientific projects for human reform and purification. In those intense pages of *Surveiller et punir* where he discusses plagues as both real and imaginary forms which give rise to dreams of purification and the disciplinary programmes which make them reality, Foucault once again creates doubt regarding the naturalness of our intellectual and moral aspirations.[55] We know that his quest entailed no search for a pure reason. There is neither stability nor purity in the emergence and activity of the thought which interested him. He succeeded in doing what he proposed in his inaugural lecture at the Collège de France, an 'introduction into the very roots of thought of notions of chance, discontinuity and materiality'.[56] This is the practice of an impure reason and, as I have indicated, Foucault's work may be thought of as a reversal of Kant's great questions.

If philosophers have often conceived their task to be the harbouring of human existence from raw exposure to the contingent, Foucault tried to drive them back out to sea. Certainly his work places us within a much more dangerous and menacing zone than we might have chosen for ourselves. But it is a zone which reflects the history of our present. And perhaps that danger and menace echo his own memory of growing up as a youth in Poitiers:

> The menace of war was our background, our framework of existence. Then the war arrived. Much more than the activities of family life, it was these events concerning the world which are the substance of our memory. . . . Our private life was really threatened. Maybe that is the reason why I am fascinated by history and the relations between personal experience and those events of which we are a part.[57]

If, at the beginning of this paper, I recalled Foucault's visit to Auschwitz, it is because I am so struck by his uncommon courage in journeying so deeply into those impure events and contingencies which have fashioned our feelings for both life and death. His excursions into that putrid history, however, did not lead him to a despair of philosophical thought and human existence. The energy of his work reminds me far more of Alyosha's reaction to the unexpected, shocking putrefication of Father Zossima's corpse in *The Brothers Karamazov*: 'Alyosha stood, gazed out before him and then suddenly threw himself down on the earth. He did not know why he embraced it. He could not have told why he longed so irresistibly to kiss it, to kiss it. But he kissed it weeping and watering it with his tears, and vowed passionately to love it, to love it forever and ever.'[58] Foucault brought philosophy closer to earth. The better to love it.

NOTES

1. Paris: Syros, 1985. The book is based on the exhibition 'Foucault' which took place in November–December 1985 at Espace Belleville. The photograph to which I refer is on page 90.
2. *La Volonté de savoir*, Paris: Gallimard, 1976, p. 188 (English translation [ET]: *The History of Sexuality I: An introduction*, transl. Robert Hurley, New York: Pantheon, 1978, p. 143). The English omitted the term 'biological' in its translation of '*seuil de modernité biologique*'.
3. 'Le jeu de Michel Foucault', *Ornicar?*, no. 10, July 1977, p. 87 (ET: 'The confession of the flesh', in *Power/Knowledge: Selected Interviews and Other Writings 1972–1977*, ed. C. Gordon, New York: Pantheon, 1980, p. 222).
4. The important recent exception to this silence is Maurice Blanchot's beautiful text *Michel Foucault tel que je l'imagine*, Montpellier: Fata Morgana, 1986.
5. John Boswell, 'How the Greeks viewed sex', *The Boston Sunday Globe* (20 October 1985) B 36.
6. Richard Wolin, 'Foucault's aesthetic decisionism', *Telos*, no. 67, Spring 1986, p. 84.
7. Martha Nussbaum, 'Affections of the Greeks' (a review of *L'Usage des plaisirs*), *The New York Times Book Review*, 10 November 1985, pp. 13–14.
8. 'Le retour de la morale', Foucault's interview with Gilles Barbedette and André Scala in *Les Nouvelles*, no. 2937, 28 June–5 July 1984, p. 38 (ET: 'Final interview', transl. T. Levin and Isabelle Lorenz, *Raritan*, no. V, Summer 1985, pp. 2–3).
9. *Les Mots et les Choses*, Paris: Gallimard, 1966, pp. 368–70 (ET: *The Order of Things*, New York: Vintage, 1973, pp. 357–8).
10. *La Volonté de savoir*, p. 206 (ET, p. 156).
11. 'Le retour de la morale', p. 41 (ET, p. 10).
12. *Ibid.* (ET, p. 13).
13. 'Politics and ethics: An interview' (1983) in *The Foucault Reader*, ed. Paul Rabinow, New York: Pantheon, 1984, p. 375.
14. *Les Mots et les Choses*,. pp. 289–91 (ET, pp. 277–8).
15. S. Freud, *Das Unbehagen in der Kultur*, in *Gesammelte Schriften*, vol. XII, Vienna: Internationaler Psychoanalytischer Verlag, 1934, p. 89.
16. *Les Mots et les Choses*, p. 386 (ET, p. 374); 'Christianity and confession', a lecture presented by Foucault in November 1980 at Dartmouth College. Foucault's criticism of Freud's death drive and its dependence upon biology was initially stated in his very first book, *Maladie mentale et Personnalité*, Paris: PUF, 1954, p. 41.
17. Foucault, 'The subject and power', in Hubert L. Dreyfus and Paul Rabinow, *Michel Foucault: Beyond Structuralism and Hermeneutics*, Chicago: University of Chicago Press, 1983, 2nd edn, p. 212.
18. *Herculine Barbin dite Alexina B*, ed. M. Foucault, Paris: Gallimard, 1978.
19. 'The Subject and power', pp. 212, 216.
20. See his course descriptions from these years in *Annuaire du Collège de France*, 76 (pp. 361–6); 78 (pp. 445–9), 79 (pp. 367–72).
21. *Annuaire du Collège de France*, 80, pp. 449–52.

22. S. Freud, *The Interpretation of Dreams*, Standard Edition, vol. IV, ed. James Strachey, London: Hogarth, 1973, p. 262.
23. 'Introduction to Pfister's *The Psycho-Analytic Method*' (1913), in *Standard Edition*, vol. XII, ed. James Strachey, London: Hogarth, 1973, p. 329.
24. *Naissance de la clinique: Une archéologie du regard médical*, Paris: PUF, 1963, pp. 154, 200 (ET: *The Birth of the Clinic*, New York: Vintage, 1975, pp. 153, 198).
25. Cf. *Histoire de la folie à l'âge classique*, Paris: Gallimard, 1978, pp. 523–30 (ET: *Madness and Civilization*, New York: Pantheon, 1965, pp. 216–22); *Naissance de la clinique*, p. 207 (ET, p. 199).
26. *Les Mots et les Choses*, p. 372 (ET, p. 361).
27. Foucault's 'Introduction' to the English translation of *Herculine Barbin*, New York: Pantheon, 1980, p. xi. See also *La Volonté de savoir*, pp. 137–9, 91, 94 (ET, pp. 104–5, 68, 70).
28. *La Volonté de savoir*, pp. 108–9 (ET, pp. 82–3); see also pp. 136–51, 172–3 (ET, pp. 103–14, 130).
29. Foucault, 'On the genealogy of ethics', in Dreyfus and Rabinow, *Beyond Structuralism and Hermeneutics*, p. 246.
30. Foucault, 'La combat de la chasteté', *Communications*, no. 35, May 1982, p. 23; 1980 course, lecture of 26 March.
31. 'Christianity and confession.'
32. Course lecture of 19 February 1975.
33. See 'Omnes et singulatim: Vers une critique de la raison politique', *Le débat*, no. 41 (Sept.–Nov. 1986), pp. 19–20; 'Christianity and confession'; Foucault's 1982 course at the University of Toronto, 'The Discourse of self-disclosure', 15 June 1982; 'Sexuality and Solitude', *Humanities in Review*, no. 1, 1982, ed. David Rieff, New York: Cambridge University Press, 1982, pp. 10, 15; *L'Usage des plaisirs*, Paris: Gallimard, 1984, pp. 74, 82 (ET: *The Use of Pleasure*, New York: Pantheon, 1985, pp. 63, 70).
34. See *Discourse and Truth: The Problematization of Parrhesia*. Notes to the Autumn 1983 seminar given by Foucault at the University of California, Berkeley. Also Thomas Flynn, 'Foucault as parrhesiast: his last course at the Collège de France', *Philosophy and Social Criticism*, vol. 12, pp. 2–3, Summer 1987, pp. 213–29.
35. *Maladie mentale et Psychologie*, Paris: PUF, 1962, p. 103 (ET: *Mental Illness and Psychology*, New York: Harper & Row, 1976, p. 87); *Les Mots et les Choses*, pp. 338–9 (ET, pp. 327–28).
36. 'Table ronde du 20 mai 1978', *L'impossible prison*, ed. Michelle Perrot, Paris: Seuil, 1980, p. 48.
37. *L'Ordre du discours*, Paris: Gallimard, 1971 p. 48; *L'Usage des plaisirs*, p. 35 (ET, p. 28).
38. *Raymond Roussel*, Paris: Gallimard, 1963, p. 14 (ET: *Death and the Labyrinth: The World of Raymond Roussel*, transl. Charles Ruas, Garden City, NY: Doubleday, 1986, p. 7).
39. *Discourse and Truth*, p. 48; cf. 'Polemics, politics and problematizations', in *The Foucault Reader*, p. 390; on Foucault's notion of practices, cf. 'Table ronde du 20 mai 1978', *L'impossible prison*, pp. 40–56.

40. 'What is Enlightenment?', *The Foucault Reader*, p. 45.
41. See Foucault's 'La grande colère des faits', in *Faut-il brûler les nouveaux philosophes?*, Paris: Nouvelles Éditions Oswald, 1978, pp. 65–6.
42. George Steiner, *In Bluebeard's Castle: Some Notes Towards the Redefinition of Culture*, New Haven: Yale University Press, 1971.
43. *Hitler's Secret Conversations 1941–1944*, New York: Octagon Books, 1976, p. 6.
44. Himmler's speech in *Trial of the Major War Criminals Before the International Military Tribunal*, vol. XXIX, Nuremberg, 1948. For similar expressions, see Himmler's speech two days later in Himmler, *Discours secrets*, Paris: Gallimard, 1978, pp. 159–84.
45. *Trial of the Major War Criminals*, vol. XXIX, p. 146: '*Und wir haben keinen Schaden in unserem Inneren, in unserer Seele, in unserem Charakter daran genommen.*'
46. An example of such an approach is Saul Friedländer, *Reflets du Nazisme*, Paris: Seuil, 1982.
47. *Trial of the Major War Criminals*, vol. XXIX, p. 146: '*Wir hatten das moralische Recht, wir hatten die Pflicht gegenüber unserem Volk, dieses Volk, das uns umbringen wollte, umzubringen.*'
48. *Hitler's Secret Conversations*, pp. 33, 578. For a study of the scientific claims in National Socialism, see Daniel Gasman, *The Scientific Origins of National Socialism*, London: Macdonald, 1971. One of the most promising utilisations of Foucault's ethic for thought will be an analysis of the operation of such sciences as biology and genetics in the political programmes of National Socialism.
49. See *Discours secrets*, pp. 204, 54–5.
50. Among other studies, see the collection edited by Michel Adam, *Souillure et pureté*, Toulouse: Privat, 1972; Albert Sicroff, *Les controverses des statuts de pureté de sang en Espagne du xve au xviie siècle*, Paris: Librairie Marcel Didier, 1960; Mary Douglas, *Purity and Danger*, New York: Praeger, 1966.
51. Bradley F. Smith, *Heinrich Himmler: A Nazi in the Making, 1900–1926*, Stanford, CA: Stanford University Press, 1971.
52. Robert Jay Lifton, *The Nazi Doctors: Medical Killing and the Psychology of Genocide*, New York: Basic Books, 1986, pp. 17, 483.
53. *The Nazi Doctors*, p. 133. See also, the recent article by Benno Müller-Hill, 'Genetics after Auschwitz', *Holocaust and Genocide Studies*, vol. 2, no. 1, 1987, pp. 3–20.
54. *Inside the Third Reich*, New York: Avon, 1970, p. 35.
55. *Surveiller et punir*, Paris: Gallimard, 1975, pp. 199–201 (ET: *Discipline and Punish*, New York: Pantheon, 1977, pp. 197–200).
56. *L'Ordre du discours*, Paris: Gallimard, 1971, p. 61.
57. 'Michel Foucault: An interview', conducted by Stephen Riggins on 22 June 1982, *Ethos*, vol. 1, no. 2, Autumn 1983, p. 5.
58. F. Dostoevsky, *The Brothers Karamazov*, New York: New American Library, 1957, p. 334.

SUMMARY OF DISCUSSIONS

André Glücksmann stressed that in the speech quoted by James Bernauer, Himmler, also says that the glorious acts with which the SS were honouring themselves in the death camps were not such as to tolerate publicity. The German people themselves, devoted to Hitler as they were, would not be able to bear the spectacle. In other words, *Nacht und Nebel* was necessary to the construction of the death camps.

There is a problem with the visibility of the intolerable. There were two aspects to the conditions of possibility of Auschwitz: the historical production of Nazism on the one hand, but also the blinding of the authorities of democratic powers: the silence of the Pope, the Red Cross, Roosevelt, the American Jewish community – a silence which made it possible for the intolerable to happen.

There is also the problem of determining the extent to which democratic, idealistic and well-meaning discourses might actually form part of the conditions which make silence and obscuration possible in the face of the intolerable. This question exercised Foucault. It is not possible to reply by saying that if there had been more democracy, Nazism would not have been possible. Foucault's question goes deeper than ideals: though ideals might stop us from being Nazis, they make it possible for others to remain in 'night and fog'. Foucault's question with regard to Nazism concerns not only the historical causes of Auschwitz but also the production of the possibility of Nazism in well-meaning democracies. Thinking in terms of the universal was not one of the conditions of the production of Nazism but one of the conditions of possibility of the production, by abstention, of the *laissez-faire* attitude which made it possible.

James Bernauer replied that biologism and Darwinism were factors which explain Nazism. Since the Second World War it has no longer been possible to talk using biologistic vocabulary, since the legitimacy of this latter has been completely destroyed. Foucault teaches us not to talk in terms of a nation in general but in terms of different groups who think in response to a given situation. What Himmler said teaches us that if the concentration camps had been publicised there would have been resistance amongst the German people. The secret of the concentration camp lasted only three years. But what was the real secret? It was not only the fact of death. Foucault can help us to reply to this question to the extent that he challenges our nature as a moral individual.

5 RATIONALITIES AND HISTORIES

one

Rationality, force and power
Foucault and Habermas's criticisms

Dominique Janicaud

The question of power can be put in at least three ways:

1. The purpose might be to measure, understand or master physicochemical and energy exchanges, either within a given system or on a macroscopic level.

2. The purpose might be to understand and master the excesses of force in a moral or political sphere (which, according to Eric Weil's terminology, would be manifest in the first instance as *violence* exterior to reasoned discourse).

3. Finally, the purpose might be to reflect on the role of *power as such*, from the point of view of the individual and of society, linked with the growing efficiency of scientific and technological strength since the beginnings of industrialisation. This is the point of view established by Max Weber which goes by the name of *rationalisation*. Yet this can and must be developed beyond Weber's own ethnosociological field.

The debate with which I am going to deal here is more circumscribed. It should probably be rooted at a point beginning with Nietzsche, who meditated on the ensemble of power relations and organised his genealogical project on the basis of the third point of view – that is to say, on the basis of the historical forms of domination by means of which man comes to see the increase of power (over nature and society) as his only end. Habermas, for his part, has recourse to the term *Macht* in his discussions of Michel Foucault's ideas and thus gives the tenth chapter of his book *Der philosophische Diskurs der Moderne* (*The Philosophical Discourse of Modernity*)[1] the title 'The aporias of a theory of power' [*Machttheorie*]; but the word *Macht* is ambiguous, designating at the same time strength [*puissance*] and power [*pouvoir*]. In French, on the other hand, although one can speak of the physical *pouvoir* and of the *puissance* of a king, the term *puissance* is used primarily in the first sense mentioned above (or, more rigorously, in terms of the *general* conditions of the exercise of the excess of energy of strength, domination, and so on), whilst the use of *pouvoir* is reserved to *specific* juridical-political forms and moralities. Foucault is in fact interested in *pouvoir* (in the forms, structures and rules adopted by power), not in power [*puissance*] in the general sense (nor in the physical or metaphysical sense). One does not find in Foucault a theory of *puissance*, but there are elements of a theory of power [*pouvoir*], since he replies explicitly to the following questions: Why should power be studied? In what way is it exercised? In what does the specific nature of power relations consist? Foucault sums it up as follows: '. . . power can only be said to be exercised by *some* over *others*; power exists only in action, even if, of course, it is inscribed in a field dense with possibilities which depend on permanent structures'.[2]

This terminological elucidation of power has no meaning in itself unless it is referred to the philosophical elaboration of the understanding (and the intelligibility) of power in the modern contemporary world – say, for the century since the death of Nietzsche. Even if it is to become more specific, the context of Foucault's study of the forms of power is a project which derives its momentum and coherence from its reference to Nietzsche. This '*après-Nietzsche*' is to be understood neither in a purely historical sense nor in a purely biographical sense, despite the personal tone in which Nietzsche proclaims it in *Ecce Homo*:

> A day will come when the memory of a formidable event will be linked with my name, the memory of a unique crisis in the history of the earth, the most profound collision of consciousnesses, of a decree given forth against everything that had been believed, demanded and sanctified up to our time. I am not a man, I am dynamite.[3]

What was for his contemporaries no more than an arbitrary provocation, a symptom of imminent madness, takes on for us, looking back over a century (and what a century!), worrying proportions: it is of course always possible to debate the truth of Nietzsche's affirmations; yet one cannot deny that they mark, in our history, a considerable break which has affected and continues to affect consensus about truth itself and the meaning of this consensus – that is to say, the will to truth. From the second of these *Intempestives*, Nietzsche showed that the systematic search for historical truth is no more 'innocent' than the search for theoretical truth; from *Vérité et mensonge au sens exta-moral* onwards he interpreted the concern for truth in terms of the mastery which language gives over things, generalisation on the basis of metaphorisation; he placed the notion of 'pure truth' back in its context of relative efficiency. It is from the starting point of this undermining of rational self-justification that Foucault's study of the forms of power proceeds. A further terminological elucidation could be added at this point: just as Foucault prefers the term *pouvoir* to *puissance*, he also speaks of discourse rather than rationality: 'I think that the word *rationalisation* is dangerous. What we should be doing is to analyse specific rationalities rather than ceaselessly invoking the progress of rationalisation in general.'[4]

The meaning of this warning will become clearer in the context of what follows. There is no way to understand it except by untangling the threads of the debate which has imposed itself as being the most urgent and the most decisive at the end of this century: the debate about the rationality of power [*puissance*], given that the rational finds its former ideals in confrontation with the most recent forms of its *own* powers. Habermas is the one contemporary philosopher who in the recent past has taken up this question in an extremely methodological way and who, supported by an already considerable body of work, has undertaken a systematic criticism of Foucault's positions (and his Nietzscheanism). For the sake of clarity I shall start with this criticism, which was recently set out in Chapters IX and X of *Der philosophische Diskurs der Moderne*; and when I have summarised and analysed this I shall confront it with the texts of his 'adversaries', Foucault and Nietzsche himself. Work on these texts will make it possible to take up and relaunch the one question which continually occupied these authors and those who followed them: what rationality is there in power [*puissance*], and what can be made of what goes on in this relationship?

THE SYSTEMATIC AMBIGUITY OF THE COUNTER-DISCOURSE ABOUT POWER

It is almost at the end of his book that Habermas criticises Foucault, at the end of a succession of philosophers in which the great names are Hegel and Hegelians on the right and Nietzsche, Horkheimer, Adorno, Heidegger, Derrida and Bataille on the left. This is not without significance: Habermas's project is presented explicitly as a genealogy of modern philosophy and therefore, as far as Foucault is concerned, as the genealogy of a genealogy (if, that is, one goes along with Dreyfus and Rabinow, as Habermas does, in maintaining that Foucault's archaeology changes into a genealogical project in the proper sense of the term in the 1970s.

This first observation makes it possible to anticipate the nature of Habermas's reading: for him the point is not so much statements which he considers to be completely erroneous but rather the analysis of their ambiguities and presuppositions. So the critique proceeds with a mixture of sympathy and irritation (in which the second finally wins out) in the two chapters which in general terms deal with the two parts of Foucault's work (the break is situated between *Les Mots et les Choses* and *Surveiller et punir* – that is to say, about 1970): the enterprise which aims to 'unmask' human sciences in a rational-critical way (Chapter IX) and the aporias of a theory of power (Chapter X). These aporias, which are to a large extent consciously assumed by Foucault, explain the difficulties in the first part of the work. So Habermas is *redoubling* the critical effort which Foucault has already directed at his own work; but he wants to enforce this criticism even more radically – so radically that a *different* theory seems finally to impose itself.

Let us go straight to the heart of the objection. This is directed at a 'systematic ambiguity' (also referred to as a 'paradoxical link') between an approach which is empirical and even positivistic on the one hand, and claims which are critical and even metatheoretical on the other.[5] This 'systematic ambiguity' is deployed throughout the work, as we shall see, but it is rooted in the very concept of *power* which most particularly guides Foucault's work in his last years. 'Systematic ambiguity' obviously means a lot more than drifts between the empirical and the meta-empirical or even an ambivalence *of fact*, due either to uncontrolled slippage from one level to another or to a sort of literary pleasure in double-dealing. 'Systematic ambiguity' means that one *ascertains* a disconcerting and even irritating 'double role' in the concept of *power*, to which one adds the double function of structure and the instance of regulation. Yet it means in particular that this double play makes it possible for Foucault, through the joining of forces between 'the idealist thought of a transcendental synthesis' with the 'presuppositions of an empirical ontology',[6] first to dispense with justifying his position and secondly to mask his 'empirical shortfalls'. In fact: 'The empirical shortfalls are reflected in the unclarified methodological problems.'[7]

It is not enough to draw attention to the presence of an ambiguity (for even if he is tempted to think it, Habermas does not go so far as to claim that ambiguity *in itself* should be banished); it is also necessary to try to understand the *systematic* of this ambiguity from both sides.

First the empirical side. One might wonder how appropriate it is to use this term in relation to Foucault. Habermas insists on it, although he also speaks of a *descriptive historiography*, which would seem a more appropriate name for enquiries which refuse to be moulded by the disciplinary framework of philosophy and history but slip into its 'interstices' – as Foucault puts it at the end of *L'Archéologie du savoir*. At the time there were some who were surprised that a philosopher should consult prison archives, work laboriously at the registers of asylums; that he should look up seventeenth- and eighteenth-century grammar books, theological manuals, and so on, instead of rereading the *Méditations métaphysiques* or the *Critique of Pure Reason*. It should be remembered, though, that Foucault saw himself as following in the tradition of his master Canguilhem, the French tradition (since the eighteenth century) of a critical, positive philosophy concentrating on patient documentary investigation (especially in the field of the history of science and technology) rather than on certainties too quickly drawn from metaphysics.

Yet just remembering is not enough. Nor is it enough just to recall the undeniable documentary (and literary) interest of *Histoire de la folie*, *Surveiller et punir*, and so on. Habermas speaks of the 'innocence' of the concept of power (he does not say this is apparent, but allows it to be supposed) which is then 'descriptively utilisable' in the service of an 'empirical analysis' of the techniques of power [*pouvoir*]. He adds that from the methodological point of view this empirical analysis 'cannot be distinguished in any striking way from a functionalist sociology of knowledge which has been directed towards the historical'.[8] If this is the case, then the methodological procedures are no more 'innocent' here than in a sociology of that nature. Taking a positive viewpoint (even 'positivistic', as Foucault himself puts it, proclaiming himself a 'happy positivist'[9]) does not immediately equip one in the human sciences, and even less so in their 'archaeology', with some kind of certificate of objectivity such as one might claim for oneself in the exact sciences. That is why Habermas believes himself to be in a position to articulate three criticisms against Foucault's major 'enquiries': unwarranted reference to the present (which he calls *Präsentismus*), relativism and 'crypto-normativism'.[10]

I should like first to examine 'presentism'. This is the name Habermas gives to a form of methodological behaviour which Foucault claims to be eliminating, yet will never succeed in eliminating: the retrospective projection of *our* vision of things on to attitudes and events which can be explained neither in terms of eternal value-functions nor in terms of the function of our present feelings. Whilst the hermeneuticist approach presupposes a hidden origin and therefore keeps in reserve a point from which judgements can be made, the 'archaeologist' is supposed to take into account only the substitution of one technique of power for another, and to consider only the logic internal to each of these techniques. For example, Louis XIV, at the time of the Great Confinement of 1656, did not create the General Hospital for humanitarian reasons such as we would today but for specific reasons which it is precisely the task of the historian to reconstitute. Another example is given by Paul Veyne and taken up by Habermas: the interdiction of gladiatorial combats in late Rome was not due to the humanitarian influence of Christianity but to the replacement of one archetype of power by another: the Emperor becomes a Father who has to protect his children.[11] According to Habermas, Foucault does not succeed in reaching this objectification of power formations. Why?

Because the 'radical historicist' cannot dispense with comparisons between the different complexes of power which he studies, and for this reason cannot avoid working on a hermeneutic basis. Habermas gives an example in support of this argument: the chronological separation of the Middle Ages, the Renaissance and the classical age. This separation cannot but be referred back to the disciplinary power, the 'biopolitics' which Foucault identifies as 'the destiny of our present'.[12] Therefore this viewpoint, which links decisive historical changes to an economy of disciplines exercised over bodies, this alleged objectivity which denudes the discursivity of practices in terms of what claims to be the interiority of meanings, is just as datable and partial (in view of its very historicism) as the modifications of power complexes which it claims to be reconstituting. Thus it can be explained how *Histoire de la folie* – just like *Surveiller et punir*, limiting ourselves to these two examples – played the double role of documentaries and manifestos against psychiatry as well as for the struggle for the change in conditions of detention. For Habermas the reason is clear: Foucault is caught in a game of negation; he gives in to the 'presentism' he claims to banish because his scientific objectivism (weighed down by 'anti-science') collapses into an 'incurable subjectivism'. Because of the way he impugns all hermeneutics of *signification*, he finds himself divided, as a radical historicist, between objectivism and subjectivism.

The second criticism is that of relativism. The reference point shifts from *signification* to *truth*; but – as far as Foucault is concerned – the point is still to unmask the same double game of genealogical historiography. This is relativist in a double sense: to begin with in the sense that his historicism obliges him to follow the functioning of practices. Since discourses have no intrinsic validity, all that needs to be retained is their power-function. But 'all counter-power is already moving in the horizon of the power which it is combating and from the moment of its victory it transforms itself into a power complex which provokes another counter-power. The genealogy of knowledge cannot break this circle.'[13] In the shifts from discourse to practice which are supposed to found its objectivity there is still nothing to distinguish this form of relativism from historicism which always ends up caught in its own trap – that is to say, the tendency to militancy in favour of minorities (the oppressed, criminals, homosexuals, and so on). What is interesting in this argument is not that one power is seen as chasing another, which is obvious, nor that objectivity is seen as being impossible in the human sciences, another obviousness of which Foucault was more aware than anyone else. What is interesting is the way the criticism shifts from the empirical to the transcendental and the attempt to unmask a second-degree relativism which is the inverse of self-justification: a *self-reference* which is *self-defeating*. Genealogical historiography has to compensate for its (deliberate) lack of universal validity by means of a relative validity which is reduced more and more to its militant purpose, its style, and so on. We find the same reversal of objectivism into subjectivism which we previously observed. The problem is the same; it is no longer observed on the basis of practices described but on the basis of the behaviour of the historiographer himself, who is caught up in the process of his own ducking and weaving.

The third problem is that of 'crypto-normativism'. Habermas continues to drive in the same nail and to pursue the same refutation, but this time on the level of *values*: does Foucault escape from the 'crypto-normativism' to which he accuses the human sciences of falling prey? On the one hand he claims that he is being purely descriptive, jeering at the same time at traditional humanism and the 'leftist dogma' which he finds is on what he considers to be the 'right side'. On the other hand he sees himself as a dissident, his commitment impregnating his style and even his vocabulary. He does not separate, as Max Weber did so clearly, the work of the scientist from that of the man of decision, who might be heroic or otherwise, but who chooses his values. We might well concede that the point is a *tactic* to avoid simply reinforcing the major dominant discourses, as did the Marxists and Freudians, who are easily 'recuperated' by the enterprise of normalisation. Yet still the question formulated by Nancy Fraser regarding the origin of the choice in favour of this tactic remains to be answered:

> Why is struggle preferable to submission? Why should domination be resisted? It is only through the introduction of some sort of normativity that Foucault was able to begin to answer this question. It was only the introduction of normative notions which made it possible for him to begin to tell us what is wrong with modern power (the regime of *connaissance*) and why we should oppose it.[14]

The way this goes back to the unavoidable necessity of a choice of values seems to be quite a classical move, but the originality of Habermas's criticism lies in the way he traces this choice process (and the negation of this choice) back to Foucault's practice of genealogical history. In so doing Habermas concedes that Foucault is able to justify his 'crypto-normativism' in terms of an *asymmetry* which resides in power complexes themselves at the heart of which Foucault does not principally see a struggle between dominators and dominated (as in the Marxist schema) but tensions between disciplinary powers and mute bodies. The genealogical historiographer is therefore introducing support from the biological-somatic into the play of the biopower (this being particularly the case in *Histoire de la sexualité*). But Habermas suggests that far from being a real justification (an assumed norm), this reference to the body indicates and betrays a *vitalism* in the 'self-experience of the body'.[15]

The time has now come to conclude this summing up of Habermas's criticism by going right to the very heart of it before submitting it in turn to discussion. From Habermas's point of view it is fair game (and here he uses the most classical form of refutation) to show that Foucault does not succeed in his own enterprise, that he is caught in his own trap: the empirical shortcomings of his work are traced back to the unconsidered transcendental element, and this is used to explain the nature of the bias of genealogical history. The three points of view which Habermas chooses (signification, truth and value) therefore reappear in Foucault *in spite of himself*. As in an involuntary confession made by a denial, one witnesses in Foucault, at the same time as the 'repression of fundamental concepts' (in particular those quoted above), the impossibility of eradicating them from the 'counter-discourse' which claims to banish them.[16]

The empirical shortcomings are not clarified by a transcendental synthesis, since the refusal to admit concepts of signification, of truth and of value is fundamental. One can finally join Habermas in questioning the systematic nature of this denial and this counter-discourse before trying to step back from and look at Habermas's own enterprise.

The concept of *power* is burdened with a double role which, as we saw, irritates Habermas: how can an objective or objectivisable structure structure itself? This can be explained only if in the concept of power one hypostasises an instance which is at the same time transcendental and historical, and whose metaphysical origin is the will to truth. For Habermas, Foucault is wrong to postulate *a* will constitutive of truth for all times and all societies; he is also wrong in his failure to differentiate between the will to power and the will to knowledge.[17] He believes that this difficulty can be resolved by substituting a *genealogy* of the practices of power for an *archaeology* of knowledge [*savoir*]; but his own genealogical historiography is not itself thought of in genealogical terms.[18] To sum up: Habermas is claiming through his criticism to be providing the genealogy of the Foucauldian genealogy. This second-order genealogy reveals the genealogical foundation on the basis of which Foucault practises his counter-discourse, ducking and weaving as he does so. This origin (which is hidden from Foucault himself) is on the one hand the dialectic internal to the discourse of the modern subject since Kant and Fichte, and on the other the Nietzschean model of the overturning of Platonic–Christian values and universal rationality. Whilst the Nietzschean heritage is fully recognised by Foucault, the dialectic of reflexivity and of the opaque non-self is shifted and fixed in an empirical–transcendental dual relationship which Foucault (in *Les Mots et les Choses*) imputes only to the human sciences but not to his own archaeology. According to Habermas, the contradictions in the concept of power in Foucault, his oscillation between the will to knowledge [*savoir*] and contingent discursive formations, demonstrate and exemplify in the historiographic practice the character of the *counter-discourse* of Nietzsche's own debunking procedure. Did the 'death of God' bring about that of man, and with this latter also the death of the sovereign notions of meaning, truth and value? For Habermas this debunking procedure seems to be the historical avatar of a more fundamental constitution: historicism, caught in its own trap, has to confess its origin; and argumentation – in this philosophical crisis – rediscovers all its rights, thus profiting a new theory: that of the intersubjective communication professed by Habermas.

If Habermas, the philosopher of communication, took the trouble to make such a meticulous criticism of Foucault, this was certainly not in order to have the last word; it was, to be sure, to score a few points, but also to seek clarification and to obtain Foucault's entry – whether or not he made important concessions – into a dialogue. Now there has not been such a dialogue. Paul Veyne kindly confirmed that Foucault did not reply to Habermas's initial criticisms (he died before he received them in their definitive version); but he did not exclude all dialogue, since he had accepted the principle of a joint seminar with Habermas in Berkeley.

Because Plato – and for good reason – failed to reply to Aristotle, this does not mean to say that there should be no dialogue between Platonism and Aristotelianism. What would be the main lines of force of a reply given to Habermas? I now wish to sketch what this might be both from Foucault's point of view and also from that of Nietzsche who, as is well known (and this is one point on which the two interlocutors agree), profoundly shook Western thought, which suddenly had to become aware of its destiny regarding power.

THE POWERLESSNESS OF A NEW FORM OF INSTRUCTIVE DISCOURSE

I should like first to point out a few weak points in Habermas's own criticisms. In the 'presentism in spite of himself' which he imputes to Foucault, Habermas seems *himself* to confuse two processes: one is *scientific* in its intent (the elimination of prejudices due to the historical situation of the observer), the other is, properly speaking, philosophical (the refusal to rely on a hidden originating signification); as a result, one cannot see clearly the cause of the shortcomings of Foucault's historicism, nor how any history can escape historicism. The two other criticisms are largely redundant: it is in fact the same criticism shifted from the point of view of signification to that of truth and then value. The *ad hominem* arguments interfere with the methodological criticisms: does Foucault's militancy compromise the scientific nature of his work? Not only is this not obviously the case (Foucault did, after all, separate the two activities: one would seek in vain any militancy in *L'Archéologie du savoir*, in *L'Ordre du discours* or even in *Les Mots et les Choses*), but the suspension of value judgements and the retreat of subjectivity are sometimes such that they cause one to doubt whether any political commitment could be possible on the basis of these works (the ambiguity then is not the ambiguity which Habermas analyses): for example in *Surveiller et punir*, the development of the Panopticon for surveillance is described in minute detail, almost with fascination, in a way which has nothing to do (at least on this level) with a 'topical' struggle. Finally, Habermas does not confess that the source of these criticisms is often Foucault himself: not only did Foucault never deny that his work had 'empirical shortcomings' (he undertook a commendable self-criticism at the beginning of the second volume of *Histoire de la sexualité*), but it was he who defined his own work explicitly in terms of the decentring and the constant shifting of the 'ground which might give him support'.[19] Why should this constant shifting, which has a positive value for Foucault, have a negative connotation for Habermas? Is it not up to Habermas to explain and to make clear the extent to which he appropriates Foucault's methodological lucidity (even his self-criticism) and what it is that gives him the right to turn this against Foucault himself?

Yet there is a more serious problem. It is necessary to get to the bottom of the misunderstanding. If this is a complete misunderstanding, it is not enough simply to state it (one could make lists of quotes and examples); it is necessary to go right to the heart of it. Then it will be possible to understand what it was that made the debate between the two men so difficult, almost impossible; thus we shall also be able to *learn* philosophically from this confrontation.

Let us begin with a sentence from Habermas, aimed at Nietzsche but just as applicable to Foucault (and, moreover, repeated almost word for word in the criticisms he addresses to him): 'Behind apparently universal truth claims are hidden the subjective claims to power of value judgements.'[20] This pseudo-résumé of Nietzsche's thought shows that Habermas *does not understand* Nietzsche (in any case, that he does not understand Nietzsche's most interesting and overdetermined thoughts). The will to power becomes, according to Habermas, the *truth* of the claim to truth: the rationalist affirms the universal validity of his judgements; the Nietzschean unmasks this latter as a form of will to power. This is a continuation of the confrontation between Socrates and Callicles. The Nietzschean is taken to be the one who in general terms denies the universal validity of rational judgements, preferring a statement which is just as general as his (subjective) will to power ('It is true, it is just, because I desire it'). Nietzsche would thus be sustaining an anti-rational, anti-universal *thesis* in favour of a subjective imposition of strength. 'There is no rationality; there are only the effects of power': such would be the substance of Nietzsche's teaching faithfully applied by Foucault in his historiography of discursive practices.

It is obvious that if Nietzsche's thought could be reduced to this anti-rationalist thesis (or to this brutal antithesis of the claim of universal validity) it would be easily refuted: not only because a subject's will to power could be denied from one instant to another by another subject in the most arbitrary way, but also because it contradicts itself; for by denying truth (in general terms) it affirms (in general terms) non-truth, which boils down to affirming the truth of this non-truth called the will to power. The Nietszchean (just like Callicles) is caught in the trap of an implicit truth judgement which cannot subtend its own negation: 'I affirm (I put forward as truth) that there is no truth.' This is self-contradictory relativism! We have seen that this is how Habermas defines and criticises the claim to scientific status of a genealogical historiography whose only object is the kaleidoscope of power formations.

But what is being refuted? Nietzche or his shadow? Foucault or his caricature? Is it necessary to go over the 'demonstration' again, this time on Nietzsche's side? It would be necessary to deal with a lot of texts in order to take stock of the extent of the real situation. I shall keep to the essential.

In Nietzsche the questioning of rationality can by no means be reduced to a naive dispute on the surface level between the intrinsic and formal validity of truth judgements. Nietzsche never contested either the coherence or the interest of the logical, mathematical or scientific *corpus* Rather, he affirmed the eminent *disciplinary* value of the spirit of analysis and observation and the critical value of the exercise of reason in sciences. It is well known that he dedicated *Humain trop humain* to Voltaire, that he admired the Encyclopédistes and that he made plans to pursue scientific studies in Paris. Even if this leaning towards positivity grew less marked during the latter years of his lucidity, it would be an untenable misinterpretation to reduce Nietzsche's thought to a challenge to rationality made by life or to the destruction of objectivity by the *pathos* of subjectivity.

If the Nietzschean procedure is not anti-rational in this first sense, on what level should it be understood? It seems that the heart of the matter is reached if one investigates the *prescriptive* character of rationality. Rigorous reasoning might constrain me to admit something. But what is meant here by 'constrain'? The mechanism of syllogism has been used in positive ways, more formal ways and others which are aberrant. The question bears less on the veracity of logic than on the modality of its appearance and the contexts in which it was received and put into practice. Nietzsche is not asking if we have to recognise and apply logical principles and the principles of argumentation, but rather: 'How could it be that a noble and intelligent humanity could have had a quite different relationship from ours regarding these principles and these rules? Why have they become so constraining for Western man and what are the consequences which result for the link with the experience and the constitution of modern civilisation? . . .'

It is not enough to say that the Nietzschean project was not only theoretical but practical; not only assertoric but deontological; and so on. From *The Birth of Tragedy* onwards the question which preoccupied Nietzsche was that of the potentiality of great art as a civilising force. The Greeks were at the centre of the debate because the flowering and then the rapid decline of the tragic enigmatically sealed our destiny and caused us to measure our weaknesses as possibilities. From the *Intempestives* to the late fragments the main question remained that of the destiny of the West and the civilising resources attendant on it. This, then, is a genealogical question with hermeneutic requirements which have to be grasped (which Foucault tried to do in his Royeaumont lecture on Nietzsche in 1964, in which hermeneutics as the communication of communications appears as an infinite task[21]).

Genealogy is not directly prescriptive: it acquires its density from a narrative which gives one something to think about, like a fable. 'How, finally, the *real world* became a fable. The history of a mistake': have we really understood this famous text from the *Twilight of the Idols* if we flatten out its dramatic nature and its irony and make of it the equivalent of 'There is no more truth', even if a fable (for the rational spirit which Nietzsche *also* is) is also something in which one no longer believes? Nietzsche is proposing nothing less than measuring the scope of Western history against the history of truth. This means the foundation of the *episteme*, the profound change of the 'becoming-world' of this truth, the devaluation of this 'true world': that is as many phases as it takes for history to become destiny which Nietzsche, as a 'subject', can set out only by himself talking in the name of Western man from a point of view which is beyond his own 'subjectivity'.

In Habermas there is nothing (or almost nothing) about this hermeneutic contribution to Nietzschean genealogy, at least not in the book I am dealing with. The chapter on Nietzsche in *Der philosophische Diskurs der Moderne* is to say the least schematic, if not caricaturing. Even the title sets the tone: 'Nietzsche als Drehscheibe':[22] Nietzsche as turntable! Not only is this (false) understanding of Nietzsche worthy of a railway engineer; it is also purely historicist. Nietzsche is seen as opening the way to postmodernism like a link between the Romantic quest for a new mythology and the radical criticism of reason carried out by Heidegger and Bataille. In this chapter on Nietzsche there is almost nothing on Nietzsche's actual work, his method, his style, the interruptions in his work – everything one would have expected to be revealed by a thorough reading by this great stylist, even if his tone had been critical or polemical. Nietzsche's Dionysianism is seen simply in terms of his Romanticism, and his thought is reduced to a 'theory' which 'hypostasises' the aesthetic which it sees as 'the other of reason'.[23] Nietzsche is even criticised for not having been able to carry out an *Idealogiekritik*, a rather hasty accusation which seems totally to disregard his pitiless criticism of the Christian morality of asceticism. His critical side which is open to science is mentioned only in passing,[24] announcing the advent of French 'postmodernism'.

It is not surprising therefore that we get a distorted view of Foucault from Habermas's criticism. I have begun to demonstrate this; it is now time to bring to light, with regard to Foucault's work, the fundamental misunderstanding which made it possible for these criticisms to appear. Habermas imputes to Foucault the desire to construct a theory of power which would arrive at definitive and complete 'solutions'; it is as if he is attributing to Foucault the project of completing a systematic philosophy, as if Dreyfus and Rabinow (the merits of whose work I by no means wish to call into question) were more familiar to him than Foucault's actual questions. Now Foucault, to my knowledge, never characterised his itinary as a *parcours philosophique*, a philosophical 'journey' (the subtitle of the French translation of Dreyfus and Rabinow's book); he even removed the word 'philosophy' from the title of Jean Hyppolite's Chair at the Collège de France: the Chair of 'History of philosophical thought' became the Chair of 'History of thought systems'. It is therefore necessary to go back to the specific nature of Foucault's thought and style if one's criticisms are to be tighter and more fruitful. Let me give some examples.

As early as 1964, in his lecture to the Royaumont 'Nietzsche' colloquium entitled 'Nietzsche, Freud, Marx', Foucault confessed that he was uncertain; he suggested an 'indirect approach' to his subject – that is, 'certain themes concerning the *techniques of interpretation* of Marx, Nietzsche and Freud'. It seems to me that this tactic of taking an *indirect approach* can be found throughout the whole of Foucault's work. When he had to give the customary inaugural lecture at the Collège de France and eulogise his predecessor, Jean Hyppolite, the great Hegelian, what did Foucault do? Exactly the opposite of what was expected. He spoke of Hyppolite and Hegel *in fine*. He succeeded in disconcerting his audience. I should like to read out the admirable beginning of *L'Ordre du discourse*:

> I should have liked to slip surreptitiously into the speech that I have to give today, and into those that I shall have to give, perhaps for years. Rather than making the speech, I should rather have preferred to be enveloped by it and carried beyond the point of any possible beginning. I should have liked to have noticed the moment I spoke that a nameless voice had preceded me for a long time: then all I would have had to do would have been to continue, to carry on the sentence, to take up position, without anyone noticing, in the interstices, as if it had beckoned to me, holding itself for a moment in suspense. There would not then be any beginning . . .[25]

How significant this beginning is in the way it attempts to dodge solemnity! Foucault, whose death came after only a short illness, *also* wanted to avoid the ceremonial of death: 'Let us try rather to give meaning and beauty to death-effacement', he wrote.[26] Already, in the way he began the speech, the 'subject' tries to find a sort of anonymity; this is, however, such a personal way of carrying out a duty without giving in to convention. The infinite insistence of discourse and the density of language allows man only some 'breathing space'. The timescale is not that of *ego cogito*, which attempts to hold eternity at bay in a radical new beginning; it is the timescale of an incessant and sometimes indiscernible continuity, of a duration which lasts the length of its murmurings and holds attention by the whispered consciousness of its fragility, more than by the eloquence trumpeted forth by its presence. And then there is this bold conditional: 'There would not then be any beginning . . .', as if it were permissible to dream in the very bosom of the Collège de France and under such solemn circumstances. But this distance which is introduced by the conditional is in response to the irony of the institution (which 'gives' the right to speak), the irony which Foucault *bestows on* this latter. This dramatisation joining discourse and institution makes it possible, without one realising it, for the problem of the power of language (for ordered discourse also gives orders) to be posed. Hence the question implicitly formulated at the end of the introduction: 'But what is so perilous in the fact that people speak and that their discourse proliferates indefinitely?'

Proceeding in this way, Foucault could not have been unaware of the fact that he would be accused of a 'systematic ambiguity', especially with regard to the problem of power. Yet could one not reply to such a criticism from a censor hungry for coherence that power is precisely the moving locus of unexpected exclusions, mutations and shifts which make any *grand theory* of power abstract, indeed utopian? When Foucault considers the opposition between true and false as a 'system of exclusion' (alongside interdiction and the reason–madness divide) he knows that he is shocking his audience, especially if this latter is a philosopher, by going against the self-constitution which seems to define the true [*verum index sui*]. If the truth is traced back to a violent division imposed from the outside, would we not be altering it to an extent that would make it completely unrecognisable? Foucault is conscious of this objection: he was the one who formulated it. And he replies in a way which it will be necessary to quote in order to show how much more subtle it is than the way Habermas presents it:

> Of course, if one places oneself on the level of a proposition, on the inside of a discourse, the divide between the true and the false is neither arbitrary nor modifiable, nor institutional, nor violent. But if one situates oneself on a different level, if one seeks to know what the nature was, and still is, through our discourse, of this will to truth which has gone through so many centuries of our history, or what is, in a very general form, the type of division which orders our will to know, then what one sees taking shape is perhaps something like a system of exclusion (a historical, modifiable, institutionally constraining system).[27]

The *if* is the most important thing. In this there is a working hypothesis. One can choose *a different scale* from the traditional perspective, which can act as the *revealer* of something non-said lodged in the relations of submission, exclusion and violence which are not manifested by the self-envelopment of discourse, nor by the self-reference of philosophy as a sovereign *logos*. Is Foucault here giving way to an anti-rationalist *pathos* and to a will to invalidate rational discourse? The point is rather to broaden the horizon, to make archaeologically apparent this 'will to truth' which underlies the self-constitution of the true according to relations which are perhaps not simple and which need precisely to be deciphered. Alas, it cannot be denied that the *universal Geltungansprüche*, the claims of universal validity dear to Habermas, are not those which have regulated the course of history. Even Hegel did not claim this – Hegel who saw war, in a way for which he has continually been reproached, as the *ultima ratio regum*; what is more, he avoided the confusion of argumentation (the production of a *Grund*) and intersubjective recognition (remaining on the phenomenological level of *Selbstbewusstsein*) with the plenary and speculative deployment of reason.

There is nothing more difficult than constructing a theory of power in the present world; yet nothing is more necessary, at least in principle (for it is necessary to ask whether a *theory* would be enough to deal with such complexity). Power, like quicksilver, is hard to grasp: incessantly taking shape, destroying itself and then restructuring on the microscopic level what Richard Bendix, following Max Weber, calls *constellations of interest*.[28] Yet a theory of power also has to take account of domination [*Herrschaft*], '*the authoritarian power of command*', which is exercised essentially in the modern and rationalised Western world by means of this elaborate mediation which is called the State and which reserves to itself the right to legitimate violence as a means.[29] Finally – and it is at this point that Weber's contribution has to be seen in terms of an extension of Nietzsche's perceptions – new and specific problems result from the considerable growth of power due to the development and universal diffusion of scientific and technical procedures in the State, on its periphery and outside it. Rational potentialisation is no longer exercised *a priori* (in its core of intelligibility), nor even *a posteriori* (transforming experience through the way it operates, principally mathematically), but is capable of a third order which is of a paradoxical nature. Here what rational potentialisation itself puts into practice comes back at it like a boomerang in the form of the pure effects of force which are exposed to (but not controlled by) its own reflexive-critical-normative potential.

If this present contribution is to be situated in the 'line of descent from Nietzsche', this is because Nietzsche discerned with extraordinary lucidity (not to mention, especially in his latter years, some terrifying flashes of genius) the new dangers of the (scientific) will to truth and the hitherto unthought-of possibilities open to the future. If 'the most sacred and powerful thing the world possessed to this day bled beneath our knife',[30] there is no doubt that the scalpel was that of *Wissenschaft*; for the latter can also be used to regulate the redistribution of vital energies: it would be necessary to 'use clear-sighted science to warn of the dangerous consequences of too-pressurised heating' (of instincts, passions and illusions).[31] Hence the question put in *Le Gai Savoir*: 'Is science capable of *giving* goals to the lives of men when it has proved that it can remove and destroy them?'[32]; it 'has not yet built its Cyclopean monuments; yet the time will come for this too';[33] 'its prodigious ability to open new universes of stars to the joy of humans'[34] will be discovered.

Not only is the Nietzschean vision of scientific rationalisation not a flat and brutal criticism of reason giving preference to subjective or vital *pathos*, but Habermas also fails to discern that if in Nietzsche there is a criticism of reason, it is a *self-criticism*. It is *us* that he is addressing, this *us* being the whole of Western humanity. When Nietzsche asks: 'Why do we believe in truth?' it is not an *exterior* instance that he is criticising; he is trying to untangle the knot of rationality which has become destiny. On this subject it is worth looking closely at Paragraph 344 of the *Gay Science*, [35] an extremely questioning text: 'This unconditional will to truth: what is it . . . ?' Why 'truth at any cost?' The Nietzschean meditation suggests a suspicion: '*To want the truth* could be secretly to want death' and a certainty: 'our faith in science still rests on a *metaphysical* faith'. Nietzsche thus arrives at a mode of questioning the presuppositions of both the rationalisation which is integral to life and also the metaphysical foundation of science which is in fact hyper-rational because of its profoundly philosophical nature.

The sole point of this return to Nietzsche was to call to mind the wealth of inspiration to be found in his work for any meditation on the destiny of the force of reason, and correlatively the danger of schematising Nietzsche's genealogical contribution in favour of a simple reformulation of rationalism. Is the change in model suggested by Habermas from a philosophy of consciousness to a philosophy of communication sufficient? The edification of a complex, non-functionalist theory of communication is a worthy enterprise; but does it not run the risk of remaining abstract and even edifying in a purely useless sort of way, so long as its recourse to a *normativity* interior to rationality sees this rationality in terms of a comfortable and artificial autonomy, turning away from the most disturbing power effects of scientific rationality itself?

Yet for all that, the picture is not altogether satisfactory on Foucault's side either. In fact Foucault himself recognised the still imperfect and indeterminate nature of his theory of power; he wisely chose to study power in its *open relationships*,[36] but the parenthesising of Weber's problematic (and the increase in rationalisation) stopped him from taking into consideration the power effects resulting *directly* from scientific-technical developments; there was still less chance of his approaching this in his later years because of the fact that his work was moving towards the genealogical study of the Self and the analysis of modes of *subjectification*. It seems to me none the less unfair to accuse Foucault of being a 'vitalist', since the concept of *biopower* implies not an unconditional exaltation of the life principle but a new way of thinking of the disciplinisation and objectification of life.

Foucault and Habermas bear witness, each in his way, to the difficulty of dealing with the *double demands* of *geneaology* and *rationality*. If one ignores the requirements of genealogy, one ends up with a form of rationality which is too pure or exclusively argumentational, casting power back into 'outer darkness' in a way which is incapable of explaining how we became 'prisoners of our own history' (according to Foucault's expression). If we ignore purely rational requirements, we are exposed to historicism or relativism; we also run the risk, in a world which is becoming more and more marked by techno-scientific power, of depriving ourselves of any recourse when faced with technological functionalism.

Rather than continuing this criticism, which by no means claims to be putting a full stop to a debate which is still open,[37] I should like to end this contribution in a more measured way. Even if he did not recognise the full scope of Nietzsche's, Foucault's and Heidegger's hermeneutics, Habermas himself did after all sketch a genealogy of modern consciousness in *Der philosophische Diskurs der Moderne*; it remains to determine the degree of necessity (or meaning) of the genealogy in relation to the theory of communication acts, and particularly the methodological and philosophical limitations of this latter. In his self-criticism of the first volume of *Histoire de la sexualité* (*La Volonté de savoir*) Foucault renounces any attempt to make sexuality into a discursive practice closed in on itself; he opens his genealogy of sexuality to a 'hermeneutic of the self' and in consequence deepens its field and makes it more philosophical. His history becomes an 'analysis of *truth games*, of games of truth and falsehood through which the being is historically constituted as experience, that is to say, as able and having to be thought of'.[38]

The dialogue between truth as game and truth as pure normative requirement becomes impossible only if reason forgets that it is only ever truly itself when it criticises itself and attempts to grasp its own limitations. Power imposes itself on rationality as an enigma, and therefore as the sign of a task to be done, precisely because thought recognises then that there cannot be (and perhaps must not be) any final solutions – only aporias.

NOTES

1. Jürgen Habermas, *Der philosophische Diskurs der Moderne*, Frankfurt-am-Main, Suhrkamp, 1985.
2. Hubert L. Dreyfus and Paul Rabinow, *Michel Foucault: Un parcours philosophique*, Paris: Gallimard, 1984, p. 312.
3. Nietzsche, *Ecce Homo*, French transl. A. Vialatte, Paris: Gallimard, 1942, p. 163.
4. Dreyfus and Rabinow, p. 300.
5. Habermas, *Der philosophische Diskurs der Moderne*, p. 318.
6. *Ibid*., p. 322.
7. *Ibid*., p. 344.
8. *Ibid*., p. 317.
9. Declaration dating from 1974, quoted by Habermas, *ibid*., p. 292.
10. Habermas, *ibid*., p. 325.
11. *Ibid*., 325–6. See Paul Veyne, 'Foucault révolutionne l'histoire', in *Comment on écrit l'histoire*, Paris: Éditons du Seuil, coll. 'Points', 1979, pp. 210–11.
12. Habermas, *Der philosophische Diskurs der Moderne*, p. 326.
13. *Ibid*., p. 330.
14. Nancy Fraser, quoted by Habermas, *ibid*., p. 333.
15. *Ibid*., p. 335.
16. *Ibid*., p. 336.
17. *Ibid*., p. 317.
18. *Ibid*., p. 316.
19. Michel Foucault, *L'Archéologie du savoir*, Paris: Gallimard, 1969, p. 267.
20. Habermas, *Der philosophische Diskurs der Moderne*, IV.
21. Michel Foucault, 'Marx, Nietzsche, Freud', in *Nietzsche*, Paris: Éditions de Minuit, 1967, pp. 183–92.
22. Habermas, *Der philosophische Diskurs* . . ., IV, 23. See *ibid*., pp. 109, 118, 120.
24. *Ibid*., p. 120.
25. Michel Foucault, *L'Ordre du discours*, Paris: Gallimard, 1971, p. 7.
26. Quoted by Paul Veyne, 'Le dernier Foucault et sa morale', *Critique*, August–September, 1987, p. 941.
27. Michel Foucault, *L'Ordre du discours*, p. 16.
28. Richard Bendix, *Max Weber: An intellectual portrait*, London: Methuen, 1966, p. 290.
29. *Ibid*., pp. 291–2. See Max Weber, *Staatssoziologie*, Berlin, Duncker-Humblot, 1956, p. 27.
30. Nietzsche, *Le Gai Savoir*, § 125.
31. Nietzsche, *Humain, trop humain*, I, § 251.
32. *Le Gai Savoir*, § 251.
33. *Ibid*.
34. *Ibid*., § 12.
35. Entitled *Inwiefern auch wir noch fromm sind* ('The degree to which we are still pious').
36. Dreyfus and Rabinow, p. 265.

37. Bernard Waldenfels tried to present a critical reading of Habermas and Foucault in his article 'Division ou dispersion de la raison?' (*Les études philosophiques*, October–December 1986, pp. 473–84); apart from the fact that he does not really take account of *Der philosophische Diskurs der Moderne*, this article wrongly presupposes what the main question is: a unified concept of 'reason' which is supposed to be 'divided' in Habermas and 'dispersed' in Foucault. This approach seems to me to be too schematic, in any case less elucidating than that of Rainer Rochlitz ('Des philosophes allemands face à la pensée française', *Critique*, January–February 1986, pp. 7–39.)

    If the debate is to be continued, Foucault himself indicated the direction it should take in his 1983 lecture on Kant's *Was ist Aufklärung?* (*Magazine littéraire*, May 1984, pp. 34–9) Habermas echoes this in his brief homage 'Mit dem Pfeil ins Herz der Gegenwart', in *Die Neue Unübersichtlichkeit*, Frankfurt-am-Main Suhrkamp, 1985, pp. 126–31 ('Une flèche dans le cœur du temps présent', French transl. C. Bouchindhomme, *Critique*, August–September 1986, pp. 794–9).

    I should like to observe that in spite of these equally 'reasonable' philosophers' attempts at *rapprochement* – claiming to be in the same tradition (except Nietzsche) – there is a major divergency between their attitudes: one attitude supposes that *taking sides* with reason is still required (cf. the end of *Raison et Légitimité*, in which Habermas sees his own thought as being at the heart of 'a practice which is attached to a rational will, in other words to a practice which does not duck out of the requirements of foundation and justification' (*Raison et Légitimité*, French transl. J. Lacoste, Paris: Payot, 1978, p. 193); the other attitude (not found only in Foucault) refuses to *redouble* the rational thrust towards another metaphysical idealisation (or partiality) and ducks, avoids, and decentres the process involving the need to learn about new modes or rationality – and also advances towards the boundaries of these rationalities and of the rational.

    The question facing us remains more than ever: 'What is Enlightenment?' – that is to say: 'What is rationality today? Being at once ideal and destiny, formal coherence and discursive and functional autonomisation, rationality today is disjointed, yet the way it is disjointed is still questioned in a unitary – albeit concerned – way by the question 'What is Enlightenment?'.
38. Michel Foucault, *L'Usage des plaisirs*, Paris: Gallimard, 1984, pp. 12–13.

SUMMARY OF DISCUSSIONS

François Wahl asked what the criteria would be for the appreciation of the new; we do not have any. The criteria of rationality are still internal to certain practices of discourse. The same goes for truth. Foucault would seem to be suggesting rather that there are successive truths. Deleuze, moreover, saw an aesthetic in this. Is it possible to speak of a structure of truth?

François Boulant said he was surprised by the attention paid to Kant's text on the Enlightenment. It is an enigmatic text which is difficult to penetrate and does not necessarily admit of Foucault's reading of; it was as if he were pursuing an absent question: What is the present? What is our present?

But the debate was dominated by **Manfred Frank's** contribution. He thanked Dominique Jacinaud for having in some way pacified the discussion and reintegrated the Germans into the debate. Germans are not necessarily irrational, even if for them disobedience might come too late. Relationships between French and German philosophers are difficult, poisoned with suspicion; a recent conference ended in disaster, also as a result of German stubbornness. Hence the pleasure of renewed contact this morning. This background explains the obliqueness in the relationship between Habermas and Michel Foucault. Jacinaud speaks of the 'fundamental difference of attitude'; but divergence does not exclude complementarity. Universalist discourse is not possible without its Other. Habermas and Foucault were both formidable polemicists and one would have liked to see them meet, as had in fact been planned.

Gérard Lebrun asked about how the universal was perceived by Michel Foucault. Following on from Nietzsche, Foucault insisted on seeing all thought about the universal as subject to the work in which it is contained, as can be seen in *Histoire de la folie* and in his reflection on the Enlightenment.

According to **Dominique Jacinaud**, Michel Foucault in particular asks us not to forget the extent to which the universal is an instance of something else. Would he have gone so far as Gilles Deleuze, whose contribution tends to make the non-universal into a system? He would probably have been more careful.

Dominique Jacinaud stressed the importance of style in Foucault, a point which was elaborated by **Raymond Bellour**, showing Foucault as being vigilant in his will to understand 'God's grammar rules' as in Brisset, and passionately interested in art. Between Habermas and Foucault, perhaps, the question is one of style; Habermas never seems to have left modernism behind him. Foucault advances in terms of a form of understanding like that applied to movements in art.

two

Foucault, the present and history

Mark Poster

Foucault's historical work initiates a thematic of discontinuity.[1] That much is well known. What is less well recognised is that his work also implies a discontinuity in the present social formation, a discontinuity that resituates the historian's relation to the past, suggests a theoretical reorientation of the historical discipline and calls for a re-examination of the appropriate topics of historical investigation. Foucault's work enacts this second type of discontinuity, without fully recognising and conceptualising its contours and significance.

The topics Foucault investigated exemplify a restructuring of historical priorities. Insanity, language, medicine, punishment, sexuality – these have been marginal topics for historians. By placing them at the centre of the historical stage, Foucault reversed the fundamental theoretical assumptions of the discipline, a reversal that derives its power not only from the strength of Foucault's texts but also from a large-scale social transformation in the second half of the twentieth century, one that has led to what I call 'the mode of information'. My paper will explore this theme and assess its value for the historical discipline.

One's estimate of the significance of Foucault's writings for the discipline of history depends in every way on which of Foucault's texts one takes to represent his position. It is possible, of course, to discover a fundamental unity in his writings. That strategy gives a central role to the author, a position that Foucault himself rejected. A more fruitful interpretation begins with the recognition of a diversity of themes and strategies in his texts, a diversity that is suggested by the marked differences in the spate of studies of his works that have appeared in English in recent years. Books on Foucault by Lemert and Gillan, Major-Poetzl, Dreyfus and Rabinow, Smart, Cousins and Hussain, Rajchman, Racevskis, myself and others present sharply contrasting interpretations of their nature and significance.[2]

My interest in Foucault derives from my sense that Marxism no longer provides a basis for critical social theory. I have become increasingly troubled by the inability of historical materialism to present an adequate account of the structures of domination in modern society, and therefore of its deficiencies as a guide to the social critic and historian. Yet critiques of Marxism often run aground because (1) they fail to specify with appropriate complexity a historical field (usually the political) that cannot be accounted for by the theory of the mode of production; and (2) they are unable to provide an epistemological position that would acknowledge the viability of Marxist analyses within a regional domain. In my view *Surveiller et punir* and associated writings by Foucault from the 1970s go a long way towards overcoming the customary limitations of the critiques of historical materialism on both these counts.

The great achievement of *Surveiller et punir* is to theorise and historically analyse a structure of domination in modern society which is beyond the field of investigation opened by the traditional Marxist notion of the mode of production. After *Surveiller et punir* it is no longer possible for Marxist historians to maintain that they alone are able to present a critique of liberal institutions, one that reveals both their structures of domination and their historical specificity. Foucault's history of prisons undermines the liberal view that prisons constituted a humane advance over earlier systems of punishment and the Marxist view that they are no more than a secondary elaboration of the mode of production. *Surveiller et punir* unveils a specific discourse/practice of domination in modern prisons, one Foucault terms a 'technology of power', a structure of domination that is invisible when modern history is read through the categories of the mode of production.

The Panopticon, as Foucault calls the system of domination specific to prisons, cannot be analysed from the Marxist historical standpoint because the Marxist categories of alienation and exploitation address only those features of domination that concern the act of labour. Other forms of domination are recognised by Marxist discourse only to the extent that they are rooted in the domination of labour. This limitation of Marxist history is not necessarily a fatal deficiency, since it is characteristic of all theoretical perspectives to open up only particular fields for exploration. There may be problems with the manner in which Marxist theory addresses labour practices (such as the theory of the 'false consciousness' of workers who fail to recognise their class interests) but these problems can be corrected by revising the theory; they do not undermine its heuristic value.

The more troubling difficulties with historical materialism derive not so much from the particular categories it generates to enable a critique of the capitalist organisation of labour but from the way Marxist theory attempts to monopolise the historical field. When Marx proclaims that the sufferings of the working class are universal, and when he contends that domains of practice other than that of labour are superstructural, he is totalising the historical field, improperly excluding other critical perspective. In short, he flagrantly reduces all domination to the level of labour. By totalising the historical field, Marxist history introduces a form of domination at the level of theory and works against the very interests of emancipation it claims to promote.

How is it possible that a theorist who formulated the principle that theory is rooted in the social world, situated in the finitude of practice, should go on to cancel this advance in self-reflectiveness and pretend to elevate his position to that of a universal science? Marx maintained both that his theory was rooted in the standpoint of the working class and that the position derived from that standpoint is universal in character. His failure to sustain the conditioned, particular and limited character of the knowledge generated by historical materialism is the source of a theoretical slide back into what Derrida terms the 'logocentrism' of the Western philosophical tradition'[3] the theoretical cause of its regression back to claims of certain truth or, put differently, its appropriation of the surplus-value of reason. The implications of this regression are vast for critical theory, Marxist historiography and much of socialist practice.

The emancipatory interests promoted by historical materialism are sustained only with a detotalised theoretical stance such as that proposed by Foucault, a theoretical asceticism that severely restricts the truth claims of texts. Two constraints are of particular importance: (1) that the historian acknowledge his or her political orientation; and (2) that the historian's text does not claim to exhaust the meaning of the field to be investigated. *Surveiller et punir* exemplifies both these self-limiting principles, though it does better with the second than the first, and even regarding the second there are points where the text flirts with totalisation.

In *Foucault, Marxism and History* I demonstrated in detail how *Surveiller et punir* detotalises the historical field in relation to these self-limiting principles.[4] Here I shall discuss another work, Foucault's essay 'What is Enlightenment?'. I shall then return to a feature of Foucault's work that concerns a restructuring of the historical field in relation to language. I shall do this by contrasting Foucault's position with that of Marx.

Foucault's short essay 'What is Enlightenment?' is a remarkably dense statement of position. It outlines nothing less than a new critical theory (reluctant as Foucault was 'to theorise'), one that attempts to go beyond the limits of existing positions such as that of the Frankfurt School. The return to Kant, and in particular to his *Was ist Aufklärung?*, signals by itself a re-examination of the fundamental premisses of critical theory and points specifically to an effort by Foucault to differentiate his stance from that of Jürgen Habermas. Perhaps most surprising of all to followers of recent French theory is Foucault's willingness, in 'What is Enlightenment?', to argue for the value to contemporary theory of certain Enlightenment strategies of thought.

The return to Kant, and therefore to the Enlightenement, is also associated with the recent work of Jean-François Lyotard.[5] Lyotard, like Foucault, examined one of Kant's 'minor' historical essays, but in this case it was 'The Dispute of the Faculties'.[16] Lyotard sought a logical basis of support for epistemological multiplicity, for the positive value of non-totalising argument. Lyotard's terms 'phrase' and later '*le différand*' mark the boundaries between discourses that are unbridgeable by the ambitions of a total theory. While Foucault's project is similar to Lyotard's it is at once broader in scope and more politically rooted. A detailed comparison of the recent work of Foucault and Lyotard would reveal interesting similarities and contrasts.

Foucault is most sensitive in 'What is Enlightenment?' to the problem of rooting his own project in the Enlightenment. He finds something of interest there, but he does not want his work to be associated too intimately with eighteenth-century thinkers. Too many people, he complains, put things in the black-and-white terms of pro and contra. He sharply attacks the 'blackmailers' who do so because they limit discourse to 'a simplistic and authoritarian alternative'.[7] Foucault's touchiness on this issue derives from an unresolved issue that is at the heart of his essay. The point at stake has to do with his strategy of rooting theory in the present in both ethical and political terms, without, however, adequately determining the relationship between the present and the past.

Foucault extracts from the Enlightenment – and from Kant in particular – the problematic of the constitution of the self, relating this to Kant's 'dare to know'. He contends that Kant introduced into philosophy the novelty of connecting the issue of the 'public' freedom to know with 'a reflection on history and a particular analysis of the specific moment at which he is writing and because of which he is writing'.[8] In other words, the ability to constitute oneself as the subject of knowledge is related to one's intervention in the present as well as one's estimate of the relationship between the present and the past. On this formulation rests the achievement of Kant that Foucault would emulate. (In the light of Foucault's unfortunately interrupted history of the constitution of the self, it is especially important to analyse Kant's formulation of the problem in relation to the history of modernity.) Foucault carefully delimits his debt to Kant to a particular proposition – a proposition, moreover, that is not characteristic of Kant's major works. The charge that Foucault had become a Kantian, much less a *philosophe*, would appear to be remote. Then why all the fuss about 'blackmail'?

For one thing, Foucault is somewhat uncomfortable in the *philosophe*'s garb. He had, after all, devoted many of his early works to a critique of humanist rationalism. From *Histoire de la folie à l'âge classique* to *Les Mots et les Choses*, he participated in an intellectual current that was animated by the rejection of the Enlightenment. In 'What is Enlightenment?' Foucault distinguishes humanism from the Enlightenment – a distinction to which not everyone would agree – reserving his criticism for the former.

> Humanism . . . can be opposed by the principle of a critique and a permanent creation of ourselves in our autonomy: that is, a principle that is at the heart of the historical consciousness that the Enlightenment has of itself. From this standpoint, I am inclined to see Enlightenment and humanism in a state of tension rather than identity.[9]

Such a definition of the Enlightenment, while arguable, is not widely accepted.

Another issue that disrupts an easy appropriation of the Enlightenment by Foucault concerns his relation to Habermas. In recent works such as *The Theory of Communicative Action*,[10] 'Modernity versus postmodernity'[11] and 'The entwinement of myth and Enlightenment',[12] Habermas defends the Enlightenment, against thinkers like Foucault, precisely on the issue of rationalism. The project of an emancipated society, for Habermas, is impossible without the extension of Enlightenment rationality throughout the space of politics and everyday life. In 'Modernity versus postsmodernity' he defends modernity, based on the Enlightenment, against postmodernity which, he claims, leads to conservatism. In 'The entwinement of myth and Enlightenment' he rejects as superficial any similarity between the critique of the Enlightenment in Derrida and Foucault, on the one hand, and that in Horkheimer and Adorno,[13] on the other, contending that the pessimism of the latter thinkers is recuperable while that of the former is not.

An important change occurred in Habermas's position on this issue with *The Theory of Communicative Action*. Habermas now recognised that the defence of the Enlightenment would have to be modified: no longer could it be based on reason as an attribute of consciousness. Instead, Enlightenment rationality must be defended by translating it into a linguistic model. Habermas defined rationality as a capacity for speech in a certain linguistic–social setting. This 'ideal speech situation' is conceptualised as a stage in human evolution. Mankind – or at least Western society – is now capable of making a project of constituting the 'ideal speech situation', and therefore of constructing an emancipated society.[14] The more recent work elaborates more fully the linguistic character of the concept of reason.

One can plausibly read *The Theory of Communicative Action* in a way that suggests that Habermas is closer to the positions of Lyotard and Foucault than might at first appear. Although communicative rationality presumes a goal of consensus – a goal with which neither Lyotard nor Foucault has much sympathy – it includes a moment of difference as well. The speaker, in Habermas's discourse, must be able to contest the proposition of another in order for rationality to be effective in a communication. Support for this reading of *The*

Theory of Communicative Action comes in a recent interview with Habermas by Perry Anderson. Here Habermas denies that his defence of rationality on the basis of linguistic consensus leads to 'a fully transparent society'. On the contrary, he claims that consensus is attained 'by means of the criticism of validity-claims [and] does not conflict therefore with the pluralism of life-forms and interest.'[15] Habermas's emphasis on criticism in communication puts him close to Lyotard's notion of *le différand* and to Foucault's notion of oppositional self-constitution, even as it is borrowed from Kant. Foucault's notion of 'the constitution of the self as an autonomous subject'[16] bears considerable resemblance to Habermas's notion of communicative rationality as a critcal speech act. An additional similarity in the thought of Foucault and Habermas is that they both develop their ideas in relation to the project of emancipation.

The crucial divergence in their ideas, however, concerns the problem of historical framing. Habermas, the dialectician, sets the notion of communicative rationality within the context of the total evolution of mankind. His is, in short, a teleological position. Foucault, the genealogist, roots his position in a detotalised confrontation with the present. On the question of historical framing, Habermas retreats to an assumption of epistemological certainty: the critical theorist must be able to reconstruct the entire past. Foucault's position requires a much more modest claim for the critic: that he or she can dare to know and constitute him- or herself in political opposition to present structures of domination. Foucault's position therefore goes further than Habermas's in abandoning the traditional, essentialist view of the subject as centred in knowledge.

The main theoretical problem at stake in the appropriation of the Enlightenment, however, is the issue of how to change the present. Foucault argues very powerfully for a new kind of criticism, one he calls 'a limit attitude'. The new criticism will seek to determine what is and what is not possible. In many ways, Foucault's proposal is closer to Marx than to Kant. Kant defined what reason could *not* do, thereby rejecting earlier forms of metaphysical discourse. The powers of rationality that remained after Kant's philosophical house-cleaning were determined through the strategy of the transcendental deduction, which rooted pure reason in universality. By contrast, both Marx and Foucault place temporal limits on reason, restricting it by its contingency, its presentness. The limits of reason are determined by the finitude of the thinker, by his or her situation.

In addition, both Marx and Foucault orientate, however differently, the task of criticism to the 'positive' goal of transgression. Foucault was never more clear on this issue then in 'What is Enlightenment?'. The project of criticism is associated with the labour of freedom: reason unmasks pretensions to universality, reveals the boundaries of social and cultural forms and points to the possibility of alternative forms that are not yet associated with domination. Where Foucault goes considerably beyond Marx is in the connection he makes between the transgressive critique of the present and the constitution of the self. Much more clearly than Marx, Foucault insists that historical writing is a form of self-determination as well as a practice of social critique. In Foucault's words:

> I mean that this work done at the limits of ourselves must, on the one hand, open up a realm of historical inquiry and, on the other, put itself to the test of reality, of contemporary reality, both to grasp the points where change is possible and desirable, and to determine the precise form this change should take.[17]

Marx, in many ways a son of the Enlightenment, never saw that the critique of the present was authorised by the contingency of the constitution of the self of the critic. Instead he presumed the universal validity of the dialectic, which is a variation on the theme of essentialist rationalism.

'What is Enlightenment?' synthesises two strains in Foucault's work since the early 1970s. *Surveiller et punir* and *Histoire de la sexualité*, Volume I present critiques of domination by providing detotalised histories of particular discourse/practices. Subsequently Foucault worked on the problem of the constitution of the self, exploring that theme in Volumes II and III of *Histoire de la sexualité*. But the connection between these two lines of research were not drawn out until 'What is Enlightenment?'. The enigmatic proclamation in *Surveiller et punir* that Foucault's history is a history of the present now becomes clear. Criticism – of which historical writing is one form – begins with the critic's self-constitution, and that occurs through the recognition of one's contingency and, at the same time, the recognition that social domination is contingent. Foucault's formulation is worth repeating:

> I shall thus characterize the philosophical ethos appropriate to the critical ontology of ourselves as a historico-practical test of the limits that we may go beyond, and thus as work carried out by ourselves upon ourselves as free beings.[18]

The weak point of Foucault's new history rests with the problem of the generality of the historian's work, a problem that Foucault recognises and addresses but does not completely resolve. The historian's work begins with his or her recognition of contingency and subsequent constitution of self as historian. The historian's work is ultimately one of self-examination. With an interior focus having priority over the labour of reconstructing the past, the historian is subject to the blind spot of social determination. Historical writing is rooted in the inward investigation of limits; its strategy of outward investigation of social domination may therefore lack systematicity, lack a grasp of the general structures that work to determine the contingency of the individual. Foucault grapples with this problem by outlining what he regards as the 'generality' of his problematic:

> This philosophical attitude has to be translated into the labor of diverse inquiries .... [which] have their theoretical coherence in the definition of the historically unique forms in which the generalities of our relations to things, to others, to ourselves, have been problematized.[19]

Foucault here maintains that historical writing, however 'monographic' or limited in scope, implicates large theoretical issues. These issues ('relations to things, to others, to ourselves') are definitions of general questions. The problem with Foucault's position is that he privileges the historian's relations to others and things in comparison to the historian's relation to him- or herself.

Part of the contingent situation of the historian is the world in which he or she attempts the constitution of self. Yet in Foucault's essay there is no attempt to characterise the general patterns of this world – or, better, no attempt to determine the particularity of the social world which gives force to the historian's investigations. What the reader confronts in Foucault's text is a world in which there are diverse forms of domination and diverse forms of resistance to domination. One finds no recognition of a special character of the contingent present that makes pertinent a form of historiography such as the one Foucault develops.

It is my conviction that there have emerged in the recent past new language experiences, which I call the mode of information, and that these language experiences work to detotalise the social world, providing the impetus for a decentred form of historiography such as Foucault's. It is also my conviction that the explicit recognition and analysis of the mode of information provides supplementary force to the main lines of Foucault's work, giving it a power that it otherwise lacks. His position, as it stands, remains subject to the charge that it generates projects that are arbitrary; that its problematic is unable to argue for the general value and applicability of its conclusions.

The additional force that might be added to Foucault's position by incorporating the perspective of the mode of information can be briefly sketched in a few remarks. The problematic of the constitution of the self in contemporary social space must take account of electronically mediated communications. These are increasingly being substituted for both face-to-face and written communications. Today television takes over the role of the confessional and the therapy session of earlier times. In the act of watching television, 'discourses' are presented which operate to 'constitute the self' of the viewer. Television is a complex phenomenon in which network serials and news, advertisements and tapes of movies played on VCRs have very different effects on the question of the subject. In the case of advertisements, the viewer is fashioned into a consumer-subject by the visual and aural rhetoric, with floating signifiers attached to commodities not by an intrinsic relation to them but by the logic of unfulfilled desire that is at once imprinted in the subject's fantasy and already there through the limits of the social order.

In the case of computer mail and teleconferencing,[20] temporal and spatial distance structures the subject continuously to constitute him- or herself in the discourse. Electronic mediation heighten the 'artificiality' of communication, extending to the ultimate degree the *différance* of writing., Self-constitution is built into the structure of the communication. With the mode of information, the question of the subject is no longer limited to the opposition consciousness/structure. Instead, the subject becomes a multiplicity of self-constitutions, with one identity as the receiver of television advertisements, another as operator of an automatic teller, another as a reader of novels, and so forth. Foucault's problematic of self-constitution is the appropriate strategy for the mode of information, finding its most extensive field in that context.

Foucault's reluctance to problematise the character of the social world stems no doubt from the failures of the characterisation provided by Marxists, and the epistemological implications of that failure.[21] But the impasses at all levels of the theory of the mode of production and the dangers of totalisation inherent in the project of characterising the social world are not adequate excuses. A detotalised analysis of the social world, one that defines emergent structures in our social space, remains both possible and necessary. For without such an analysis Foucault remains unable to distinguish the difference in the respective situations of Kant and himself, and therefore remains uneasy in returning to Kant because of the danger that an identity of positions might appear to result. Yet if Foucault had defined his present in its difference from Kant's (post-modern versus modern; mode of information versus mode of production), the danger of the confusion of positions would disappear and the return would become a graceful exchange, one not subject to 'blackmail' of any sort.

It is necessary to theorise, therefore, as one moment in the constitution of the historian's subjectivity and discourse, a characterisation, however provisional, of the historian's social world. To summarise, there are two benefits of this endeavour: (1) to provide specificity and difference to the historian's situation; (2) to give generality to his or her transgressive investigations. I will now illustrate these themes by comparing Marx to Foucault and indicating how a theory of the mode of information enhances both their historical perspectives.

Marx constitutes the historical field as one predominantly of action, specifically labouring action. In contrast, Foucault gives priority to discourse, a form of language, without severing the relation of discourse to practice. Foucault carried out this paradigmatic shift in the context of the strong current of structuralism in France. Structuralists not only privilege linguistic phenomena, they tend to reduce the entire field of the human sciences to language. Foucault rejects the structuralist totalisation of language with his insistence on the couplet discourse/practice, thereby avoiding the danger of formalism. The problem, however, is that he accepts the paradigm shift towards language without questioning the social factors (such as the mode of information) that give urgency to this move.

Marx shifted the field from politics to labour, arguing not only that labour had not yet been adequately theorised but that the current social formation *draws attention to labour as a problem* in that capitalism transforms the labour process. Foucault shifted the field from labour to discourse *without a rigorous examination* of how the contemporary field problematises language. He contextualised the shift to language partially in that he drew attention to the new role of the human sciences in structures of domination, a Nietzschean theme that he renewed with great success. But he never examined thoroughly the drastic transformations of linguistic experience in the contemporary field. The result is that his texts do not reveal as fully as they might the powerful social forces that justify the emphasis on language as a focus of historical investigation.

I have been developing the concept of 'the mode of information' to accomplish just that purpose. I use the term not to designate a new period of history, such as 'the age of information'. Conceptualised in that way, the mode of information would totalise the field, reintroducing the problem that plagues Marx's concept of the mode of production. I employ the concept of the mode of information to designate the field of linguistic experience, a field whose basic structural relations change from period to period, just like those of the mode of production. But Marx's concept of the mode of production tends to slide in its usage from one that stipulates that there are different modes of production at different times to one that posits the modern epoch (capitalism) as a social system dominated by the forces and relations of production. The simple theoretical observation that all societies include structures through which human beings produce objects to satisfy their needs is transformed into a reductive totalisation that centres the historical field in the system of production. This theoretical slippage must be avoided in the development of the concept of the mode of information. This category must not be theorised in such a way that it appears that the current period substitutes a mode of information for a mode of production.

The need to develop a historical field of investigation constituted by the mode of information derives both from the failure of historical materialism (as well as other positions, such as Max Weber's) to elaborate a theory of language and from fundamental changes in linguistic experience that have occurred in the twentieth century. Due to the limitations of this paper, I will focus only on the second issue. An adequate theory of the mode of information crucially depends upon the way the context of language is envisioned. It is true that the human sciences in the twentieth century have become associated with systems of social control. It is true that the mode of production has been significantly altered in recent years by the introduction of information-processing systems. But neither of these contextual changes is an adequate starting point for developing a concept of the mode of information because they both fail to come to terms with the general problem of the position of language in social relations – they fail, in short, to formulate a theory of the relation of language to action.

The theory of the mode of information must take into account the critiques of the representationality, intentionality and univocality of language that have developed in so many varieties in recent decades. The structuralists derive meaning not from the consciousness of the language-speaker but from the system of binary opposites at a synchronous level of analysis.[22] Semiologists demonstrate that meanings can 'float' in social space and be attached to objects in a manner that is out of phase with their 'utility' or referentiality.[23] Deconstructionists argue for the 'textuality' of spoken language, the systematic gap between intention and discourse.[24] Speech-act theorists insist on the performative component of utterances, denying that statements are reducible to the function of truth.[25] Bakhtin uncovers a dialogic dimension of language in which polyvocity and polysemy disrupt the illusion of semantic stability.[26] Each of these positions contains impressive arguments against positivism and formalism.

However valuable these 'post-rationalist' theories of language may be, they do not offer the historian the principles of structural variation that constitute a linguistic field *at the temporal level*.[27] While many of the above positions include suggestive analytic perspectives on the question of context, they do not elaborate its internal complexity and differences. By this I mean that they do not specify the uniqueness of linguistic experience in the present conjuncture. Their categories tend to capture language in a way that presents it as a structurally unchanging phenomenon. What is required for a theory of the mode of information is a set of categories that prepares for the analysis of historical difference.

This large theoretical task cannot be approached in the context of a short paper, but I do want to indicate the kinds of linguistic phenomena that appear to have recently arisen and require historical analysis. If, beginning in the sixteenth century, the printing press transformed linguistic experience, so, in the twentieth century, have electronic forms of information storage and transmission. A great body of linguistic interaction now occurs at tremendously expanded space and time distances. The telephone, radio, television and computer all encourage a dispersal of communicating groups. Although this process began with printing, it may be asked if the new media institute a qualitative transformation of social interaction by extending the distancing process so vastly? I would argue that subjects are constituted differently when a good part of their communicative experience is mediated by electronic discourse/practice. In his last years Foucault worked on the question of the constitution of the subject; his project must be extended to include the mode of information.

One structural feature of the electronic media that makes them different from printing is their complex multidirectionality. Print sends signifiers out from a source; the computer *collects* signifiers from everywhere. Print extends the 'influence' of a communicating subject or text; the computer allows the receiver of signifiers to monitor the transmitter. Centres of power become panoptical addressees whose 'memory' is a new structure of domination. A landlord in Los Angeles entered into his computer information about the behaviour of his tenants and made that available to other landlords, at a price.[28] Communicational experience has been altered: the electronic media encourage the dispersal of the community, but at the same time facilitate its surveillance.

The market is also transformed. Semiologists like Baudrillard have analysed the structure of signification in advertising, stressing the separation of the signifier and its subsequent recoding of commodities. The electronic media promote this process. Anything can be associated with anything else for a viewing subject who is structured by the rhetoric of the commercial. President Reagan, a media person *par excellence*, attempted to associate a visit to SS graves with US–West German alliance. He was surprised that many groups held on to signifiers about the graves that contradicted that move of reconciliation. What is germane here is not only the resistance of communicational communities whose 'data storage' read out SS = murderers. In addition Reagan re-enacted the new structure of the mode of information in which meanings are manipulated by transmitters. It is necessary also to analyse labour and leisure in terms of the new mode of information.

The relationship between the computer and its user requires study. The computer is not written upon like a blank sheet of paper. First, the patterned, lighted pixels on the screen are not like marks of ink or graphite. They are 'immaterials'[29] not inertial traces. The user's mind is confronted not by the resistance of matter but by a screen with a new ontological status: half matter, half idea. The text on a computer screen is as evanescent as a speaker's words, instantaneously available for correction or change. So an individual creates texts in a computer by interacting with an 'object' that is more like the writer's brain than a piece of paper.

Next, the computer can be the brain – that is, it can access databases that resemble memory but vastly extend some of its capabilities. The computer can make available, in principle, the corpus of the world's texts, transforming in practice the user's memory. In addition the computer can substitute for the speaker in a conversation. Besides regulating machines, it can act communicationally in place of people. The traditional, Cartesian view of the human subject as speaker who acts on the world of nature must be modified to account for these new 'agents'.

The electronic means of communication explode the space–time limits of messages, permit the surveillance of messages and actions, complete the process of the automation of production, despatialise certain kinds of work, enable signifiers to float in relation to referents, become a substitute for certain forms of social relations, provide a new relationship between author and text, infinitely expand human memory and undermine the Cartesian ontology of subject and object. In these ways 'reality' is constituted in the 'unreal' dimension of the media. In this domain there are no longer pure acts, only linguistically transformed representations, which are themselves 'acts'. These features of the new mode of information are suggested as a tentative outline, nothing more. Even in this preliminary form they depict a drastically new character of linguistic experience, one with inestimable significance for the reconstitution of the social world including entirely new structures of domination. Historians committed to the project of emancipation in its liberal, Marxist or any other form need to concern themselves with the analysis of the mode of information, a project in which the theory of the mode of production will be of minimal assistance.

NOTES

1. Allan Megill read this essay and provided me with many valuable comments.
2. Charles Lemert and Garth Gillan, *Michel Foucault: Social theory as transgression*, New York: Columbia University Press, 1982; Pamela Major Poetzl, *Michel Foucault's Archaeology of Western Culture*, Chapel Hill, NC: University of North Carolina Press, 1983; Hubert L. Dreyfus and Paul Rabinow, *Michel Foucault: Beyond structuralism and hermeneutics*, Chicago: University of Chicago Press, 1982; Barry Smart, *Foucault, Marxism and Critique*, London: Routledge & Kegan Paul, 1983; John Rajchman, *Michel Foucault*, New York: Columbia University Press, 1984; Mark Cousins and Althar Hussain, *Michel Foucault*, New York: St Martin's Press, 1984; Karl Racevskis, *Michel Foucault and the Subversion of Intellect* Ithaca, NY: Cornell University Press, 1983; and Mark Poster, *Foucault, Marxism and History*, New York: Blackwell's, 1985.
3. See Jacques Derrida, *Of Grammatology*, transl. Gayatri Spivak, Baltimore, MA: Johns Hopkins University Press, 1976.
4. My book *Foucault, Marxism and History* devotes considerable attention to this question. See Chapter 4.
5. See especially *Le Différand*, Paris, 1984.
6. See 'Judiciousness in dispute or, Kant after Marx', published in French as 'Judiceux dans le différand,' in *Le Faculté de jugement*, Paris, 1985. See also 'Philosophy of phrases', unpublished manuscript.

7. What is Enlightenment?', transl. in Paul Rabinow, ed., *Foucault Reader*, New York, 1984, p. 43.
8. *Ibid*., p. 38.
9. *Ibid*., p. 44.
10. Transl. Thomas McCarthy, Boston, MA, 1984.
11. *New German Critique*, no. 22, Winter 1981, pp. 3–18.
12. *New German Critique*, no. 26, Spring/Summer 1982, pp. 13–30.
13. See Max Horkheimer and Theodor Adorno, *Dialectic of Enlightenment*, transl. John Cumming, New York: Seabury, 1972.
14. This theme was developed as early as *Communication and the Evolution of Society*, Boston, MA, 1979. The German texts were published in 1976.
15. 'Jürgen Habermas: A philosophico-political profile', *New Left Review*, no. 151, May–June 1985, p. 94.
16. *Ibid*., p. 42.
17. *Ibid*., p. 46.
18. *Ibid*., p. 47.
19. *Ibid*., p. 50.
20. I am indebted to Andrew Feenberg and Rob Kling for stimulating this line of thought.
21. That is that the revolutionary subject and the subject of revolutionary theory cannot be the basis of a project of universal emancipation.
22. Perhaps the most interesting text to consult for this position is Roland Barthes, *The Fashion System*, transl. M. Ward and Richard Howard, New York: Hill & Wang, 1983 (1st edn 1967).
23. See Jean Baudrillard, *The Mirror of Production*, transl. Mark Poster, St Louis, MO: Telos, 1975 (1st edn 1973).
24. Jacques Derrida, *Of Grammatology*, transl. Gayatri Spivak, op. cit.
25. J. L. Austin, *How to Do Things with Words*, Cambridge, MA: Harvard University Press, 1962.
26. M. M. Bakhtin, *The Dialogic Imagination*, transl. Michael Holquist, Austin: University of Texas Press, 1981.
27. For a different opinion see Dominick LaCapra, *Rethinking Intellectual History*, Ithaca, NY: Cornell University Press, 1983.
28. Gary Marx, 'The new surveillance', *Technology Review*, May–June 1985, pp. 43–8.
29. This term was coined by Jean-François Lyotard for his Beaubourg exhibition in 1985.

three

Foucault, morality and criticism

Christian Bouchindhomme

What probably most strikes the reader is the kind of ubiquity and polymorphism which seems to characterise Foucault's production and which today still makes any attempt at a global view of it a perilous enterprise. As a resolutely Nietzschean Marxian, a philosopher as much as a historian and as a (happy) positivist who defines historiography as an anti-science, Foucault certainly made full use of his right to non-identicality. One might recall the reproach he addresses to himself in *L'Archéologie du savoir* [*AS*], placing himself in the position of his critics: 'You are already preparing a way out so that in your next book you will be able to pop up elsewhere and toy with us as you are doing now: no, no, I'm not where you expected me to be; I'm over here looking at you, laughing' (*AS*, p. 28); or again the statement he makes at the end of the same work: 'The thing is that at the moment my discourse, and I cannot foresee any end to this, far from being able to determine the point from which it is speaking, avoids any ground which might give it support' (*AS*, p. 267). But this was as much as to say: 'Do not ask me who I am and do not ask me to stay the same' (*AS*, p. 28). This somewhat ironic 'ubiquity' certainly helped Foucault to his greatness; it is probably through it that he was able – nomad-like, so to speak – to touch on the most sensitive and painful points of our time. But then a question must be asked: to be a philosopher and as such to 'grasp one's time by means of thought' (Hegel), should we understand, following on from Foucault, that philosophy which submits itself to the rules of rational discourse is a historically situated figure which today is out of date? Or should we understand Foucault's nomadism as being linked with multiple attempts to construct a form of critical thought? It is to this second question that I wish to attempt to give an affirmative reply – which will of course permit me to regard the preceding question as obsolete.

'If I were pretentious, I should give what I do the general title: a genealogy of morality', Foucault told J.-J. Brochier in 1975.[1] In 1984, in the interviews in

Concordia[2] and in the *Nouvelles*,[3] he said, rather, that he was working on a theory of the subject. The formulation differs, yet I think that in saying this Foucault gave a very precise framework through which his work should be perceived. Although one might see the sort of relationship which could be set up to deal with the subject and morality, it is far bolder on Foucault's part to make an association between a *genealogy* of morality and a *theory* of the subject. The ambiguity – indeed, contradiction – escaped no one; especially since Foucault, particularly in his interview with *Concordia*, seemed to be suggesting that he had always been working towards a positive theory of the subject. This, we have to admit, might seem surprising. Apart from the probable provocation and guile in this (such as he admits to in his interview in *Nouvelles*), in the face of it we obviously do have to adopt a different perspective if we are to understand this vision which Foucault has of his own work; and I think that it is to the desire to put forward an embryonic normative basis that the claim to positivity in his procedures should be attributed.

In order to see this more clearly, I should like to go back to the 'general title' which Foucault gave his work in 1975. Beyond the reference to Nietzsche, by which one should not be led astray, the purpose of this abridgement is principally to create a shock effect by designating the asylum, the clinic, human sciences and prison as manifestations of morality. In other words, if Nietzsche's intent is to designate 'the origin of moral prejudices', and if in so doing he creates a typology and critique of reactive forces inasmuch as these create an obstacle to the exercise of thought, nothing so clear could be said of Foucault's work, which none the less seems at the same time more modest and more precise. If Nietzsche takes up position on the level of principle in order to oppose Kant, Foucault takes up position on the level of experience and the mode of life as lived, and this is not so as to set himself up in opposition to an author but to face up to a mentality. Now, observing the periodisation of the set of works written between 1954 and 1975 – amongst which could be included *La Volonté de savoir*, which appeared a year later – a hint could be taken from the cover of the fourth edition of *Surveiller et punir* [*SP*], which talks of a 'genealogy of *modern* morality'. Thus, to the extent that the morality whose genealogy Foucault wants to draw up is not the morality of moral theories but that which characterises, impregnates and regulates modern social reality, it can be said that Foucault's style of genealogy is a genealogy of modern social morality.

But then what can be done with this genealogy? For Nietzsche, drawing up the genealogy of morality (in its entirety) would tend towards the total criticism of a form of reason which emasculates creative thought and negates the will to power. Can we impute the same aspiration to Foucault? The question should not really be asked in these terms, since we are not on the level of principles which reign over Western thought but on the level of tacit norms which regulate a circumscribed social experience. If genealogy can be seen as having any critical scope, for Foucault as for Nietzsche, on the one hand there is the problem that because of the nature of its object, this criticism is not founded in such a way that it could be seen as rooted in the creation of and the will to power; and, on the other hand, there is the problem that through the scrupulous periodisation which Foucault respects, the instance at which his criticism aims has necessarily to be specific to modernity. The distance from Nietzsche is therefore important in spite of the affinities to which Foucault bears witness, and in any case the basis of Foucault's actual criticism is necessarily different from that put forward by Nietzsche.

Even before we try to find out what this basis might be, it would perhaps be appropriate to wonder if in Foucault's case any critical potential actually exists. It seems to me that on an initial level the answer begins to take shape in a negative form because of the very nature of the problematic of Foucault's work. Beyond the reference to genealogy, which thus supposes criticism, what he chooses to describe are not processes of agreement, comprehension or integration but processes of rejection, separation and exclusion, and in particular processes which take place in a hidden way and are established under the auspices of the natural. Denunciation (at least up to *Surveiller et punir*) is therefore latent, and so is criticism; the style, however, indicates that these dimensions are present, and a number of readers at the time were not mistaken in their immediate view that Foucault was a committed philosopher. It is well known that Foucault confirmed this in his practice, committing himself on a political level, alongside the Marxists (at the beginning of the 1970s) and particularly in the context of what can be called 'civil' or 'civic' issues (with reference to *civil rights*) on behalf of prisoners and minorities (at the end of the 1970s).

It is well known that there are those nowadays who see this commitment as a form of self-contradiction. Yet again, for the contradiction to be obvious it would be necessary for Foucault to be committed to a 'total criticism of reason', or for his theoretical work to have no place from which to speak. To these detractors I concede that Foucault's ubiquity, his shifts and his irony could give them grounds for argument. If one is prepared to look closely enough, however, traces of a 'normative base' (this expression is probably by nature too strong) do appear in his work in a way which is extraordinarily permanent. It is found in different forms, sometimes verging on the insubstantial, yet it is certainly present just about everywhere. It was probably more marked by the time of the final volumes of *Histoire de la sexualité*, but – and this bears witness to its permanent nature – it was in Foucault's first work, *Maladie mentale et Psychologie* [*MMP*] (1954), that it is formulated most clearly. Here this conclusion can be found:

> The psychological dimensions of madness . . . have to be situated on the inside of the general relationship which Western man established nearly two centuries ago with himself and to himself. . . . This relationship, which provides the philosophical foundation for all possible psychology, could have been defined only from a precise moment in the history of our civilisation: the moment at which the great confrontation between Reason and Unreason *ceased to take place in the dimension of liberty* and *reason ceased to be an ethics for man and became a nature.* (*MMP*, p. 103)

For Foucault this normative base was freedom, considered less as a formal right than as an ontological dimension. It is this that gives a sense of direction to the ensemble of his works – that is, his genealogy of modern social morality. The nature of his procedure suddenly becomes clear – as, moreover, does the reference to Nietzsche and the limits regarding how far this reference can be taken.

Why draw up a genealogy? The answer is, of course, to find the historical origins of a process. Why draw up a genealogy of modern social reality? Because, following Nietzsche's view of morality in its totality, modern social morality reveals itself as a reactive force. At the same time this shows the whole difference from Nietzsche, to the extent that the origin of this reactive process is not necessarily to be found in reason itself (we see, moreover, in 1954 an invocation of an *ethical reason* as opposed to a *natural reason*) but in the change of status in reason which characterised modernity and saw the intelligibility of nature (determinism) become the model of ethical relationships founded essentially, for Foucault, in liberty.

In other words, it is the interiorisation of modern reason, and as such the establishment of the modern subject, which leads, on the one hand, to an alienation from essential liberty and to the way it is shifted forcibly from the body in the direction of the soul, where it is sublimated into a 'liberation'; and, on the other, to a perversion of ethics into a social morality which sets this liberation to work against liberty:

> The ideal asylum . . . is intended to reconstitute around the insane person a quasi-family in which he is supposed to feel at home; in fact he is subject to an uninterrupted social and moral control; curing him means reinculcating in him the feelings of dependence, humility, guilt and recognition which are the moral armoury of family life. . . . In the new world of the asylum, in this world of punishing morality, madness has become something which essentially concerns the human soul, its blameworthiness and its liberty; it is henceforth inscribed within a dimension of interiority; and as such for the first time madness receives psychological status, structure and meaning. . . . All one discovers in the designation of madness as psychological is the result of the processes through which it came to be seen as such. This whole psychology would not exist without the *moralising sadism* in which the 'philanthropy' of the nineteenth century enclosed it, in the hypocritical guise of 'liberation'. (*MMP*, pp. 84–7)

The genealogy of modern social morality therefore proceeds to bring to light this production of the modern 'soul' inasmuch as this becomes the nature of man and the 'prison of the body' (*SP*, p. 34) – such that the doctor is no longer charged 'with therapeutic intervention so much as ethical control' (*MMP*, p. 85). It identifies the mechanisms of this production (through the human sciences, the order of discourse, transformations in the penal system); it plots the route of this naturalisation as it takes on institutional form (the birth of the asylum, the clinic and the prison); and as it does so (as is shown by the progression in the above text) it makes itself a critic of what guarantees this adulteration of morality and freedom – that is, of the nineteenth-century humanism and philanthropy which are guarantors of the institutionalisation of exclusion.

This being the case, it can be seen that Foucault's critical aspirations now intersect with Nietzsche's only to a very limited extent; while the shifts which Foucault brings about (the movement from a total critique of reason to a criticism of modern reason and the appeal to liberty rather than to the will to power) save him from Nietzsche's extremism, they also deprive him of Nietzsche's breadth and radicality of criticism.[4] Nietzsche's practice of the genealogy of morality criticises the philosophical institution since Plato (indeed since Socrates) by situating moral prejudices in the reason–thought alliance; by fixing this historically he tends to rediscover an originating potential which in fact serves the myth on which our civilisation depends and is as such situated outside history. This is why the Nietzschean model is both credible and acceptable. For Foucault to have respected this model it would at least have been necessary for him to show – this being what is at stake in genealogy – that there was a full and effective freedom exactly where, as a result of liberation, there is nothing left but perverted freedom: *Histoire de la folie* incessantly suggests this (see Chapter III, third part 'Du bon usage des libertés'), yet it by no means establishes it. There is good reason for this: the periodisation on which Foucault's genealogy rests does not permit him to step outside history, so he has to found the reality of an effective liberty anterior to modernity *historically*. Now Foucault was well aware that such an attempt would have been scientifically unacceptable and, even if it had succeeded and been accepted, it would have been of only secondary philosophical interest since this liberty would not have been very effective as far as its mythical potential was concerned. Aware of this, Foucault entered this domain only implicitly, but because of this his criticism, real as it might have been, also remained on the stylistic and lexical level, basically relying on an appeal to the ethical sense of the reader (cf. above the [italicised] 'moral sadism' of the philanthropists). To my mind, the weakness of the normative base and the will to compensate for it explain many aspects of Foucault's evolution.

This should probably all be set out in terms of more detailed analyses, but it can still be noted that following on from its clearly stated presence in *Maladie mentale et Psychologie*, this normative base becomes more diffuse in *Histoire de la folie* and in *Naissance de la clinique*, then disappears in succeeding works (although it leads to involvement in political and civic struggles) and finally resurfaces again in his theoretical production, this time setting out his production as a publicist in a way which transforms it. This being the case, I should like to move directly to this re-emergence in the latter period of his work. But before I can get to this period, I still need to make an observation essential to my purpose.

In fact, if we consider the period which Foucault studies and his intention in carrying out his study – to bring to light the effects of alienation, reification, double-talk and pathologisation which have generated and continue to generate the dominant social morality in modern Western society – one cannot help but be struck by the proximity of Foucault's project to that of Marxism, which also sees bourgeois society as a source of alienation and reification.

I should say that this proximity is in fact only a relic. The role played by Marxism in Foucault's early studies is well known, and traces of it can clearly be found in *Maladie mentale et Psychologie*, as Pierre Macherey shows so well.[5] From this point of view it is not by chance that Foucault's normative base is infinitely less implicit in this work than in those that follow. In a minimal way which he does not talk about, Foucault retained a normative base from French Marxism of the 1950s, which is necessarily close to his own (to the extent that it explicitly formulated the aspiration to a non-alienated society which would thus be *a priori* free) which he was nevertheless already tempering with a genealogical perspective, this being both a mark of his originality and a promise of renewal of the Marxist perspective. But obviously between 1954 and 1961 came 1956; and it was then that the real problem was posed to Foucault's normative base. The entry of Soviet tanks into Budapest in fact appeared to the most consistent of French Marxists (who were at the same time often positivists) as a falsification of the historical determinism which was to lead to a free society, and as the bankruptcy of the normative basis of historical materialism. This – although not without analogy to Nietzsche's – differed essentially in its teleological dimension, by nature of its stake in the future in the form of the society to come which acted as a regulating end and authorised the criticism of present society; although it was never something he adhered to – at least there is no thematisation of this nature in *Maladie mentale et Psychologie* – Foucault is none the less very careful from *Histoire de la folie* onwards to flush out any teleological structure which could induce any form of regulatory utopia – and it is well known that this process continued in the subsequent works.

Up to *La Volonté de savoir*, Foucault therefore preserves from Marxism a periodisation (the modern period), an object of study (Western bourgeois society) and to a large extent a discipline (history)[6] which he is led to overdetermine for theoretical and epistemological reasons. But parallel to this he attempts to cut himself off radically from it on the normative level – hence not only his retreat to a weak form of genealogy but also the increased precariousness of his normative base which is caught, as it were, between two irreconcilables.

As I said above, Foucault's solution was to suggest his normative base by style and insinuation and to make implicit appeal to the ethical sensibility of his reader. Would it in fact be possible to read *Histoire de la folie* or *Surveiller et punir* without seeing in them criticisms of the world of the asylum or the world of the prison? The procedure was obviously precarious to the extent that there was always the risk that the implied criticism, being based on nothing more than Foucault's love of liberty, would be anaemic on the theoretical level because of the logic of the description. Moreover, one might wonder whether in *La Volonté de savoir* Foucault did not finally give way to this logic, delegating – as I suggested above – all responsibility to the publicist in himself. But I should like to leave that to one side and return to the point. It all looks very much as though Foucault had been constrained to saw away at the branch he was sitting on and at the same time, as the normative base was wasting away, the philosopher in him came to the fore. He thought that factual modernity had turned down the option of a 'tribunal of modern reason' – which then ceased to be a tribunal and became instead an instrument – yet at the same time he was unable to draw on the only two critical philosophical possibilities open to him; it was at this point that it seemed impossible to Foucault that philosophy could be assumed to be what it purported to be. This is the reason why I think that, for a time at least, he attempted to thematise and consolidate two poles which had collapsed – the origin and the end of history – and came to think of the role of 'philosopher' today as having a dual modality: historian and journalist, the first replying to the questions of the second. But this solution was not viable. For though the historian was able to invest the past with meaning, the a-teleological journalist was drowned in the meaning of a present without a future.[7] The objectivism of the first, his happy positivism, was undermined by the subjectivism of the second, this leading to a 'morality of discomfort'.[8]

It is to these problems and to the lack of an underlying normative base that the last two volumes of *Histoire de la sexualité* attempt to reply, by means of what appears to be a spectacular 'return of morality'.[9] I shall not go into detail on these texts,[10] but I shall stress several points. These texts appeared as yet another considerable discontinuity in Foucault's work. There is no doubt that there is discontinuity here. For all that, this discontinuity results from the accumulation of problems and does not perhaps correspond to the sum total of Foucauldian ambitions.

These two books seem to me to make significant advances in two areas. On the one hand they present a by no means negligible thematisation of liberty, which is something really new in Foucault since for the first time the normative base is finally put forward as such in a way which makes possible a subtle analysis of the dialectic of liberty – which Foucault would call ontological – and that of 'liberation'.[11] On the other hand – and also for the first time – Foucault breaks with his periodisation: in other words, with the vicious circle which placed him between two irreconcilable poles, Marxism and Nietzscheanism; and resolutely takes the side of genealogy, thus opening an important door.

However, through so doing he is then confronted with the problem he had thus far avoided. As with Nietzsche, the point was to rediscover the origin of moral prejudices, in this case with regard to sexual ethics, showing that Christianity was the basic cause of these prejudices. As I said, for Nietzsche, genealogy provided the possibility of joining forces with Dionysus and the myth of the original power of creation. In a post-Hölderlin context this had both meaning and credibility in a way which remains the case today, although we do not often think in these terms. But what has become of the liberty of the Ancients? With what mythical value is it charged? What is its potential for our present? These are questions which Foucault can answer only by making reference to the present, though at the cost of a large hermeneutic gap. 'Genealogy means that I carry out the analysis on the basis of a present question', he says.[12] This may well be so. But in what way is the liberty of the Greeks ours? For Foucault's genealogy to have any meaning here it would be necessary for us to have lost this liberty, for Christianity to have deprived us of it in the same way that, according to Nietzsche, creation was *effectively* annihilated. Now this is not Foucault's opinion, of course. He deals with the practices of liberty in *our* context. This is how he replies to François Ewald's question ('What then is the present question here?'):

> For a long time there have been those who have imagined that the rigour of sexual codes in the form in which we recognised them were indispensable for so-called 'capitalist' societies. Now the lifting of these codes and the dislocation of the prohibitions came about much more easily than had been believed (which seems to me to indicate that their *raison d'être* was not what had been thought); and the problem of an ethics as a form to give to one's conduct and one's life arises again. All in all it was a mistake to believe that all morality was contained in interdictions and that the lifting of these would in itself resolve the question of ethics.

This seems to me to be an excellent self-criticism as far as the work he had so far produced was concerned, but I do not see anywhere in this a need for a genealogy. *On the contrary*. What is being stated here is that modernity has a potentiality which is ignored and an aptitude for liberty which is poorly understood. This is what should have been studied and analysed – especially since it is because this potentiality exists that these two books of Foucault none the less speak to us and are not simply history books. Now it is clear that from 1954 until 1975 Foucault had already been making use of the ethical sensibilities of his readers – their sense of freedom – in order to construct his negative criticism through his style, his choice of words and his implication. In other words, he was playing on a normative potential which was at a point where he could not see it, and it is on this same potential that he played again in 1984 – but this time in order to carry out a positive criticism. Using Habermas's terms, I would say that Foucault glimpsed a post-conventional ethics in the present but that his actual work, with its lack of a normative base and the problems this caused him, made it impossible for him to formulate it. In this respect *L'Usage des plaisirs* and *Le Souci de soi* are a coherent and effective response to the problems posed by the internal economy of his work, but they leave the question of the relationship to the present untouched.

It would have been possible for Foucault – and the passage quoted affirms this retrospectively – when he found himself deprived of any recourse to what was to come and to that which came before, to seek and to find *in* modernity itself a normative basis which would make it possible for him, at the same time, to carry on the criticism of subjective reason and to respect his own philosophical requirements. But in order to do this he would probably have had to question the genealogical method.

I should like to conclude by making two observations. The first bears on the well-known polemic aimed at Foucault regarding the theory of the subject. When Foucault began to reuse the concept of the subject, those who upheld the cause of reason centred on the modern subject immediately saw the mark of a contradiction, as if the very philosopher who had been the detractor of the modern subject were suddenly contradicting himself. Foucault obviously intended to theorise a much broader notion of the subject which, moreover, would have had to comprise the criticism of the modern subject. Yet it is still symptomatic of Foucault that he did not let go of this particular conceptualisation. This might have been in order to provoke, but still. . . . To my mind it is an indicator of Foucault's lucidity and at the same time of the limits which he was constantly running up against because of his theoretical approach.

My second observation is to do with the actual exercise of philosophy. Foucault knew more acutely than anyone else in France what the limits of contemporary philosophical discourse are, and in my opinion he was an authentic philosopher, as I have constantly tried to demonstrate in this paper; the doggedness with which he 'stuck with' problems – which I believe that I have revealed in his work – is the proof of this. It was Foucault's style each time to give a completely new twist to each new work, even at the expense of having to re-cover ground which had already been gone over in the previous one; hence the impression of ubiquity that I mentioned at the beginning. Though the general thrust of his work was in the direction of 'otherwise', it still seems to have demonstrated an attachment to the requirements of philosophical discourse in a way which makes it impossible to place him amongst the ranks of those who nowadays want to use him as inspiration to escape from philosophy rather than redefining it.

NOTES

1. Interview in *Magazine littéraire*, 1975, pp. 27–33; here p. 33.
2. Interview on 20 January 1984, *Concordia*, no. 6.
3. *Les Nouvelles littéraires*, 28 June–5 July 1984.
4. It must be understood that the French context favoured a successful transference of Nietzschean criticism, to the extent that the post-Revolutionary society was in fact instituted through a *hypostasised* reason which provided support for the values of Catholicism in a way which was simultaneously *political* and *social* and which arose out of the (Counter-) Reformation. In this respect, all Foucault's work, including his theory of power, could be analysed as a total critique of this reason and its institutional manifestations.
5. Pierre Macherey, 'Aux sources de l'*Histoire de la folie*', in *Critique*, 'Michel Foucault: du monde entier', no. 471–2, pp. 761 ff.
6. Thus in the 1975 interview, a little before referring to his production of a 'genealogy of morals', he declared: 'One could go so far as to ask what difference there could be between being a historian and being a Marxist' (*Magazine littéraire*, p. 33).
7. Cf. the articles on Iran in which Foucault really lost his way.
8. The title of an article on Jean Daniel's book *L'Ère des ruptures*. This article, which appeared in *Le Nouvel Observateur* on 23 April 1979, could be taken as a prefiguration of the remarkable lecture on Kant's *Was ist Aufklärung?*, where Foucault seems at the same time to be stumbling on the present, as if confronted with the opacity of modernity, yet none the less affirming the ontological thought of the present day. (Cf. *Magazine littéraire*, 'L'art du dire vrai', no. 207, May 1984, pp. 35 ff.)
9. Title of the interview in *Nouvelles*.
10. See Rainer Rochlitz's text (pp. 248–59) for a more precise analysis.
11. Interview in *Concordia*.
12. Interview of Michel Foucault by François Ewald, 'Le souci de la vérité', *Magazine littéraire*, p. 21.

SUMMARY OF DISCUSSIONS

Two questions dominated the debate: What is the specific nature of Foucault's procedure? What is it that motivates the absence of 'normative bases' in his thought?

François Ewald took up the Habermas–Foucault comparison. They have an analogous point of departure: the diagnostic of a crisis in reason. But thereafter their ways part. Habermas reconstructs a traditional, classical philosophy; Foucault thinks that it is not possible to do philosophy in a traditional way. This can be seen in his use of irony, which has been so much talked about, and also in his criticism of Socrates, another thinker in a divided world. Foucault's outlook on history is that of Yalta: the division of a world. This poses a problem analogous with the end of the Wars of Religion in the sixteenth century. How can order be thought of in a divided world? In his analysis of the Enlightenment he certainly sees a way of linking knowledge and power. In the same way one could ask how truth and freedom could be linked today. This, according to Foucault, is the task of the philosopher today.

Michel Karkeits thought that there is a normative base in Foucault. He made reference to an interview which Michel Foucault gave to German students in 1984 – apparently little known about in France – which is to a large extent on the subject of books he was going to publish. In this interview Foucault gave the following definition of ethics: 'a considered practice of freedom'.

Christian Bouchindhomme replied that he would have preferred to have a more pronounced theorisation than that, although in fact more could probably be found in recent interviews. Without the power of his style Foucault's normative base would have been weaker, and the same is true in a way of his genealogical method which succeeds only imperfectly in showing what it is that is going wrong, and which is unable to rediscover an original form of freedom.

four

Moral identity and private autonomy

Richard Rorty

Vincent Descombes has pointed out that attempts to appropriate Foucault's work have given us an American Foucault and a French Foucault. He contrasts the two as follows. The American Foucault 'sought to define autonomy in purely human terms', without the notion of a universal law. This Foucault can be read, with only a little strain, as an up-to-date version of John Dewey.[1] Dewey was the philosopher who said that liberal democracies would work better if they stopped trying to give universalistic self-justifications, stopped appealing to notions like 'rationality' and 'human nature', and instead viewed themselves simply as promising social experiments.

But, as Descombes says, the American Foucault is Foucault with most of the Nietzscheanism drained away. The French Foucault is the *fully* Nietzschean one. For this Foucault, Descombes says, the project of autonomy requires us to have 'inhuman thoughts', to have no 'worries about sharing our beliefs with our fellow citizens'.[2] In so far as the French Foucault has any politics, they are anarchist rather than liberal.

I think that the contrast Descombes draws catches a real tension among Foucault's mixed and complicated motives. This tension is one characteristic of the Romantic intellectual who is also a citizen of a democratic society. Such an intellectual finds his moral identity – his sense of his relations to most other human beings – in the democratic institutions he inhabits. But he does not think that his *moral* identity exhausts his self-description, for he does not think his conduct towards other human beings is the most important thing about him. What is *more* important is his *rapport à soi* (relationship to himself), his private search for autonomy, his refusal to be exhaustively describable in words which apply to anyone other than himself. This is the search summed up in Blake's exclamation: 'I must create my own system, or be enslaved by another man's.'

Blake and Baudelaire share with Nietzsche and Heidegger the need to have a self which is autonomous, in the sense of being self-invented. To invent one's own self one must indeed think, in Descombes's words, 'inhuman thoughts' – in the sense that one must have thoughts which no human being has yet had, write books unlike any books yet written. So one must cut the links which bind one's vocabulary to the vocabularies so far used by mankind.

But cutting those links does not *necessarily* mean cutting the social bonds which, for purposes of public action, unite one with one's fellow citizens. Nor does it necessarily mean ceasing to use in good faith, for public purposes, the political vocabulary used by the mass of one's fellow citizens. Just as Kierkegaard's knight of faith looks like a bank clerk, and in public acts like one, so the Romantic intellectual can be, for public purposes, your ordinary bourgeois liberal. It is only when a Romantic intellectual begins to want his private self to serve as a model for other human beings that his politics tends to become anti-liberal. When he begins to think that other human beings have a moral duty to achieve the same inner autonomy as he himself has achieved, then he begins to think about political and social changes which will help them to do so. Then he may begin to think that he has a moral duty to bring about these changes, whether his fellow citizens want them or not.

Foucault was, for much of the time, a 'knight of autonomy'. He wanted to invent his own self as much as Nietzsche did. But, unlike Nietzsche, he did not urge anybody else to engage in this effort. He did not think that human beings *in general* have a moral duty to be Baudelairean or Nietzschean self-inventors. He did not envisage a politics which would help – or force – them to become more autonomous. Like a good liberal, he was willing to leave them alone to be as self-inventive, or as banal, as they liked. In an interview, he said: 'The search for a form of morality acceptable by everyone in the sense that everyone would have to submit to it, seems catastrophic to me.'[3] Much of the time, his only politics was the standard liberal's attempt to alleviate unnecessary suffering.

Only much of the time, however. At other times, Foucault ran together his moral and his ethical identity – his sense of his responsibility to others and his *rapport à soi*. At these times, like Nietzsche, he projected his own search for autonomy out into public space. In both his and Nietzsche's case, the results were bad. Those were the times when Foucault wrote the passages which upset his American admirers; for example: 'I think to imagine another system is to extend our participation in the present system.'[4] That is the sort of passage about which Michael Walzer says: 'The powerful evocation of the disciplinary system gives way to an antidisciplinarian politics that is mostly rhetoric and posturing.'[5] Yet these are the 'anarchist' passages which many of his French admirers seem to like best.

We liberals in the USA wish that Foucault could have managed, just once, what Walzer rightly says he always resisted: 'some positive evaluation of the liberal state'. So do our Canadian and German counterparts. Habermas echoes Charles Taylor's complaint about Foucault's 'amazing one-sidedness'[6] when he says that Foucault's history of the power formations which shaped modern subjectivity 'filters out all the aspects under which the eroticization and internalization of subjective nature also meant a gain in freedom and expression'.[7] You would never guess, from Foucault's account of the changes in European social institutions during the last three hundred years, that during that period suffering had decreased considerably; nor that people's chances of choosing their own lifestyles had increased considerably.

So Walzer, Taylor, Habermas and I have the same mixed reaction to Foucault. On the one hand there is admiration and gratitiude, for Foucault highlighted a new set of dangers to democratic societies. He served such societies well by telling them about tendencies and patterns they needed to watch out for. As Taylor rightly says – and as Habermas might agree – Foucault 'offered the Frankfurt School an account of the inner connection between the domination of nature and the domination of man which is rather more detailed and more convincing than what they [the Frankfurt School] came up with themselves.'[8] On the other hand, we liberal reformists think that Foucault's work is pervaded by a crippling ambiguity between 'power' as a pejorative term and as a neutral, descriptive term. In the first sense, to quote Taylor again, '"power" belongs in a semantic field from which "truth" and "freedom" cannot be excluded.' In the second sense, the term has the vacuity which Nietzsche, at his worst, termed *Wille zur Macht*. In this broad and vacuous sense, any study of anything (of chemical or mathematical relationships, of chess-playing, of social institutions) will be a study of 'strategies of power', just as it will be a study of 'the exploitation of structural possibilities'. Both phrases are resounding only because they are empty.

When a first-rate thinker gets hung up on the ambiguity between a pejorative and an empty sense of a crucial term, we have reason to suspect that he is trying to do two things at once. Foucault was trying to serve human liberty, but he was also, in the interest of his personal autonomy, trying to be a faceless, rootless, homeless stranger to humanity and to history. As a citizen, he was trying to achieve the same political consequences which a good humanitarian bourgeois liberal would wish to achieve. As a philosopher trying to invent himself, he was, to quote Taylor yet again, 'tossing aside the whole tradition of Augustinian inwardness'.[9] This tradition says that one's *deepest* identity is the one which binds one to one's fellow humans, that there is something common to all men, and that getting in touch with this common element is getting in touch with one's real self. Foucault, as I understand him, wanted to do good to his fellow humans while at the same time having an identity which had nothing whatsoever to do with them. He wanted to help people without taking their vocabulary as the one in which he spoke to himself. He wanted to help them while inventing a self which had nothing much (indeed, as little as possible) to do with theirs.

My own view is that this is a feasible, if difficult, project: that one *can* do both the things Foucault was trying to do; one *can* be 'a knight of autonomy'. But I wish that Foucault had been more willing to *separate* his two roles – more willing to separate his moral identity as a citizen from his search for autonomy. Then he might have resisted the temptation to which Nietzsche and Heidegger succumbed – the temptation to try to find a public, political counterpart to this latter, private search. This, I think, was the temptation which led to his quasi-anarchism, to his refusal to be 'complicit' with 'power', even when that term 'power' is stretched so far that it loses any contrastive force and becomes vacuous. That anarchism seems to me the result of a misguided attempt to envisage a society as free of its historical past as the Romantic intellectual hopes to be free of his private past.

The Romantic intellectual's goal of self-overcoming and self-invention seems to me a good model (one amongst many other good models) for an individual human being, but a very bad model for a society. We should not try to find a societal counterpart to the desire for autonomy. Trying to do so leads to Hitler-like and Mao-like fantasies about 'creating a new kind of human being'. Societies are not quasi-persons, they are (at their liberal, social-democratic best) compromises between persons. The point of a liberal society is not to invent or create anything, but simply to make it as easy as possible for people to achieve their widely different private ends without hurting each other. To work out the details of the continually shifting compromises which make up the political discourse of such a society requires a common, banal, moral vocabulary – a vocabulary which is no more relevant to one individual's private self-image than to another's. In a liberal society, our public dealings with our fellow citizens are not *supposed* to be Romantic or inventive; they are supposed to have the routine intelligibility of the marketplace or the courtroom.

Publicly discussable compromises require discourse in a common vocabulary, and such a vocabulary is required to describe the *moral* identities a liberal society asks its citizens to have. They are asked to have this moral identity for public purposes, and to have it irrespective of whatever other, private identities they may also have. Only if one refuses to divide the public from the private realm will one dream of a society which has 'gone beyond mere social democracy', or of 'total revolution'. Only then will anarchism begin to seem attractive. Only then will one be tempted to use a pejorative term like 'power' to describe the results of *any* social compromise, *any* political balancing act.

The attempt to break down the distinction between the private and the public sphere is characteristic of a long-standing tradition in social philosophy. This is the tradition which, with Plato, sees society as man writ large. Most philosophers in this tradition try to isolate some central, ahistorical, non-contingent core (e.g. 'reason', or 'a specifically moral motivation') within us, and to use the presence of this element within us as a justification for certain political arrangements, certain social institutions. Foucault inverts this attempt. Since he sees human subjectivity as a contingent product of contingently existing forces, he does not believe that there is any such ahistorical non-contingent core. So he concludes – at least in his anarchist moments – that every social institution is equally unjustifiable, that all of them are on a par. All of them exert 'normalising power'. From the failure of the Platonic attempt to find something deep within us which will let us answer Thrasymachus, he comes close to concluding that there is no interesting difference between Pericles and Critias.

It seems to me that we should drop the assumption which Plato and Foucault share. This is the assumption that unless there is some interesting connection between what matters most to an individual and his purported moral obligations to our fellow human beings, then he has no such obligations. If we drop this assumption, we can say that Romantic intellectuals, religious mystics, sexual fetishists, and others whose private self has nothing much to do with their public self are under the same moral obligations as all the rest of us. No deep philosophical reason can be given to explain the fact that they are under such obligations, so Thrasymachus can never be answered to Plato's satisfaction. But an inability to answer Thrasymachus has no political consequences of the sort which Nietzsche and Foucault are sometimes inclined to draw. A sense of human subjectivity as a centreless bundle of contingencies, of the sort which both Foucault and Dewey shared with Nietzsche, is compatible with *any* sort of politics, *including* liberal politics.

Foucault's projection of the desire for private autonomy out on to politics seems to me the inverse of the insistence by my fellow liberal, Habermas, on notions like 'rationality' and 'the true self'. Habermas would like to ground moral obligation, and thus social institutions, on something universally human. Conversely, Foucault's radical Nietzschean anti-Platonism leads him to infer, from the absence of anything which might serve as such a ground, the absence of the need for social institutions, to anarchism. I should prefer to split the difference between Foucault and his liberal critics by saying that Nietzsche and Foucault are right against Plato, but that this anti-Platonism does nothing to show that there is something wrong with liberal societies. More generally, it does nothing to show that there is something wrong with whatever networks of power are required to shape people into individuals with a sense of moral responsibility.

Unlike Habermas, I do not think that Foucault needs to answer charges of 'relativism'. He does not have to answer Socratic questions like 'Why should domination be resisted?'[10] If one is willing, as Dewey and Foucault were, to give up the hope of universalism, then one can give up the fear of relativism as well. I agree with Ian Hacking that 'it won't be long before the solemn clamor of the intellectuals about Foucault [asking "where do you stand?"] sounds as quaint as the baying of the Edinburgh mob [around Hume, asking "have you recanted your atheism?]'.[11] I think Foucault should have answered the questions 'Where do you stand? What are your values?': 'I stand with you as a fellow citizen, but as a philosopher, I stand off by myself, pursuing projects of self-invention which are none of your concern. I am not about to offer philosophical grounds for being on your side in public affairs, for my philosophical project is a private one which provides neither motive nor justification for my political actions.'

Such a reply would sound less shocking if one replaced 'philosopher' with 'poet'. For philosophers, as opposed to poets, are traditionally supposed to offer a 'basis' for our moral obligations to others. They are supposed to have what Fraser calls 'an adequate normative perspective'.[12] Unlike poets, philosophers are supposed to be 'rational', and rationality is supposed to consist in being able to exhibit the 'universal validity' of one's position. Foucault, like Nietzsche, was a philosopher who claimed a poet's privileges. One of these privileges is to rejoin 'What has universal validity to do with *me*?' I think that philosophers are as entitled to this privilege as poets, so I think this rejoinder sufficient.

Nevertheless, I think it is important to notice that one can ask that rhetorical question without going on to ask, as Nietzsche did, 'What has the suffering of my fellow humans to do with me?' For one can be humanitarian without being universalist, without believing either that it is 'rational' to be concerned with the sufferings of others or that there is a 'common humanity' which binds you to those others. One can want to relieve suffering without having an interesting answer when Socrates asks you *why* you desire this, and also without believing that this desire is the deepest and most important thing in your life. Foucault, I think, found himself in this position – the position which I have described as that of 'the knight of autonomy'. This meant that, whether he wanted to be or not, he was a useful citizen of a democratic country, one who did his best to make its institutions fairer and more decent. I wish he had been able to be more comfortable with that self-description than he in fact was.

NOTES

1. I have sketched such a reading of Foucault in my *Consequences of Pragmatism*, Minneapolis: University of Minnesota Press, 1982, pp. 203–8.
2. Descombes, review of David Hoy, ed., *Foucault: A Critical Reader*, *London Review of Books*, 5 March, 1987, p. 3.
3. *Les Nouvelles*, 28 June 1984, p. 37. Quoted by Dreyfus and Rabinow in their 'What is Maturity?', in Hoy.

4. This quotation comes from a 1971 interview with *Actuel*. It appears on p. 230 of the English translation of that interview in *Language, Counter-Memory, Practice: Selected Essays and Interviews*, ed. Bouchard, Ithaca, NY: Cornell University Press, 1977.
5. Hoy, p. 65.
6. *Ibid.*, p. 81.
7. Habermas, *The Philosophical Discourse of Modernity*, p. 292.
8. Hoy, p. 77.
9. *Ibid.*, p. 99.
10. See Habermas, *The Philosophical Discourse of Modernity*, p. 284, where he cites Nancy Fraser as posing this question.
11. Hoy, p. 238.
12. Nancy Fraser, 'Foucault on modern power: Empirical insights and normative confusions', *Praxis International*, no. 1, 1981, p. 91. For a thoughtful reply to Fraser, Habermas and Taylor on Foucault's behalf, see Chapter 4 of David R. Hiley, *Philosophy in Question: Essays on a Pyrrhonian theme*, Chicago: University of Chicago Press, 1988.

SUMMARY OF DISCUSSIONS

At the heart of the discussions on Rorty's contribution was the question of Foucault's 'anarchism'.

Michel Karkeits asked what the distinction between 'public' and 'private' means in modern times. Is it anything other than historical invention? **Rorty** replied that if so, it is a very good historical invention.

On the notion of 'it is me speaking', **François Ewald** insisted on the interdependency in Foucault's work of the relationship to the self and the relationship with others: if there is such a thing as concern for the self, it is precisely because there is such a thing as concern for others. Foucault demonstrates this in his reading of the *Alcibiades* and develops it in the last part of *L'Usage des plaisirs*, showing how the governing of the other – governance – is dependent on concern for the self.

Ewald went on to say that Rorty's notion of an 'anarchistic Foucault' does not in any case correspond to the French reading. This latter reading would rather reproach Foucault for his representation of a power which it is not possible to go beyond or free oneself from. This pessimism with regard to an absolute power would not, however, have anything to do with Foucault. Indeed, we are not always linked to power, we are in the element of power; but we do have a responsibility with regard to the way we exercise power: we must not lose the idea that we could exercise it differently.

Foucault is also reproached for a perceived failure to pronounce obligations, as if the foundation of morality resided in the notion of our being 'obliged . . .' but there is no lack of obligations. They are always there. What Foucault is suggesting is not that we should create them but that we should ask: given that we are in a state of obligation, how can we think of obligations and how can we carry them out?

In a way, what Richard Rorty reproaches Foucault for is the fact that he is not the *philosophical civil servant* of the democratic State. That is certainly one thing Foucault would not have wanted to be.

Manfred Frank thought that there was an ethics in Foucault's work; but he claims the right to dispute this, and on a number of points he sides with Rorty. He shares his pessimism regarding the catastrophe of modernity and the importance of the norm. The norm should not be confused with obligation. Obligation is the province of the State and the police (things like traffic lights, for example); the norm obliges people because they oblige themselves in accordance with their convictions. In the face of power, Foucault evokes the possibility of revolt; though this is something one might well have to remain hungry for.

For **John Rajchman**, there was a certain nationalism underlying Rorty's ideas; he seemed to be putting forward the notion of a 'good' Foucault close to the American liberals and a 'bad' Foucault in the French tradition. Rajchman sees this categorisation as more appropriate to the nineteenth century. On the one hand, a lot of American liberals were not nationalists and American liberalism owed a lot to immigrant Jews who were very internationalist; on the other hand, Michel Foucault never intended to write as a Frenchman; he wanted to be a 'faceless man'.

five

Michel Foucault's nihilism

André Glücksmann

The term nihilism can be understood in three ways. (1) Relativism of values: there is no supreme good. Was Foucault a nihilist in this sense? Certainly. (2) Refusal to create supreme values. God, being dead, cannot be replaced. Was Foucault a nihilist in this sense? Certainly. (3) The reign of absolute subjectivity, loss of the world and a-cosmic existence. Was Foucault a nihilist in this third sense? Yes and no. Foucault is an a-cosmic thinker, yet he upholds no form of absolute subjectivity. Foucault invites us to question this last way of seeing nihilism.

The question of nihilism is put to Foucault as if he were before a tribunal. Foucault is condemned as a result of an ethic, because of the way nihilism is present in his work. Foucault, however, teaches us to turn that which appears to be negative into something positive. He would say that not only is nihilism in the first two senses neither immoral nor amoral, but rather that it is the condition of any ethic for the present day.

At the centre of the moral problem is the intolerable. The intolerable is the privilege of no person, no country and no nation. It is a first condition which precedes the existence of all European countries. The possibility of Auschwitz and of genocide is affirmed and described in the *Iliad*: the fall of Troy is the first genocide in Western thought.

The first definition of nihilism, the relativism of values, is not characteristic of Foucault. The anti-humanist climate of the 1960s should be borne in mind. This anti-humanism goes back to Gide or Sartre. It does not designate an eternal opposition to an eternal humanism but a very precise form of humanism, that which belonged to the end of the nineteenth century and the beginning of the twentieth. This was a positive humanism which attributed knowledge concerning supreme values to European man. For people like Gide, Sartre or Foucault this alleged knowledge produced a blinding effect regarding colonialism, fascism, Siberian camps and Stalinism. This led to the idea – which was quite simple, though difficult enough to put into practice – that it might perhaps be possible to develop commitments and moralities not on the basis of a positive idea of the good which would be universally and eternally valid but on the basis of a perception, of an obviousness *index sui* of the intolerable. This obviousness was at the heart of events like the Calas affair or the Dreyfus affair. On this point Foucault is not original, but he is rigorous. Using Foucault's work as a starting point, it would be possible to replace the Weberian opposition between the two ethics of responsibility and conviction with an opposition between, on the one hand, a morality of extreme urgency which analyses the cases of what is intolerable and, on the other, a kind of edifying, fine-thinking thought or morality aiming to resolve all problems at once and for the eternity of ages.

Foucault's practice bears witness in favour of this possibility, the background to which, however, remains to be considered. Negative humanism, commitment on the basis of negative evidence, is written into the Declaration of the Rights of Man of 1793. It is said here that the notion of the rights of man can be understood only in terms of the recent memory of despotism. It is the consideration of despotism which founds the necessity to affirm the rights of man. It is inhumanity which founds the rights of man as a defence against this inhumanity and not as a definitive, universal and eternal idea of man. The rights of man can be founded without any need of an idea of man; all that is necessary is to face up to recent despotism. One could go back further. Montaigne used to say: 'I do not know what I am [in the sense that I have no ideal] but I do know what I am fleeing [that is to say, I know what I reject, what I refuse to accept].' Aeschylus in *Orestes* says that the *pathein*, the painful experience of the injustice of sickness and evil, is the condition of the *mathein* of knowledge and perception [*savoir* and *connaissance*].

The apprehension of the intolerable yields to several interpretations. It could be said that consideration of the intolerable is the *ratio cognoscendi* of an intuition of the good which comes after us, but which also founds this intuition and is as such the *ratio essendi*. One could also go along with Deleuze in saying that the intolerable is grasped within the context of social apparatus and that if such apparatus becomes universal, so too does the intolerable: when the barbed wire of ideologies spreads, evil moves in everywhere along with it. One could also go along with Lévi-Strauss in saying that the prohibition of incest means the pronouncement of something which must not be done anywhere and that this becomes, as it were, the act by means of which societies are constituted. Finally, it could be said that the question of philosophy is not that of being but that of non-being. Thus Plato warns us that the consideration of mud and dirt founds the work of the philosopher and the education of citizens at least as much as the idea of the good.

The second definition of nihilism can again be turned round. It is because man puts nothing in the place of God that moral action becomes possible, just as it is because man grasps the intolerable before he knows what a good society is that moral action becomes possible and has an object: resistance to the intolerable. The counter-example to this is Heidegger. Heidegger analyses technology as the creation of a counter-world, as demiurge, this technology making moral action impossible. In his interview with *Der Spiegel* Heidegger says: 'Only a God could save us from our situation, only a God could get us out of the soup'. This is obviously not the way Foucault would have formulated it. In fact Foucault did not have the same conception of technology. For Foucault, technology could not be reduced to the domination of nature – that is, to the application of modern mathematisation to the sciences of nature. It has its own truth status. The strategies are not pure domination, pure application or pure devastation. For Foucault technology is a strategy and a duel, whilst for Heidegger it is a struggle for the domination of nature. It would be wrong to ignore Foucault's struggle against Heidegger, or to think that their views are identical because of their common rejection of anthropocentrism. Foucault's and Heidegger's conceptions of technology are not the same. And this is why Foucault conceives of the possibility of moral action, whilst Heidegger cannot do so.

I wish now to deal with the third view of nihilism: the reign of absolute subjectivity and the disappearance of the being into the world; the a-cosmic situation of modern man. What do Foucault's last two books offer us on this point?

There are three ways of understanding nihilism. That of the Thomists, or that of Léo Strauss, consists in seeing modernity as cut off from the Middle Ages or Antiquity: the subjective right is opposed to the objective or natural right. Nihilism can thus be understood as a discontinuity between the Christian world (Nietzsche) or the devastated Latin world (Heidegger), and the Greek world. Using Foucault's analysis, it would be necessary rather to reverse the schema: the opposition is no longer between the Greek and the Latin world but between two forms of the erotic: the dualist erotic defined in *L'Usage des plaisirs* and the monist erotic the expression of which is found in the texts of Plutarch. From the point of view of nihilism this opposition causes problems: the absolute subject, having denied the world, finds himself on the side of the second form of eroticism, although he has not lost the world since he finds himself in harmony with this monist, balanced, reciprocal and symmetrical relationship, the harmony of a conjugal relationship within the context of the cosmos. With this distinction between the two forms of eroticism Foucault does not refute Heidegger or Nietzsche; he completely reformulates the question.

Foucault's last two books lead back to a global reinterpretation of Western thought, and to a reinterpretation of nihilist thought. The following have to be brought together: (1) that the relativism of values is the condition of the perception of the intolerable and hence of moral action; (2) that the non-creation of absolute values is also the condition of moral action; and (3) that the non-existence of a world which surrounds us, wraps round us and protects us is also a condition of the possibility of an ethic. The possibility of an ethic is to be found less in the second erotic, the monist erotic, than in the second erotic, which allows dissymmetries, imbalances, aporias and impossibilities to appear, these being precisely the object of all commitment.

six

Foucault and going beyond (or the fulfilment of) nihilism

Paul Veyne

You find me in complete agreement with what André Glücksmann has just said, and flattered at this convergence of our views. Still, lacking Glücksmann's talent, I propose to edify you by means of a homily, on a different subject: Foucault and going beyond (or the fulfilment of) nihilism. A large number of the ideas you are about to hear come from Gianni Vattimo – I shall say this loud and clear, once and for all; but this exposé, though I do not make this explicit, also traces Michel Foucault's evolution from the bitter rage of his years of dark youth at the *École normale* (following a childhood which was perhaps too full of guilt and too humble) through the courageous serenity, to the happy laughter and equanimity of his mature years.

A spectre haunts the Western world, or at least the nights of its thinkers – that of nihilism. Yet our grandchildren will probably laugh at us, saying: 'They spent their lives in a state of fear, yet it was not the wolf, only its shadow'.

Nihilism is a name we can give to periods of history where thinkers feel that truths are without truth and without foundation; this state is so much the one in which we find ourselves that we talk about it in terms of proverbs: Malraux said that our societies were the first to find out that myths were myths; it is also well known that one of our intellectual difficulties is our awareness of the relativity of civilisations. This certainly does not disturb the vast majority of people for an instant, and governments even less, so that it is ridiculous to talk in terms of decadence, but this none the less does constitute a problem for philosophers. There exists, then, an uneasiness in thought which is referred to as historicism or relativism. Now this uneasiness is a false uneasiness since philosophers, as men, have very clear opinions on racism, the rights of man and even the choice between Mitterrand and Barre. All that remains is for them to accept that this is the case and to learn that one can get along very nicely without foundations and even without truth.

How, then, can one escape from nihilism? By discovering ways of making us believe in ourselves? No, by ridding ourselves of a prejudice which has caused us a lot of trouble – that is, a prejudice about time. To suffer from historicism is still to believe in an opposition between time and eternity; now something which is opposed both to time and to eternity is our validating present; the past is not the present in the past, it has experienced neither our interpretations nor our values. The present is no longer opposed to the erroneous but to the obsolete. As such the historicist confusion fades away: relativism turns out to be only a moment of decay.

What I am undertaking to preach to you – for one can preach only what everyone knows already – is that one emerges from nihilism when one has thought it through serenely to the very end (a lot of you will think of Nietzschean serenity, this *Heiterkeit* which one senses in Foucault's last two books, which are so full of equanimity). The same is true for nihilism as for the north-facing slopes of the Alps: one can get down from them only by going further up.

One can get beyond nihilism if one learns to defend oneself from passive nihilism and from reactional nihilism or the nihilism of resentment. It is reactional if what one draws from nihilism is self-irony; or again when one reacts to the loss of values through the cultivation of second-order values, like minimal art or underground culture. It becomes passive if the absence of foundation and truth without finitude stops us from daring to want anything and, for example, paralyses us when we are faced with thoughts which are alien to us yet which we do not dare to condemn (whoever 'understands' his enemy too well is lost, and perhaps I might be permitted to doubt the purity of motive of professional 'understanders'). Serenity with no bad conscience, which remains fearless in the face of the collapse of infinitude, is what Nietzsche called 'the health of the man of good character', who 'conserves nothing in himself of the sort of resentment of those who have grown old in fetters'; he who is no longer afraid. And yet at the time of Nietzsche a lot of people thought that because they had lost God, they were themselves lost and cried out in fear, like little children who had lost their nanny.

The same goes nowadays for the loss of truth which provokes the same wild reaction as 'idealism' in the last century. If philosophers believed that the 'outside world does not exist', why would they take an umbrella with them on rainy days? How could a historian who is dedicated to the truth claim that there is any form of truth other than saying what is true? Apparently Nietzsche hesitated to approach this problem for fear of the 'rigid seriousness, which leads one to stumble and fall because of one word': it is well known also that he largely skirted round the issue. Foucault's pronouncements on the subject were also elliptical, though clear. We are all aware, for example, of how frequently the words 'this is neither true nor false' appear in his journalistic writing. The transcendental historic, as he used to say in earlier days – or rather, *positive finitude* – means that questions escape our understanding, or rather our *episteme*, which makes it impossible to know what *true* democracy is from an eternal point of view. Since the question has no present perspective, a reply to it cannot be either true or false (the only good reply being to find out what we want in this domain).

Serenity also supposes (and here I am sketching a portrait of Foucault himself) a benign, curious, even-minded attitude towards the obsolete truths of the past. We remember Foucault's decisiveness, the unhesitating way he would take sides and intervene in events going on around him; yet we remember also the sort of kind, excited joy with which he considered not only dreams or madness but the most strange and frightening doctrines of past or present. Before the formidable otherness of these different truths he was happy to appreciate, not to censure; happy that the boldness of passing time should have gone so far. He felt neither melancholy nor disdain in the face of dead truths, nor was he afraid of the fragility of our own truths; on the contrary, he was stoically happy to see the past confirm to him that the extent of the possible is indefinite and that all this is the Fable, neither true nor false, which Nietzsche did not see as being in opposition to reality.

If there is such a Fable, then metaphysics is no more than an old fable and there is no more to know than that the Fable is fabulous; could Foucault still be called a philosopher if metaphysics is dead? What is more, he preferred to preach by example, to exemplify his method in history books rather than setting it out. This was done for strategic reasons (to avoid words which might shock, since the thing is not shocking, because people are already living out the death of truth without knowing it); but it was done also for reasons of hygiene: he preferred the obsolete to concepts and he preferred not to subject the idea of finitude to too much scrutiny, for it is made rather to be lived out.

When we are forced to accept that nothing can be founded, one thing remains: us. It is true, as has been said here, that Foucault cannot found norms; he cannot appeal to a nature, or to a reason, or to a functionalism, or to an essence, or to intersubjectivity. But nor could anyone else. In this inability to find foundations, should we see a gap in Foucault's thought, since it does not respond to our hunger to know? What a criticism of this nature unknowingly implies is something enormous: that hunger is sufficient to prove the existence of food. For the non-existence of norms to be seen as an absence, it would be necessary in advance to know that norms were foundable in some way or another. But why should they necessarily be foundable? Would this be because we wish it to be so? But nothing has been promised to us. Again, for this to be a philosophical gap it would have to be the case that the only conceivable role of philosophy would be to provide norms and tell us what we have to do. For Foucault the worry about finding foundations was specific to the 'anthropological age': it was from Kant to Husserl that attempts were made to found, to get back to the unquestionable *arche*; to get beyond the anthropological age is to abandon the project of foundation in favour of something else.

If philosophy cannot found, what remains is to live and to want what one wants without justifying oneself and saying that one is right. The only thing that would lose out from the disappearance of big words would be polemics; yet precisely, as Nietzsche would say, the very healthy man is never emphatic. The anthropological philosopher asked: 'How can one lay foundations?'; Foucault's position would be rather: 'Let us draw the consequences from the impossibility of finding foundations and in doing so take note that finding foundations would be as useless as it is impossible.'

As a non-philosopher I had the perhaps naive impression during this conference that there was a confrontation between two attitudes: one consisted in 'finding oneself good reasons, so that one could be right'; the other in 'knowing what one wants, and that is enough, especially since there is nothing more one can do'.

Around 1900 Jules de Gaultier, an unjustly forgotten if somewhat verbose author, gave the name Bovaryism to the tendency to believe that knowledge and action are founded on a world ideally made for the sake of their 'happy end'.

SUMMARY OF DISCUSSIONS

Jacques Rancière returned to the question, which had so often been referred to, of the so-called need for foundations. He said that freedom cannot be founded and democracy cannot be founded. All that can be founded is domination. Democracy is precisely the regime which functions through an absence of foundation. Democracy is an aberrant object in relation to philosophical attempts at founding it. Following the Greeks, it could be said that for Plato, as for Aristotle, democracy is what happens when politics does not work. Liberty and the rights of man are declared and redeclared but not founded. Richard Rorty was saying that the French are Nietzscheans. . . . They are probably more like Greeks; they think either that democracy is the worst of the good forms of government, or that it is the best of the worst. On the other hand they agree to a pact, which is also what made Foucault possible – this being the revolutionary pact, which provides a card which can always be replayed. The rights of man are practised, played out over again, like liberty. There is nothing in this which makes a catastrophe bound to happen, nor is there anything which makes a common language [*langage*] impossible. There probably is a need for a common language and for the universal, but there is no lack of such things; it is always possible to found a language [*langage*] of this nature, but this has nothing to do with the idea that there is a need to found a democracy or a common reason. In one sense democracy can always be founded; the French did it: Alain made a very fine speech about the foundation of democracy. But this does not always work, as was shown between the wars, when democracy met its other.

Rorty spoke of the philosopher and of the privilege of the poet. In fact the philosopher assumes this position. But people like Foucault give a different sense to what is meant by this. It is not for nothing that René Char's sentences punctuate Foucault's texts, notably in the titles of his books. This is a question of synonymy. The point is to contradict synonyms of a single word. The possibility of struggling against the intolerable is conceived of on the basis of work done on limits, of work on synonyms. René Char spoke – in 1940, to be precise – about a return of the void of the Father. Now it seems to me that the void of the Father is the void of foundation. In times of war, poetry makes it possible to give the same words to the same things and yet to make something different of them.

Pasquale Pasquino whilst agreeing with this, wanted to mention a small difference. The non-foundation of juridical thought cannot be overstressed. A judge has to give arguments, to found what he has to say on values which have a universal status. He put forward the case of the Supreme Court in the United States, to which Richard Rorty made reference. Since the war the Supreme Court has been the principal agent of social reform. Dewey was its principal inspiration, moving not towards worries about foundation but towards action. Dewey was the poet of American democracy; but also in some ways the 'philosopher of the civil service of democracy'.

Rainer Rochlitz wondered if the debate about Foucault was not situated in the shade of a question which is no longer asked: the end of metaphysics. Is not all the pathos surrounding nihilism an anachronism? In our modest attempts to explain why we do not accept the intolerable, we can none the less wonder what the guiding values are. Foucault can be read either generously or in a way which is niggardly. It can also be said that there are things in his work which are hard to accept; thus, what he has to say about the aesthetics of existence is perhaps inadequate in relation to his own diagnostics. Yet in the last analysis, interventions and reflections on the validity of these interventions and their possible foundations are not antithetical.

Manfred Frank contradicted the thesis that God is dead. God is not dead, because He was never alive. The heavens are still just as dark; we have always been in a state of dereliction.

He wondered if we could agree on the idea that the maximum degree of intolerability would be the idea that anyone could do anything in any situation.

Walter Seitter asked Paul Veyne what distinction he would establish between the 'present' and the 'obsolete'. How, he said, could one spend one's life dealing with things which were obsolete? 'I thought that was what everyone did!' retorted Paul Veyne. Maybe the obsolete is not totally obsolete? One would have to ask the poets, he said.

On this eulogy of obsoleteness, of non-obsoleteness, and poets, the debate closed in a way which Foucault would probably have enjoyed.

Note on the Michel Foucault Centre

It was necessary to make some sort of provision so that Michel Foucault's premature death should not interrupt work which could be done on his work and on the basis of it. At the same time, though, it was necessary to avoid any proselytism. So there was a need to maintain the present identity of Michel Foucault's work without constructing any form of orthodoxy. The solution was to create an association with the goal of bringing into being a *Michel Foucault Centre*. The purpose of this was – borrowing one of Michel Foucault's own expressions – to be a kind of 'tool-box' for researchers who wanted to use it.

Thus it happened that on 31 May 1986 thirty or so university teachers and researchers who had worked alongside Michel Foucault created an association (under the law of 1901) in order to bring the Michel Foucault Centre into being. The second article of its statutes defines its object as follows: 'The purpose of this association is to create, manage and represent the Michel Foucault Centre. The objectives of the Centre are to assemble documents, archives and writings which constitute Michel Foucault's work, using for this purpose all means necessary: conferences, particularly international meetings, broadcasting, publication and teaching.'

The essential objective on which the others depended was to assemble the 'Fonds Michel Foucault' (Michel Foucault's work together with work relating to it) in order to ensure dialogue about it and make it available to researchers. This is a longer and more difficult task than it seemed at first, because of the 'geography' of Michel Foucault's work, which is very diverse in its forms and very widely dispersed as far as its location is concerned.

The Association for the Michel Foucault Centre is therefore neither a friendly society nor a school. The Association makes it possible for the Centre to exist, though it should not be confused with it. No one can say that they are a member of the Michel Foucault Centre, only of the Association. The Michel Foucault Centre cannot take up a position in a public, philosophical or political debate. This was requested by the founders of the Association, so that the

Michel Foucault Centre could not become the object of any personal or partisan act of appropriation. The Michel Foucault Centre is an instrument which is at the disposal of researchers and a means of communication for those working on or on the basis of Michel Foucault's work.

The Association for the Michel Foucault Centre is governed by a council of which Maurice Blanchot, Pierre Boulez, Georges Canguilhem, Gilles Deleuze, Paul Veyne and Georges Dumézil are members.

The Fonds Michel Foucault is located at the Bibliothèque du Saulchoir (43 *bis*, rue de la Glacière, 75013 Paris), where it can be consulted. It consists of the whole of Michel Foucault's work in whatever form it exists – books, articles, tape-recordings or videos, in all the languages in which it is published. It will progressively be completed by the totality of texts, theses and articles written on Michel Foucault's work or in areas relating to it. A detailed catalogue of the Fonds Michel Foucault is in preparation.

To consult the Fonds Michel Foucault located at the Bibliothèque du Saulchoir, one should make a request to the Association. Consultation takes place according to the general conditions of access to the Bibliothèque du Saulchoir and respecting the conditions of Michel Foucault's will.

All correspondence should be addressed to the Bibliothèque du Saulchoir, Association pour le Centre Michel Foucault, 43 *bis*, rue de la Glacière, 75013 Paris.

Notes on contributors

Étienne Balibar is Maître de Conférences (philosophie), Université de Paris-I

Blandine Barret-Kriegel is Professeur de Philosophie politique at the Université Jean Moulin de Lyon

Raymond Bellour is Directeur de Recherche at the Centre National de la Recherche Scientifique

James W. Bernauer is Associate Professor in the Department of Philosophy, Boston College

Christian Bouchindhomme is Translator and Head of Seminars at the Université Europeanne de la Recherche

Georges Canguilhem is Professor honoraire Université Pantheon Sorbonne à Paris

Gilles Deleuze is a philosopher and critic

Michael Donnelly is Member, School of Social Science, The Institute for Advanced Study, Princeton

Hubert L. Dreyfus is Professor of Philosophy at the University of California at Berkeley

François Ewald is Directeur de Recherche, Centre National de la Recherche Scientifique

Manfred Frank is Ordentlicher Professor für Philosophie at the Philosophischen Seminar of the Universität Tübingen

André Glücksmann is a philosopher and critic

Pierre Hadot is Professeur at the Collège de France, Chair d'Histoire de la Pensée hellènistique et romaine

Denis Hollier is Professor in the Department of French, Yale University

Christian Jambet is Professor of Philosophy, Lycée Jules-Ferocy (Khâgne), Paris

Dominique Janicaud is Professor of Philosophy at the University of Nice, France

Gerard Lebrun is a philosopher and critic

Robert Machado is Professor Titular at the The Institute de Filosofia & Ciencias Sociais da Universidade Federal do Rio de Janerio

Pierre Macherey is Maître de Conférences, Université de Paris I

Jacques-Alain Miller is a philosopher and critic

Miguel Morey is a philosopher and critic

Alessandro Pizzorno is a philosopher and critic

Mark Poster is Professor of History in the University of California at Irvine

John Rajchman is Professor, Collège International de Philosophie

Rainer Rochlitz is Chargé de Recherche au Centre National de la Recherche Scientifique

Richard Rorty is University Professor of Humanities at the University of Virginia

Walter Seitter is a politologist and philosopher

Paul Veyne is Professor au Collège de France

François Wahl is a philosopher and critic

Note on Foucault's texts

A selected bibliography

The following list comprises English translations of books by Michel Foucault that are cited by the contributors in this collection of essays.

Maladie mentale et personalité (1954) [retitled (1955) *Maladie mentale et psychologie*]. *Mental Illness and Psychology*, trans. A. Sheridan (Vintage/ Random House, 1979).

Folie et déraison. Histoire de la folie à l'âge classique (1961) [second edition with new material, 1972]. *Madness and Civilization: A History of Insanity in the Age of Reason*, trans. R. Howard (Vintage/Random House, 1973).

Raymond Roussel (1963). *Death and the Labyrinth: World of Raymond Roussel*, trans. C. Raus (Athlone Press, 1987).

Naissance de la clinique. Une archéologie du regard médical (1963). *Birth of the Clinic*, trans. A. M. S. Smith (Tavistock, 1976).

Les Mots et les Choses. Une archéologie des sciences humaines (1966). *The Order of Things: An Archaeology of the Human Sciences*, trans. A. M. S. Smith (Tavistock, 1974).

L'Archéologie du Savoir (1969). *The Archaeology of Knowledge*, trans. A. M. S. Smith (Harper Colophon, 1972).

L'Ordre du discours (1971). 'Order of Discourse', trans. R. Sawyer; republished as 'The Discourse on Language' in *The Archaeology of Knowledge*.

Ceci n'est pas une pipe (1973). *This is Not a Pipe*, trans. J. Harkness (California UP, 1983).

Surveiller et punir. Naissance de la prison (1975). *Discipline and Punish: Birth of the Prison*, trans. A. Sheridan (Penguin, 1979).

L'Historie de la Sexualité. Vol. I, La volonté de savoir (1976); *Vol. II, L'Usage des plaisirs*; *Vol. III, Le souci de soi. The History of Sexuality. Vol. I, An Introduction*, trans. R. Hurley (Vintage, 1978). *Vol. II, The Use of Pleasure* (Viking, 1986). *Vol. III, The Care of the Self* (Allen Lane, 1988).

Herculine Barbin (1979). *Herculine Barbin: Being the Recently Discovered Memoirs of a Nineteenth Century Hermaphrodite*, ed. Michel Foucault (Harvester, 1981).

English translations of some of Michel Foucault's essays that are cited by the contributors to this collection can be found in the following books.

Bouchard, Donald F. (ed.) *Language, Counter-Memory, Practice* (Cornell UP, 1977).

Dreyfus, Hubert L. and Paul Rabinow (eds) *Michel Foucault: Beyond Structuralism and Hermeneutics*, 2 edn (Chicago UP, 1983).

Gordon, Colin (ed.) *Power/Knowledge: Selected Interviews and Other Writings* (Harvester, 1981).

Hoy, M. (ed.) *Foucault: A Critical Reader* (Blackwell, 1986).

Kritzman, Lawrence (ed.) *Politics, Philosophy, Culture: Interviews and Other Writings* (Routledge, 1990).

Rabinow, Paul (ed.) *A Foucault Reader* (Pantheon, 1984).